Nostradamus:
The Illustrated Prophecies

By The Same Author

The Armageddon Script
Beyond All Belief
The Cosmic Eye
Gospel Of The Stars
The Great Pyramid Decoded
The Great Pyramid: Your Personal Guide
The Healing Of The Gods
This New Age Business
Nostradamus: The Final Reckoning
The Nostradamus Encyclopedia
The Essential Nostradamus
Nostradamus Beyond 2000/Nostradamus And Beyond
Decoding The Great Pyramid
Nostradamus In The 21st Century
The Unknown Nostradamus

Translations by The Same Author

Through Music To The Self (Hamel)
Zen In The Art Of The Tea Ceremony (Hammitzsch)
The Healing Power Of Illness (Dethlefsen & Dahlke)
Harmony Is The Healer (von Rohr)

Peter Lemesurier is well known in the uneasy world of Nostra-
damians as a conscientious and accurate researcher. Probably his
strong point is that he investigates the Prophecies of Nostradamus
in the context of the time when they were composed. His translation
of the quatrains is based on an impartial analysis of 16-century-
related materials and strict observance of the available historical
sources.

Alexey Penzensky, prominent Russian Nostradamus scholar

NOSTRADAMUS

The Illustrated Prophecies

*The New and Authoritative Translation to
commemorate Nostradamus' 500th Anniversary*

Peter Lemesurier

BOOKS

Winchester, UK
New York, USA

Neither the author nor the publishers are responsible for the expressed views or predictions of Nostradamus, nor do they necessarily subscribe to them. Readers' reactions to the prophecies are entirely their own responsibility. While all interpretations are offered in good faith, no guarantee is implied or should be inferred regarding their predictive validity.

Superscript numbers and lower-case letters refer to the Reference-Bibliography at the end of the book.

Superscript 'P' denotes an illustration in the color-plate section.

Copyright © 2003 John Hunt Publishing Ltd
46A West Street, Alresford, Hants SO24 9AU, U.K.
Tel: +44 (0) 1962 736880 Fax: +44 (0) 1962 736881
E-mail: office@johnhunt-publishing.com
www.o-books.net

Text and original pictures: © 2003 Peter Lemesurier

Cover design: Echelon Design, UK
Typography: Jim Weaver Design, UK

ISBN 1 903816 48 3

Printed in the USA by ????

Acknowledgement

Frontispiece (opposite page 1): Courtesy of Michel Chomarat, Bibliothèque Munipale de Lyon

Any sufficiently advanced technology is
indistinguishable from magic.

Arthur C. Clarke: *Profiles of the Future*

Cette édition représente un premier effort.
La qualité des résultats obtenus devrait encourager
d'autres chercheurs à la reprendre et à étendre l'entreprise
au restant des centuries.

Pierre Brind'Amour (d. January 1995),
Introduction to *Nostradamus: Les*
premières centuries ou prophéties

Contents

Introduction

NOSTRADAMUS, THE WORLD-FAMOUS SIXTEENTH-CENTURY FRENCH MAGE, wrote not just one book, but a whole series of them. Most of these are completely unknown to the general public. They ranged from a best-selling medical cookbook at one end of the scale, through a variety of academic works and a long series of annual almanacs designed to predict the weather, the harvest, and a variety of political, military and other events along the way, to the book for which he is most famous today. This was entitled *The Prophecies* (*Les Propheties*).

Not, note, *Prophecies*, but **The Prophecies**.

There was good reason for this rather strange formulation. It was that the majority of them were simply *not his* – 'even though (as he himself put it in his dedicatory letter to King Henri II) there be many who attribute to me what is as much mine as nothing of the kind.' Contrary to what has been popularly supposed for some five centuries now, he was, in effect, merely re-interpreting whole rafts of ancient end-time prophecies by prominent saints and divines – most of which were Bible-based and had been in circulation for a very long time indeed – then amplifying them by projecting into the future a range of appropriate events and omens taken from well-known historical accounts, and finally superimposing on them a fairly vague astrological framework to add to their sense of seeming inevitability.

We know all this because we have the full texts of those ancient prophecies, and can consequently identify with reasonable certainty which of them he has borrowed; because it has similarly become possible to identify many of the historical events and omen-reports that he was projecting into the future (and often, especially in the earlier verses, even the specific texts that he was plundering); and because the astrological principles on the basis of which Nostradamus and his contemporaries habitually worked have now likewise been unearthed.

The subject of his book was thus not *his* prophecies, but *the* prophecies!

No wonder, then, that on no fewer than three occasions in his two dedicatory letters to it he specifically denies that he himself is a prophet. True, he constantly encourages the reader in the subtlest terms to wonder whether he is not just being modest. He even suggests that the prophecies are divinely inspired – without making it any too clear that he does not in fact claim that *he* is.

Yet that much was inevitable. His main underlying source, after all, was quite clearly the celebrated *Mirabilis Liber* ('Marvelous Book') of 1522, possibly in its better-known 1523 edition.[45] This was not only Bible-based, but written by a whole bevy of famous saints and divines into the bargain. It was thus theoretically 'divinely inspired' twice over. Mostly in impenetrable Latin Gothic script, and replete with scholarly abbreviations, it was a huge anthology of ancient prophecies stretching right back to the seventh century and even – via its direct biblical antecedents – far beyond that. Its list of unwitting contributors was impressive:

- ✧ Bishop Bemechobus (better known as Pseudo-Methodius – Syrian, seventh century)
- ✧ The Tiburtine Sibyl (Syrian, ninth century)
- ✧ 'St Augustine of Hippo' (actually the tenth-century Adso of Montier-en-Der)
- ✧ 'St Severus' (in fact a fifteenth-century composition)
- ✧ Johann Lichtenberger (a composite collection from various named sources, first printed in 1488)
- ✧ A set of papal prophecies (fourteenth century)
- ✧ Telesphorus of Cosenza (fourteenth century)
- ✧ Another composite source combining (among others) St Brigid of Sweden, St Hildegard of Bingen, the Cretan Sibyl, the Hermit Reynard, and the celebrated Abbot Joachim of Fiore
- ✧ Joannes de Vatiguerro (sixteenth century)
- ✧ Joachim of Fiore himself (twelfth century)
- ✧ 'St Vincent' (actually a sixteenth-century compilation from St Thomas Aquinas and other sources)
- ✧ 'St Catuldus' (actually a sixteenth-century prophecy)
- ✧ Jerome of Ferrara (Savonarola – late fifteenth century)
- ✧ Fra Bonaventura (sixteenth century)
- ✧ Johannes de Rupescissa (Jean de la Roquetaillade – fifteenth century)
- ✧ St Brigid of Sweden (fourteenth century)

  plus, in French, an anonymous composite source including a collection of late thirteenth-century prophecies elsewhere attributed to 'Merlin'

But, of all these, it was Bishop Bemechobus – i.e. Pseudo-Methodius – who had laid down the basic scenario.

Published some thirty years before Nostradamus even began to write *The Prophecies*, the *Mirabilis Liber*'s version of this will be astonishingly – if not worryingly – familiar to connoisseurs of Nostradamus (see the annotations to verses I.9, I.47, I.75, II.9, II.24 below, for example). The Arabs (i.e. the Muslims) would invade the rest of the world – led, in some accounts, by the Antichrist in person. They would prove absolutely invincible. Turkey, Syria, North Africa, Greece, Italy, Spain, France, Germany, even the isles of the sea would be overrun, their cities laid waste, their churches burnt, their treasures stolen, their priests and monks put to the sword, their women raped, their children murdered, their corpses strewn about the countryside. Subsequent accounts filled in the picture yet further. Among other things, there would be fire, plague, famine, floods, earthquakes, and droughts. Beneath louring comets, there would be brutal occupations and bloody oppressions. As the Church collapsed, the Pope would be forced to flee Rome. And all this by way of Divine vengeance on a Christendom that had allowed its morals to decay, its religion to become decadent, its systems of justice to become corrupted, its sexuality to become depraved.

Then would follow an equally bloody counter-invasion on the part of Christendom, led by a young and brilliant king of France who would push the Muslims all the way back to the Middle East and, with the aid of an 'Angelic Pope', even convert them to Christianity (see, for example, the annotations to I.10, I.55 and I.92 below). After a period of world peace under the new ruler, a fresh invasion of the Christian world would follow, this time led by the dreaded northern tribes of Gog and Magog. This would prove yet worse, even extending to cannibalism. No sooner would this gruesome invasion in turn have been repulsed after some years of tribulation than the Antichrist (or, in some accounts, a second Antichrist) would appear in Jerusalem. At this, God would resurrect the biblical Enoch and Elias to testify against him. A bloody massacre of the faithful would follow, whereupon the returning Christ would at last appear in the clouds of heaven, surrounded by legions of angels, and put the Antichrist to death. The Last Judgment would follow, and then amid a rain of universal fire (to say nothing of a universal flood!) the earth would finally be dissolved. The righteous would at last enter into everlasting glory, while the wicked would be consigned to endless torment.

It was a dramatic, if familiar sixteenth-century catalogue of apocalyptic events, compiled in response to a growing general feeling that, in the light of truly dire current developments, the End of the World must surely be at hand. It was not just that the climate was deteriorating rapidly, as what is now known as the 'Little Ice Age' steadily encroached on Europe; Famine, too, was consequently becoming widespread and ever more frequent; the Plague was on the rampage; and War and Death – to say nothing of a whole range of worrying celestial phenomena – threatened on every side.

The Four Horsemen of the Apocalypse, in other words, were definitely abroad.

Yet even all this was still not enough to fill out the thousand prophecies that

Nostradamus and his publisher planned to produce. And so, in order to put some flesh on the bare bones of the *Mirabilis Liber's* grisly account, Nostradamus now ransacked the history books in order to find detailed events that, projected into the future, would more or less fit its overall scenario and help bring it to life. Classical histories and mythologies, the great medieval chronicles, even accounts of quite recent events – all provided grist to his mill; indeed, in his later verses, these last would take over almost completely.

Like any Renaissance man, after all, Nostradamus always looked to the past for his answers – and it went almost without saying that it would eventually repeat itself.

Among the classical works he can be shown to have plundered, often almost verbatim, were:

✧ Virgil's *Eclogues* (42-37 BC), *Georgics* (37-30 BC) and *Aeneid* (19 BC)
✧ Julius Caesar's *Gallic War* (first century BC)
✧ Pliny the Elder's histories (first century BC)
✧ Strabo's *Historical Memoirs* (first century BC to first century AD)
✧ Livy's *History of Rome* (first century BC to first century AD)
✧ Petronius's *Satyricon* (first century AD)
✧ Suetonius's *The Twelve Caesars* (AD 120)
✧ Plutarch's *Parallel Lives* (first to second century AD)
✧ Lucian's *True History* (second century AD)
✧ Eusebius's *Ecclesiastical History* (fourth century AD) and especially
✧ Julius Obsequens's *On Omens* (fourth century AD)

No doubt this massive classical content was why the *Propheties* were, according to Garencières, actually used as a reader in early seventeenth-century French schools. Certainly it can hardly have been for their grammatical correctness or stylistic elegance!

Among the great medieval chronicles from which Nostradamus also borrowed[60] were:

✧ Villehardouin's *La Conquête de Constantinople* (1209–13)
✧ Joinville's *Histoire de Saint-Louis* (1270–1309), first printed in 1547
✧ Froissart's celebrated *Chroniques* (1358 onwards), first printed 1504
✧ Commynes' *Memoires* (1489–98)
✧ D'Auton's *Chroniques de Louis XII* (1499–1508)
✧ The *Rozier historial de France* (1522)

Finally, by way of giving some kind of possible timescale to all this, Nostradamus consulted the published astrological tables, checked the positions of the planets at the time of some of the historical events in question and, looking up when these would recur in the future, suggested when they might have the most likely chance of repeating themselves. Once again his astrological sources are well known, not least because he himself actually named, owned, and quoted directly from some of them:

- ✧ Manilius's *Astronomica* (first century BC to first century AD)
- ✧ Claudius Ptolemy's *Tetrabiblos* (second century AD), republished by Cardano (d.1576) in his *Commentaries*
- ✧ Albumasar (ninth century), often referred to by Nostradamus as *le grand Albumasar: De magnis conjunctionibus*, reprinted in 1515
- ✧ Alcabitius's *Praeclarum Summi in Astrorum Scientia Principis* (tenth century, reprinted in Lyon in the 1520s)
- ✧ Abraham Ibn Ezra (twelfth century – known to Nostradamus as *Avenezra*): translated into French as the *Livre du Monde et des Conjonctions* (thirteenth to fourteenth century)
- ✧ Jean de Murs' *Alfonsine Tables* (fourteenth century, republished by Gaurico in 1545)
- ✧ Apianus's *Astronomicum Caesareum* of 1540 (which included tables for calculating planetary positions up to 7000 years into the past and future, and even offered little disc-type computers for making the job easier) and especially
- ✧ Richard Roussat's immensely influential *Livre de l'estat et mutation des temps* (1549-50), 'proving by the authority of Holy Scripture and by astrological reasoning that the end of the world is at hand.'

Such, then, were the main sources of *The Prophecies*. To these we must add Petrus Crinitus's *De honesta disciplina* of 1504, a book that is known to have finished up in his son's personal library – as well as Gasparus Peucerus's *Teratoscopia* ('Monstroscopy') of 1553, Marcus Frytschius's *De Meteoris* ('On Meteors') of 1555, and Jobus Fincelius's *De miraculis sui temporis* ('Concerning the Wonders of his Times') of 1556, all of which, hot off the presses at the time of writing, would be reflected in his pages. In the latter stages, too, Conrad Lycosthenes' massive *Prodigiorum ac ostentorum chronicon* of 1557,[44] which duly collected all three sets of omen-reports and others too, seems to have played a role – and all of them claimed, of course, to represent yet further warnings sent by God Himself.

But what of the book itself and its author?

History of *The Prophecies*

Born in 1503 in St-Rémy-de-Provence, Michel de Nostredame had spent most of his time as a wandering apothecary before he finally settled down in 1547 with his second wife in nearby Salon to begin a career as a writer. Having started on a series of annual *Almanachs* in 1550 – now under the more 'academic' name of Nostradam*us* – it seems to have been a series of 'omens' in early 1554 that prompted him finally to embark on the composition of the rather larger-scale work that would become *Les Propheties*.

The plan that he evidently cooked up with his publisher Macé Bonhomme of Lyon was to produce the book in three installments of 300 or so verses each, after the pattern of an earlier book that Bonhomme had produced in four 'centuries' of a hundred verses each. The first installment of 353 verses duly appeared as a tiny pocketbook in the spring of 1555, together with a dedicatory preface to Nostradamus's one-year-old son César. It was distributed unbound, so as to save both space and weight on the backs of the pack-horses: retailers and customers were evidently expected to await the two further installments before binding all three together under whatever cover they pleased.

However, by the time Nostradamus had the second installment of 289 verses ready in 1557 he had changed publishers, and his new publisher, Antoine du Rosne of Lyon, evidently unwilling (as publishers usually are) to publish what was, in effect, a sequel to another publisher's book, decided to make a new start and publish both installments together for himself, finishing at verse VII.42. When, however, Nostradamus finally completed his third and final installment in 1558, he had changed publishers yet again, and this time his new publisher (who seems to have been Jean de Tournes – though no copy of this edition has come down to us) decided to cut his losses and publish just the last three 'centuries' as a separate book (so leaving the seventh 'century' of the second edition incomplete to the extent of 58 verses) and with a new dedication of its own, this time to King Henri II himself.

However, King Henri was killed while jousting shortly afterwards, and with Nostradamus still producing at least one *Almanach* a year, nobody seems to have felt it worthwhile to publish a complete edition of *The Prophecies* during the latter's lifetime. Only after his death did his secretary Jean de Chavigny seemingly put matters in hand in co-operation with his late Master's widow Anne Ponsarde, issuing via Benoist Rigaud of Lyon a new, omnibus edition that simply bound the two previous editions together, each with its own title page and page-numbering. It is with this edition that *The Prophecies* come to a close as far as this present volume is concerned.

From 1605 further editions followed, each more corrupt and inaccurate than its predecessor, and introducing yet more material gleaned from Nostradamus's *Almanachs* and a collection of 58 six-line verses that may or may not have been his. Numerous rank forgeries appeared, too, as more and more editors and commentators discovered that, with a bit of verbal twisting, Nostradamus could be made to say virtually anything they liked, while his

name guaranteed good sales. It is this lamentable tradition, which has persist-
ed to the present day (especially in English-speaking countries) that the current
book is designed finally to lay to rest.

The present edition

In this book the prophecies are presented in their original order (which seems
to have been purely arbitrary, though sometimes influenced by which of his
textual sources Nostradamus had been reading most recently) and in the form
in which each appeared in its original edition – though transliterated, as is normal, into modern lettering. This means that the original spelling and punctuation are preserved – even though all the evidence suggests that these are the
copyright of the printer, not of Nostradamus. Typesetting at the time, after all,
tended to be done purely by dictation – a recipe, if ever there was one, for unin-
tended misspellings and unhelpful homonyms, especially where the syntax
was (as so often in Nostradamus) none too clear – and each publisher in any
case had his own favorite spelling and punctuation conventions. Perhaps it was
because of this that, on the evidence of his *Orus Apollo*, Nostradamus almost
certainly neglected to punctuate or accent his verses at all. He did, however, set
a few words out in block capitals – presumably ones that he wanted to ensure
that the compositor would set exactly as spelt, whether because they were ana-
grams (a fashionable device at the time, especially for encoding sensitive proper names) or merely because they were likely to be unfamiliar to the printer.

As a result, the compositor set them in capitals, too, as compositors will.

In the text that follows, simple notes are next appended to indicate the suggested modern French equivalents of any words and phrases that may seem
'difficult'. This may be because of unfamiliar sixteenth-century 'spellings' (no
such concept as 'correct spelling' in any case existed at the time), because the
context makes it clear that they are obvious misprints, because they contain
abstruse historical or mythological references, because of the constant use of
the Latinate words and constructions that were then all the rage, or because
Nostradamus was self-evidently modeling his verse itself closely on that of his
age's idol, the Roman poet Virgil who – Latin being Latin – used few pronouns
or prepositions, and no articles at all.

A proposed English verse-translation is then offered which, like the original,
is normally in lines of ten syllables and usually rhymes in the same *abab* pattern typically affected by the French. The latter's general 'feel' and artistic
impression (often a relatively crude and clumsy one) is thus preserved as far as
possible, and the common impression avoided that Nostradamus's verses are
in reality some kind of legal document in meticulously drafted prose. True, re-
presenting the result in verse necessarily involves (as does any verse-translation) a certain amount of re-wording and even 'padding' at times, but nothing

of any great significance is either omitted or added.

A further feature of the verse – a fairly rigid *caesura*, or hiatus, after the fourth syllable of each line – is not reproduced in the English, where it is less common. However, since it can sometimes prove extremely helpful in working out the sense of the original French, the sign *[/]* is sometimes inserted into the French in order to indicate just where the 'break' occurs.

Finally, a note is appended to indicate the source (or, more often, a range of possible sources) from which each verse is evidently taken or on which it is based (where known), so enabling readers, by referring back to those sources, to assess for themselves their applicability or otherwise to the future. Some of these are classical, some medieval. Original woodcuts relating to the latter are included at relevant points, as are contemporary English translations of them, thus helping to reflect the essentially medieval nature of much of the work. It should be borne in mind, though, that identifying the exact sources is sometimes no easier than it is to tease out the sense of the words. Nostradamus's memory (which is what he seems to have preferred to work from) was often imperfect. Indeed, he was quite prepared to be 'creative' even with the originals, to say nothing of freely combining them with other, quite different sources of ideas, none of which he bothered to identify. Research consequently continues.

Some readers may be surprised to find translations here that are somewhat at variance with my earlier versions, as published in my more speculative works on the seer such as *Nostradamus in the 21st Century* (Piatkus, 2000). If so, they may care to reflect (a) that there is no such thing as '*the* translation' of a foreign text, but only '*a* translation', (b) that research into the *Prophecies* is, as I have just pointed out, ongoing, and (c) that a strictly academic reading cannot permit itself quite the same sort of exegetical freedoms that a more speculative work both demands and allows. Nevertheless, by comparing the two, readers may sometimes gain a fuller insight into the possible implications of the original texts . . .

Superscript numbers refer to the Reference-Bibliography at the end of the book. Verse-references in the text are designed to point the reader to the earliest verse for which I have cited the relevant sources in full, so avoiding unnecessary duplication. A superscript P refers to a photograph in the color section.

In all of this I have been grateful for the support and advice of Michel Chomarat, 'guardian of the Nostradamus texts' at the Bibliothèque Municipale de Lyon, which boasts an unparalleled collection of over 2000 original items; to Jacqueline Allemand and the staff of the Maison de Nostradamus at Salon-de-Provence for much guidance, encouragement and friendly conversation; to Bernard Chevignard, Professor of Language and Communication at the University of Burgundy in Dijon for his supporting documentation and comradely advice; to Dr Jennifer Britnell, Head of French at the University of

Durham, for kindly making available her painstaking research into the *Mirabilis Liber*; to Roger Prévost for his inspiration and assistance; to my distinguished friend and colleague Joseph Bain for helping to check my French; to Mario Gregorio for his unstinting documentary research and long-term online collaboration; to our colleague Markus for kindly making and supplying a copy of Lycosthenes; to Jason Jamieson for his work on Nostradamus's astrology; to Monique Roussy for her French textual research; to Samuel Oak for his collaboration in translating parts of the *Mirabilis Liber*; to Gary Somai for his original research into quatrains IX.76 and X.86; to the late and much lamented Ted Johnson for his bequest of valuable historical materials; and to my many other Internet correspondents who, even when they have not been particularly informative, have never ceased to question and provoke.

LES
PROPHETIES
DE M. MICHEL
NOSTRADAMVS.

A LYON,
Chés Macé Bonhomme.

M. D. LV.

La permiſſion eſt inſérée à la page ſuiuante.
AVEC PRIVILEGE.

Century I

1. Original 1555 text

ESTANT assis [/] de nuict secret estude,
Seul repousé sus la selle d'aerain,
Flambe exigue sortant de solitude,
Faict proferer qui n'est à croire vain.

Read as modern French:

à étudier la nuit en secret
Seul, en repos sur le siège de bronze

Fait prophétiser ce qu'il n'est pas vain de croire

    Seated, he studies secretly at night,
    'On tripod bronze', at ease, alone again:
    A tiny, lonely flame that shines so bright
    Makes prophesy what none should count as vain.

Source: The fourth-century Iamblichus's *De Mysteriis Aegyptiorum*, as reprinted in Latin by Petrus Crinitus in his *De honesta disciplina* of 1504, republished in Lyon by Gryphius in 1552, and almost certainly in Nostradamus's personal library, given the frequency with which he quotes from it (and the fact that his son César would report as much): 'The prophetess at Delphi . . . being seated in the inner shrine on a bronze seat [*super sedem aeneam*] having three or four legs . . . would expose herself to the divine spirit, whence she was illuminated with a ray of divine fire [*radio divini ignis*].' Nostradamus is evidently evoking the Delphic oracle in the hope of impressing the reader with his own prophetic credentials.

2. Original 1555 text

La verge en main mise au milieu de
    BRANCHES
De l'onde il moulle & le limbe & le pied.

Un peur & voix fremissent par les manches,
Splendeur divine. Le divin prés s'assied.

Read as modern French:

à la main; dans le saint des saints de Branchis

De l'eau il mouille et le bord du vêtement et le
    pied
Vapeur, et voix

    Wand placed in hand as once at Branchis' heart,
    He wets his hem with water, and his feet.
    Vapors: voices him in his gown that start.
    Then light divine! The god assumes his seat.

Source: Once again Iamblichus's *De Mysteriis Aegyptiorum*, as reprinted in Latin by

Petrus Crinitus in his *De honesta disciplina* of 1504: 'The female oracle at Brancis . . . either holds a wand in her hand [*vel manu tenet virgam*] or dips her feet or the hem of her robe in the water [*vel pedes, aut limbum tingit in aquam*] . . . or inhales some of the vapor arising from the water [*vel ex aqua qadam vaporem haurit*] . . . and in this way is filled with a divine light [*impletur splendore divino*] . . . and predicts what is to come . . . the god becomes externally present . . . and the prophetess . . . is inspired.' As before, Nostradamus, this time quoting some of the ancient text word-for-word, is likening his own efforts to those of the ancient Greek oracles, in this case with that of Branchidai (now Didyma) in Asia Minor, once consulted by Alexander the Great in person.

3. Original 1555 text

Read as modern French:

Quant la lictiere du tourbillon versée,   sera versée
Et seront faces de leurs manteaux couvers,   couvertes [accord typique de proximité]
La republique par gens nouveaux vexée,   L'état [lat. res publica]; troublée
Lors blancs & rouges jugeront à l'envers.   Alors les juges [ainsi identifiés par Nostradamus[9]]

When litter by the whirlwind is upset,
And face is covered by protecting cloak,
Then shall new folk the very state beset
And judges shall perversely laws invoke.

Source: Presumably Julius Obsequens's *On Omens* (18) for 152 BC: 'The columns on the precinct before the temple of Jupiter were knocked down by the force of a whirlwind, together with the golden image itself; and when the soothsayers responded by saying that the ruin of the magistrates and priests was at hand, all the magistrates resigned forthwith' – but modified to fit a related event that had perhaps occurred recently in Provence, the country of the *Mistral*. In his *Prodigiorum ac ostentorum chronicon* of 1557,[44] Conrad Lycosthenes would similarly illustrate the event in terms of what

is clearly medieval Christian Europe (see woodcut). As for Nostradamus, he is evidently projecting this whole tale of whirlwinds and magistrates into the future as an omen of the expected change of legal climate during the *Mirabilis Liber*'s anticipated Muslim invasion of Europe: 'The men of those days shall be rapists, liars, shameful, proud, enemies of justice, and even the Roman judges shall be corrupt; depending on the day of the week, their judgments shall be changed for money; if one of their eyes is good, the other shall be evil: and for money there is nothing that the magistrates shall not be prepared to do. While swearing to do good, they shall do ill; falsity shall preside over their utterances' (The Prophecy of the Tiburtine Sibyl); 'Thenceforward the book of the gospels shall not be in force. For the judges shall do justice only in exchange for money . . . ' (The Book of Merlin).

4. Original 1555 text

Par l'univers sera faict ung monarque,
Qu'en paix & vie ne sera longuement:
Lors se perdra la piscature barque,
Sera regie en plus grand detriment.

Read as modern French:

Pour/A travers le monde entier
Qui en
la barque du pêcheur [St Pierre]

O'er all the world a monarch shall be crowned
Whose life – and peace – shall not too long endure.
Then shall St Peter's barque at sea be drowned,
And shall be steered towards overthrow most sure.

Source: The *Mirabilis Liber*: 'But towards the year of Our Lord 1515, or shortly before or after, these provinces shall be rescued by a young captive, who shall regain the crown of the lily and shall spread his dominion over the whole World . . . ' (Prophecy of Joannes de Vatiguerro); 'There shall come forth a monarch of the illustrious lily [France] . . . No one shall be able to resist him, because he shall always have the strong arm of the Lord beside him, who shall bestow on him sovereignty over the entire world' (Anonymous sixteenth-century prophecy); 'More than one peril shall threaten the Church of the Lord and the barque of Peter . . . The barque of Peter is the Roman Church' (Prophecy of Abbot Joachim of Fiore); 'Under the great eagle that shall nourish the fire in its breast, the Church shall be ravaged and trampled underfoot . . . and then the barque of Peter, attacked by powerful enemies, shall be shaken . . . ' (Prophecy of St Brigid of Sweden). Both the last two prophets quoted by the *Mirabilis Liber*, however, are rather less pessimistic about the Church's ultimate prospects than is Nostradamus.

5. Original 1555 text

Chassés seront sans faire long combat
Par le pays seront plus fort grevés:
Bourg & cité auront plus grand debat,
Carcas. Narbonne auront cueurs esprouvés.

Read as modern French:

Ils seront chassés
accablés
se battront mieux
Carcassonne; coeurs

Pursued they'll be, nor shall they fight much longer,
In country districts even more oppressed.
Cities' and towns' resistance shall be stronger,
Carcassonne's, Narbonne's hearts put to the test.

Source: The continuing wars with Spain in the south-west, probably assimilated to the *Mirabilis Liber*'s general scenario of future Arab invasion, as detailed by its Prophecy of Pseudo-Methodius.

6. Original 1555 text   **Read as modern French:**

L'œil de Ravenne sera destitué,   *Le roi de Ravenne [voir lettre à Henri II, App. B]*
Quand à ses pieds les aesles fallliront,   *les ailes failliront*
Les deux de Bresse auront constitué,   *Les ducs [jeu de mots habituel sur lat. dux/duces]*
Turin, Verseil que Gauloys fouleront.

> **Ravenna's regal 'Eye' shall be plucked out**
> **When wings at last shall fail his speeding feet:**
> **French forces shall Turin, Vercelli rout,**
> **Once chiefs from Bresse have placed them on their seat.**

Source: Unknown. The exact sense of the last two lines is unclear, though the context seems to be the eventual Christian counter-invasion against the Muslim occupiers of Europe, as anticipated by the *Mirabilis Liber*. The 'Eye', as elsewhere in Nostradamus, seems to be a local ruler.

7. Original 1555 text   **Read as modern French:**

Tard arrivé l'execution faicte
Le vent contraire, letres au chemin prinses   *lettres; prises*
Les conjures. xiiij. dune secte   *conjurés; d'une*
Par le Rosseau senez les entreprinses.   *Rousseau/Rouge ; signées/autorisées*⁹

> **Too late arrived, the execution done,**
> **Things gone awry, the letters seized en route,**
> **Conspirators fourteen, yet sects but one:**
> **By the Redhead the matter set afoot.**

Source: Two separate recent events possibly related to the *Mirabilis Liber*'s prediction of the coming collapse of Catholic Christianity: the burning of the humanist Louis Berquin on the very day of his condemnation in 1528, before King François I could intervene as he had on previous occasions, and the repression of the fourteen reformers of Meaux in 1540, linked with the covert Protestantism of Bishop Roussel of Oloron.⁶⁰

8. Original 1555 text   **Read as modern French:**

Combien de foys prinse cité solaire   *prise*
Seras, changeant les loys barbares & vaines.   *Seras-tu; dispensations musulmanes*
Ton mal s'aproche: Plus seras tributaire   *Toujours/Encore/D'avantage*
La grand Hadrie reovrira tes veines.   *La grande [forme invariable à l'époque] Venise*

> **How oft, Sun City, you shall captured be**
> **Your laws replaced by barbarous edicts vain!**
> **Your doom draws near. E'en more you'll bend the knee**
> **When mighty Venice opes your every vein!**

Source: The long historical struggle between Turks and Venetians over Rhodes (which was formerly dedicated to the sun-god Helios, whom its famous Colossus of course represented), projected into the future as an episode in the eventual Christianization of the entire Middle East, as confidently (if surprisingly) predicted by the *Mirabilis Liber*: 'The king of the Franks, Greeks, and Romans, reclaiming for himself the whole empire of Christendom, shall devastate all the pagan islands and cities, shall overthrow the temples of idolatry, and shall summon all the pagans to baptism. The cross shall be raised in all the temples, and whoever shall not adore it shall be punished with the sword' (Prophecy of the Tiburtine Sibyl). Hadria, just to the south of Venice, was (as so often in Nostradamus) merely the name of that city's former classical equivalent, which it of course gave to the Adriatic Sea on which it stood.

9. Original 1555 text

Read as modern French:

De l'Orient viendra le cueur Punique,
Facher Hadrie & les hoirs Romulides,
Acompaigne de la classe Libycque,
Trembler Mellites: et proches isles vuides.

le courage des Arabes/des Africains du nord
Venise et les héritiers de Romulus/habitants de Rome
Accompagné de la flotte libyenne
Malte; vides

> **From th' East shall Afric hearts a passage beat**
> **To harass Venice, Rome itself to try,**
> **Accompanied by all the Libyan fleet:**
> **Malta shall quake; emptied each isle nearby.**

Sources: (a) The *Mirabilis Liber*'s vision of a coming Arab invasion of Europe via the Mediterranean islands: '. . . the children of Ishmael [i.e. the Arabs] . . . shall, however, renew their enterprise, they shall destroy the land, shall invade the globe from the East unto the West, from the South to the North, as far as Rome. Their yoke shall weigh heavy on the heads of the people. There shall be no nation or realm that can fight against them, until the Times shall be accomplished . . . Massacre and captivity await the Greeks . . . The Spanish shall perish by the sword. France, Germany, and the land of the Goths, eaten up by a thousand scourges, shall see a host of their inhabitants carried off. The Romans shall be killed or put to flight; and pursuing their enemies as far as the islands of the sea, the sons of Ishmael shall invade at one and the same time the North and the East, the South and the West . . . The way of the Saracens shall spread from sea to sea . . . ' (Prophecy of Pseudo-Methodius); 'The Turks and Albanians shall destroy many Christian islands' (Prophecy of Joannes de Vatiguerro); (b) Livy's account of the Carthaginian ('Punic') general Hannibal's devastating invasion of Italy in 218–6 BC.

10. Original 1555 text

Read as modern French:

Serpens transmis dens la caige de fer
Ou les enfans septains du roy sont pris:
Les vieux & peres sortiront bas de l'enfer,
Ains mourir voir [/] de son fruict mort & crys.

Sergents [?]; dans la cage
sont emprisonnés par le roi
du bas de l'enfer
Mais ils les verront mourir

Into the iron cage sergeants [?] inserted
Where, captured by the King, seven youngsters lie:
Old folk and fathers, depths of hell averted,
Shall watch their offspring as they scream and die.

Source: Two historical accounts – (a) the contemporary *Journal d'un bourgeois de Paris*'s description of how seven Protestant heretics ('serpents'?) were condemned to be burned at the stake on 10 November 1534 and held in the dungeon of the Châtelet (Paris's police headquarters), which was popularly referred to as 'hell' at the time – a fact memorialized in a famous poem by Clément Marot;[60] and (b) a further account in the *Mémoires* of Philippe de Commynes (one of Nostradamus's known sources) of how such cages (generally some eight feet square) had been used in the fifteenth century, as he had known from first-hand experience (VI.xi).[9] Whether 'snakes' or 'sergeants', then (one has to suspect a misprint, since *sergens* goes much better with *transmis* – literally 'dispatched' – and it is rather difficult to imagine how 'snakes' could be retained by the bars of a cage), Nostradamus is conceivably assimilating both accounts to the *Mirabilis Liber*'s account of the eventual Christian defeat and repression of Islam: 'There shall emerge from Gaul [interpolation by the sixteenth-century French editor!] a race of Christians who shall make war on them and shall pierce them with the sword, shall take away their women captive and shall slaughter their children' (Prophecy of Pseudo-Methodius).

11. Original 1555 text

Le mouvement de sens, cueur, pieds, & mains
Seront d'acord. Naples, Leon, Secille,
Glaifves, feus, eaux: puis aux nobles Romains
Plongés, tués, mors par cerveau debile.

Read as modern French:

coeur
d'accord; Lentini [?]; Sicile
Glaives [épées]; aux puits [plongés]

In minds, hearts, feet and hands whate'er transpires
Is one in Naples, Leon, Sicily.
Rome's lords in wells thrown – swords, then waters, fires –
And killed stone-dead through brainless idiocy.

Source: The *Mirabilis Liber*'s frequent descriptions of a future Muslim invasion of Europe via the Mediterranean islands. See I.9 above.

12. Original 1555 text

Dans peu dira faulce brute, fragile,
De bas en hault eslevé promptement:
Puys en instant desloyale & labile
Qui de Veronne aura gouvernement.

Read as modern French:

l'on dira de la fausse bête brute inconstante
Qu'il a été élevé
et vacillant
Vérone

Shortly, they'll say, the false and fickle beast
Has been too quickly raised from low on high:

> At once he'll faithless prove, fitful at least,
> He who Verona's government shall ply.

Source: Unidentified Italian annals, possibly relating to the Veronan tyrant Ezzelino da Romano (1226–1259).

13. Original 1555 text

Read as modern French:

Les exiles [/] par ire, haine intestine,   *Les exilés*   '
Feront au roy grand conjuration:
Secret mettront ennemis par la mine,   *En secret*
Et ses vieux siens contre eux sedition.

> The exiles shall for rage and inner hate
> Against the king a major plot devise,
> In secret sending foes in 'neath the gate,
> And stir sedition 'gainst his old allies.

Source: A familiar sixteenth-century problem where banished noblemen were concerned,[9] presumably related by Nostradamus to the *Mirabilis Liber*'s predictions: 'In addition, in the year of our Lord 1503, great ills shall be prepared for sometime in the future: at that time insurrections and horrible conspiracies shall be plotted that, in these years, shall not produce all their effects, for some shall only break out later . . . and then shall be revealed judicial seditions, and conspiracies, and unheard of confederations of plebeian cities, and there shall be in the world such great dissension that no one shall know what to make of it' (Prophecy of Joannes de Vatiguerro). Nostradamus takes up the same theme again in his *Almanach* for 1566.

14. Original 1555 text

Read as modern French:

De gent esclave chansons, chantz & requestes,
Captifs par princes & seigneur aux prisons:
A l'avenir par idiots sans testes   *sans instruction/sans cerveau*
Seront receus par divins oraisons.   *Ils seront compris comme*

> The hymns and songs and prayers of those enslaved
> And into jail by lords and princes cast
> Shall come to be by idiots depraved
> As prayers and songs divine received at last.

Source: Evidently a commentary on the likely future success of the contemporary Protestant Huguenot cause in France, as well as an interesting sidelight on the Catholic (albeit Franciscan-orientated) Nostradamus's attitude to it.

15. Original 1555 text

Mars nous menasse par sa force bellique
Septante foys fera le sang espandre:
Auge & ruyne de l'Ecclesiastique
Et plus ceux qui d'eux rien voudront entendre.

Read as modern French:

menace; guerrière
Maintes fois
Apogée

With warlike force Mars threatens us right sore.
Full seventy times he'll spill blood everywhere.
The Church shall rise, then ruined be the more;
So, too, those who to listen shall not care.

Source: The *Mirabilis Liber*'s familiar scenario of a future Muslim invasion of Europe (see I.9 above) and the consequent destruction of the Catholic Church: 'All the treasures and ornaments of the churches made of gold, silver, and precious stones shall become their property; the desolation shall be great, the churches burnt, and the corpses of the faithful shall be thrown where no one shall be able to find them to bury them . . . They shall even be seen putting pregnant women to the sword point and immolating the priests in the sanctuary. They shall desecrate their churches, cohabiting there with women, and they shall bedeck themselves, both themselves and their spouses, with sacred ornaments. They shall attach their horses to the tombs of the faithful as though to a bush. There shall be a general tribulation among the Christians who inhabit the earth' (Prophecy of Pseudo-Methodius); 'Then shall emerge from Babylon a king, a supporter of Satan who, in his infernal power, shall put the saints to death, and shall destroy the churches. There shall be many wars and tribulations. The children of Agar shall seize Tarento, and spreading through Apulia, shall sack a host of towns. They shall be determined to enter Rome, and nobody in the world shall be able to resist them, unless it be the Lord God himself' (Prophecy of the Tiburtine Sibyl); 'Indeed, the mischief and profanity of the Huns and the cruel inhumanity of the Vandals shall be nothing in comparison to the new tribulations, calamities, and sufferings that in a short while shall oppress the holy Church; for the altars of the holy Church shall be destroyed, the floors of the temples desecrated, the monasteries polluted and despoiled, because the hand and anger of God shall take their vengeance on the world on account of the multiplicity and continuity of sins' (Prophecy of Joannes de Vatiguerro).

16. Original 1555 text

Faulx a l'estang joinct vers le Sagitaire
En son hault AUGE de l'exaltation,
Peste, famine, mort de main militaire:
Le siecle approche de renovation.

Read as modern French:

[Le faux] Saturne à Jupiter [l'étain]
apogée
mort par force militaire
L'âge/Le cycle

Jove joined with Saturn near the Archer bright
Is at his highest point of exaltation:
Plague, famine, death by military might –
The mighty cycle nears its renovation.

Source: Richard Roussat's *Livre de l'estat et mutation des temps* (1549–50):[67] 'Then Saturn and Jupiter shall be conjoined in Sagittarius . . . Saturn, in the Fire Sign, shall be raised and exalted at its apogee . . . Whereby pestilence, famine, and all kinds of corruptions, both of body and possessions, shall abound during this Cycle.'

17. Original 1555 text

	Read as modern French:
Par quarante ans l'Iris n'aparoistra,	*l'arc-en-ciel; apparaîtra*
Par quarante ans tous les jours sera veu:	*il sera vu*
La terre aride en siccité croistra,	*sécheresse*
Et grans deluges quand sera aperceu.	*quand il sera aperçu*

> **For forty years no rainbow they shall know,**
> **Then forty years it light shall daily shed.**
> **First arid land shall yet more arid grow,**
> **Then, when it's seen, great floods there'll be instead.**

Source: Once again Richard Roussat's *Livre de l'estat et mutation des temps* (1549–50):[67] 'The Venerable Bede (no less) states that Iris (that is to say the Rainbow, or Bow of Peace) shall in no wise be seen for the space of forty years before this incineration, on account of the great dryness of the celestial influences and stars, they being dependent on the divine wisdom and providence' – a wonderful example of Nostradamus's characteristic garbling of his sources, probably as a result of working from memory rather than from the printed text.

18. Original 1555 text

	Read as modern French:
Par la discorde negligence Gauloyse,	*françaises*
Sera passaige à Mahommet ouvert:	*Le passage sera livré aux Musulmans*
De sang trempé la terre & mer Senoyse	*Siennoises*
Le port Phocen de voiles & nefs couvert.	*Le port de Marseille*

> **Through negligence and discord French shall be**
> **To Muslim forces passage free allowed:**
> **Siena's lands bloodsoaked by land and sea,**
> **And sails and ships shall Marseille's harbor crowd.**

Source: The *Mirabilis Liber*'s forecast of a massive Muslim invasion of Europe by sea (see I.9), assimilated to François I's surprise 1543 alliance with the Ottomans that allowed their fleets to overwinter at Toulon and Marseille, their crews virtually occupying both ports.

19. Original 1555 text

	Read as modern French:
Lors que serpens viendront circuir l'are,	*l'autel*
Le sang Troien vexé par les Hespaignes	*La famille royale; Espagnes*
Par eux grand nombre en sera faicte tare,	*perte*
Chief, fuyct cache [/] aux mares dans les saignes.	*fuit, caché; aux marais*

> When serpents wind the altar round about
> Shall royal blood by Spaniards harrowed be.
> By them shall many be condemned to rout:
> Their leader, hid in ponds and reeds, shall flee.

Source: Julius Obsequens's *On Omens* (42) for 105 BC: 'At Trebula Mutusca, before the games began, as the flautist was playing, black snakes circled the altar . . . The Roman army was defeated by the Lusitanians [Portuguese]'; plus Plutarch's account in his *Parallel Lives* of the flight of the old Roman general Gaius Marius many years later: 'At Marius's wish, he bore him into the marshes and bade him hide himself in a hollow by the riverside, where he laid upon him many reeds . . . But within a short time he was disturbed . . . Whereupon Marius, arising and stripping himself, plunged into a pool full of thick muddy water.'

20. Original 1555 text   Read as modern French:

Tours, Orleans, Bloys, Angiers, Reims, & nantes
Cités vexées par subit changement:
Par langues estranges seront tendues tentes
Fluves, dards Renes, terre & mer tremblement.   *Fleuves d'arènes*

> Tours, Blois, Reims, Angers – towns whom change immense
> With Orléans and Nantes shall fast o'ertake.
> About them foreign speakers pitch their tents,
> While sandy rivers, land and sea shall quake.

Source: The *Mirabilis Liber*'s forecast of a vast Arab invasion of Europe (see I.9 above), accompanied by a range of worrying natural phenomena: 'Many towns and strong military posts on the Po, the Tiber, the Rhône, the Rhine, and the Loire shall be razed by extraordinary floods and earthquakes' (Prophecy of Joannes de Vatiguerro). All the above towns except Reims stand on the largely sandy river Loire.

21. Original 1555 text   Read as modern French:

Profonde argille blanche nourir rochier,   *rocher*
Qui d'un abysme istra lacticineuse,   *sortira laiteuse*
En vain troubles [//] ne l'oseront toucher   *troublés, ils*
Ignorans estre au fond terre argilleuse.

> The deep white clay that nourishes the rock
> And milky from a chasm takes its birth
> Shall needless those who dare not touch it shock,
> Not knowing clay soil lies beneath the earth.

Source: Contemporary excavations of the ancient Gallo-Roman *oppidum* of Constantine, near Lançon, just south of Salon, as noted by Nostradamus elsewhere.[63] See V.7.

22. Original 1555 text

Ce qui vivra & n'aiant aucun sens,
Viendra leser à mort son artifice:
Autun, Chalon, Langres & les deux Sens,
La gresle & glace fera grand malefice.

Read as modern French:

ayant
artificier/créateur

dommage

That which shall live, yet be without a mind
Shall wound to death [her] who did it create:
At Autun, Langres, Chalon and Sens (each kind)
Shall hail and ice cause devastation great.

Source: Reports (possibly purely oral) of a contemporary omen and its 'result' – a woman who has died giving birth to a brain-damaged child, followed by severe winter weather around Lyon.

23. Original 1555 text

Au mois troisiesme se levant le soleil,
Sanglier, liepard, au champ mars pour combatre.
Liepard laisse, au ciel extend son œil,
Un aigle autour du soleil voyt s'esbatre.

Read as modern French:

sur le champ de bataille
lassé

In the third month scarce ere the sun is high
Leopard and Boar enter the field to fight.
Leopard, exhausted, glances at the sky
And sees an Eagle round the sun in flight.

Source: A whole raft of contemporary reported omens, later catalogued by Conrad Lycosthenes in his *Chronicle of omens and portents* (1557).[44] In this case the original source for both authors (albeit slightly garbled in the case of Nostradamus who – as ever – was probably working from memory) was evidently the *Teratoscopia* ('Monstroscopy') of Gasparus Peucerus, and specifically its description of the omens that had allegedly been observed during 1534. As the 1581 English translation of Lycosthenes by Dr Stephen Batman[5] renders it: *The third day of July (as afore sayde, but more at large by a seconde Authour), in the town of Schesvie [Schevitz] in the South, in fayre weather there were seene in the aire Lions running together from divers places to a conflicte . . . a little while after there was seene a Bores head tusked . . . Afterwarde in a large playne there appeared two burning Castels neare to a high hill, to the whiche stoocke a greate Eagle hiding the halfe of his body behind the side of the hill: there appeared also certayne yong Eagles of a brighte white coloure, likewise the head of a Lyon lying upright, having a Crowne uppon his head, a Cocke striking and digging the heade with his Bill untill it was loose and fell from the body, and so vanished away, the body remayning a long tyme to be seene. There stoode by also other Lyons, and by the Bores heade there was a Unicorne which by little and little turned into a Dragon, and there were very many creatures of forme and greatnesse not usuall.* Compare I.35 below.

24. Original 1555 text   **Read as modern French:**

A cité neufve pensif pour condemner,
Loysel de proye au ciel se vient offrir: *L'oiseau*
Apres victoire a captifs pardonner,   *il pardonnera*
Cremone & Mantoue [/] grands maulx aura   *[Cremo. & Mant. dans l'éd. de nov. 1557] à*
    souffert   *souffrir*

> **At his new city, thinking to condemn,**
> **An eagle in the sky to him shall show:**
> **Victor with captives, he shall pardon them.**
> **Cremona, Mantua woes shall undergo.**

Source: A classical omen, this time from Livy's *History of Rome* (I.34), reported as befalling the future King Tarquin (always an enthusiast for such phenomena) as he arrived for the first time before his new city of Rome at the behest of his ambitious wife Tanaquil: as though to confirm her intention and remove any doubts on his part by seemingly crowning him in advance, 'an eagle swooped down, gently snatched his cap from his head . . . and then neatly replaced it on his head as though in the service of the divine'; amplified with a passage from Virgil's *Eclogues* (IX.28): 'For Mantua, alas, huge miseries through the closeness of Cremona!'

25. Original 1555 text   **Read as modern French:**

Perdu, trouvé, caché de si long siecle   *âge/de si longue date*
Sera pasteur demi dieu honore,   *honoré*
Ains que la Lune acheve son grand cycle   *Avant que*
Par autres veux sera deshonoré.   *il sera*

> **Hidden for many an age, first lost, then found,**
> **The shepherd shall be demigod acclaimed.**
> **Before the moon completes its mighty round**
> **Shall he by other wishes be defamed.**

Source: Either the checkered history of Christianity – the cult of the Good Shepherd himself[9] – or the alleged discovery by a Spanish shepherd of the tomb of St James at Compostella in the early ninth century, which then became a place of cult pilgrimage until overrun by the Moors in the eleventh, only to become the 'Mecca of the West' once more only shortly before Nostradamus's birth and the beginning of the 'age of the moon' (according to Roussat[67]) in 1535 (compare I.48).[60] The end of this age would come in 1887, and this and other statements suggest that Nostradamus expected it to mark a collapse of established religion, as foretold in the *Mirabilis Liber*: 'All the Church in all the World shall be persecuted in a lamentable and grievous manner; it shall be stripped and deprived of all its temporal possessions . . . For all the churches shall be polluted and desecrated, and all public worship shall cease because of fear and because of a most rabid and uncontrolled madness. The nuns, quitting their convents, shall flee here and there, demeaned and insulted. The pastors of the Church and the hierarchy, hunted and stripped of their dignities and their positions, shall be cruelly manhandled; the flocks and subjects shall take flight, and shall remain dispersed without pastor and without leader . . . for the altars of the holy Church shall be destroyed, the floors of the temples desecrated, the monasteries polluted and despoiled, because the hand and anger of God shall take their vengeance on the world on account of the multiplicity and continuity of sins' (Prophecy of Joannes de Vatiguerro).

26. Original 1555 text

Read as modern French:

Le grand du fouldre tumbe d'heure diurne,
Mal & predict par porteur postulaire

tombe
Mal est prédit par un messager porteur des
   protestations des dieux offensés[9]

Suivant presaige tumbe d'heure nocturne,
Conflit Reins, Londres, Etrusque pestifere.

tombe
pestiféré

> **The lord felled by a bolt in broad daylight**
> **Bodes ill, conveying anger of the gods.**
> **The next great omen falls amidst the night:**
> **Plague in Etruria: London and Reims at odds.**

Source: Julius Obsequens *On Omens* (28) for 130 BC: 'The Praetor of the Roman people was struck dead by lightning'; plus Petrus Crinitus, *De honesta disciplina* (1504), itself based on the classical Festus: 'For they called [these lightning bolts *fulgura*] *postularia* for this reason: because [the gods] were demanding redress for the fact that, whether through contempt or merely non-observance, the ritual prayers or sacrifices had not been offered.'

27. Original 1555 text

Read as modern French:

Dessoubz de chaine Guien du ciel frappe,
Non loing de la est caché le tresor,
Qui par longs siecles avoit este grappé,
Trouve mourra, l'œil crevé de ressort.

chêne portant du gui [?]; frappé
là
depuis de longs âges; volé
Une fois l'ayant trouvé, il mourra

> **'Neath mistled oak by lightning long struck dead –**
> **The hidden, stolen treasure lies nearby**
> **Which through the ages had been plunderèd.**
> **Who finds it dies, a spring stuck in his eye.**

Source: The ancient story (reported by the Romano-Greek geographer Strabo, among others) of the *aurum tolosanum*, the sacred treasure of Toulouse first allegedly looted by the local Tectosagi tribesmen from the Greek treasuries at Delphi, then pillaged anew by the consul Quintus Servilius Caepio in 106 BC, which inexplicably disappeared before reaching Marseille on its way back to Rome, and which Caepio himself was suspected of having buried somewhere near Toulouse. His subsequent exile to Asia Minor and various other calamities resulted in the hoard's being associated with bad luck (*cf* Erasmus: *Adages*). Always fascinated by buried treasure and artifacts, Nostradamus would take up the theme again at VIII.29, as well as in a letter to two treasure-seekers of 1562, in which he specified in an appended quatrain that *A my chemin d'or reluisant la broche/Le percera* ('Half-way there, the pin of shining gold shall pierce him').

28. Original 1555 text

La tour de Bouq gaindra fuste Barbare,
Un temps, long temps apres barque
*   hesperique,*
Bestail, gens, meubles tous deux feront
*   grant tare*
Taurus & Libra quelle mortelle picque!

Read as modern French:

hissera [la voile] ; la petite galère de Barbarie
une barque de l'ouest/de l'Espagne

attaque!

> **Off Tour de Bouc shall galleys all sail make**
> **From Barbary then, later on, from Spain.**
> **Great toll shall both of beasts, men, chattels take.**
> **'Neath Taurus, Libra, what dread raids again!**

Source: Current events. Muslim pirates from North Africa continually raided the Mediterranean coast just south of Salon (guarded by the Tour de Bouc, now a lighthouse[P]) during Nostradamus's lifetime, notably between 1526 and 1531, in 1534 and in 1536. With the Mirabilis Liber's predictions of an eventual Muslim invasion of Europe, in part via Spain, it was logical to expect such attacks later on from further west, too – whether or not in April/May (Taurus) or September/October (Libra).

29. Original 1555 text

Quand le poisson terrestre & aquatique
Par forte vague au gravier sera mis,
Sa forme estrange suave & horrifique,
Par mer aux murs bien tost les ennemis.

Read as modern French:

When fish aquatic and terrestrial
By mighty waves upon the beach is cast,
In form horrific, sleek, fantastical.
The seaborne foes the wall shall reach
**   at last.**

Source: Apparently an extremely confused memory of the unnamed source also quoted by Conrad Lycosthenes in his *Prodigiorum ac ostentorum chronicon* of 1557,[44] describing the ominous events of 1553. As later translated into English by Dr Stephen Batman,[6] *The river*

of Rhine the 19th of June through many shoures did so exceede his channell, that it did much harme, not onely to Corne and Pasture, but to many Cities by the river side. Basill was in some daunger whiche standeth full upon the Rhine, whilest the violence of the raging river didde touche the walles of the lesser Citie, and touched almost the fishmarket of the greater Basill . . . by the means of that greate overflowing Fishes were taken in Meddowes and Sellers, the violence of the flood being past. In Nostradamus's version, this has become a fish-omen portending an attack on the walls by enemies from the sea . . . Compare III.21.

30. Original 1555 text   Read as modern French:

La nef estrange par le tourment marin
Abourdera pres de port incongneu,   *Atterrira; inconnu*
Nonobstant signes de rameau palmerin   *de palmier*
Apres mort, pille: bon avis tard venu.

> **The foreign ship 'midst mighty waves at sea**
> **Shall come to land at last at port unknown,**
> **Though warned by palm-branch waved frenetically.**
> **They'll kill and loot: too late the truth is known.**

Source: Unknown historical incident.

31. Original 1555 text   Read as modern French:

Tant d'ans les guerres en Gaule dureront,
Oultre la course du Castulon monarque,   *Au delà de; castillan*
Victoire incerte trois grands couronneront *trois nobles*
Aigle, coq, lune, lyon, soleil en marque. *à remarquer*

> **The wars in Gaul shall last the decades down**
> **Beyond the life-course of the king of Spain,**
> **Uncertain victory shall three lords crown:**
> **Cock, Eagle, Moon, Lion, Sun are seen again.**

Source: The current political and military adventures of Charles V of Hapsburg in his capacity as King of Spain (with his motto of *PLUS ULTRA*, or 'Further beyond'), simply projected into the future. The last line seems to refer to the various rivalries and squabbles between France, Germany, the Ottomans, England, and Rome.

32. Original 1555 text   Read as modern French:

Le grand empire sera tost translaté   *transféré*
En lieu petit qui bien tost viendra croistre: *s'aggrandira*
Lieu bien infime d'exigue comté
Ou au milieu viendra poser son sceptre.   *Où; il posera*

> Transferred right soon shall be the great Empire
> *To a small place which soon shall grow apace –*
> A tiny place within a tiny shire –
> Where, at its heart, his scepter he shall place.

Source: The former transfer of papal rule from Rome to Avignon at the time of the Great Western Church Schism of 1378 to 1417 (see V.46, V.49, V.92, VI.13, VII.22, VII.23, VII.35, VIII.62, IX.4), assimilated to the *Mirabilis Liber*'s: '. . . and then the barque of Peter, attacked by powerful enemies, shall be shaken. Terrified, Peter shall be forced to flee, in order not to incur the infamy of servitude' (Prophecy of St Brigid of Sweden); 'For all the malice of men shall turn against the Catholic Church, and as a result she shall be without an advocate for twenty five months and more, because, throughout the said space of time, there shall be neither Pope nor Emperor in Rome, nor any Regent in France' (Prophecy of Joannes de Vatiguerro).

33. Original 1555 text	Read as modern French:
Près d'un grant pont de plaine spatieuse,	
Le grand lyon par force Cesarées	
Fera abbatre hors cité rigoreuse,	*entêtée*
Par effroy portes luy seront reserées.	*ouvertes*

> Near a great bridge upon a spacious plain
> The mighty Lion with full imperial power
> Shall train his cannon on the city vain:
> For fear the gates they'll open, and shall cower.

Source: A projection into the future of any one of a number of known successful sieges – possibly that conducted by the English Henry VIII in person at Thérouanne or at Tournai in 1513, not long before the death of King Louis XII.

34. Original 1555 text	Read as modern French:
L'oyseau de proye volant a la senestre	*à gauche*
Avant conflit faict aux Francoys pareure	*apparaît*
L'un bon prendra, l'un ambigue sinistre,	
La partie foyble tiendra par bon augure.	*faible; le prendra pour*

> The bird of prey that leftwards takes its flight
> Before the fight shall to the French appear.
> Some good shall think it, some bad, some unclear.
> The weaker side shall think that it bodes right.

Source: Projection into the French future of the standard ancient Roman doctrine of omens: 'Had not, on the left, the crow warned me from the hollow holly-oak' (Virgil, *Eclogues*, IX.15); 'I shall lead my legions, the bird on the left being a clear omen that accords with my wishes' (Plautus, *Pseudolus*).

35. Original 1555 text

Le lyon jeune le vieux surmontera,
En champ bellique par singulier duelle,
Dans caige d'or les yeux luy crevera:
Deux classes une, puis mourir, mort cruelle.

Read as modern French:

il lui crèvera
Deux flottes/armées réunies, puis il mourra

The younger lion shall surmount the old
'Midst martial battlefield in single duel.
His eyes he'll put out in a cage of gold –
Two forces joined – and then a death most cruel.

Source: A report (seemingly supplied originally by Marcus Frytschius,[24] and later requoted by the Swiss Conrad Lycosthenes in his *Chronicle of Omens and Portents*[44]) of a notable Swiss omen of 1547: 'In Switzerland two armies were seen in the sky, and two lions also fighting hard against each other, of which one bit off the head of the other.' (It is perhaps worth remembering that Nostradamus seems to have preferred working from memory rather than directly from the printed texts, and so was always prone to get his details slightly wrong.) Compare VIII.34.

This in turn is assimilated to Villehardouin's account in his *Conquest of Constantinople* of the deposing and blinding of the old Emperor Isaac II Angelus of Constantinople by his brother and successor Alexius III in his golden throne-room adorned with a famous battlefield fresco, at the very moment when Crusader and Venetians fleets were combining to attack the city.[60] Compare VIII.69, where Nostradamus appears to refer to the same event. No doubt, too, there is a sideways look at the *Mirabilis Liber*'s: 'New phenomena shall be seen in the air in Austria, in Italy, and in all the Eastern quarter' (Prophecy of the Angelic Pastor, attributed to St Cyril); as well as at 'The lily, partner of the great eagle, shall sweep from the West to the East against the lion; the lion, defenseless, shall be overcome by the lily' (Prophecy of St Brigid of Sweden) – to Nostradamus a possible presage of eventual victory, somewhat on the earlier Byzantine model, by the younger King Henri II over his older enemy, the Emperor Charles V.

36. Original 1555 text

Tard le monarque se viendra repentir
De n'avoir mis à mort son adversaire:
Mais viendra bien à plus hault consentir
Que tout son sang par mort fera defaire.

Read as modern French:

sa famille; détruire

Too late the monarch shall himself repent
Of having failed to put to death his foe,
Yet to one higher still he shall consent
To have his whole kin put to death, e'en so.

Source: Unknown, unless related to the previous verse.

37. Original 1555 text

Read as modern French:

Ung peu devant que le soleil s'esconse　　*Un peu; se cache*
Conflict donné, grand peuple dubieux:
Proffligés, port marin ne faict responce,　　*Abattus*
Pont & sepulchre en deux estranges lieux.　　*Pompe et sépulture*

Shortly before the sun at last goes down,
A mighty race unsure, the battle rages.
Defeated: no response from harbor town:
Their funerals on two quite different stages.

Source: The Battle of Actium in 31 BC (Suetonius: *The Twelve Caesars*, II.17): 'The battle went on so late that he [Augustus] spent the night aboard ship'; assimilated to the *Mirabilis Liber's* various predictions of a future Muslim seaborne invasion of Europe, with the last line reflecting the respective burial places of the original participants.

38. Original 1555 text

Read as modern French:

Le Sol & l'aigle au victeur paroistront:
Responce vaine au vaincu l'on asseure,
Par cor ne crys harnoys n'arresteront
Vindicte, paix par mort si acheve à l'heure.　　*Rétribution; s'y achève*

Eagle and Sun to th' victor shall appear:
Mere vain assurance to the beaten shown.
Nor shouts nor bugles shall the armed men steer
From vengeance: peace assured by death alone.

Source: Indeterminate, but with a hint at the traditional omens in line 1. See I.23, I.24 above.

39. Original 1555 text

Read as modern French:

De nuict dans lict le supresme estrangle　　*étranglé*
Pour trop avoir subjourné, blond esleu:　　*séjourné*
Par troys l'empire subroge exancle,　　*réclamé; épuisé*
A mort mettra [//] carte, pacquet ne leu.　　*non pas lus*

Abed at night, strangled the mighty chief
For having stayed too long; the fair elect
(By three the empire being claimed and wrecked)
Puts him to death, unread the unoped brief.

Source: The over-long reign of Charles V and the claims of his 'blond' brother Ferdinand, his own son Philip and Ferdinand's son Maximilian, with a sly and somewhat menacing reference to Suetonius's account in his *The Twelve Caesars* (I.81) of the assassination of Julius Caesar and his succession by the ruling triumvirate of Octavian, Mark Antony, and Lepidus: 'Caesar set out at about the fifth hour and added to other letters that he was holding in his left hand, as though intending to read them shortly, a letter warning him of an ambush.'

40. Original 1555 text   Read as modern French:

La trombe faulse dissimulant folie   *trompette*
Fera Bisance un changement de loys:
Hystra d'Egypte qui veult que l'on deslie   *Sortira*
Edict changeant monnoyes & aloys.   *alois*

   False trumpetings that madness' face disguise
   In Istanbul a changed regime shall cause.
   From Egypt a reformer shall arise:
   On money and alloys he'll make new laws.

Source: The edicts on the reform of the currency issued by Louis IX in 1263, following his return from captivity in Egypt between 1250 and 1254,[9] assimilated to conditions under the *Mirabilis Liber*'s expected eventual regime in France: 'Fake jewelry, false metals' (Anonymous Latin prophecy). The 'trumpetings' are those of Discord: compare I.57.

41. Original 1555 text   Read as modern French:

Siege en cité, & de nuict assaillie,
Peu eschapés: non loing de mer conflict.
Femme de joye, retours filz defaillie
Poison & lettres cachées dans le plic.   *cachetées; pli*

  The town, besieged, by night they shall attack.
  Few shall escape the battle near the sea.
  Mother shall faint with joy that son is back.
  In th' envelope shall poisoned letters be.

Source: Unknown, but the idea of poisoned letters was a popular one at the time.

42. Original 1555 text   **Read as modern French:**

Le dix Kalendes d'Apvril de faict Gotique   *par le calendrier Julien*
Resuscité encor par gens malins:
Le feu estainct, assemblée diabolique
Cherchant les or du d'Amant & Pselyn   *les ordures décrites par Adamantius et Psellus*

> **March twenty-third in Gothic style, anew**
> **The rite's revived by evil-minded men:**
> **Out goes the light, and then this devil's crew**
> **Seek out that filth in Psellus, Origen.**

Source: Petrus Crinitus's *De honesta disciplina,* published in 1504 and reprinted by Gryphius of Lyon in 1552, citing Psellus and Origen (who was also known as 'Adamantius'[9]) on the practices of the ancient Gnostics. In the words of Psellus's *De daemonibus,* 'They gather on the evening of the Passion of Our Savior and . . . having put out the lights, copulate promiscuously either with their sisters or with their daughters . . . reckoning that this will . . . facilitate the entry of the demons.' French Catholics at the time were prone to apply this passage directly to the contemporary Protestants.[9]

43. Original 1555 text   **Read as modern French:**

Avant qu'avienne le changement d'empire,   *advienne; l'échange*
Il aviendra un cas bien merveilleux,   *un événement*
Le champ mué, le pilier de porphyre,
Mis, translaté sus le rochier noilleux.   *noueux*

> **Ere the great empire shall supplanted be**
> **A thing miraculous shall hap: the land**
> **Disturbed by quake, a shaft of porphyry**
> **Transferred upon a gnarlèd rock shall stand.**

Source: An unidentified seismological omen presaging the downfall of a mighty empire. Originally, no doubt, this was the Roman Empire, but Nostradamus now projects it into the future on the back of the *Mirabilis Liber's* prediction of a massive Muslim invasion and occupation of Europe, and thus the collapse both of the Roman *Church* and of the contemporary Holy Roman Empire under Charles V. See I.9, I.15, I.75, II.24.

44. Original 1555 text   **Read as modern French:**

En brief seront de retour sacrifices,
Contrevenants seront mis à martyre:
Plus ne seront moines abbés ne novices: *ni novices*
Le miel sera beaucoup plus cher que cire.

> **Soon pagan sacrifices shall come back again,**
> **Those who resist be martyred as before.**

No abbots, monks, no novices to train:
Honey than candle-wax shall cost far more.

Source: The looming religious wars, assimilated to *Mirabilis Liber's* forecasts of a general decay and collapse of the Church (see I.4 and I.15 above) and, more specifically: 'All the Church in all the World shall be persecuted in a lamentable and grievous manner; it shall be stripped and deprived of all its temporal possessions, and there shall be nobody in all the Church who does not feel fortunate at having escaped with his or her life. For all the churches shall be polluted and desecrated, and all public worship shall cease because of fear and because of a most rabid and uncontrolled madness. The nuns, quitting their convents, shall flee here and there, demeaned and insulted. The pastors of the Church and the hierarchy, hunted and stripped of their dignities and their positions, shall be cruelly manhandled; the flocks and subjects shall take flight, and shall remain dispersed without pastor and without leader . . . Alas! the suffering caused by all the tyrants, emperors, and unfaithful princes shall be renewed by those who shall persecute the holy Church. Indeed, the mischief and profanity of the Huns and the cruel inhumanity of the Vandals shall be nothing in comparison to the new tribulations, calamities, and sufferings that in a short while shall oppress the holy Church; for the altars of the holy Church shall be destroyed, the floors of the temples desecrated, the monasteries polluted and despoiled, because the hand and anger of God shall take their vengeance on the world on account of the multiplicity and continuity of sins' (Prophecy of Joannes de Vatiguerro).

45. Original 1555 text

45. Original 1555 text	**Read as modern French:**
Secteur de sectes grand preme au delateur:	*Le persécuteur [donnera] grande récompense*
Beste en theatre, dressé le jeu scenique:	
Du faict antique ennobli l'inventeur,	*le producteur/metteur en scène*
Par sectes monde confus & scismatique.	

The sect-finder shall every spy reward,
With beast and games the stage set up again.
The antic show's deviser made a lord,
The world by sects confused and split in twain.

Source: The contemporary *Journal d'un bourgeois de Paris*: 'On the Saturday following (4 June 1530) it was also promulgated that anybody who knew of any secret Lutherans should come and reveal them to the Court of Parliament, and they would be given twenty gold crowns',[9] combined with the ennoblement by King Henri II of the poet Étienne Jodelle in 1553 following a performance of his ground-breaking classical verse-tragedy *Cléopâtre captive* and the subsequent ritual sacrifice by himself and his friends of a goat in celebration, after the proper pagan manner.[60]

46. Original 1555 text

Tout aupres d'Aux, de Lectore & Mirande
Grand feu du ciel en troys nuicts tumbera:
Cause aviendra bien stupende & mirande:

Bien peu apres la terre tremblera.

Read as modern French:

Auch; Lectoure
tombera
Une chose se produira bien étonnante et
*   merveilleuse*

> **Near Auch, Lectoure, Mirande, the folk shall see**
> **Three nights' tremendous fire from heaven fall –**
> **Marvelous and stupendous it shall be –**
> **Then shortly earth shall quake and heave withal.**

Source: Recent regional meteorological events, reflecting Julius Obsequens *On Omens* (20) for 147 BC: 'At night the sky and earth were seen to burn'; (38) for 113 BC: 'In Gaul the sky was seen to burn'; (51) for 94 BC: 'A torch appeared in the sky and all the heavens were seen to burn'; and (54) for 91 BC: 'Around Reggio part of the city and its walls were shattered by an earthquake', and assimilated to the numerous predictions of 'fire from the sky' and earthquakes in the *Mirabilis Liber*: 'There shall be earthquakes in divers places . . . Fire shall devour the land, the sea, and the sky at a single stroke . . . A rain of fire and sulfur shall descend from heaven . . .' (Prophecy of the Tiburtine Sibyl); 'Nearly all the major part of the West shall be destroyed by its enemies; that is why extraordinarily violent earthquakes shall be felt in many places . . . All the elements shall be debased, because it is necessary that the whole nature of the age be changed; indeed, the earth, petrified with fear, shall suffer frightening quakes in many places, and shall swallow up the living; a number of towns, fortresses, and strong castles shall collapse and be flattened by earthquakes . . . In the sky shall be seen numerous and most surprising signs' (Prophecy of Joannes de Vatiguerro).

47. Original 1555 text

Du lac Leman les sermons facheront:
Des jours seront reduicts par les sepmaines,
Puis moys, puis an, puis tous deffailliront,
Les magistrats damneront leurs loys vaines.

Read as modern French:

semaines

> **Of Lake Geneva shall the sermons bore:**
> **Days shall become like weeks, and weeks in turn**

Like months, months years, till all fall to the floor.
The magistrates their empty faith shall spurn.

Source: The *Mirabilis Liber*: 'Then a prince of iniquity shall emerge from the tribe of Dan; he shall be called the Antichrist . . . The child of perdition, full of pride and of insane malice, he shall perform a host of prodigies on the earth, in order to reinforce the errors that he shall teach: through his magic arts he shall shake the good faith of many who shall see in his voice fire descending from heaven. Years shall be shortened like months, months like weeks, weeks like days, and days like hours' (Prophecy of the Tiburtine Sibyl). Nostradamus is identifying John Calvin, with his controversial pruning of the religious calendar, as the Antichrist in person, while making a wry comment on the typical Protestant sermon by standing the *Mirabilis Liber*'s prophecy on its head.

48. Original 1555 text   Read as modern French:

Vingt ans du regne de la lune passés
Sept mil ans autre tiendra sa monarchie:
Quand le soleil prendra ses jours lassés   *laissés/qui restent*
Lors accomplir & mine ma prophetie.   *s'accomplira et terminera*

These twenty years the moon it has been reigning.
By year seven thousand then another's king.
When next the sun takes up its time remaining
My prophecy's fulfillment it shall bring.

Source: Richard Roussat's *Livre de l'estat et mutation des temps*[67]: 'As for the present work and treatise, it will be divided into four parts: the first will show the conjunction marking the End of the World and Last Times . . . which will take place after a period of seven thousand years . . . The second part will demonstrate the end of the world through the movement and rule of the seven planets that are called wandering stars, each of which governs the world for the space of 354 years and four months, as Abraham Avenara writes in the punultimate chapter of his book *Liber rationum* . . . Next Mars was in control, up to 6732 years and four months [from the Creation as dated by Roussat – i.e. AD 1533] for the third time; and finally the Moon, which governs at present, took over its rule, which it should maintain (in order to complete its normal course of 354 years and four months) until the year 7086 and eight months [i.e. AD 1887]'; and the Sun after it until the year 7441 [i.e. AD 2242].' It was evidently by inexplicably adding the date of writing to this final figure (1555 + 2242) that Nostradamus seems, in his *Preface to César*, to have arrived at the surprising date of '3797' for what he expected to be the final fulfillment of the prophecies.

49. Original 1555 text   **Read as modern French:**

Beaucoup beaucoup avant telles menées
Ceux d'Orient par la vertu lunaire   *par la puissance*
L'an mil sept cent feront grand emmenées
Subjugant presques le coing Aquilonaire.   *la partie nord [de l'Europe]*

> **Long, long before such things shall come to pass,**
> **Those from the East with all their lunar strength**
> **In seventeen hundred shall come forth, alas,**
> **And subjugate near all the north at length.**

Source: A somewhat rash attempt to date the *Mirabilis Liber*'s constant warnings of a Muslim invasion of Europe: ' . . . So God delivered the sons of Israel from the slavery of the children of Ishmael. These [i.e. the Arabs] shall, however, renew their enterprise, they shall destroy the land, shall invade the globe from the East unto the West, from the South to the North, as far as Rome. Their yoke shall weigh heavy on the heads of the people. There shall be no nation or realm that can fight against them, until the Times shall be accomplished . . . This new invasion of the Ishmaelites shall be a punishment without measure or mercy. The Lord shall deliver all the nations into their hands because of the transgressions that we have committed against his laws . . . Thus it is that all the earth shall be delivered to the children of Ishmael, who shall bring dissolution in their wake' (Prophecy of Pseudo-Methodius); 'Their rage against the Christians of the north and of the west shall surpass the ferocity of all the cruelest beasts; the Christians, full of gentleness, shall be crushed by them' (Prophecy of Raymond Lolhardus, as quoted by Johann Lichtenberger). Nostradamus constantly associates the moon with Islam, whose prime symbol it of course is.

50. Original 1555 text   **Read as modern French:**

De l'aquatique triplicité naistra
D'un qui fera le jeudy pour sa feste:
Son bruit, loz, regne, sa puissance croistra, *Son renom, louange*
Par terre & mer aux orients tempeste.   *chef de guerre*

> **Of trigon watery, he'll take his birth**
> **From one who'll take a Thursday for his feast:**
> **His fame, praise, rule and power shall grow on earth,**
> **By land and sea the warlord of the East.**

Source: Roussat's *Livre de l'estat et mutation des temps*: 'It is time to say more about the aquatic triplicity [Cancer, Scorpio and Pisces] under which we are living at present . . . this triplicity started under Scorpio in the year 1402. Its extent includes the present year 1548 . . . only 94 years of this triplicity remain . . . the conjunction of Jupiter and Saturn in Scorpio signifies and shall signify the depopulation of a great part of Christendom, its desolation and perdition, should God in his immense and immeasurable goodness not intervene, for this aquatic triplicity is, moreover, most contrary to the Christian religion . . . It therefore seems likely in the nature of things that we should expect the Antichrist (if he is not already come) under the influence of the aquatic triplicity'; combined with contemporary expectations that the future Antichrist would celebrate Thursday as his 'sabbath'.[8]

51. Original 1555 text

Read as modern French:

Chef d'Aries, Juppiter & Saturne,   *Au premier point d'Aries*
Dieu eternel quelles mutations!   *bouleversements*
Puis par long siecle son maling temps retourne,   *pendant un long âge*
Gaule & Itale quelles esmotions!   *perturbations*

Saturn and Jove at Point of Aries show:
Eternal God, what changes are in train!
Then the slow round brings evil times again:
In France and Italy what stirrings grow!

Source: Roussat's *Livre de l'estat et mutation des temps*: 'Thereafter the most famous approach and union of Saturn and Jupiter, which will take place near the Point of Aries in the year of our Lord 1702, shall show throughout the world astonishing signs and more than great changes and upheavals.'

52. Original 1555 text

Read as modern French:

Les deux malins de Scorpion conjoints,
Le grand seigneur meurtry dedans sa salle:
Peste à l'eglise par le nouveau roy joint,
L'Europe basse & Septentrionale.   *En Europe du sud et du nord*

Saturn and Mars are met in Scorpio:
The mighty lord is murdered in his hall:
Plague on the Church a new king shall bestow
In southern Europe and the north withal.

Source: Roussat's *Livre de l'estat et mutation des temps*: 'To sum up, seeing that the stellar nature of Scorpio is identical to that of Mars, it follows that a conjunction of Jupiter and Saturn in Scorpio will signify the depopulation, desolation, and perdition of much of Christendom . . .' The reference is thus presumably to the Pope.

53. Original 1555 text

Read as modern French:

Las qu'on verra grand peuple tormenté   *Hélas!*
Et la loy saincte en totale ruine:
Par aultres loyx toute Chrestienté,
Quand d'or d'argent trouve nouvelle mine.   *Trouvé[e]*

Alas, a mighty race shall be sore tried
And Holy Law cast down upon the ground!
O'er Christendom shall other laws preside,
Of gold and silver new supplies once found.

Source: The *Mirabilis Liber*'s usual predictions of the destruction of Christendom by invading Muslims (I.9, I.15, and see previous quatrain), apparently related to the recent inflow of massive amounts of gold and silver looted by the Spanish Conquistadors from the New World in the wake of Cortés's expedition of 1519.

54. Original 1555 text

Deux revolts faits du malin falcigere,
De regne & siecles faict permutation:
Le mobil signe à son endroict si ingere
Aux deux egaux & d'inclination.

Read as modern French:

Dix [?] revolutions de Saturne et âges
à son tour; s'y

Two revolutions of dread Saturn's sphere
Shall changes bring of age and government,
When it in th' mobile sign shall interfere,
To both at angle quite equivalent.

Source: Roussat's *Livre de l'estat et mutation des temps*: 'Albumasar, that famed and renowned Astrologer, teaches and demonstrates . . . that sects, and the duration of kingdoms and their changes, come and last in accordance with the movement and duration of the ten revolutions of Saturn: especially when the change occurs under the mobile signs – that is to say, under Aries, Cancer, Libra, or Capricorn.'

55. Original 1555 text

Sous l'opposite climat Babylonique
Grande sera de sang effusion,
Que terre & mer, air, ciel sera inique:
Sectes, faim, regnes, pestes, confusion.

Read as modern French:

Sur la latitude proche [lat. oppositum] de Babylon

Over against where Babel used to stand
Great shall the bloodshed be, and full of evil
For air and sky, for sea and for the land:
For sects, starvation; kingdoms, plagues, upheaval.

Source: The *Mirabilis Liber*'s predictions of the eventual Christian backlash against the Muslim Middle East: 'Weep, alas! unhappy Babylon, what sad days await you! Like the ripened harvest, you shall be cut down on account of your iniquities. The kings of the four corners of the world shall advance against you . . .' (Anonymous sixteenth-century prophecy); 'There shall emerge from Gaul [interpolation by the sixteenth-century French editor!] a race of Christians who shall make war on them and shall pierce them with the sword, shall take away their women captive, and shall slaughter their children. In their turn, the sons of Ishmael shall encounter both sword and tribulation. And the Lord shall return to them the evil that they shall have done in sevenfold measure' (Prophecy of Pseudo-Methodius); 'The king of the Franks, Greeks, and Romans, reclaiming for himself the whole empire of Christendom, shall devastate all the pagan islands and cities, shall overthrow the temples of idolatry, and shall summon all the pagans to baptism' (Prophecy of the Tiburtine Sibyl).

56. Original 1555 text

Read as modern French:

Vous verrés tost & tard faire grand change
Horreurs extremes, & vindications,   *et vengeances*
Que si la lune conduicte par son ange
Le ciel s'approche des inclinations.   *de la fin de ses inclinations*

Sooner or later you'll see changes great:
Huge horrors, vengeance cruel the signs portend
As did its angel to the moon dictate.
Then heaven shall see its trepidation end.

Source: Roussat's *Livre de l'estat et mutation des temps*: 'At present . . . the moon is governing the world with the Angel Gabriel . . . under it shall occur great wonders and unusual events . . . it also signifies wondrous changes, inconstancy among men, diversity, the breaking of faith, violence, and deformity, for a multitude of monsters shall be born [compare Lycosthenes' book!44], not having the full form or stature of times of yore . . . Know therefore, friendly readers, that the Kingdom of God is at hand: that is to say, during the seventh millennium in which we [currently] are, when the eighth Sphere (which is the highest altitude of the Firmament, and the splendor of God) shall accomplish a full revolution: and the heavenly bodies shall return to the place from whence they first started their movement, and shall move no more.'67

57. Original 1555 text

Read as modern French:

Par grand discord la trombe tremblera.   *la trompette vibrera*
Accord rompu dressant la teste au ciel:
Bouche sanglante dans le sang nagera: *il nagera*
Au sol la face ointe de laict & miel.

Discord shall cause the trumpet note to sound.
Broken the pact, she'll raise her head on high:
Bleeding her mouth, in her own blood half-drowned:
Face-down, and milk-and-honey smeared, she'll lie.

Source: Petrus Crinitus, *De honesta disciplina,* quoting Petronius's *Satiricon*:

The trumpets blared, and Discord, shorn of hair,
Raised to the heavens her head, and with her mouth

All caked with blood, she wept with bruisèd eyes . . .
For the last line of the quatrain, compare VI.89.

58. Original 1555 text

Trenché le ventre, naistra avec deux testes,
Et quatre bras: quelques ans entier vivra:
Jour qui Alquilloye celebrera ses festes
Foussan, Turin, chief Ferrare suyvra.

Read as modern French:

Aquilée
Fossan

> **Sliced at the belly, with two heads and loins,**
> **Four-armed, it shall live several years at least;**
> **The day that Aquileia holds its feast**
> **Ferrara's lord Fossano, Turin joins.**

Source: Any one of a number of near-contemporary cases of monstrous births reported at the time, and in due course collected together by chroniclers such as Lycosthenes (1557).[44] The closest is the case reproduced and illustrated by him from reports for 1544, and in due course translated into the English of the day by Dr Stephen Batman:[5] *At Hedelberg standing by the river Neccarus, on Whitson Sonday was borne two boyes joyned togither, having two bodies closed by the belly part, two heades, foure handes and feete, whose mother was called Catherine: and* [whose father was called] *Gasper Besler* [an artisan.] *sayth* [This word is not in the Latin at all!] *they were christened, one*
called John the other Jerome and lived a day and a halfe: when they were dead [and the interior parts were seen by the doctors on cutting them apart], *they found in the belly but one hart.* If this report was indeed the origin of the verse, Nostradamus's recollection of the conjoined twins' lifespan was no more accurate than was Batman's translation (see my bracketed interpolations from the original Latin) – which makes me feel rather less guilty about adding 'and loins' to line 1 to make the rhyme! Whatever the details, however, Nostradamus is using the incident as an omen for an unidentified historical event, possibly connected with Hercule II d'Este of Ferrara's pro-French policies, which aligned him with Fossano and Turin during the early sixteenth century.

59. Original 1555 text

Les exiles deportés dans les isles
Au changement d'ung plus cruel monarque,
Seront meurtrys: & mis deux des scintilles
Qui de parler ne seront estés parques.

Read as modern French:

exilés

dedans/dans les scintilles [?]
économes

The exiles who to th' islands were outcast
Upon the advent of king more cruel
Shall murdered be, and in the flames be cast
Whoever shall their tongue not curb or rule.

Source: Unidentified incident from the history of Rome, which routinely banished its high-born exiles to various of the Mediterranean islands.

60. Original 1555 text

| | Read as modern French: |

Un Empereur naistra pres d'Italie, — *en Italie ['près de' pour 'à' ou 'en' est très normal chez Nostradamus]*

Qui a l'Empire sera vendu bien cher,
Diront avecques quels gens il se ralie — *Ils se moqueront*
Qu'on trouvera moins prince que boucher. — *Qu'on le chantera*

An Emperor is born near Italy
Who'll cost the Empire dear: and ever since
They'll scorn the types with whom he shall ally
And call him more a butcher than a prince.

Source: Unidentified medieval account of the life and dramatic career of the Holy Roman Emperor Frederick II von Hohenstaufen (1194–1250), who was also king of Sicily.

61. Original 1555 text

Read as modern French:

La republique miserable infelice
Sera vastée du nouveau magistrat: — *dévastée*
Leur grand amas de l'exil malefice — *[Lors?]*
Fera Sueve ravir leur grand contract. — *Suèves/habitants allemands du Jura; renier*

That miserable, wretched state shall sack
A master new, who'll see it ruined and racked:
Then a great force, from exile grim come back,
Shall force the Swabians to annul their pact.

Source: Unknown.

62. Original 1555 text

Read as modern French:

La grande perte las que feront les letres: — *les sciences*
Avant le cicle de Latona parfaict, — *de Diane [la lune]*
Feu, grand deluge plus par ignares sceptres
Que de long siecle ne se verra refaict. — *âge*

What mighty loss shall learning know, alas,
Before the cycle of the moon is done!

Through fire and flood and, worse, by monarchs crass
Which for long ages shall not be re-won.

Source: The *Mirabilis Liber*: 'Alas! the suffering caused by all the tyrants, emperors, and unfaithful princes shall be renewed by those who shall persecute the holy Church . . . The sea shall rage and shall rise against the world, and it shall swallow many ships and their crews . . . The pomp of the nobles shall disappear, even the sciences and arts shall perish, and for a short space of time the whole order of the clergy shall remain in humiliation' (Prophecy of Joannes de Vatiguerro). The thought was shared by Rabelais and other scholars of the time, who feared that a resurgence of popular ignorance might yet threaten the fragile plant of Renaissance learning. According to Roussat,[67] the end of the Age of the Moon would come in 1887.

63. Original 1555 text

	Read as modern French:
Les fleaux passés diminue le monde	*diminué*
Long temps la paix terres inhabitées	*habités [lat. inhabitare]*
Seur marchera par ciel, terre, mer, & onde:	*On marchera sûr*
Puis de nouveau les guerres suscitées.	

The woes once past, smaller the populace;
With lands re-peopled, peace shall long remain.
Through sky, o'er land and sea they'll safely pace,
Then wars once more shall be stirred up again.

Source: The *Mirabilis Liber*: 'The land . . . shall then be pacified. The prisoners . . . shall once again see their homelands, and the population shall grow and multiply . . . Peace and tranquility shall be reborn on earth, a peace such as there has never been, and such as there shall never be; happiness and rejoicing shall be everywhere. The world shall rest from its tribulations . . . In the very midst of this calm, there shall suddenly emerge from the north with Gog and Magog a nation which shall make the whole world tremble. Horrified, all men shall hide themselves in the mountains and among the rocks in order to flee their presence' (Prophecy of Pseudo-Methodius). Note the apparent prediction of air travel in line 3, possibly on the basis of the thirteenth-century predictions of Friar Roger Bacon, or even the near-contemporary speculations of Leonardo da Vinci.

64. Original 1555 text

	Read as modern French:
De nuit soleil penseront avoir veu	*ils penseront avoir vu*
Quand le pourceau demy-homme on verra,	
Bruict, chant, bataille, au ciel battre aperceu	
Et bestes brutes a parler lon orra.	*l'on entendra*

The sun at night they'll think that they espy
When pig half-human shall alive appear.

Songs, loud alarums, battles in the sky,
And of brute beasts that speak the sound they'll hear.

Source: Julius Obsequens's *Book of Omens* (12) for 166 BC: 'In Casino . . . the sun was seen at night for a few hours; (14) for 163 BC: 'In Caere a pig was born with human hands and feet . . . in Cephalonia a war-trumpet was seen sounding in heaven'; and (43) for 104 BC: 'Celestial arms were seen to fight at a variety of times, places, and occasions' (see II.85); plus, at sections 15, 26, 27, 43, 53, 'an ox spoke' – possibly assimilated to the *Mirabilis Liber*'s 'In the sky shall be seen numerous and most surprising signs (Prophecy of Joannes de Vatiguerro). Conrad Lycosthenes[44] would similarly report a whole rash of such apparitions in the sixteenth century – not, admittedly, talking beasts, but the sound of battles in the sky (notably in 1520 and 1526), actual visions of the combatants (in 1535, 1538, 1547 and 1554), the sun seen in the middle of the night (notably in 1532 near Babylon), and a pig born with a human face in 1523: as Dr Stephen Batman would later translate this last text into the English of the day:[5] *A Calfe Monke, a terrible Monster was borne at Watersodorsi, a mile from Friberg, a village belonging to the Lordshippe of Cellen, at a Farmers house called Stecker, of which Monster Mayster Martin Luther hathe sette forthe hys opinion: we knowe also that a Pigge-prieste was farrowed with a bald Crown in Saxonie upon Easter day.*

65. Original 1555 text   Read as modern French:

Enfant sans mains jamais veu si grand foudre:
L'enfant royal au jeu d'oesteuf blessé. *au jeu de paume*
Au puy brises: fulgures alant mouldre: *brisés*
Trois sous les chaines par le milieu troussés: *chênes [?]*

A handless child: lightning as ne'er befell:
The royal prince at tennis shall be wounded:
Men struck by bolts milling beside the well:
Three 'neath the oaks, their waists with rope surrounded.

Source: A series of contemporary omens linked (inexplicably, at first sight) to the death of the young Dauphin François at Tournon in 1536, after he had complained of feeling unwell during a game of tennis, and his resultant immediate replacement as first in line of succession by his younger brother Henri. The first two omens seem to be among those reported for 1548 by Marcus Frytschius in his *De Meteoris* of 1555, as later reprinted by Conrad Lycosthenes in his *Prodigiorum ac ostentorum chronicon* of 1557[44] and then translated into English by Dr Stephen Batman in his *The Doome, warning all men to the Judgemente* of 1581. Immediately

above the entry: *The tenth of Februarie there was* **1548**
seene in Saxony a fire in ye Elemente, falling upon cer-
taine cities came the words: *The 18. of the Kalendes*
of Maye betweeen sixe and seven a clock, at Mysena, a
childe was borne with the skul devided in the forehead,
w one thigh, without lippes, having in the place of his
mouth a little hole, and maimed in the reste of hys
bodye. The accompanying woodcut showed the
result more dramatically and explicitly. The pre-
sumed link with the French succession would then
duly appear just six entries later (on the opposite
page, in Lycosthenes' anthology), albeit a year behind the times. Again in Batman's
words: *Fraunces the French King died, whome his Sonne Henry the second of that name*
succeeded: so uppon the death of King Henrye the eighte King of Englande, Edwarde suc-
ceeded being yet but a Chylde, as before is sayde.

66. Original 1555 text   Read as modern French:

Celui qui lors portera les nouvelles,
Apres un peu il viendra respirer.
Viviers, Tournon, Montferrant & Pradelles,
Gresle & tempestes les fera souspirer.   soupirer

> **He who shall then the news both bring and tell**
> **Shall, after a short while, his breath regain.**
> **At Viviers, Tournon, Montferrand, Pradelles**
> **Both hail and storm shall make them sigh amain.**

Source: Unknown contemporary events. Reports of prodigious hailstorms were
frequent in omen-collections of the day, as later recorded by Lycosthenes – but few
of his, at least, were for places in France.

67. Original 1555 text   Read as modern French:

La grand famine que je sens approcher,
Souvent tourner, puis estre universele,   retournera souvent
Si grande & longue qu'on viendra arracher
Du bois racine, & l'enfant de mammelle.

> **The mighty famine whose approach I feel**
> **Shall oft return, then reign from east to west,**
> **So great, so very long that they shall steal**
> **From trees their roots, babes from their mother's breast.**

Source: The *Mirabilis Liber*: ' . . . there shall be an astonishing and cruel famine
which shall be so great and of such an extent throughout the World and especial-

ly in the regions of the West, such that since the beginning of the world no one has ever heard of the like' (Prophecy of Joannes de Vatiguerro); 'There shall break out a war across the world, in the pagan lands as much as in Christendom; and this war shall last a long time, during which our Lord shall send upon the Christians, just as upon the pagans, so great a famine that when He shall see them make war on each other, He shall make them abase their pride despite themselves . . .' (Prophecy of Merlin).

68. Original 1555 text

O quel horrible & malheureux torment
Troys innocens qu'on viendra à livrer:
Poyson suspecte, mal garde tradiment
Mis en horreur par bourreaux enyvrés.

Read as modern French:

A trois innocents
gardés ; trahison

> **Oh, what grim torment, and so wretched too,**
> **Shall on three innocents be then inflicted –**
> **Treason, poor guarding, poison all suspected –**
> **When grimly murdered by that drunken crew!**

Source: Unknown event, probably contemporary.

69. Original 1555 text

La grand montaigne ronde de sept estades,
Apres paix, guerre, faim, inundation,
Roulera loing abysmant grands contrades,
Mesmes antiques, & grand fondation.

Read as modern French:

À la grande montagne

de grande fondation

> **The mighty mountain near a mile in girth**
> **Shall – after peace, war, famine – floods surround.**
> **Far they shall roll to great lands of the earth**
> **E'en old, that mighty countries once did found.**

Source: The *Mirabilis Liber*, possibly referred to the ancient Greek colonies in Sicily: 'The cities and provinces of the Islanders shall be swallowed up by floods. To the plague which shall devastate some places shall be joined the fury of enemies, and nothing shall be able to comfort them . . . There shall no longer be on earth any eminence or unevenness, for the azure waters of the sea shall roll in level with the mountaintops' (Prophecy of the Tiburtine Sibyl); 'The sea shall rage and shall rise against the world' (Prophecy of Joannes de Vatiguerro); 'He shall make the high sea mount above its shores . . . As the mountains are above the plains, if it were not for an angel, they would all drown in their sins. But this sea shall rise far above the shores quite obviously. The sea shall rise in all parts of the world: truly even the Indies shall share in it, and know that the sea shall rise greatly and miraculously . . .' (Prophecy of Merlin).

70. Original 1555 text   **Read as modern French:**

Pluie, faim, guerre en Perse non cessée
La foy trop grande trahira le monarque,
Par la finie en Gaule commencée:
Secret augure pour à ung estre parque.   *pour être économe envers quelqu'un*

> Rain, famine, endless war shall Persia know,
> Faith overdone the monarch soon ensnaring.
> What starts in France there to its end shall go:
> A secret sign to someone to be sparing.

Source: The *Mirabilis Liber*'s various descriptions of an eventual Christian counter-invasion against the Muslim Middle East. See I.55 above. The precise significance of the second and last lines is unknown.

71. Original 1555 text   **Read as modern French:**

La tour marine troys foys prise & reprise
Par Hespagnols, barbares, Ligurins: *Espagnols*
Marseille & Aix, Arles par ceux de Pise
Vast, feu, fer, pillé Avignon des Thurins.   *Dévastation*

> Three times the sea-fort's stormed, then taken back
> By Spanish, Arab and Italian thunder.
> Marseilles, Aix, Arles shall those from Pisa sack
> By sword and fire, Turin Avignon plunder.

Source: Either Andrea Doria's seaborne attack on the Tour de Bouc[P], at the entrance to the Étang de Berre, in 1536; or the three captures of Marseille and the Tour St-Jean[P], which guards its harbor by the Saracens in 735, by Charles d'Anjou in 1252 and by Alphonso V of Aragon in 1423.[60]

72. Original 1555 text   **Read as modern French:**

Du tout Marseille des habitans changée,
Course & poursuitte jusques au pres de Lyon.
Narbon. Tholoze par Bourdeaux outragee: *Narbonne, Toulouse*
Tués captifz presque d'un milion.

> Marseille a change of citizens shall know:
> Chased and pursued, towards Lyon they shall head.
> Narbonne, Toulouse by forces from Bordeaux
> Are sacked. Of captives near a million dead.

Source: Apparently the *Mirabilis Liber*'s general forecast of a future Muslim invasion of France, both from the south and from the southwest: 'The Spanish shall perish by the sword. France, Germany, and the land of the Goths, eaten up by a thousand scourges, shall see a host of their inhabitants carried off' (Prophecy of Pseudo-Methodius). Compare the previous verse.

73. Original 1555 text

Read as modern French:

France à cinq pars par neglect assailie
Tunys, Argiels esmeus par Persiens,
Leon, Seville, Barcelonne faillie
N'aura la classe par les Venitiens.

négligence
Alger

flotte/armée

> **Negligent France on five fronts to assail**
> **Shall Persia Tunis and Algiers incite.**
> **Leon, Seville and Barcelona fail**
> **To see the force that Venice them did plight.**

Source: The *Mirabilis Liber*'s general predictions of a Muslim invasion of Europe via North Africa. See previous verse.

74. Original 1555 text

Read as modern French:

Apres sejourné vogueront en Epire:
Le grand secours viendra vers Antioche,
Le noir poil crespe tendra fort à l'Empire:
Barbe d'aerain le roustira en broche.

Après un séjour [/]

Barberousse

> **Rested, on Epirus they'll set their sights:**
> **Deliverance great they'll bring to Antioch's coast.**
> **The lord with black, curled beard for th' Empire fights,**
> **But Barbarossa him on spit shall roast.**

Source: An account of the Emperor Friedrich Barbarossa's siege of Antioch in 1097 during the First Crusade, assimilated to the *Mirabilis Liber*'s account of an eventual re-invasion by Christian forces of the Muslim Middle East. See I.55.

75. Original 1555 text

Read as modern French:

Le tyran Siene occupera Savone:
Le fort gaigné tiendra classe marine:
Les deux armées par la marque d'Ancone
Par effraieur le chef s'en examine.

de Sienne ; attaquera [lat.]

> **Siena's tyrant shall attack Savona:**
> **The fort once gained, he shall the fleet control.**
> **Two hosts shall land on th' Marches of Ancona:**
> **In fright the chief his conscience shall console.**

Source: Unknown historical event, assimilated to the *Mirabilis Liber*'s general predictions of a Muslim invasion of Europe via Italy: 'The children of Agar shall seize Tarento, and spreading through Apulia, shall sack a host of towns. They shall be determined to enter Rome, and nobody in the world shall be able to resist them, unless it be the Lord God himself' (Prophecy of the Tiburtine Sibyl).

76. Original 1555 text   Read as modern French:

D'un nom farouche tel proferé sera,
Que les troys seurs auront fato le nom: *Que les trois Parques auront prédit*
Puis grand peuple par langue & faict duira   *conduira/mènera*
Plus que nul autre aura bruit & renom.

A name as fierce to him shall be decreed
As ever by the Fates, those Sisters Three.
Then a great race by word and deed he'll lead:
More than all others famed, renowned he'll be.

Source: Apparently the shock sacking of Catholic Rome in 1527 by Imperial troops (many of them Protestant) who were partly under the command of Georg von Frundsberg – to whose barbaric-looking German Gothic signature Nostradamus seems to refer on several other occasions as well (see IX.26, X.20, X.65) – assimilated to the *Mirabilis Liber*'s prophecies of the Antichrist: 'It is then that the Son of Perdition shall appear, the Antichrist' (Prophecy of Pseudo-Methodius); 'Then a prince of iniquity shall emerge from the tribe of Dan; he shall be called the Antichrist . . . From the north shall issue the most ferocious people whom King Alexander had held in check, namely Gog and Magog' (Prophecy of the Tiburtine Sibyl); 'He shall be great in the eyes of people, and one of the most respected princes since the beginning of the Church. He shall be called the Antichrist' (Prophecy on the Antichrist, quoted from Johann Lichtenberger's *Pronosticatio quedam mirabilis*).

77. Original 1555 text   Read as modern French:

Entre deux mers dressera promontoire   *une incursion/tête de pont*
Que puis mourra par le mords du cheval: *Celui qui; mors*
Le sien Neptune pliera voyle noire,   *Son amiral à lui*
Par Calpre & classe aupres de Rocheval.   *Par Gibraltar; flotte/armée; Rochevaux*

Between two seas he'll mount a great campaign,
That one who, bitten by his horse, shall die:
His admiral his black sail furls again
Gibraltar near, and ships near Rochevaux ply.

Source: Unknown historical incident, with echoes of the story of the Greek Theseus.

78. Original 1555 text

D'un chef viellard naistra sens hebete,
Degenerant par savoir & par armes
Le chef de France par sa sœur redouté:
Champs divisés, concedés aux gendarmes.

Read as modern French:

de sens hébété

> Son of old chief, a dimwit comes to birth,
> Degenerate in knowledge and in arms:
> Feared by his sister, lord of France's earth
> Shall share out fields, let out to men at arms.

Source: The subject of the first two lines is unidentified, but the last two are reminiscent of the Emperor Augustus, who remodeled the city of Arles for the Sixth Legion, veterans of his Egyptian campaigns, and parceled out the country between Arles and St-Rémy to his centurions in the form of plots known as 'centuries', watered by an aqueduct whose ruins can still be seen at Fontveille, just to the south-west of the latter. His sister Octavia, who had married his eventual rival Mark Antony, had good cause to be afraid of him, even though she subsequently divorced her husband again: but Nostradamus may be confusing her with Augustus's wife Julia.

79. Original 1555 text

Bazaz, Lectore,Condon, Ausch, & Agine
Esmeus par loys, querele & monopole.
Car Bourd. Thoulouze Bay. metra en ruine
Renouveler voulant leur tauropole.

Read as modern French:

Bazas, Lectoure, Condom, Auch et Agen
Agitées; complots
Carcassonne, Bordeaux, Toulouse, Bayonne
leurs sacrifices de taureaux

> Bazas, Lectoure, Agen, Auch and Condom
> Stirred up by laws, disputes and plots galore,
> Carcassonne, Bordeaux, Toulouse and Bayonne
> He'll ruin, who their bull-cult would restore.

Source: Étienne Dolet's 1528 accusation of idolatry directed at Toulouse, with its ancient history of animal sacrifices, which were formerly so strongly opposed by the local St Sernin.

80. Original 1555 text

De la sixiesme claire splendeur celeste
Viendra tonner si fort en la Bourgoigne:
Puis naistra monstre de treshideuse beste.
Mars, apvril, May, Juing grand charpin & rongne.

Read as modern French:

De Jupiter

déchirement; querelle

> The sixth bright splendor of the sky at night
> Shall cause such thunder there in Burgundy.
> Then shall be born a monster to affright:
> From March to June great discord there shall be.

Source: More of the familiar accounts of omens, this time linked to astrology, and particularly to the planet Jupiter – i.e. Jove The Thunderer. Lycosthenes[44] would later report a number of cases of storms coinciding with the birth of monsters, notably in 1523 (at Freiburg and Naples), in 1545 (in Switzerland and Italy) and in 1550–1 (sited vaguely 'in Germany'). Given that Burgundy was currently under the control of the Emperor Charles V, who was also King of Germany, this last may conceivably have lain at the basis of the first two lines.

81. Original 1555 text	Read as modern French:
D'humain troupeau neuf seront mis à part	
De jugement & conseil separés:	
Leur sort sera divisé en depart	*partage/distribution [?]*
Καπ, Θhita, λambda *mors, bannis esgarés.*	*Kappa, Thêta, Lambda [par gématrie, 9, 20, 30]*

> **Of human flock shall nine be set apart,**
> **All judgment and all counsel be denied.**
> **Their fate shall be decided from the start,**
> **Fifty-nine dead, the banished scattered wide.**

Source: The burning to death in Paris in 1310 of 59 Templars, arrested for alleged unnatural practices, sacrilege and heresy, who had retracted their confessions, and at Senlis of the nine whose trials were broken off.[60] See II.51.

82. Original 1555 text	Read as modern French:
Quand les colomnes de bois grande tremblée	*trembleront beaucoup*
D'Auster conduicte couverte de rubriche	*À cause du vent du sud; ocre/argile rouge*
Tant vuidera dehors grand assemblée,	*sortira*
Trembler Vienne & le païs d'Austriche.	*Trembleront*

> **As all the wooden masts shall shake and tremble**
> **In the south wind, covered with ochre red,**
> **So shall they all come forth who there assemble:**
> **Vienna and all Austria quake for dread.**

Source: The Ottoman naval invasion of Europe, leading to their invasion of Austria and their siege of Vienna in 1526, assimilated to the *Mirabilis Liber's* predictions of just such a Muslim invasion. See I.9.

83. Original 1555 text	Read as modern French:
La gent estrange divisera butins,	
Saturne en Mars son regard furieux:	
Horrible strage aux Tosquans & Latins,	*massacre*
Grecs, qui seront à frapper curieux.	*qui seront soucieux de frapper*

The alien race the booty out shall share,
Angry-eyed Saturn Mars regard, belike.
For Latins, Tuscans fearsome genocide
By Greeks who shall be anxious them to strike.

Source: Unidentified, but presumably a reference back to the *Mirabilis Liber's* anticipated invasion of Italy. See I.9, I.15, I.75.

84. Original 1555 text

Read as modern French:

Lune obscurcie aux profondes tenebres,
Son frere passe de couleur ferrugine: *pâle [pasle]; roux*
Le grand caché long temps sous les latebres,   *en cachette [lat. latebra]*
Tiedera fer dans la plaie sanguine.   *tiendra [?]*

    The moon all hidden and in shadow deep,
    Its solar brother dim, and red as rust,
    The noble who did hidden vigil keep
    Within the bloody wound his sword shall thrust.

Source: Virgil's *Georgics* (I:461–8), describing the death of Julius Caesar:

    Who shall be heard to say
    The sun is false? For he it is who oft
    Warns of blind tumults, crimes and acts of war.
    E'en he it was who at great Caesar's death
    Did Rome bewail, veiling his shining head
    In rust-red darkness . . .

85. Original 1555 text

Read as modern French:

Par la response de dame, roy troublé:
Ambadassadeurs mespriseront leur vie:
Le grand ses freres contrefera doublé   *à deux reprises*
Par deus mourront, ire, haine, envie.   *deux*

    The Lady's answer shall the monarch trouble:
    Envoys shall hold their lives in scorned estate.
    The lord shall counterfeit his brothers double.
    They both shall die midst rage and scorn and hate.

Source: Unidentified historical incident.

86. Original 1555 text

Read as modern French:

La grande royne quand se verta vaincu,   *Verra; vaincue*
Fera exces de masculin courraige:
Sus cheval, fluve passera toute nue,   *fleuve*
Suite par fer: à foy fera oultrage

> The mighty queen, seeing herself subdued,
> Shall show man's courage to degree unheard:
> Ahorse, she'll cross the river in the nude
> Pursued by arms, flouting the given word.

Source: Livy, *History of Rome*, II.13; Valerius Maximus, *Memorable deeds and Sayings*, III,2,2; Plutarch, *Life of Poplicola*, 19 and *On the Virtue of Women*, chapter 52; Françoys de Billon, *Le fort inexpugnable de l'honneur du sexe feminin*, Paris, 1555 – all recounting an incident in the early history of Rome when, in 509 BC, a noble young Roman hostage called Cloelia managed, while bathing in the Tiber, to escape the clutches of the besieging Etruscan King Lars Porsena by swimming back to the city on horseback, in breach of an agreement between the two sides.[9] By including it here, Nostradamus is presumably drawing a parallel with the *Mirabilis Liber's* predictions of an eventual Muslim invasion of Europe via Italy: 'The children of Agar shall seize Tarento, and spreading through Apulia, shall sack a host of towns. They shall be determined to enter Rome, and nobody in the world shall be able to resist them, unless it be the Lord God himself' (Prophecy of the Tiburtine Sibyl).

87. Original 1555 text

Ennosigée feu du centre de terre
Fera trembler au tour de cité neufve:
Deux grands rochiers long temps feront la
  guerre
Puis Arethusa rougira nouveau fleuve.

Read as modern French:

Poseidon [gr. Ennosigaios, 'ébranleur du sol']
autour de Villeneuve/Cita Nova/Naples
Deux nobles 'feront la guerre aux rochers'

Puis Arethuse [/] fera jaillir un nouveau fleuve
  rouge

> Earth-shaking fires from the world's center roar:
> Around 'New City' is the earth a-quiver.
> Two nobles long shall wage a fruitless war,
> The nymph of springs pour forth a new, red river.

Source: A so-far-unidentified account of one of the dozen or soknown eruptions of Mount Vesuvius overlooking Naples (Greek *Neapolis* = 'New City') following the one that destroyed Pompeii in AD 79 – given that this produced mainly ash, rocks, and pumice, rather than the lava flow evidently described in the last line. The most recent of these before Nostradamus's time occurred in 1500 (his most likely source). Julius Obsequens (29) reports a similar eruption – though of Etna – in 126 BC: 'Mount Etna, with an earthquake, sprayed forth fire from its summit . . .'. Like the 'omens' of 1554 (a two-headed kid, a two-headed infant, and the celebrated

Salon meteorite), Nostradamus is projecting the eruption into the future as an omen of an imminent civil war that will, like the volcano, produce a 'red river', but this time presumably of blood. Possibly, too, he is associating it with the *Mirabilis Liber*'s prediction of: ' . . . battles, tribulations, bloodshed, earthquakes, cities in captivity' (Prophecy of the Tiburtine Sibyl).

88. Original 1555 text

	Read as modern French:
Le divin mal surprendra le grand prince	*L'apopléxie*
Un peu devant aura femme espousée,	*avant*
Son puy & credit à un coup viendra mince,	*appui*
Conseil mourra pour la teste rasée.	*Consul [?]*

> Apoplexy the prince shall strike again:
> Shortly before, he shall his wife have wed.
> At once his credit and support shall wane,
> He'll die as Consul through the shaven-head.

Source: The life and death of Julius Caesar, a known sufferer from apoplexy – though the 'shaven-head' is unidentified.

89. Original 1555 text

	Read as modern French:
Touts ceux de Ilerde seront dedans Mosselle,	*de Lérida*
Metants à mort tous ceux de Loyre & Seine:	
Secours marin viendra pres d'haulte velle	*à haute voile*
Quand Hespagnols ouvrira toute vaine.	

> All those from Lerida by the Moselle
> Shall put to death all those of Loire and Seine:
> Sea-going help at hand with full-pressed sail,
> When Spaniards shall slit open every vein.

Source: Contemporary wars between France, England, and the Spanish Netherlands.

90. Original 1555 text

	Read as modern French:
Bourdeaux, Poitiers, au son de la campane'	*du tocsin*
A grande classe ira jusques à l'Angon,	*à grande force*
Contre Gauloys sera leur tramontane,	*tempête/attaque*
Quand monstres hydeux naistra pres de Orgon.	

> When sounds the tocsin, Poitiers and Bordeaux
> Shall send a mighty force towards Langon:
> Against the French their great north wind shall blow
> When hideous monster's born hard by Orgon.

Source: The salt-tax revolt of 1548, almost exactly as later described by Thomas Cormier in his Latin *Of the Deeds Performed by Henri II* of 1584, and linked with the ominous birth of a deformed child at Sénas, just south of Orgon and north of Salon, in 1554, as eventually celebrated in César Nostradamus's *Histoire et Chronique de Provence* of 1614.

91. Original 1555 text   Read as modern French:

Les dieux feront aux humains apparence,
Ce quils seront auteurs de grand conflit:
Avant ciel veu serain espée & lance,   *sera vu*
Que vers main gauche sera plus grand afflit   *vers le nord [voir II.99]; affliction*

> **The gods to men shall show well in advance**
> **That of a mighty war they'll be the source.**
> **Before the sky seems clear shall sword and lance**
> **To northward turn with even greater force.**

Source: More ancient reports of omens in the clouds (see I.23, I.35, I.64 above), and particularly Julius Obsequens's *On Omens* (68) for 44 BC: ' . . . the sun being enclosed in a kind of orb amid a pure and serene sky, an outer circular line, like a bow stretched amid the clouds, surrounded it . . . Between Caesar and Antony civil war broke out.' The words 'left' and 'right', applied to geographical directions, traditionally applied to an observer facing due east. See the passage from Virgil's *Aeneid* quoted at II.85.

92. Original 1555 text   Read as modern French:

Sous un la paix par tout sera clameé,   *partout*
Main non long temps pille & rebellion,
Par refus ville, terre & mer entamée,
Morts & captifz le tiers d'un milion.

> **'Neath one shall peace be everywhere proclaimed,**
> **But not for long. Sack and rebellion**
> **Shall his rejection cause by land and sea.**
> **Of dead and captives near a third-million.**

Source: Apparently the *Mirabilis Liber*'s predictions of a future King of France who would allegedly rule the world: 'Then shall emerge in Gaul a king of the Greeks, Francs, and Romans, of lofty stature and handsome appearance; his body and limbs shall have the most beautiful proportions; he shall reign a hundred and twelve years . . . after that, peace shall reign for Christians up until the time of the Antichrist . . .' (Prophecy of the Tiburtine Sibyl); 'The land . . . shall then be pacified. The prisoners . . . shall once again see their homelands, and the population shall grow and multiply . . . Peace and tranquility shall be reborn on earth, a peace such as there has never been, and such as there shall never be: happiness and rejoicing shall be everywhere. The world shall rest from its tribulations . . . In the very midst of this calm, there shall suddenly emerge from the north with Gog and Magog a nation which shall make the whole world tremble. Horrified, all men shall hide themselves in the mountains and among the rocks in order to flee their presence' (Prophecy of Pseudo-Methodius).

93. Original 1555 text   Read as modern French:

Terre Italique pres des monts tremblera,
Lyon & coq non trop confederés,
En lieu de peur l'un l'autre saidera   *s'aidera*
Seul Castulon & Celtes moderés.

> **Near th' mountains shall the earth Italian quake,**
> **Lion not much with Cock confederate.**
> **Only for fear shall they alliance make,**
> **Only the Celts and Spain stay moderate.**

Source: The *Mirabilis Liber*: 'Now the lion shall arise, and the black eagle, flapping its shining wings above its aerie, shall take to the air: then shall commence the tribulations and battles by land and sea. The great Gallic lion shall go to meet the eagle, and shall strike it on the head (Prophecy of Saint Severus); 'O young man advancing into the land of the lily, listen to my counsels and engrave them in your heart. Consult your conscience, and see whether you are coming from the good or from the evil cockerel. For there is an old prophecy about the good cockerel that runs: The lily, partner of the great eagle, shall sweep from the West to the East against the lion; the lion, defenseless, shall be overcome by the lily, which shall spread its perfume over Germany, while the eagle, in its flight, shall carry its fame afar' (Prophecy of Saint Brigid).

94. Original 1555 text   Read as modern French:

Au port Selin le tyran mis à mort
La liberté non pourtant recouvrée:
Le nouveau Mars par vindicte & remort: *par vengeance et remord*
Dame par force de frayeur honorée.

> **The tyrant's put to death at lunar port,**
> **Yet freedom shall not be restored, perforce.**
> **The new Mars acts out of revenge and tort,**
> **His lady honored out of fear and force.**

Source: Unknown.

95. Original 1555 text   **Read as modern French:**

Devant monstier trouvé enfant besson   *monastère; jumeau*
D'heroic sang de moine & vestutisque: *vétuste*
Son bruit par secte langue & puissance son   *sonne*
Qu'on dira fort elevé le vopisque.   *jumeau prématuré survivant*[9]

    Before the cloister is a twin child found
    Of blood heroic by old, decrepit friar.
    His fame through every tongue, power, creed shall sound,
    Such as that living twin to raise yet higher.

Source: Conceivably a somewhat distorted version of the birth, upbringing, and rise to eminence of the man who would subsequently become Calvin's Protestant successor at Geneva, Théodore de Bèze.[60]

96. Original 1555 text   **Read as modern French:**

Celuy qu'aura la charge de destruire
Temples, & sectes, changés par fantasie,   *Églises; sera changé*
Plus aux rochiers qu'aux vivans viendra nuire
Par langue ornée [/] d'oreilles ressaisies.   *par langue persuasive; ressaisi [accord par*
                                                         proximité]

    He who was charged with dashing to the ground
    Churches and sects shall change upon a whim.
    The stones more than the people he shall wound,
    By flowery speech hearing restored to him.

Source: Contemporary acts by a Catholic 'sect-finder'. See I.45 above. The last line is loosely based on a description by Lucian of a Gallic painting: 'The Gauls in their mother-tongue called Hercules "Ogmion", and represented him in their paintings in a new, unheard of way . . . he was dragging after him a marvelous great company of men and women, all attached separately by the ear. The bonds were little chains of finely worked gold and amber . . . The painter, having not found anywhere to attach the ends of all these chains to . . . pierced the tongue of the God Hercules, to which all these chains were then attached.'

97. Original 1555 text   **Read as modern French:**

Ce que fer flamme n'a sceu parachever,   *su*
La doulce langue au conseil viendra faire.
Par repos, songe, le roy fera resver.
Plus l'ennemi en feu, sang militaire.   *Encore/Toujours*

    What sword and flames ne'er managed to achieve
    Shall gentle speech in Council do instead.

To th' resting king a dream ideas shall give.
Foes under fire, more soldiers' blood is shed.

Source: Current political and military events, and particularly the machinations of Chancellor Michel de l'Hospital.[60]

98. Original 1555 text
Read as modern French:

Le chef qu'aura conduit peuple infini
Loing de son ciel, de meurs & langue estrange: *Loin de son pays*
Cinq mil en Crete & Thessale fini,
Le chef fuiant sauvé en marine grange.

The chief who led abroad a mighty host
'Midst foreign ways and tongues far, far away,
In Crete and Thessaly five thousand lost,
In seaside warehouse saved, shall run away.

Source: Not known, but evidently assimilated either to the *Mirabilis Liber*'s anticipated Muslim invasion of Europe, or to the subsequent Christian re-invasion of the Middle East.

99. Original 1555 text
Read as modern French:

Le grand monarque que fera compaignie
Avecq deux roys unis par amitié:
O quel souspir fera la grand mesnie: *compagnie*
Enfans Narbon à l'entour quel pitie!   *pitié*

The mighty monarch who shall spend his days
With two more kings in friendship's bond at one --
What a great sigh his mighty host shall raise!
Pity the children round about Narbonne!

Source: Unknown, but presumably based on the continuing conflicts between France and Spain.

100. Original 1555 text
Read as modern French:

Long temps au ciel sera veu gris oiseau
Aupres de Dole & de Tousquane terre,
Tenant au bec un verdoiant rameau,
Mourra tost grand, & finira la guerre.   *bientôt; le noble*

Long shall a gray bird in the sky be seen
Near Dole and near the land of Tuscany,

With, in its beak, a branch of living green.
Soon dies the lord, and war soon past shall be.

Source: Presumably Suetonius's description of the omens warning of Julius Caesar's death in his *The Twelve Caesars* (I.81): 'On the day before the Ides a small king-bird flew into the Hall of Pompey with a laurel-twig in its beak.'

Century II

1. Original 1555 text

Vers Aquitaine par insults Britanniques,
De par eux mesmes grandes incursions.
Pluies, gelées feront terroirs iniques,
Port Selyn fortes fera invasions.

Read as modern French:

attaques
Et [?]
Territoires
salin

> **British assaults upon fair Aquitaine**
> **On their behalf shall mighty inroads make:**
> **Hostile the lands are made by ice and rain.**
> **At salt-sea port shall great invasions break.**

Source: Reports of the salt-tax revolt in western France in the summer of 1548, together with contemporary fears that the English might intervene via La Rochelle in a domain that was formerly theirs, and that had maintained close ties with England. See II.61.

2. Original 1555 text

La teste blue fera la teste blanche
Autant de mal que France a fait leur bien.
Mort à l'anthenne grand pendu sus la branche,
Quand prins des siens le roy dira combien.

Read as modern French:

L'un mort à la vergue ; à la branche
pris

> **In such degree shall blue-head harm white-head**
> **As France's good to them shall e'er amount:**
> **From branch duke hanged, on th' yard another dead,**
> **When the king of his captives gives account.**

Source: Given that 'blue-turbans' and 'white-turbans' are specifically identified by Nostradamus in his 1566 *Almanach* as feuding Muslim sects of the time (namely the Shi'ites of Persia and the Sunni of Turkey), this verse presumably has to refer back to the *Mirabilis Liber*'s frequent predictions of an eventual Muslim invasion of Europe, and particularly (in the light of line 3's reference to yard-arms) of its sea-going aspects, as already cited at I.9. See IX.73.

3. Original 1555 text   **Read as modern French:**

Pour la chaleur solaire sus la mer
De Negrepont les poissons demis cuits: *De la Mer Noire [lat. pontus]*
Les habitans les viendront entamer
Quand Rod. & Gennes leur faudra le biscuit.   *de Rhodes et Gènes; faillira*

> **Through the sun's heat upon the shining sea**
> **The Black Sea's fish shall be half-cooked alive:**
> **The local folk to cut them up shall strive**
> **When by Genoa, Rhodes half-starved they'll be.**

Source: Julius Obsequens's *On Omens* (68) for 44 BC: 'At Hostia a shoal of fishes was left high and dry when the tide went out', plus the *Mirabilis Liber*'s: 'An extraordinary drought that shall dry up even the water of the rivers. Death of the flocks and herds in mountainous countries by reason of lack of water. The land shall burn in many places, and the heat shall be intense! The fishes shall perish, being themselves consumed' (Anonymous collection of predictions) – all assimilated to Villehardouin's *History of the Conquest of Constantinople*, where an old Greek legend recounted how the fish that were in the process of being cooked in 1453 when the Turks captured the city (which was currently being starved out by having its supplies from Genoa via Rhodes cut by the Turks) jumped out of their frying pans, ready to jump back in again on the day when the city was finally freed.[60]

4. Original 1555 text   **Read as modern French:**

Depuis Monech jusques au pres de Secile   *Monaco; Sicile*
Toute la plage demourra desolée,
Il ny aura fauxbourg, cité, ne vile   *n'y; ni*
Que par Barbares pillée soit & vollée.   *Arabes/Musulmans/corsaires barbaresques*

> **From Monaco near unto Sicily**
> **The coast entire shall desolated be.**
> **There'll be no city, town or even village**
> **That has not suffered Arab sack and pillage.**

Source: The *Mirabilis Liber*'s various accounts of a future Arab sea-borne invasion of Europe, assimilated to a whole series of historical attacks on the Mediterranean coasts by Saracens and Barbary pirates dating from AD 735. See I.9, I.15, I.75 . . .

5. Original 1555 text   **Read as modern French:**

Qu'en dans poisson, fer & letre enfermée   *Quand; prison; enfermé [accord de proximité]*
Hors sortira qui puys fera la guerre,
Aura par mer sa classe bien ramée   *flotte*
Apparoissant pres de Latine terre.

He who by sword and letter had been jailed
Shall thence come forth and shall proceed to war:
Across the sea he'll well his fleet have sailed
By oar, to appear off the Italian shore.

Source: Nostradamus's personal recollection of the release in 1552, following a three-year prison sentence for his involvement in the Waldensian massacre of 1545, of his old crony the Baron de la Garde, Admiral of the Eastern Sea, who had previously been involved in operations against the Holy Roman Empire in Italy in alliance with the Turkish fleet under the terms of François I's extraordinary alliance with the Ottomans of 1543.

6. Original 1555 text

Read as modern French:

Au pres des portes & dedans deux cités   *Auprès*
Seront deux fleaux onques n'aperceu un tel,   *jamais*
Faim dedans peste, de fer hors gens boutés,
Crier secours au grand Dieu immortel.

Within each city's heart and at its portal
Of ne'er seen scourges twain shall fall the stroke.
Famine and plague within, expelled its folk,
Calling for succor on great God immortal.

Source: The biblical story of Sodom and Gomorrah (Gen. 18:16 to 19:29), including a misunderstood version of the sentence at 18:20–21 later rendered into English as: 'And the LORD said, because the cry of Sodom and Gomorrah is great, and because their sin is very grievous, I will go down now and see whether they have done altogether according to the cry of it.' The first Hebrew expression here rendered as 'the cry of' in fact means 'the outcry over'; besides, it is worth remembering that Nostradamus, as a good Catholic layman, almost certainly had no actual copy even of the Vulgate Bible in his house, given that for all practical purposes it was banned as 'seditious literature', and so he was prone to misquote and misremember it.

7. Original 1555 text

Read as modern French:

Entre plusieurs aux isles deportés
L'un estre nay à deux dens en la gorge   *L'un sera né; dents*
Mourront de faim les arbres esbrotés   *broutés*
Pour eux neuf roy novel edict leur forge.

'Midst many who to th' isles shall banished be
Shall one be born with two teeth in its craw:
They'll die of hunger, stripping every tree.
For them a new king fashions a new law.

Source: Livy's *History of Rome* (XLI.21): 'at Auximum [Osimo, near Ancona] a girl was born with teeth', assimilated to the Romans' traditional banishment of noble prisoners to the Mediterranean islands. Pliny the Elder, in his *Natural History* (VII, 16, 68–9) recounted how such physical peculiarities were considered a particularly bad omen for infant girls.

8. Original 1555 text

Read as modern French:

Temples sacrés prime façon Romaine   *Églises*
Rejeteront les goffes fondements,   *grossiers*
Prenant leur loys premieres & humaines,
Chassant, non tout, des saints les cultements.

> **Of holy temples in grand Roman style**
> **They shall the very fundaments reject,**
> **Adopt prime human principles the while,**
> **And many a former saintly cult eject.**

Source: Current efforts by Catholic Reformers, of which Nostradamus, with his known Franciscan sympathies, seems heartily to have approved. Compare the prophecies on the Angelic Pastor at VI.21.

9. Original 1555 text

Read as modern French:

Neuf ans le regne le maigre en paix tiendra,   *le stérile*
Puis il cherra en soif si sanguinaire: *tombera*
Pour luy grand peuple sans foy & loy mourra,
Tué par un beaucoup plus de bonnaire.   *débonnaire*

> **Nine years the sterile one shall rule in peace,**
> **Then into rank bloodthirstiness decline.**
> **For him shall die a lawless, faithless race.**
> **Killed he shall be by one far more benign.**

Source: The first nine relatively benevolent years of the Protestant John Calvin's reign at Geneva, before he started his persecutions of his religious opponents in 1546, assimilated to the *Mirabilis Liber*'s various descriptions of the Antichrist: 'It is then that the Son of Perdition shall appear, the Antichrist . . . the child of perdition shall come in his turn, thinking that he is God. He shall perform a thousand miracles on earth. Through him the blind shall see, the lame shall walk, the deaf shall hear, the dead shall revive, such that, if it is possible, the elect themselves shall be deceived. He shall enter into Jerusalem, and shall seat himself in the temple as if he were the Son of God, and his heart, drunk with pride, shall forget that he is the son of a man and a woman of the tribe of Dan; deceiver and forger, he shall seduce through his miracles many credulous folk. Then God shall send two of his most faithful servants, Enoch and Elias, preserved so that they may bear witness for him against his enemy. Then the first who shall believe in Judah shall be last. Elias and

Enoch shall attack him in the face of all the people, and shall convict him of imposture and falsity. The Jews of all the tribes of Israel shall then believe and shall be killed for Christ. The Antichrist, seized with rage, shall order the death of the saints of God, and of those that shall have added faith to their words. Then shall come the Son of God in person, our Lord Christ, carried on the clouds of heaven, surrounded by legions of angels and by celestial glory: immediately they shall put to death the Antichrist, the beast, the enemy, the seducer, and those that shall have lent him their support' (Prophecy of Pseudo-Methodius); 'Then the Antichrist shall reveal himself publicly; he shall seat himself in the house of the Lord in Jerusalem. During his reign, there shall appear two illustrious men, Elias and Enoch, to announce the coming of the Lord. The Antichrist shall put them to death, and two days latter the Lord shall revive them. Then shall be seen a great persecution, such as there has never been and shall never be again. God shall shorten not the measure, but the number of those terrible days – the same God of whom it is written: "The day is fulfilled by your command." For the sake of the elect, through the power of the Lord, the Antichrist shall be killed on the Mount of Olives by Michael' (Prophecy of the Tiburtine Sibyl).

10. Original 1555 text

Read as modern French:

Avant long temps le tout sera range   *rangé*
Nous esperons un siecle bien senestre: *Nous attendons un âge bien pervers*
L'estat des masques & des seulz bien changé   *des coquines et des moines; échangé*
Peu trouveront qu'a son rang veuille estre.

Before too long shall all change for the worse:
We see ahead an age that's upside-down.
Of monks and whores they shall the roles reverse:
Few shall be pleased their proper state to own.

Source: Current omens of radical religious and social upheaval, imperfectly recalling the *Mirabilis Liber*: 'Thus it is that all the earth shall be delivered to the children of Ishmael, who shall bring dissolution in their wake . . . They shall desecrate their churches, cohabiting there with women, and they shall bedeck themselves, both themselves and their spouses, with sacred ornaments' (Prophecy of Pseudo-Methodius); . . . 'for the altars of the holy Church shall be destroyed, the floors of the temples desecrated, the monasteries polluted and despoiled' (Prophecy of Joannes de Vatiguerro).

11. Original 1555 text

Read as modern French:

Le prochain fils de l'asnier parviendra
Tant eslevé jusques au regne des fors,   *forts*
Son aspre gloire un chascun la craindra,
Mais ses enfans du regne getés hors.   *jetés*

> Soon shall be raised the numbskull's son and heir
> Upwards unto the very power and throne.
> His bitter pomp shall all and sundry fear
> His children, though, out of the kingdom thrown.

Source: Possibly the reign of Augustus, of whom Suetonius writes (II.3): 'I cannot believe that Gaius Octavius, his father, was also a money-changer who gave out bribes' – a tale of dubious origins which, clearly, was believed at the time by some.

12. Original 1555 text	Read as modern French:
Yeux clos, ouverts d'antique fantasie	*fermés*
L'habit des seulz seront mis à neant,	*des moines [gr. monachos < monos, seul]*
Le grand monarque chastiera leur frenesie:	
Ravir des temples le tresor par devant.	

> Eyes closed to all but fantasies of yore,
> True monkish habit shall devalued be.
> The mighty king shall scourge their madness sore,
> And, as they watch, sack their church treasury.

Source: The *Mirabilis Liber*'s predictions of Church corruption, as per II.10 above, with its inevitable consequences: 'For the Christians shall give themselves up to a host of unlawful acts and shall defile themselves with the most disgraceful depravities, and that is why the Lord has delivered them [in advance] into the hands of the Saracens . . . All the treasures and ornaments of the churches made of gold, silver, and precious stones shall become their property; the desolation shall be great, the churches burnt, and the corpses of the faithful shall be thrown where no one shall be able to find them to bury them' (Prophecy of Pseudo-Methodius).

13. Original 1555 text (misnumbered '12')	Read as modern French:
Le corps sans ame plus n'estre en sacrifice:	*plus ne sera*
Jour de la mort mis en nativité.	
L'esprit divin fera l'ame felice	*heureuse*
Voiant le verbe en son eternité.	

> The soulless corpse shall no more suffering know:
> On th' day of death it shall be born anew.
> On it the Holy Ghost shall bliss bestow,
> As soul th' eternal Word shall plainly view.

Source: The *Mirabilis Liber*'s various portrayals of the supposedly imminent End of the World: 'Then shall come the Son of God in person, our Lord Christ, carried on the clouds of heaven, surrounded by legions of angels and by celestial glory . . .

This shall be the consummation of the ages, and the Judgment shall commence before thousands of angels and hundreds of thousands of archangels and seraphim. The saints, the patriarchs, the prophets, the martyrs, the confessors, the virgins and all the saints together shall be grouped around Christ. Then both the just and the sinners shall give an account, in the presence of the Lord, of their actions. The righteous shall be separated from the wicked. The righteous, radiant as the sun, shall follow the lamb of life and the King of heaven, whose radiance shall always be visible to them, and in whose company they shall remain forever. The wicked shall descend into hell with the beast. The righteous shall live in eternity, and shall be endlessly glorified with the King of Heaven . . .' (Prophecy of Pseudo-Methodius); 'All shall cease to be; the shattered earth shall perish. The waves and flames shall descend in destructive torrents, and from heaven shall suddenly come the gloomy sound of trumpets. The shattered globe, the gaping earth shall be no more than a horrible chaos, and the face of the Lord shall appear to all the kings of the earth. A rain of fire and sulphur shall descend from heaven. Then God shall judge everyone according to his works: the impious shall go to eternal torment, condemned forever to the flames. The just shall receive eternal life; there shall be a new heaven and a new earth that shall exist forever. The sea shall cease to be, God shall reign over the saints, and the saints shall reign with God forever and ever, amen' (Prophecy of the Tiburtine Sibyl).

14. Original 1555 text (misnumbered '13')

Read as modern French:

A. Tours, Jean, garde seront yeux penetrants   *A la Tour St-Jean*
Descouvriront de loing la grand sereyne,   *sa majesté Sérenissime*
Elle & sa suitte au port seront entrants
Combat, poulsés, puissance souveraine.

From Fort St-Jean the guards their eyes shall strain
To see His Great Serenity afar
Who then the port shall enter with his train,
His power sov'reign, banished far all war.

Source: The triumphal entry into the port of Marseille[P] (which Nostradamus may possibly have witnessed) of Pope Clement VII and his niece Catarina de' Medici in 1533, on her way to marry the young prince who would subsequently mount the throne as Henri II of France.

15. Original 1555 text (misnumbered '14')

Read as modern French:

Un peu devant monarque trucidé?   *tué,*
Castor Pollux en nef, astre crinite.   *et Nef [?]; comète*
L'erain publiq par terre & mer vuidé   *Le trésor publique*
Pise, Ast, Ferrare, Turin, terre interdicte.

> **Shortly before the monarch killed shall be,**
> **In Twins and Ship a comet shall be seen.**
> **State funds they shall exhaust by land and sea,**
> **The lands cut off from Pisa to Turin.**

Source: Probably the *Mirabilis Liber*'s forecasts of a vast Muslim invasion of Italy (see I.9, I.15, I.75): 'It has been given to the stars and meteors (for the stars cannot have been created in vain) to exert an influence on things here below' (Prophecy of Abbot Joachim da Fiore, quoting Aristotle); 'In the sky shall be seen numerous and most surprising signs . . . ' (Prophecy of Joannes de Vatiguerro). Also Julius Obsequens's *On Omens* (2) for 147 BC: 'A star burned for thirty-two days'; (68) for 44 BC: 'At the games of Venus the Generatrix. . . a bearded star that appeared at the eleventh hour towards the north drew all eyes . . . An extraordinary star burned for for seven days'. See also II.41 and II.43.

16. Original 1555 text **(misnumbered '15')**	**Read as modern French:**
Naples, Palerme, Secille, Syracuses	*Sicile*
Nouveaux tyrans, fulgures feuz celestes:	*feux*
Force de Londres, Gand, Brucelles, & Suses	*Beaucoup*
Grand hecatombe, triumphe, faire festes.	*jeux d'hécatombe [jeux olympiques]*

> **Naples, Palermo, Sicilian Syracusa –**
> **New rulers rule, fires flash aloft the sky:**
> **Many from London, Gent, Brussels and Susa**
> **Great games, a triumph, feasts for all supply.**

Source: The Norman conquest of Naples and Muslim Sicily in the late eleventh century, assimilated to the *Mirabilis Liber*'s prediction of the liberation of Europe from its future Muslim occupiers (see I.55 above), with the Holy Roman Empire re-cast in the role of the original Normans, and with 'Susa' included at the end of line 3 more for its rhyming properties than anything else. The flashes of fire in the sky appear to be no more than celebratory fireworks, which dated from the time of the Crusades: compare the 'games, rites, feasts' also mentioned in line 3 of VII.22. 'Tyrant' was simply the original title of the rulers of Syracuse, as of many other ancient Greek city states.

17. Original 1555 text **(misnumbered '16')**	**Read as modern French:**
Le camp du temple de la vierge vestale,	*Dans la plaine*
Non esloigné d'Ethne & monts Pyrenées:	*d'Elne*
Le grand conduict est caché dens la male	
North. getés fluves & vignes mastinées.	*Fleuves et vignes cultivées gelés par le vent du nord*

To vestal virgin's temple's sacred field
Not far from Elne and lofty Pyrenees
The Great One in a sack is brought concealed.
North winds shall rot the vines, the rivers freeze.

Source: In part, no doubt, Plutarch's account of the flight of Marius, son of the ageing general Gaius Marius, in his *Parallel Lives*: 'but the steward, anticipating their approach, hid Marius in a cart full of beans.' The English loan-word *north* (also used by Rabelais) was perfectly normal in contemporary French as a replacement for the former *aquilon* (north wind).

18. Original 1555 text   **Read as modern French:**

Nouvelle & pluie subite impetueuse
Empeschera subit deux exercites.   *deux armées*
Pierre, ciel, feuz, faire la mer pierreuse,
La mort de sept terre & marin subites.

A new and sudden rain so sharp shall be
That it shall stop both armies where they stand.
Stones, fires from heaven shall stony make the sea:
For seven sudden death by sea and land.

Source: Julius Obsequens's *On Omens* (3) for 186 BC: ' . . . in Picenum it rained stones, and celestial fires . . . burned the clothes of many'; (44) for 102 BC: 'There was a nine-day festival because it had rained stones in Tuscany; (51) for 94 BC: 'Among the Vestini it rained stones at a country house'; and (54) for 91 BC: 'Among the Vestini it rained stones and potsherds for seven days' (which is possibly where Nostradamus got his 'seven' from!); plus a number of similar omens in Livy's *History of Rome* including, at

XXIII.31: 'The sea burned that year . . . and it rained stones around that temple, a shower which they duly celebrated with a nine-day festival.' The expression, however, is not necessarily as dramatic as it sounds: in contemporary omen-accounts such as Lycosthenes it usually refers simply to large hailstones! As his account for the great Milan hailstorm of 1510 puts it[44] (in Batman's later translation[5]): *There fel from heaven, to the great wonder and astonishment of all men, about 1200 stones, in a field butting upon the river Abdua [Adda], one of these (as Cardanus writeth in his booke of ye varietie of things) waied 120 pound waight, another 60 pounde waight: many of them were brought to French noble men for a myracle, whose colour was like yron, & in hardnesse passed, the smell being like brimstone. There was before at 3 a clock a great fire in the element. The noise of ye stones*

falling down was heard at 5 a clock, that it is a wonder that so great a Masse coulde be held up in the ayre two houres. The military sequel, as recorded by Lycosthenes, was that 'Within twenty months the French were expelled from Milan,' and that 'Having returned three years later, fortunes having been reversed, they were expelled all over again, and were felled as they fled.'

19. Original 1555 text   Read as modern French:

Nouveaux venuz, lieu basti sans defense
Occuper place par lors inhabitable.
Prez, maisons, champs, villes prendre a plaisance,
Faim, peste, guerre, arpen long labourable.

> **Newcomers undefended towns shall fill,**
> **And people lands where none lived until now.**
> **Meadows, fields, houses, towns they'll take at will:**
> **Famine, plague, war, then acres long to plow.**

Source: The *Mirabilis Liber*'s various forecasts of a future Muslim invasion of Europe, followed by an eventual counter-invasion: 'Cappadocia, Licilia, the land of Syria, once subjected to the devastation, shall become a desert; their inhabitants shall be dragged off into captivity, while others shall perish by the sword. Massacre and captivity await the Greeks. [North] Africa shall be made desolate . . . France, Germany and the land of the Goths, eaten up by a thousand scourges, shall see a host of their inhabitants carried off . . . '; but then, eventually: 'The land, previously laid waste by them, shall then be pacified. The prisoners they had taken shall once again see their homelands, and the population shall grow and multiply' (Prophecy of Pseudo-Methodius).

20. Original 1555 text   Read as modern French:

Freres & seurs en divers lieux captifs   [Huguenots]
Se trouveront passer pres du monaque,   *monarque*
Les contempler ses rameaux ententifz,   *ses fils attentifs*
Desplaisant voir menton, front, nez, les marques.   *Mécontents de*

> **'Brothers' and 'sisters', captured here and there,**
> **Shall find themselves before the king paraded:**
> **His watching offspring, shocked, shall stand and stare,**
> **Seeing their faces vilely mutilated.**

Source: The procession, on 21 January 1535, of condemned heretics on their way to the stake, organized by François I and closely watched by himself and his sons, who were fascinated by their faces.[60]

21. Original 1555 text

Read as modern French:

L'embassadeur envoyé par biremes
A mi chemin d'incogneuz repousles:
De sel renfort viendront quatre triremes,
Cordes & chaines en Negrepont troussés.

De ses renforts [?]
en Mer Noire/en Eubée [?]

Th' ambassador, dispatched by biremes, shall
By folk unknown be beaten back half-way.
Of his escort four triremes he shall call.
Tied and chained up in Evia they'll stay.

Source: An unknown, but probably quite recent case of Mediterranean piracy.

22. Original 1555 text

Read as modern French:

Le camp Asop d'Eurotte partira,
S'adjoignant proche de lisle submergée:
D'Arton classe phalange pliera,
Nombril du monde plus grand voix subrogée.

Béotien [Lat]; pour Sparte
de Théra [?]
La vergue d'artimon [voile]
De Delphes la plus grande voix

On leaving Sparta, the Boeotian force
Near isle submerged shall set a common course:
Its sails the fleet shall furl, its course delayed,
While Delphi's voice supreme is called in aid.

Source: Episode from ancient Greek history – possibly in connection with the decisive Theban victory over the Spartans at the Battle of Leuctra in 371 BC and the subsequent invasion of the Peloponnese, as described by Pausanias in his *Description of Greece* (IX.13).[8]

23. Original 1555 text

Read as modern French:

Palais, oyseaux, par oyseau dechassé,
Bien tost apres le prince prevenu,
Combien qu'hors fleuve enemis repoulsé
Dehors saisi trait d'oyseau soustenu.

au-delà du Rhin/Rhône; repoussés
par l'oiseau

The palace birds by one bird are chased out:
Soon afterwards they shall the King forewarn:
Though foes beyond the borders he shall rout,
Seized just outside: by bird a dart is borne.

Source: A slightly misremembered, topsy-turvy version of the assassination of Julius Caesar and the omens attending it, as reported by Suetonius in his *The Twelve Caesars* (I.25, 81, 82): 'He was the first Roman to build a bridge across the Rhine and inflict severe losses on the Germans who live beyond it . . . Again, during a sacrifice, the Augur Spirinna warned him to beware of danger . . . On the day before the Ides, a small king-bird flew into the Hall of Pompey with a laurel-twig in its beak, pursued by a flock of different birds from a nearby wood which pecked it to pieces . . . Cimber Tillius . . . grabbed hold of his toga by both shoulders.'

24. Original 1555 text

	Read as modern French:
Bestes farouches [/] de faim fluves tranner:	*traverseront les fleuves à la nage à cause de faim*
Plus part du camp encontre Hister sera,	*La plupart de la bataille ; sur le front du Danube*
En caige de fer le grand fera treisner,	*il fera traîner le grand*
Quand Rin enfant [/] Germain observera.	*Quand l'Allemand surveillera le jeune Rhin*

Wild beasts for hunger shall the rivers swim,
The greater battle by the Danube's shore:
In iron cage the noble dragged for him
When infant German Rhine he shall watch o'er.

Source: Countless ancient histories of barbarian attacks on the north-eastern frontiers of the Roman Empire, which were marked by the rivers Rhine and Danube – Livy: *History of Rome* (XLI .57): 'For a few days after this the tribe of the Bastarnae, after repeated invitations, crossed the Hister [Danube] from their homeland with a great force of men and horse' – no doubt assimilated to recorded inroads of wolves in the winter, such as Julius Obsequens's *On Omens* (69) for 43 BC: 'if wolves are mad in the winter, corn is not gathered in the summer', plus several cases of wolves being 'seen in the city' (43, 49, 52, 63). These in turn were presumably seen as reflected in the *Mirabilis Liber*'s frequent warnings of a future 'barbarian' (i.e. Muslim) invasion of Europe: 'Prediction of a severe persecution visited on the Church by the Barbarians . . . Their rage against the Christians of the north and of the west shall surpass the ferocity of all the cruellest beasts . . . It is also said in Methodius: one day the children of Hagar [i.e. the Arabs], having emerged from their deserts, shall assemble in several parts of Germany, and shall govern the world for a period of eight years. They shall destroy cities and kingdoms, shall slaughter the priests at the altar, shall drink from the sacred vessels, shall surrender themselves to sleep in the churches in the arms of their women, and shall tether their horses to the tombs of the faithful' (Prophecy of Reynard Lolhardus, quoted from chapter 26 of Part 2 of Lichtenberger's 'Prognosticatio' of 1488). For the 'iron cage', see I.10.

25. Original 1555 text

	Read as modern French:
La garde estrange trahira forteresse:	*garce*
Espoir & umbre de plus hault mariage.	
Garde deceue, sort prinse dans la presse,	
Loyre, Son. Rosne, Gar. à mort oultrage.	*Saône; Garonne*

The foreign girl the fortress shall betray
For hope and dream of marriage so much higher:
Guard tricked, once out she's captured in the fray.
Deadly outrage on Rhône, Garonne, Saône, Loire.

Source: Unidentified incident, evidently assimilated to the *Mirabilis Liber*'s familiar scenario of Arab invasion. See I.9.

26. Original 1555 text　　　　Read as modern French:

Pour la faveur que la cité fera
Au gran qui tost perdra champ de bataille,　　*Au grand/noble*
Fuis le rang Po, Thesin versera　　　　　　*& Tessin*
De sang, feuz, morts, noyes de coup de taille.　*noyés*

Because the city shall a favor show
To the great lord who soon shall lose the fight
And flee, in the Ticino and the Po
He'll shed blood – drowned, to death hacked, set alight.

Source: An unidentified military push towards north-west Italy that begs to be associated with the Muslim invasion of Europe via Italy anticipated by the *Mirabilis Liber*. See I.9.

27. Original 1555 text　　　　Read as modern French:
(misnumbered '77')

Le divin verbe sera du ciel frapé,
Qui ne pourra proceder plus avant.
Du reserant le secret estoupé　　　　*étouffé*
Qu'on marchera par dessus & devant.

Lightning shall on the Holy Monstrance fall
Such that it may no longer forward go:
The secret snuffed of what 'tis meant to show –
Invaders shall march in and over all.

Source: Presumably a contemporary incident when lightning struck a religious procession, taken as an omen for the imminence of the *Mirabilis Liber*'s promised invasion of Europe. See I.9.

28. Original 1555 text　　　　Read as modern French:

Le penultime du surnom du prophete
Prendra Diane pour son jour & repos:　　*Dial=Jupiter=jeudi [?]; de repos*
Loing vaguera par frenetique teste,　　　*errera*
Et delivrant un grand peuple d'impos.　　*d'impôts*

The last but one to bear the name of prophet
Shall take Diana's day to rest in peace,
Roam madly far and wide, think nothing of it,
Yet a great race from tribute shall release.

Source: Possibly chapter 33 of part 2 of Lichtenberger's *Pronostacatio*, as reprinted in the *Mirabilis Liber*: 'After that, there shall appear in the land of Leo another prophet who shall announce astonishing things in the Roman senate. Saintly in appearance and timorous, severe as regards the sanctity of Christian life, he shall have rooted deeply within his heart a malignant spirit that shall lead him, beneath the cloak of his hypocrisy, to the very feet of the sovereign Pontiff. He shall deceive bishops, prelates and princes with a false facade of piety, and shall draw them into grave error. Even the wisest shall be misled; the most distinguished men of Italy, of Lombardy, and of Upper Germany shall let themselves be fooled.' The suggestion is that, scandalously for the time, he will take as his sabbath not Saturday (as per the Jews), nor Sunday (as per the Christians), nor even Friday (as per the Muslims), but Monday.

29. Original 1555 text   Read as modern French:

L'oriental sortira de son siege,
Passer les monts Apennins, voir la Gaule:
Transpercera du ciel les eaux & neige:
Et un chascun frapera de sa gaule.

Forth from his seat the Easterner shall go:
He'll cross the Apennines, he'll see fair Gaul.
Onward he'll press through heaven's rains and snow
And with his rod he'll strike both one and all.

Source: The *Mirabilis Liber*'s gruesome predictions of an imminent Muslim invasion of Europe via Italy and over the Alps, led in some accounts by the Antichrist in person, possibly with a side-glance at Attila the Hun. See I.9, I.15.

30. Original 1555 text   Read as modern French:

Un qui les dieux d'Annibal infernaulx	
Fera renaistre, effrayeur des humains	
Onq' plus d'horreurs ne plus pire journaux	*Jamais; ni; dire*
Qu'avint viendra par Babel aux Romains.	*Qui arriva*

One who th' infernal gods of Hannibal
Shall raise to life again shall men affright:
No greater horrors records shall recall
Than what shall Rome befall by Babel's might.

Source: Once again the *Mirabilis Liber* and its bloodthirsty predictions of an Arab invasion of Europe as symbolized by the former Roman Empire and the current Roman Catholic Church, assimilated to Livy's lengthy descriptions, in his *History of Rome*, of the Carthaginian general Hannibal's celebrated invasion of Italy via southern France of 218–203 BC. See I.9, I.15 . . . Because the historians of Livy's day liked to explain events in terms of unchanging human nature, they are known to have shared the cyclic view of history that Nostradamus and his contemporaries espoused, and that made the French seer's characteristic approach to prophecy, as demonstrated here, possible in the first place.

31. Original 1555 text

En Campanie Cassilin. sera tant
Qu'on ne verra que d'eaux les champs
 couverts
Devant apres la pluye de long temps
Hors mis les arbres rien l'on verra de vert.

Read as modern French:

à Capoue

> **In Capua, Campania, such shall be**
> **That none but water-covered fields are seen.**
> **Before and after endless rains they'll see:**
> **Apart from trees, no sight of aught that's green.**

Source: Possibly the *Mirabilis Liber*'s 'The cities and provinces of the Islanders shall be swallowed up by floods' (Prophecy of the Tiburtine Sibyl) – or even her distinctly end-of-the-world prophecy: 'There shall no longer be on earth any eminence or unevenness, for the azure waters of the sea shall roll in level with the mountaintops.' With Europe's Little Ice Age currently getting into full swing, floods were frequent at the time: Conrad Lycosthenes[44] would later catalogue and illustrate some dozens of them (see woodcut).

32. Original 1555 text

Laict, sang, grenoilles escoudre en Dalmatie
Conflit donné, peste pres de Balenne:
Cry sera grand par toute Esclavonie
Lors naistra monstre pres & dedans Ravenne.

Read as modern French:

battront le blé

> **Milk, blood and frogs beat down Dalmatia's corn:**
> **Contagion near Balennes, and joined the fray.**
> **Loud through Slavonia shall the mourners mourn:**
> **Then shall Ravenna's monster see the day.**

Source: Various contemporary accounts of blood and milk falling from the sky: Conrad Lycosthenes[44] catalogues at least nine reported cases of the former during Nostradamus's lifetime, to say nothing of frogs. Batman's 1581 translation of his report for 1549[5] (based on Peucerus[59]) reads: *In the uppermost Alsatia [not 'Dalmatia'!] not farre from Colmar a Citie of the Empyre, there fell oute of the Element [= sky] upon the ground a great number of Frogges and Toades, which being fyrst destroyed with clubbes and battes by the inhabitants of that place, afterwarde least the ayre shoulde be infected therewith, at the commaundement of the*

Magistrate they were gathered in a heape by the Hangmen, and Tanners, and cast into a ditch. That yeare died the Pope before called Alexander Farnezius, in whose place Julius the thyrde succeeded. Reports of milk and blood raining from the sky are also to be found frequently throughout Julius Obsequens's *On Omens*: (4) 'In the area of Concordia it rained blood'; (6) 'In the area of Vulcum and Concordia it rained blood'; (14) 'In Gabii it rained milk'; (27) 'In Amertinum the sun was seen at night and its light was seen for a while. An ox spoke and was suckled in public. It rained blood'; (28) 'In Rome at the Graecostasis building it rained milk'; (30) 'In Veii it rained oil and milk'; (31) 'At the Groecostasis building it rained milk'; (35) 'At Catona . . . it rained milk'; (35) 'At Praeneste it rained milk'; (39) 'It rained milk for three days'; (40) 'Twice it rained milk'; (41) 'In the area of Perugia and various places in Rome it rained milk . . . It rained blood'; (43) 'It rained milk in Lucania, blood at Luna'; (43) 'It rained milk in the Comitium'; (44) 'It rained blood around the river Anio'; (50) 'In Caere it rained milk'; (53) 'In Rome it rained milk'. The last line of the verse refers to the celebrated human 'monster' allegedly discovered by French troops in Ravenna in 1512, as likewise later described by Conrad Lycosthenes in his *Chronicle of Omens and Portents* of 1557, following the bloody Battle of Ravenna, to say nothing of heavy rains the previous year, accompanied by plague in Slavonia. In Batman's English translation for 1511:[5] *At Ravenna a Monster was borne with a horne on his heade, he had wings, no armes, one foote, as a Birde of the praye, an eye on his knee, & both kinds Ypsilon amid his breast, and the forme of the crosse. Some did interprete the hornes, pride, the wings lightnesse, and unstedfastnesse of minde, the want of armes lacke of good workes, a foote for the pray, robberie, usurie, and all kind of covetousnes. The eie on the knee, the bending of the minde only to earthli things: both kinds, Zodomerie or buggerie, and that for these vices [Italy] shold be beaten down with the sword, that the King of France shold not do it of his owne power, but that only it was gods scourge. But Ypsilon and X. were tokens of safetie, for Y is a figure of Vertue, wherefore if they had recourse to vertue, and to the crosse of Christ, they shoulde have a more desyred refeshyng and peace, from these troubles and afflictions. This have I reade im John Multi Vallis, & Gasper Hedio, in the Historie Synopsis after Sabellicus, continued untill oure time. I have seene another Portrature of the like Monster, but somewhat differing, and not answering the first in all pointes, with the interpretation set out in verse, which I also thought good to adde too in*

this place: sequel. In Italy after diverse uproares, the Pope got Ravenna. The general prophetic context, however, seems once again to be the *Mirabilis Liber*'s prediction of a future Muslim invasion of Italy (see I.9, I.15 . . .).

33. Original 1555 text   **Read as modern French:**

Par le torrent qui descent de Verone,
Par lors qu'au Po guindera son entrée,
Un grand naufraige, & non moins en Garonne
Quant ceux de Gennes marcheront leur contrée.

> **Beside Verona's torrent, rushing on**
> **Near where it winds its way into the Po,**
> **Wat'ry disaster: no less in Garonne**
> **When troops Genoan marching on them go.**

Source: Unidentified military disaster, presumably assimilated to the *Mirabilis Liber*'s forecast of a sea-borne invasion of France via Italy. See I.9, I.75 . . . The geography is slightly suspect.

34. Original 1555 text   **Read as modern French:**

L'ire insensée du combat furieux
Fera à table par freres le fer luire
Les despartir mort, blessé, curieux: *pensif/troublé*
Le fier duelle viendra en France nuire.

> **Th' insensate fury of a fierce set-to**
> **At table brothers sees draw flashing arms.**
> **Parted, one dead, one wounded, worried too.**
> **Their stiff-necked feud all France severely harms.**

Source: Possibly the murder by Cesare Borgia, Duke of Valence, of his brother-in law the Duke of Gandia following a quarrel at a banquet in 1497, and the dumping of the latter's body in the Tiber.[60]

35. Original 1555 text

Read as modern French:

Dans deux logis de nuit le feu prendra,
Plusieurs dedans estoufés & rostis.   *Beaucoup*
Pres de deux fleuves pour seur il aviendra   *sûrement*
Sol, l'Arq, & Caper tous seront amortis.   *le Sagittaire et le Capricorne*

> **At night shall lodgings twain catch fire, alas!**
> **Many within shall stifled be and fry.**
> **Near rivers twain it sure shall come to pass.**
> **Sun in the Goat and Archer: all shall die.**

Source: The celebrated occasion when a number of traders staying at the *Hôtel de la Tête d'Argent* at Lyon during the annual November fair of 1500 (when, consequently, the sun was in Sagittarius, and about to pass into Capricorn) were burnt alive by a fire that started in the kitchen, thanks to the fact that their bedroom windows were all barred.[7, 60] 'Two rivers' is a standard Nostradamus shorthand not merely for the former Babylon (between the Tigris and the Euphrates), but also for Lyon (at the confluence of the Saône and Rhône), and for Avignon (at that of the Rhône and Durance), which itself had been so memorably described by the poet Petrarch as 'the Babylon of the West'.

36. Original 1555 text

Read as modern French:

Du grand Prophete les letres seront prinses   *prises:*
Entre les mains du tyrant deviendront:
Frauder son roy seront ses entreprinses,   *Pour frauder; entreprises*
Mais ses rapines bien tost le troubleront.

> **The mighty prophet's letters' interception**
> **Shall put them in the tyrant's hands instead**
> **Whose aim shall be his monarch's rank deception;**
> **But soon his thefts shall bring him mighty dread.**

Source: Unknown. Could it be an accident that had befallen Nostradamus himself?

37. Original 1555 text

Read as modern French:

De ce grand nombre que lon envoyera
Pour secourir dans le fort assiegés,
Peste & famine tous les devorera
Hors mis septante qui seront profligés.

> **Out of the many who'll be sent to take**
> **Assistance to those in the fort beset,**
> **Famine and plague shall all of them o'ertake,**
> **Save only seventy who'll be beaten yet.**

Source: Unknown, but possibly assimilated to the *Mirabilis Liber*'s future invasion scenario. See I.9, I.75, II.24 . . .

38. Original 1555 text   Read as modern French:

Des condemnés sera fait un grand nombre
Quand les monarques seront conciliés:
Mais a l'un d'eux viendra si malencombre   *ce sera si gênant*
Que guerres ensemble ne seront raliés.   *guère*

> **Many are those who'll be condemned again**
> **When reconciled shall be those monarchs both.**
> **For one, though, it shall go so 'gainst the grain**
> **That their alliance to survive is loth.**

Source: The dramatic but brief reconciliation between King François I and the Holy Roman Emperor Charles V during 1538–9.

39. Original 1555 text   Read as modern French:

Un an devant le conflit Italique,   *avant*
Germain, Gaulois, Hespaignols pour le fort:
Cherra l'escolle maison de republique,   *Tombera*
Ou, hors mis peu, seront suffoqués morrs.   *morts*

> **A year before war Italy shall test,**
> **French, Germans, Spaniards shall the fort contest.**
> **The school collapses, founded by the state,**
> **Which all but few to death shall suffocate.**

Source: Unknown incident, probably quite recent.

40. Original 1555 text   Read as modern French:

Un peu apres non point longue intervalle.
Par mer & terre sera fait grand tumulte,
Beaucoup plus grande sera pugne navale,
Feus, animaux, qui plus feront d'insulte.   *Feux violents, qui intensifieront l'attaque*

> **Shortly thereafter – no great time, in fact –**
> **By land and sea great tumult there shall be:**
> **Much greater shall the conflict be at sea:**
> **Violent fires thrown in against th' attacked.**

Source: Possibly an account of an ancient sea-battle in which 'Greek fire' was used (a burning mixture of pitch, lime, and sulfur), presumably assimilated to the future Muslim sea-borne invasion of Europe expected by the *Mirabilis Liber*. See I.9, I.75, II.24 . . .

41. Original 1555 text

La grand' estoile par sept jours bruslera,
Nuée fera deux soleils apparoir:
Le gros mastin toute nuict hurlera
Quand grand pontife changera de terroir.

Read as modern French:

apparaître

de territoire

> **Seven days the mighty star shall burn on high:**
> **Cloud shall make two more suns shine in the sky.**
> **The whole night shall the burly mastiff cry**
> **When the great Pontiff shall his country fly.**

Source: Julius Obsequens's description (68) of the omens that accompanied the death of Julius Caesar in 44 BC: 'A remarkable star burned for seven days. Three suns shone, and around the lowest sun a corona like an ear of corn shone as though in a circle, and after the sun had returned to a single circular form, its light was faint for several months . . . Dogs were heard howling at night before the house of the Supreme Pontifex Lepidus, and the biggest of these, which was torn apart by the others, portended the disgraceful infamies of Lepidus'; compare also (32): 'In Gaul three suns and three moons were seen'; (43) In Picenum three suns were seen'; (70)

'Three suns were seen at around the third hour of the day' – assimilated to the *Mirabilis Liber*'s dire prophecies for the Church: ' . . . and then the barque of Peter, attacked by powerful enemies, shall be shaken. Terrified, Peter shall be forced to flee, in order not to incur the infamy of servitude' (Prophecy of St Brigid of Sweden). The appearance of three suns is a known atmospheric phenomenon caused by ice-crystals, technically termed 'parhelion', and would be described – and often illustrated – by Lycosthenes on at least eighteen occasions as among the portentous phenomena observed in Nostradamus's own day, not least on 10 February 1555 (above).[44]

42. Original 1555 text

Coq, chiens & chats de sang seront repeus,
Et de la plaie du tyrant trouvé mort,
Au lict d'uun autre jambes & bras rompûs,
Qui n'avoit peur mourir de cruel mort.

Read as modern French:

> **Upon the tyrant's blood and wound shall feast**
> **Cock, dogs and cats, once they shall find him dead,**
> **Arms and legs broken, in another's bed,**
> **Who ne'er feared death, though cruel, in the least.**

Source: Unknown.

43. Original 1555 text

Durant l'estoyle chevelue apparente,
Les trois grands princes seront fait ennemis,
Frappes du ciel, paix terre tremulente.
Po, Timbre undants, serpant sus le bort mis.

Read as modern French:

Pendant l'apparition de la comète

tremblante
Po, Tibre inondants; sur la rive

> **While, seen aloft, the bearded star's at hand,**
> **The princes three shall mutual hatred pledge:**
> **Lightning from heaven, and earthly peace on edge,**
> **Po, Tiber flood; snake washed up on the strand.**

Source: Julius Obsequens's continued account (68), as per II.41 above, of the events and omens following the assassination of Julius Caesar and the assumption of power by the warring Triumvirate of Octavian, Mark Antony, and Lepidus: 'At the games of Venus the Generatrix that he [Octavius] arranged for the college [of priests], a bearded star, appearing at the eleventh hour towards the north, drew all eyes . . . There was a rapid succession of earthquakes. The shipyards and many other places were struck by lightning . . . Trees were uprooted and many houses blown down . . . The Po flooded, and when it returned to its bed left behind a vast quantity of serpents. Between Caesar and Antony civil war broke out.'

44. Original 1555 text

L'aigle pousée en tour des pavillons
Par autres oyseaux d'entour sera chassée,
Quand bruit des cymbres, tubes & sonaillons
Rendront le sens de la dame insensée.

Read as modern French:

cymbales, trompettes

> **The eagle, perched around the group of tents**
> **From thence is chased by many another bird,**
> **But when bells, horns and cymbals shall be heard**
> **The lady's senses they'll deprive of sense.**

Source: Unknown hunting incident, probably quite topical – with a typical Nostradamian wordplay in the last line.

45. Original 1555 text

Trop le ciel pleure [/] l'Androgyn procrée,
Près de ce ciel sang humain respandu,
Par mort trop tarde grand peuple recrée
Tard & tost vient le secours attendu.

Read as modern French:

Près de ce pays

Tôt ou tard

> **Too much heaven weeps: an androgyne is born:**
> **Near that same place shall human blood be shed.**
> **By death o'erdue a great race is reborn:**
> **Sooner or later comes the hoped-for aid.**

Source: For the first two lines, either a mixture of contemporary events (including the ceaseless rains that
would similarly be treated as an 'omen' by the poet
Ronsard) or Julius Obsequens's *On Omens*, which
mentions a number of androgynous births: (22) 'At
Luna an androgyne was born'; (27a) 'In the area of
Ferentinum an androgyne was born and thrown into
the river'; (32) 'In the marketplace at Vessanum an
androgyne was born and carried off to the sea'; (50)
'An androgyne born at Urbinum was carried off to the sea.' Lycosthenes[44] would
similarly report various androgynous births during Nostradamus's lifetime, including, for 1519: 'At Zürich in Switzerland on the Kalens of January a hermaphrodite
was born with a large lump of raw flesh near its navel, and having a little below it
the female organs, as well as the male member in its usual place.' As for the last two
lines, numerous prominent figures had died in the years immediately prior to the
composition of the first edition of Nostradamus's *Propheties*, but the best candidate
is probably the nepotistic Pope Paul III, a possible former employer of
Nostradamus's own father, and chiefly remembered for instigating the Counter
Reformation, who had died in 1549 at the age of 82.

1519

46. Original 1555 text

Apres grand trouble humain, plus grand s'aprest[e]
Le grand mouteur les siecles renouvele.
Pluie, sang, laict, famine, fer, & peste
Au ciel veu, feu courant longue estincele.

Read as modern French:

le cycle des âges

The woes once past, yet greater are at hand:
The Mover starts a new age once again.
Famine, war, plague; both blood and milk shall rain:
Fire seen in heaven, trailing its blazing brand.

Source: The famous passage from Virgil's *Eclogues* at IV.4–7:

Now has the last great age begun
    by Cumae's seer foretold;
New born the mighty cycles run
    their course, and quit the old.
Now, too, the Virgin re-appears,
And Saturn re-controls the spheres.
    (tr. G. L. Bickersteth)

supplemented with details from Julius Obsequens's *On Omens* (20) for 147 BC: 'A
star burned for thirty-two days'; and (68) for 44 BC: 'A bearded star appearing in
the north drew all eyes . . . A remarkable star burned for seven days', to say nothing of the numerous contemporary reports of similar omens that would later be
collected by Lycosthenes.[44] For famine, war, and plague, see I.9, I.67, I.75, II.24,
IV.48. For rains of blood and milk, see II.32. For fire from the sky, see I.46, II.16.

47. Original 1555 text

L'ennemy grant viel dueil meurt de poison:
Les souverains par infinis subjuguez.
Pierres plouvoir, cachés sous la toison:
Par mort articles en vain sont allegués.

Read as modern French:

infimes

À l'article de la mort [lat: in articulo mortis]

> **The mighty foe, long-wailed, of poison dies:**
> **The kings by lesser folk are overcome,**
> **Pelted with stones, 'neath fleeces hiding eyes,**
> **Falsely accused, as to death's point they come.**

Source: Apparently Nostradamus's own premonitions of incipient revolution, not in fact borne out by contemporary events. The allegedly 'poisoned foe' is unidentified, but may be intended for the Emperor Charles V.

48. Original 1555 text

La grand copie que passera les monts.
Saturne en l'Arq tournant du poisson Mars
Venins cachés sous testes de saulmons:

Leur chief pendu à fil de polemars.

Read as modern French:

La grande armée qui
dans le Sagittaire; Mars rétrogradant
sous le couvert ; psaumes [A.F. saume,
*   Gr. psaumos]*
à fil de polemar

> **Over the mounts such mighty hosts proceed!**
> **In th' Archer Saturn, Mars from Fishes back,**
> **'Neath cloak of psalms they'll hide their poisoned creed,**
> **Their leader hung by string of parcel-pack.**

Source: Presumably the bloody crusade against the Protestants of the Lubéron mountains in 1545, who were known and detested by the Catholics for their heretical hymns: Saturn was in Sagittarius, and Mars in Pisces, from November 1544 until January 1545: the same situation again applied from May 1546 to July 1546, and again (with Mars now retrograde) from August to October, when Mars once again became direct. The Waldensians' leader, Marron, was imprisoned at Cabrières and subsequently hanged at Avignon.[60]

49. Original 1555 text

Les conseilliers du premier monopole,
Les conquerants seduits pour la Melite:
Rodes, Bisance pour leurs exposant pole:
Terre faudra les poursuivants de fuite.

Read as modern French:

de la première ligue
par
ciel

> **The councilors of that, th' initial league,**
> **The conquerors, whom Malta shall intrigue,**
> **Leaving Byzantium and Rhodes quite free,**
> **Shall lack a home, being hunted as they flee.**

Source: The almost contemporary story of the Knights of St John – who were finally granted refuge in Malta by the Holy Roman Emperor Charles V in 1530 – possibly assimilated to the *Mirabilis Liber's* frequent predictions of a Muslim invasion of Europe via the Mediterranean. See I.9, I.75 . . .

50. Original 1555 text   Read as modern French:

Quant ceux d'Ainault, de Gand et de Brucelles   *d'Hainaut*
Verront à Langres le siege devant mis
Derrier leurs flancz seront guerres crueles,
La plaie antique fera pis qu'ennemis.   *peste [lat. bibl. plaga]*

> **When those from Hainaut, Brussels and from Gent**
> **The siege of Langres duly laid shall see,**
> **Behind their flanks shall lands by wars be rent,**
> **The ancient plague worse than the enemy.**

Source: Unidentified military incident, evidently taken from the contemporary wars between France and the Holy Roman Empire to the east.

51. Original 1555 text   Read as modern French:

Le sang du juste à Londres fera faute
Bruslés par fouldres de vingt trois les six.   *Touchés par excommunications/anathèmes*
La dame antique cherra de place haute: *tombera*
De mesme secte plusieurs seront occis.   *tués*

> **No just blood they shall spill in London town:**
> **Anathemas singe six times twenty-three.**
> **The ancient dame from high shall tumble down.**
> **Of that same sect shall many murdered be.**

Source: The celebrated 'Affair of the Templars' of 1307 to 1314, in the course of which 138 (i.e. 6 x 23) French Templars were accused of heresy and unnatural practices, many of them being tortured and burned alive, whereas, by contrast, those arrested in England were neither tortured nor condemned. The French trials, meanwhile, were interrupted in 1510 by the appearance of various heretical sects, and in particular of an Englishwoman who claimed to be inspired by the Holy Spirit: needless to say, *she* was burned, too.[60] See I.81 above.

52. Original 1555 text   Read as modern French:

Dans plusieurs nuits la terre tremblera:
Sur le prinstemps deux effors [feront] suite:
Corynthe, Ephese aux deux mers nagera:
Guerre s'esmeut par deux vaillans de luite.

For many nights the earth shall heave and quake:
In spring shall two successive spasms follow.
Ephesus, Corinth in two seas shall wallow:
Two doughty champions bloody war shall make.

Source: The *Mirabilis Liber*'s 'Prophecy of Merlin' ('There shall be a King in Gaul called R. And this king shall be the [Crusaders'] champion, or golden chief: and there shall be another as good as the champion . . .'), supplemented by what is evidently a somewhat confused memory (or possibly a garbled oral account from nearly half a century earlier) of the great Constantinople earthquake of 1509, as later reported by Lycosthenes[44] and translated into English by Dr Stephen Batman[5]:

This yeare the 14. of September, a verye grievous Earthquake for eighteene dayes togither shaking the wall of the Citie of Constantinople to the seaward overthrew it, with all the houses that were neare to it, and filled the ditch full of Rubbish, and made it playne with the grounde, it destroyed the Castel wherein the Emperours treasure in five strong towers were kept, and a notable house wherin the Lions are inclosed, and so shoke the Conduit pipes, which being made with exceeding great labour and cost doe carry the water into the Citie from River Danubus, throughe mountaines and long journeies, that they could not be repayred with great treasure, and the arme of the Sea, lying between Constantinople and Pera made suche a great noyse with the violence of the Earthquake, that the Sea cast the water over the wals into both Cities . . . At Galliopolis a very strong Castel was rent in pieces, and no house there remained whole, it is reported that there were slain in Constantinople at that time 13000 men.

53. Original 1555 text   **Read as modern French:**

La grande peste de cité maritime
Ne cessera que mort ne soit vengée
Du juste sang, par pris damne sans crime   *comme prix*
De la grand dame par feincte n'outraigée.   *feinte*

The mighty plague of city maritime
Shall cease not ere avenged the death shall be
Of scapegoats innocent, yet blamed for crime,
Nor great dame shocked at the pretense she'll see.

Source: The Plague epidemic that ravaged Marseille and the rest of Provence following the brutal 1545 massacre of the Waldensians of the Lubéron (a mountainous region just north of Nostradamus's Salon), whose eminent patroness was the Dame de Cental.[60]

54. Original 1555 text	**Read as modern French:**

Par gent estrange, & Romains loingtaine
Leur grand cité apres eaue fort troublee,   *auprès de l'eau*
Fille sans main, trop different domaine,
Prins chief, sarreure n'avoir esté riblée.   *serrure; verrouillée [allem. riegeln?]*

> **Through alien folk far from the Roman shore**
> **Their mighty seaside city's vexed amain.**
> **A handless girl: through differing domain,**
> **The chief is held, not having locked the door.**

Source: Unidentified incident linked to the *Mirabilis Liber's* constant warnings of a Muslim invasion of Europe via the Mediterranean coast (see I.9, I.75), plus Julius Obsequens's *On Omens* (14) for 163 BC: 'A girl of Privernum was born without hands', no doubt recalled by more recent occurrences of the type such as that later reported by Lycosthenes[44] for 1528. In Batman's English translation:[5] *There was borne a Childe which had no armes at all . . . A Woman also . . . was seene at Franckeford situate on the river Menus in the yeare of Christ 1556 who having no handes at all, tooke a pen in hir feete, and did not onelye write exceeding well, but also was able to handle the distaffe, spinne, tell money, and doe all fine worke with her toes.* The inclusion of the report at this point suggests that she, likewise, must have been born in or about 1528.

55. Original 1555 text	**Read as modern French:**

Dans le conflit le grand qui peu valloyt,   *valait*
A son dernier [/] fera cas merveilleux:
Pendant qu'Hadrie verra ce qu'il falloyt,   *Venise*
Dans le banquet pongnale l'orguilleux.   *il poignarde*

> **The lord whose battle skills were little heeded**
> **At his last gasp shall do a deed to stun,**
> **With Venice well aware of what was needed,**
> **When at the feast he stabs the haughty one.**

Source: Unidentified.

56. Original 1555 text	**Read as modern French:**

Que peste & glaive n'a peu seu definer   *n'aura pas pu achever*
Mort dans le puys, sommet du ciel frappé.   *du sommet*
L'abbé mourra quand verra ruiner
Ceux du naufraige [/] l'escueil voulant grapper.

> What neither plague nor war could e'er devise,
> Dead in the well, thunderstruck from on high,.
> When he shall see the shipwrecked sailors try
> To anchor on the reef, the abbot dies.

Source: Unknown incident.

57. Original 1555 text

Read as modern French:

Avant conflit le grand mur tumbera:	*tombera*
Le grand à mort, mort trop subite & plainte:	
Nay imparfaict: la plus part nagera:	*Né*
Aupres du fleuve de sang la terre tainte.	

> Before the fight the great wall falls asunder:
> The lord's too-sudden death they shall deplore.
> A birth deformed: then most of them go under:
> Beside the river, earth all stained with gore.

Source: The sack of Rome by the forces of Charles V in 1527, which was presaged by the collapse of the wall joining the Vatican to the Castel Sant' Angelo, and accompanied by the rapid death of the Duke of Bourbon and the spilling of much blood beside the Tiber. Deformed births were part of the standard omen-currency of the time, later catalogued by Lycosthenes[44] on at least forty different occasions.

58. Original 1555 text

Read as modern French:

Sans pied ne main par dend ayguë & forte	*ni; dent*
Par globe au fort de porc & laisné nay:	*au front; et mouton [lat. lanata]*
Pres du portail desloyal se transporte	
Silene luit, petit grand emmené.	*La lune*

> Handless and footless, sharp of tooth and strong,
> With lump on brow, born of a pig and sheep.
> Th' betrayer near the gate is borne along:
> The little lord's abducted, moon a-peep.

Source: An abduction, probably contemporary, announced by an equally contemporary animal omen sufficiently local to be unknown to the later Lycosthenes.[44]

59. Original 1555 text

Read as modern French:

Classe Gauloyse par apuy de grand garde	*Flotte/Armée*
Du grand Neptune, & ses tridents souldars	*Du grand amiral [terme normal chez Nostradamus]*
Rousgée Provence pour sostenir grand bande:	*Rongée; soutenir; grande [invariable à l'epoque]*
Plus Mars Narbon. par javelotz & dards.	*Et aussi la Narbonne de Mars [lat. Narbo Martius]*

The Gallic fleet supported by la Garde,
That Neptune with his trident acolytes,
To feed its horde lays waste Provence right hard.
Narbonne with javelins and arrows fights.

Source: The contemporary exploits of the Baron de la Garde, Admiral of the Eastern Mediterranean, and a known crony of Nostradamus – even though, with the Baron d'Oppède, he had also been in charge of the massacre of the Waldensian Protestants of the Lubéron in 1545 – presumably assimilated to the *Mirabilis Liber*'s expected Muslim invasion of France via the Mediterranean. See I.9, I.75. The third line recalls François I's extraordinary agreement for the Ottoman fleets to overwinter at Toulon and Marseille in 1543–4 and the resulting much-resented drain on local accommodation and provisions. Compare II.5. Line 4 refers to the simultaneous campaigning of the Dauphin in the south-west.

60. Original 1555 text

La foy Punicque en Orient rompue
Gang. Iud. & Rosne, Loyre & Tag. changeront,
Quand du mulet la faim sera repue,
Classe espargie, sang & corps nageront.

Read as modern French:

Ganges, Indus, Rhône, Loire et Tage
mulâtre [?]
Flotte dispersée

The Afric pact once broken in the East,
Indus, Rhône, Loire and Tagus changed shall be.
Once the mulatto's appetite has ceased,
Fleet scattered, corpses float upon the sea.

Source: The breaking of the Ottomans' agreement with France in 1554, and the half-caste Baron de la Garde's consequent impatience with them (compare previous verse), assimilated to the Sibylline Oracle's:

You'll waste your efforts, straitly though you write,
When you of th' West shall see what th' East shall do:
Ganges and Indus change, the Tagus, too . . .

61. Original 1555 text

Euge Tamins, Gironde & la Rochele:
O sang Troien! Mars au port de la flesche
Derrier le fleuve au fort mise l'eschele,
Pointes a feu grand meurtre sus la bresche.

Read as modern French:

Bravo! [lat.]
O sang français royal

Les arquebuses feront

Hail, you of Thames in Gironde and Rochelle!
O Trojan blood! War at Port de la Flèche!
Beyond the river they the fort shall scale:
By arquebus great slaughter o'er the breach.

Source: Historical military campaigns in the west of France. See II.1.

62. Original 1555 text

Mabus puis tost alors mourra, viendra
De gens & bestes une horrible defaite:
Puis tout à coup la vengence on verra
Cent, main, soif, faim, quand courra la comete.

Read as modern French:

destruction

Sang humain

> **Then, Mabus shortly dying, there shall be**
> **Of man and beast a massacre most dread.**
> **Then suddenly they'll awful vengeance see:**
> **Thirst, famine, blood, with comet overhead.**

Source: Accounts of the events of 1532, when a notable daylight comet (not Halley's) marked the death of the prominent Flemish painter Jan Gossaert de Mabuse in October and the bloody repulsing of the Ottoman invaders in Hungary by the Holy Roman Emperor Charles V. What was subsequently to become known as Halley's comet had already been observed, and would duly be recorded by Lycosthenes, if possibly for the wrong year:[44] 'This year in the middle of August a Comet was seen in Germany, Italy, and France in the west for three weeks from around 6 August . . . before sunrise and at dusk after sunset. It passed through Cancer, Leo, Virgo, and Libra, where it ceased to be visible, and did not appear any more thereafter. In the same year . . . the greater part of the forces of Soliman were captured or cut down . . . There are those who say that this Comet bodes ill and portends calamitous war for the Swiss . . . Apianus [chief astrologer of the Emperor Charles V] has recorded his observations of the motion of this Comet. There also exists an [astrological] assessment of this Comet by Theophrasus Paracelsus.' Then, in a further passage subsequently translated by Batman:[5] *In the moneth of September a Comet was seene again in Virgo, and in ye house of Mercury for certayne weekes, two houres in the morning before the sunne rising, and in the East part which lasted 3. whole moneths, the flame was very terrible, for in greatnesse and continuance he surpassed the other Comet which we saw the yere past. The famous Doctor of Phisick Achilles Gassarus and John Virdungus Hastiodus a notable Astrologer hath described and interprete this Comet.* Charles's victory over the Turks in Hungary in 1532 was followed only three years later by his triumphant attack on the Muslim pirate Barbarossa at Tunis and his freeing of thousands of Christian captives (see II.79, VI.70) – reflecting the *Mirabilis Liber*'s prediction of a vast Muslim invasion of Europe (see I.9, I.75, II.24) followed eventually by a triumphant Christian counter-attack (see I.55).

63. Original 1555 text   **Read as modern French:**

Gaulois, Ausone bien peu subjugera:
Po, Marne, & Seine fera Perme l'urie   *fera à Parme tuerie*
Qui le grand mur contre eux dressera
Du moindre au mur le grand perdra la vie.

> **Not much of Italy shall France o'erfall:**
> **At Parma, Po, Marne, Seine in bloody strife,**
> **Who shall against them mount a mighty wall:**
> **The least on th' wall shall cost the lord his life.**

Source: A somewhat confused account of the War of Parma of 1551.

64. Original 1555 text   **Read as modern French:**

Seicher de faim, de soif gent Genevoise
Espoir prochain viendra au deffaillir,
Sur point tremblant sera loy Gebenoise.   *cévenole*
Classe au grand port ne se peult acuilir.   *accueillir*

> **Genevans shall for thirst and hunger wilt:**
> **Their last and brightest hope at last shall fail.**
> **Cévennian power shall in the balance tilt:**
> **No fleet succeeds into the port to sail.**

Source: The expectation of a collapse of the various contemporary 'heretical' religious movements in Switzerland and south-western France, despite English attempts to support them via La Rochelle or Bordeaux. Apparently a rare attempt at an independent prophecy, no doubt motivated by Nostradamus's own sincerely held Catholic religious convictions.

65. Original 1555 text   **Read as modern French:**

Le parc enclin grande calamité   *Le p. arc. [Les latitudes du pôle arctique][9]*
Par l'Hesperie & Insubre fera: *Par l'Espagne/l'Italie; la Gaule cisalpine*
Le feu en nef, peste & captivité: *dans l'église/le Vatican*
Mercure en l'Arq Saturne fenera.   *moissonnera/fauchera*

> **The northern lands sow great calamity**
> **Milan and all of Italy o'ersweeping,**
> **The Church aflame, plague and captivity.**
> **In Archer Mercury, and Saturn reaping.**

Source: Presumably the Imperial military campaign under Charles de Bourbon that resulted in the brutal sacking and occupation of Rome in 1527, with the Pope virtually imprisoned in the Castel Sant' Angelo until December: Mercury was indeed in Sagittarius that year from 20 November until 8 December. The prophet-

ic context is presumably once again the *Mirabilis Liber*'s forecast of a mighty counter-invasion of Muslim-occupied Europe. See I.55.

66. Original 1555 text

Read as modern French:

Par grans dangiers le captif echapé:
Peu de temps grand la fortune changée.   *du grand/noble; abîmée/ruinée*
Dans le palais le peuple est atrapé
Par bon augure la cité est assiegée.

> **Through dangers great the captive 'scapes afar:**
> **Then shortly dashed the noble's fortunes are.**
> **Caught are the folk within the palace gate,**
> **The town besieged by presage fortunate.**

Source: Unknown, and all the more difficult to identify because of the verse's lack
of clarity.

67. Original 1555 text

Read as modern French:

Le blonde au nez forche viendra commetre   *en viendra aux prises*
Par le duelle & chassera dehors:
Les exiles dedans fera remetre
Aux lieux marins commetants les plus forts.

> **The blond with furrowed nose shall go to war**
> **By duel, chase his adversary out:**
> **The exiles back within he shall restore,**
> **But ban to exile overseas the stout.**

Source: Almost certainly one of the numerous classical accounts (e.g. by Livy) of
the exiling of political opponents to the Mediterranean islands and the restoration
of exiles of the ruler's own persuasion.

68. Original 1555 text

Read as modern French:

De l'Aquilon les effors seront grands: *Du nord*
Sus l'Ocean sera la porte ouverte,
Le regne en l'isle sera reintegrand:
Tremblera Londres par voile descouverte.

> **Throughout the North their efforts shall be great,**
> **Upon the sea the door be opened wide.**
> **The island kingdom he'll re-integrate:**
> **Trembling at London when the sail's espied!**

Source: Possibly the anticipated restoration of the Stuart kings in Scotland, with their French connections and their ultimate designs on England, in the form of the anticipated son of Mary Queen of Scots. If so, a genuine prophecy.

69. Original 1555 text   **Read as modern French:**

Le roy Gauloys par la Celtique dextre
Voiant discorde de la grand Monarchie,
Sus les trois pars fera fleurir son sceptre,
Contre la cappe de la grand Hirarchie   *du pouvoir ecclésiastique*

> **The King of France upon the Celtic right,**
> **Seeing at odds the mighty Monarchy,**
> **In all three parts of Gaul shall press his might**
> **Against the cope of Roman hierarchy.**

Source: The struggles of François I and his son and successor Henri II against the Holy Roman Empire to the east. The 'three parts' reference goes back to the celebrated opening sentence of Julius Caesar's *Gallic War*: 'The whole of Gaul is divided into three parts.'

70. Original 1555 text   **Read as modern French:**

Le dard du ciel fera son extendue   *La comète*
Mors en parlant: grande execution.
La pierre en l'arbre, la fiere gent rendue,   *La foudre*
Brut, humain monstre, purge expiation.   *purification et expiation*

> **The mighty comet o'er the sky shall sprawl:**
> **Killed in mid-sentence, many shall have died,**
> **Blasted the tree, the haughty race shall fall:**
> **Brute human monsters, expiation tried.**

Source: Evidently the *Mirabilis Liber*'s predictions of events surrounding either its anticipated Muslim invasion of Europe or the expected counter-invasion, supplemented by various classical accounts of notable omens. For comets, see II.15, II.41, II.43; for the invasion itself, see I.9, I.75, II.24; for the counter-invasion see I.55; for 'monsters' of various kinds, see the numerous reports of ominous deformed births (mainly irregular numbers of hands and feet) throughout Julius Obsequens's *On Omens*; for lightning-strikes regarded as omens, see I.46, plus Julius Obsequens's *On Omens* (1) for 190 BC: 'The temple of Juno Lucinae was struck by lightning'; (3)

for 188 BC: 'The temple of Jupiter on the Capitol was struck by lightning'; (5) for 182 BC: 'The temple of Apollo at Caieta was struck by lightning'; (7) for 179 BC: 'Rome and many places around it were struck by lightning'; (12) for 166 BC: 'Many things at Cassino was struck by lightning'; (14) for 163 BC: 'Many things at Palatio was struck by lightning'; (14) for 163 BC: 'There was lightning at Crebrum'; (15) for 162 BC: 'Many things were struck by lightning'; (17) for 154 BC: 'Many things were struck by lightning'; (20) for 147 BC: 'Many things at Rome and around it were struck by lightning'; (24) for 137 BC: 'Many things were struck by lightning'; (25) for 136 BC: ''Many things were thrown down by lightning'; (27) for 134 BC: 'In the temple of Queen Juno the shield of the Ligurians was touched by lightning'; (28) for 130 BC: 'In Apulia a flock of sheep was killed by a single stroke of lightning'; (29) for 126 BC: 'Many things at Rome and around it were struck down by lightning'; (31) for 124 BC: 'At Crotona a flock of sheep with a dog and three shepherds were killed by lightning'; (36) for 117 BC: 'Many things at Rome and around it were hit by lightning'; (37) for 114 BC: 'In a field at Stellatum a girl sitting on her horse was struck by lightning and killed'; (41) for 106 BC: 'In a field at Trebulanum a married Roman woman was struck by lightning and killed'; (43) for 104 BC: 'The vultures on a tower were struck by lightning and killed'; (44) for 102 BC: 'The enclosure of the temple of Jupiter was struck by lightning'; . . . Similar reports are just as frequent in the contemporary chronicle of Conrad Lycosthenes,[44] who records at least sixteen comets and a similar number of lightning strikes causing major damage during Nostradamus's own lifetime. Moreover, as the latter's private correspondence and I.27 (above) also show, Nostradamus himself, true to his Gallic background, had a particular *penchant* for blasted oaks. Meanwhile, as I.26 recalls, lightning was regarded in classical times as a direct warning from the gods that the services due to them had been neglected, and that some form of ritual expiation was therefore expected.

71. Original 1555 text

Les exilés en Secile viendront
Pour delivrer de faim la gent estrange:
Au point du jour les Celtes luy faudront:
La vie demeure à raison: roy se range.

Read as modern French:

Sicile

    The exiles then to Sicily shall sail
    To save from famine sore the alien race.
    At break of day the Celts to show shall fail.
    Life's granted then – the King shall reason face.

Source: Unknown military campaign, possibly assimilated to the *Mirabilis Liber*'s predictions of a European counter-invasion against the future Muslim occupiers of Europe. See I.55.

72. Original 1555 text   **Read as modern French:**

Armée Celtique en Italie vexée
De toutes pars conflit & grande perte:
Romains fuis, ò Gaule repoulsée!
Pres du Thesin, Rubicon pugne incerte.   *Tessin [Ticino]; une bataille indécise*

> **In Italy the French host they'll attack.**
> **Great loss and heavy fighting many-sided.**
> **Flee those from Rome, O France so far pushed back!**
> **Ticino's Rubicon is undecided.**

Source: The disastrous Battle of Pavia of 1525, in which the flower of French chivalry was slain and King François I carted off to imprisonment in Madrid, contrasted with Julius Caesar's successful crossing of the Rubicon in 49 BC – all assimilated to the *Mirabilis Liber's* expectation of a future Muslim invasion of Europe via Italy. See I.9, I.75.

73. Original 1555 text   **Read as modern French:**

Au lac Fucin de Benac le rivaige   *Au lac de Garde [Garda]*
Prins du Leman au port de l'Orguion: *Pris; au port d'Hercule [Port'Ercole]*
Nay de troys bras predict belliq image,   *Né*
Par troys couronnes au grand Endymion   *à l'amant de la lune [à Henri II?]*

> **Seized on the banks of Garda's wat'ry lake**
> **Léman shall him to Port'Ercole take:**
> **Child with three arms a premonitiòn**
> **Of war: three crowns to great Endymion.**

Source: An unidentified incident linked to the contemporary struggles of Henri II with the Holy Roman Empire, with a reference to Julius Obsequens's *On Omens* (50) for 95 BC: 'A lamb with two heads and a boy with three hands and as many feet was born at Atestis. The spears of Mars moved into the palace.' The reference was possibly sparked by the omen-report by Stumphius from 1536 that would duly be recorded amd illustrated by Conrad Lycosthenes in his *Prodigiorum ac ostentorum chronicon* of 1557[44] and translated by Dr Stephen Batman in his *The Doome,*

warning all men to the Judgemente (1581): *Not farre from Tygstre [Zürich] a Childe was borne . . . with one bodye, two heades, three handes and three feete.*

74. Original 1555 text

De Sens, d'Autun viendront jusques au Rosne
Pour passer outre vers les monts Pyrenées:
La gent sortir de la Marque d'Anconne:
Par terre & mer le suivra à grans trainées.

Read as modern French:

Rhône
au-delà
sortira

> **From Sens and Autun come, the Rhône they'll reach,**
> **To pass on out towards the Pyrenees.**
> **The folk advancing from Ancona's beach**
> **Shall follow in long files o'er land and seas.**

Source: The *Mirabilis Liber's* predictions of a vast Arab invasion of Europe. See I.75, II.24, and especially I.9: ' . . . the children of Ishmael [i.e. the Arabs] . . . shall, however, renew their enterprise, they shall destroy the land, shall invade the globe from the East unto the West, from the South to the North, as far as Rome. Their yoke shall weigh heavy on the heads of the people. There shall be no nation or realm that can fight against them, until the Times shall be accomplished . . . Massacre and captivity await the Greeks . . . The Spanish shall perish by the sword. France, Germany, and the land of the Goths, eaten up by a thousand scourges, shall see a host of their inhabitants carried off. The Romans shall be killed or put to flight; and pursuing their enemies as far as the islands of the sea, the sons of Ishmael shall invade at one and the same time the North and the East, the South, and the West . . . The way of the Saracens shall spread from sea to sea . . . ' (Prophecy of Pseudo-Methodius).

75. Original 1555 text

La voix ouye de l'insolit oyseau,
Sur le canon du respiral estaige.
Si hault viendra du froment le boisseau,
Que l'homme d'homme sera Anthropophage.

Read as modern French:

Sur le canon dur et spiral étage [?]

Que les hommes deviendront des cannibales

> **Heard is the unaccustomed bird that calls**
> **On the stern law-book and the winding stair!**
> **So dear the peck of wheat that man shall dare**
> **His fellow man to eat, like cannibals.**

Source: For lines 1 and 2, Julius Obsequens's *On Omens* (26) for 135 BC: 'The voice of an owl was heard first in the Capitol, and then in the city around' (Lycosthenes' illustration of the bird[44] looks distinctly strange!); and (27a) for 133 BC: 'In Rome an owl and other unknown birds were seen,' with a covert dig at Henri II's appointment in 1554 of *sénéchaux* (Lieutenants General) to preside over legal and administrative matters throughout southern France.

The concomitant inflation was a perennial theme of the day, and had been posing major problems for the low-paid ever since the 1530s. The 'winding stair' reference is presumably to the still-famous spiral staircase that his father King François had had built at the royal castle of Blois[P].

76. Original 1555 text

	Read as modern French:
Foudre en Bourgoigne fera cas portenteux,	prodigieux
Que par engin [oncques?] ne pourroit faire	
De leur senat sacriste fait boiteux	sacristain
Fera savoir aux ennemis l'affaire.	

> **Thunder in Burgundy of such portènt**
> **Far beyond what mere artifice might do:**
> **Their chapter's sacristan, who limping went,**
> **Shall to the foe reveal what is ado.**

Source: Unknown contemporary omen, linked to shady Church doings at some unspecified monastery or cathedral.

77. Original 1555 text

	Read as modern French:
Par arcs feuz poix & par feuz repoussés:	
Cris, hurlemens sur la minuit ouys.	entendus
Dedans sont mis par les ramparts cassés	
Par cunicules les traditeurs fuis.	Par tunnels; traîtres

> **Repulsed by burning pitch, by fire and bow,**
> **Of shouts and screams is heard the midnight sound.**
> **Through broken walls instead within they'll go,**
> **The traitors flee through tunnels underground.**

Source: Unknown siege and battle, possibly assimilated to the *Mirabilis Liber's* expectation of a future invasion of Europe. See I.9, I.75, II.24.

78. Original 1555 text

	Read as modern French:
Le grand Neptune du profond de la mer	amiral
De gent Punique & sang Gauloys meslé,	africain
Les Isles à sang, pour le tardif ramer:	
Plus luy nuira que l'occult mal celé.	le secret; caché

> **The mighty Neptune of the ocean flood**
> **Of Afric blood and French commingled is.**
> **He sailing late, the Isles shall swim in blood:**
> **E'en secrets told shall harm him less than this.**

Source: The late arrival in 1554 of Nostradamus's crony the Baron de la Garde, Admiral of the Eastern Mediterranean – and reportedly of mixed descent – in support of Pietro Strozzi and his mixed French and Florentine forces against those of the Holy Roman Empire around Siena, and the consequent devastation of Corsica and Sardinia by the Imperial admiral Andrea Doria, thanks to half-hearted co-operation on the part of the Ottoman fleet under the celebrated Dragut;[60] no doubt assimilated to the *Mirabilis Liber*'s forecast of a massive Muslim invasion of Europe (see I.9, I.75, II.24).

79. Original 1555 text

Read as modern French:

La barbe crespe & noire par engin	*par ruse*
Subjuguera la gent cruele & fiere.	
Le grand CHYREN ostera du longin	*du cachot puant*[9]
Tous les captifs par Seline baniere.	*pris par ceux de la banniére au croissant lunaire*

By ruse he of the curly beard and black
The race so cruel and proud shall subjugate:
Great CHYREN from their dungeons shall bring back
All those by lunar flag incarcerate.

Source: The Emperor Charles V's triumphant expedition to Tunis of 1535, in which he succeeded in freeing thousands of Christian prisoners held by the Ottoman pirate Barbarossa, subsequently being feted throughout Europe as the hero of the hour (see also VI.70, VI.85). As Batman[5] would later translate Lycosthenes' terse report of it,[44] *Charles the Emperour tooke Tunis in Affricke.* This in turn is then projected into the future in connection with the *Mirabilis Liber*'s predictions of the liberation of Europe from its future Muslim invaders: 'There shall emerge from Gaul a race of Christians who shall make war on them and shall pierce them with the sword, shall take away their women captive and shall slaughter their children. In their turn, the sons of Ishmael shall encounter both sword and tribulation. And the Lord shall return to them the evil that they shall have done in sevenfold measure' (Prophecy of Pseudo-Methodius); 'The king of the Franks, Greeks, and Romans, reclaiming for himself the whole empire of Christendom, shall devastate all the pagan islands and cities, shall overthrow the temples of idolatry, and shall summon all the pagans to baptism' (Prophecy of the Tiburtine Sibyl). That this quatrain involves a clear case of the prophetic re-application of history is demonstrated by the fact that, in Nostradamus's day, it was *Henri II of France* (or, in his secretary Chavigny's day, Henri IV) who was sometimes referred to as 'Chyren', and not the Holy Roman Emperor Charles V; at some future date it was a new Henri of France, in other words (in latter-day versions, Henri V), who would take over the role of the mighty Hapsburg Emperor who, in his day, ruled over the greatest empire the world had ever seen, spanning both the Old and the New Worlds.

80. Original 1555 text

Apres conflit [//] du lesé l'eloquence
Par peu de temps se tramme faint repos:
Point l'on n'admet les grands à delivrance:
Les ennemis sont remis à propos.

Read as modern French:

du vaincu

> **After the fight, the loser's clever speech**
> **Shall for a space devise some slight repose:**
> **Yet not a noble shall deliverance reach,**
> **Back in their rightful place be put the foes.**

Source: Negotiations in the wake of an unidentified historical battle, with the word 'foes' suggesting a reference to the *Mirabilis Liber*'s prophecies of the future liberation of Muslim-occupied Europe (see I.55).

81. Original 1555 text

Par feu du ciel la cité presque aduste:
L'Urne menasse encor Deucalion:
Vexée Sardaigne par la Punique fuste
Apres que Libra lairra son Phaëton.

Read as modern French:

brûlée
Le Verseau; Deucalion [homologue Grec de Noé]
par les galères venant d'Afrique du Nord
le soleil

> **Fire near consumes the city from the sky:**
> **Aquarius bodes a new Deucalion.**
> **Sardinia's coast shall Afric vessels try**
> **Once from the Scales has passed their Phaëthon.**

Source: Julius Obsequens's copious records of 'fire from the sky' omens (see I.46), no doubt recalled by the disaster at Milan in 1521, later recorded by Lycosthenes[44] and translated into English by Batman:[5] *There hapned at Milan the 28. of June, a horrible chaunce, there was over the Arch of the Castell gate the Towre of Jupiter, not only very strong for the defence, but also very goodly to behold . . . And when by chaunce there were kept within ye Towre for ye use of Guns, many vessels of Brimstone in pouder, a lightning stroke it from heaven, and cutting the wall, kindled the fierie matter, whose violence did not only overthrow the tower from the foundation, but the walles also, and beate down to the grounde the Castle Chambers and other apurtenaunces . . . in so much that of 200. souldiours scarcely twelve escaped that grievous misfortune, neither was the noyse of so greate a fall unknowen to the Citie, which was shaken with so strong an Earthquake that it made many greatly afrayd, least it would all fall down . . . And then,*

only two years later: *The fifth of the Calendes of November in the kingdome of Naples a Comet appeared, and the Elemente by often lightning, thunder, and firie beames, falling to the Earth, seemed to be a fire, the Earth trembled, and there folowed by the breaking of the cloude so great a floude, that it caryed away for 30. Italian miles stones from the mountaines, waying six hundred hundered waighte, with houses and Castelles, with fifteene thousande and fiftie three houses and Castelles, and with an infinite number of men, heards, and Cattel.* All this is then assimilated to the *Mirabilis Liber*'s continual forecasts of a future Muslim invasion of Europe via the Mediterranean islands (see I.9, I.75), together with its prediction of a great world flood in the run-up to the end of the age: 'The cities and provinces of the Islanders shall be swallowed up by floods. To the plague which shall devastate some places shall be joined the fury of enemies, and nothing shall be able to comfort them . . . There shall no longer be on earth any eminence or unevenness, for the azure waters of the sea shall roll in level with the mountaintops' (Prophecy of the Tiburtine Sibyl); 'The sea shall rage and shall rise against the world' (Prophecy of Joannes de Vatiguerro); 'He shall make the high sea mount above its shores . . . As the mountains are above the plains, if it were not for an angel, they would all drown in their sins. But this sea shall rise far above the shores quite obviously . . . The sea shall rise in all parts of the world: truly even the Indies shall share in it, and know that the sea shall rise greatly and miraculously . . .' (Prophecy of Merlin). Deucalion was the Greek equivalent of the biblical Noah; Aquarius the sign that ruled over the winter months of January and February; Libra the sign of autumn; Phaëthon the ancient *alter ego* of the sun.

82. Original 1555 text   **Read as modern French:**

Par faim la proye fera loup prisonnier,
L'assaillant lors en extreme detresse.
Le nay ayant au devant le dernier,   *le derrière*[9]
Le grand n'eschappe au milieu de la presse.

> The prey shall seize the wolf by starving it,
> Th' attacker be consigned to great distress:
> The new-born child's behind in front shall sit,
> The lord retreat, but not escape the press.

Source: Two omens applied to two historical incidents: for the second omen, pos-

sibly a garbled version of Julius Obsequens's *On Omens* (40) for 108 BC: 'At Nursia twins were born of a free-born woman, the girl having all her members intact, the boy with the front of his belly open such that his intestines could be seen, and with his hinder parts whole, who expired after letting out a cry.'

83. Original 1555 text

Read as modern French:

Le gros trafficq du grand Lyon changé
La plus part tourne en pristine ruine,
Proye aux souldars par pille vendange   *vendangée*
Par Jura mont & Sueve bruine.

> **Great Lyon's mighty commerce shall decline:**
> **Most of it into ruins shall revert**
> **While troops maraud, and plunder every vine.**
> **Swabia and Jura's mount with drizzle girt.**

Source: Possibly the *Mirabilis Liber*'s predictions of a future Muslim invasion of Europe from the south (see I.9, I.75).

84. Original 1555 text

Read as modern French:

Entre Campaigne, Sienne, Flora, Tuscie   *Toscane*
Six moys neufz jours ne plouvra une goute.
L'estrange langue en terre Dalmatie
Courira sus: vastant la terre toute.   *dévastant*

> **From Tuscany to Naples there shall fall**
> **No drop of rain for six months and nine days.**
> **The alien tongue Dalmatia's country shall**
> **O'errun, and all the country it shall raze.**

Source: The *Mirabilis Liber*'s forecasts of a Muslim invasion of Europe via Italy (see I.9 and especially I.75), presaged by a drought.

85. Original 1555 text

Read as modern French:

Le vieux plain barbe sous l'estatut severe,   *l'édit*
A Lyon fait dessus l'Aigle Celtique: *l'emporte sur*
Le petit grand trop outre persevere:
Bruit d'arme au ciel: mer rouge Lygustique: *Ligurienne*

'Neath statute strict the old, full-bearded man
Shall worst at Lyon the Celtic Eagle's head.
The minor lord too far pursues his plan:
Arms sound in heaven: th' Genoan sea is red.

Source: Unknown military incident, probably assimilated to the *Mirabilis Liber*'s future invasion-scenario, and certainly to Julius Obsequens's *On Omens* (14) for 163 BC: ' . . . in Cephalonia a war-trumpet was seen sounding in heaven'; (17) for 154 BC: 'At Compsa arms were seen flying in heaven'; (41) for 106 BC: 'A celestial roaring was heard and javelins were seen to fall from heaven'; (43) for 104 BC: 'Celestial arms were seen to fight at a variety of times, places, and occasions'; (69) for 43 BC: 'A vision of swords and spears was seen being borne from earth to heaven with a great din' – to say nothing of Virgil's *Aeneid* (VIII.524–9):

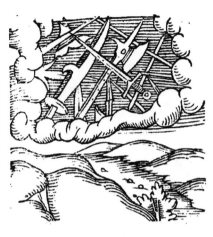

For on a sudden, shuddering from the sky,
It flashed and thundered. Almost 'twas as if
The whole world crashed down on their cowering heads
Or as if trump Tyrrhenian o'er the heavens
Did rudely blare. And as they raised their eyes
E'er and anon the thunderous din did roar
Prodigiously. And there between the clouds
Where clear did shine a space of sky serene
They arms did spy like fire all glowing red
And heard the clanging as they loudly clashed.

Such reported visions were also quite common in Nostradamus's day, as witness I.35 above.

86. Original 1555 text

Naufraige a classe pres d'onde Hadriatique:
La terre esmeuë sus l'air en terre mis:
Egypte tremble augment Mahommetique
L'Herault soy rendre à crier est commis.

Read as modern French:

flotte; dans la mer

devant le croissant Musulman [?]
de se rendre

A fleet is wrecked near th' Adriatic sea,
Lifted by earthquake, cast upon the land.
Egypt shall quake the Muslim flag to see:
A herald sent, surrender in his hand.

Source: Unidentified historical *tsunami* incident, assimilated to the *Mirabilis Liber*'s predictions of a future Muslim invasion. See I.9, I.75, II.24.

87. Original 1555 text	Read as modern French:
Apres viendra des extremes contrées	
Prince Germain dessus le throsne doré:	
La servitude & eaux rencontrées	*ès feaux [?]⁹/par eux [?]*
La dame serve, son temps plus n'adoré.	*servante*

> **Then from a distant land to sit shall come**
> **A German prince upon the throne of gold:**
> **Yet even them shall slavery o'ercome,**
> **Nor vassal lady longer dear he'll hold.**

Source: Possibly the accession of the Burgundian Charles V to the throne of the Holy Roman Empire in 1520.

88. Original 1555 text	Read as modern French:
Le circuit du grand faict ruineux	*La marche*
Le nom septiesme du cinquiesme sera:	
D'un tiers plus grand l'estrange belliqueux,	
Monton, Lutece, Aix ne guarantira.	*Mouton [?]⁹*

> **So ruinous the campaign of the lord,**
> **The fifth they'll one third greater rate than e'er**
> **The seventh's name: the warlord from abroad**
> **Shall with his ram nor Aix nor Paris spare.**

Source: Unidentified, but possibly referring obliquely to kings or popes – such as the Roman pope, Innocent VII (1406) contrasted with the Avignon pope, Alexander V (1409–10).

89. Original 1555 text	Read as modern French:
Du jou seront demis les deux grandz maistres	*Du joug seront libérés; officiers du roi*
Leur grand pouvoir se verra augmenté:	
La terre neufve sera en ses haults estres	*La terre dont on renouvelle/augmente le loyer; les hautes salles du château ayant une vue extérieure⁹*
Au sanguinaire le nombre racompté.	

> **Both high officials from the yoke dismissed,**
> **Their mighty power is seen to be increased:**
> **Of th' newleased land the value they'll recall**
> **To th' bloody one in th' high rooms of his hall.**

Source: Unidentified contemporary political and economic moves.

90. Original 1555 text   **Read as modern French:**

Par vie & mort changé regne d'Ongrie: *ruiné/abîmé*
La loy sera plus aspre que service,   *plus sévère*
Leur grand cité d'urlemens plaincts & crie,   *hurlements; cris*
Castor & Pollux ennemis dans la lyce.

> **Through life-death change of Hungary's regimes**
> **Shall come laws harsher than rank servitude.**
> **Their capital shall ring with cries and screams**
> **When in the lists its Heavenly Twins shall feud.**

Source: The celebrated Battle of Mohács of 1526, when the twin cities of Buda and Pest were captured by the Ottomans under Suleiman the Magnificent and rulership was then disputed between John Zapolya and Ferdinand of Hapsburg.[41]

91. Original 1555 text   **Read as modern French:**

Soleil levant un grand feu lon verra,   *l'on*
Bruit & clarté vers Aquilon tendant: *vers le nord*
Dedans le rond mort & cris lont orra   *l'on entendra*
Par glaive, feu, faim, mort les attendants.

> **At sunrise shall a mighty fire appear,**
> **Its roar and glare towards the northward tending:**
> **Within the circle mortal screams they'll hear,**
> **Famine, fire, death and sword them all attending.**

Source: Julius Obsequens's *On Omens* (54) for 91 BC: 'At sunrise a ball of fire appeared in the northern part of the sky with a prodigious sound', re-applied as an omen of military disaster to come, presumably associated with the *Mirabilis Liber*'s predictions of a future Muslim invasion (see I.9, I.75, II.24).

92. Original 1555 text   **Read as modern French:**

Feu couleur d'or du ciel en terre veu:
Frappé de hault, nay, fait cas merveilleuz:
Grand meurtre humain: prins du grand le nepveu,   *le neveu du seigneur est pris*
Morts d'expectacles eschappé l'orgueilleux.   *au cours de spectacles*

> **From heaven golden fire to earth shall fall:**
> **A birth prodigious: lightning from on high:**
> **Lord's nephew ta'en: slaughter shall men befall:**
> **Deaths at a show: the haughty one shall fly.**

Source: Julius Obsequens's *On Omens* (54) for 91 BC: 'At Spoletinum a globe of fire the color of gold rolled down to the ground, and increasing in size, was seen to be borne towards the east, where it was big enough to cover the sun . . . The enclosure of the temple of Piety in the circus Flaminius was struck by lightning'; plus numerous other omens in the form of deformed births, equally reflected in reports from Nostradamus's own day – all re-evoked as omens for imminent disasters of various kinds.

93. Original 1555 text

Bien pres du Tymbre presse la Libytine,
Ung peu devant grand inundation:
Le chef du nef prins, mis a la sentine:
Chasteau, palais en conflagration.

Read as modern French:

la déesse de la mort
Un

Death besets all hard by the Tiber's flow
Shortly before the mighty inundation,
The Bark's commander taken, sent below,
Castle and palace both in conflagration.

Source: The sacking of Rome by troops of the Holy Roman Empire in 1527, when the Tiber was in flood, with the fleeing Pope virtually imprisoned in the dungeons of the Castel Sant' Angelo, assimilated to the *Mirabilis Liber*'s expected invasion of Italy by vast Muslim forces. See I.9, and especially: 'The children of Agar shall seize Tarento, and spreading through Apulia, shall sack a host of towns. They shall be determined to enter Rome, and nobody in the world shall be able to resist them, unless it be the Lord God himself' (Prophecy of the Tiburtine Sibyl). Compare X.27.

94. Original 1555 text

GRAN. Po, grand mal pour Gauloys recevra,
Vaine terreur an maritin Lyon:
Peuple infini par la mer passera,
Sans eschapper un quart d'un milion.

Read as modern French:

Grand/Noble; par
au Lyon ailé de Saint Marc de Venise[9]

Po's lord through France endures great woes and loss;
Venice's Lion at sea false terrors bind.

A race unnumbered shall the ocean cross,
But quarter million no escape shall find.

Source: The *Mirabilis Liber's* prediction of a brutal European counter-attack against the continent's future Muslim occupiers. See I.55.

95. Original 1555 text   Read as modern French:

Les lieux peuples seront inhabitables:
Pour champs avoir grande division:
Regnes livrés a prudents incapables:
Lors les grands freres mort & dissension.   *entre les frères nobles*

> **Where once lived crowds, now nobody can live:**
> **The fields must be re-marked and split apart.**
> **Kingdoms to cautious bunglers they shall give:**
> **Between great kinsmen deadly feuds shall start.**

Source: The *Mirabilis Liber's* expectation of an eventual return of refugee populations to a devastated and depopulated Europe following the final expulsion of its future Muslim occupiers. See I.55.

96. Original 1555 text   Read as modern French:

Flambeau ardant au ciel soir sera veu
Pres de la fin & principe du Rosne: *et source*
Famine, glaive: tard le secours pourveu,
La Perse tourne envahir Macedoine.

> **A flaming torch at dusk in heaven they'll spy**
> **Near to the head and source of th' river Rhône.**
> **Famine and war; too late shall help come by.**
> **Th' returning Persian falls on Macedon.**

Source: Julius Obsequens's *On Omens* (11) for 167 BC: 'At Lanuvium a burning torch was seen in the sky'; (12) for 166 BC: 'At Lanuvium a remarkable torch was seen in the sky at night'; (24) for 137 BC: 'At Praeneste a burning torch was seen in the sky'; (41) for 106 BC: 'At Rome a torch was seen by day flying in the air'; (45) for 100 BC: 'At Tarquinii a burning torch was widely seen'; (51) for 94 BC: 'A torch appeared in the sky and the whole heavens were seen to burn'; (53) for 92 BC: 'A torch was seen in the sky'; (68) for 44 BC: 'A torch

was seen to be borne towards the western sky'; (71) for 17 BC: 'A celestial torch whose light spread from the south to the north turned the night as though into day'; assimilated to the *Mirabilis Liber*'s 'Discord shall once again brandish its torch on the banks of the Rhine in Germany [not untypically, Nostradamus, evidently working from memory, is confused about which of the two major rivers is involved]. Severe disorders shall take place . . . A burning fever shall consume the inhabitants of the Rhine, and great tribulations shall come to devastate the clergy and people' (Anonymous prophecy). No doubt, too, there is considerable input from Nostradamus's own quite recent experience of the famous Salon meteor of 1554 and the tardy French aid for Pietro Strozzi of the following year (see II.78 above): 'This fire, being very great, did by all accounts look like a great burning staff or torch, gave out from itself a wondrous brightness, and flames did spurt from it like a glowing iron being worked by a smith. And such fire did sparkle greatly, glowing aloft like silver over an immense distance like St James's Road in the sky, known as the *Galaxy* [Milky Way], and raced overhead very fast like an arrow with a great roaring and crackling which the poets call *immensum fragorem* [a thunderous din] and as though it were being blown hither and thither by the [raging and roaring] of a mighty wind' (Letter to the Governor of Provence, 19 March 1554). Conrad Lycosthenes' *Prodigiorum ac ostentorum chronicon* of 1557[44] would duly illustrate such phenomena, notably for 1542. All this is evidently referred to the *Mirabilis Liber*'s prediction of a coming Muslim invasion of Europe (see I.9, I.75, II.24), on the model of the Persian Xerxes' massive invasion of Greece in 480 BC.

97. Original 1555 text	Read as modern French:
Romain Pontife garde de t'approcher	
De la cité qui deux fleuves arrouse,	*que deux fleuves arrosent [?]*
Ton sang viendras au pres de la cracher,	
Toy & les tiens quand fleurira la rose.	

> O Roman Pope, beware lest you come near
> The city that shall water either flood!
> When blooms the rose, those who to you are dear
> Nearby – like you yourself – shall cough up blood.

Source: The coronation of Pope Clement V in 1305 at Lyon (at the confluence of the major rivers Saône and Rhône), in the course of which a wall collapsed under the weight of spectators, killing many of them, and the Pope himself, bareheaded, had to retrieve his tiara from among the corpses and debris.[60] The first of the medieval French popes, he ruled from Avignon – another city standing at the confluence of two great rivers (the Rhône and Durance). The 'rose' reference may be to the *Roman de la Rose* of the previous century and the associated age of the Troubadours, which had only recently drawn to a close. See also VI.51.

98. Original 1555 text   **Read as modern French:**

Celuy du sang resperse le visaige   *aspergé*
De la victime proche sacrifiée:
Tonant en Leo augure par presaige: *Jupiter*
Mis estre à mort lors pour la fiancée.

Who in the face with blood shall spattered be –
Blood of the victim sacrificed nearby,
Jove thundering in Leo portentously –
For his betrothed shall then through others die.

Source: Livy's *History of Rome* (XXI.63) for 217
BC: 'A few days later [Flaminius] entered on his
magistracy, and while he was sacrificing a calf
that had already been struck with the knife, it
escaped from the hands of the sacrificial attendants and spattered many of the bystanders
with blood. Those who were unaware of the
cause of the [resulting] alarm and trepidation
immediately fled. Many took it as an omen of
great dread'; together with numerous portentous lightning-strikes from Julius Obsequens's
On Omens (see II.70), and notably (3) for 188
BC: 'The temple of Jupiter on the Capitol was
struck by lightning.'

99. Original 1555 text   **Read as modern French:**

Terroir Romain qu'interpretoit augure,
Par gent Gauloyse seras par trop vexée:
Mais nation Celtique craindra l'heure,
Boreas, classe trop loing l'avoir poussee.   *Le vent du nord; flotte*

The Roman lands by oracle marked out
Shall by the French be vexed more than enow:
But let those self-same Celts the hour redoubt
When the north wind their fleet too far shall blow.

Source: Livy's *History of Rome* (I.18), describing the inauguration of the semi-legendary King Numa in around 710 BC: 'Looking out over the city and the country
around, [the augur], having prayed to the gods, took in the whole region from east
to west and declared the southern part to be "right" and the northern part "left":
then he . . . placed his right hand on Numa's head and prayed thus: "Father Jupiter,
if it be Heaven's will that this man, Numa Pompilius, whose head I am holding,
should be King of Rome, give us clear signs within the boundaries that I have established." Then he spelled out the exact signs that he wished to be sent. These hav-

ing duly been sent, Numa, proclaimed King, came down from the temple.' Compare V.75. The last two lines may relate to the *Mirabilis Liber*'s familiar counter-invasion scenario (see I.55).

100. Original 1555 text   Read as modern French:

Dedans les isles si horrible tumulte,
Rien on n'orra qu'une bellique brigue,   *entendra; qu'une lutte guerrière*
Tant grand sera des predateurs l'insulte,   *l'attaque*
Qu'on se viendra ranger à la grand ligue.

> **Among the isles such dreadful tumult roars,**
> **That nought is heard but sound of martial fray:**
> **So great the onslaught of the predators**
> **That all shall join the mighty league that day.**

Source: The *Mirabilis Liber*'s forecasts of a massive future Muslim invasion of Europe via the Mediterranean islands. See I.9, I.75.

Century III

1. Original 1555 text

Apres combat & bataille navale,
Le grand Neptune à son plus haut beffroy,
Rouge aversaire de fraieur viendra pasle,
Metant le grand ocean en effroy.

Read as modern French:

Le grand amiral; à sa plus haute puissance
adversaire; pâle

> **After the fight and battle under sail**
> **Great Neptune shall attain his highest power:**
> **His foe, once red, shall then for fear grow pale**
> **And terror spread the mighty ocean o'er.**

Source: The successful and almost unprecedented passage of the Strait of Gibraltar by Nostradamus's friend the Baron de la Garde, Admiral of the Eastern Mediterranean, with 25 galleys in 1545 (in his annual *Almanachs* Nostradamus routinely refers to admirals as 'Neptune', and especially the Baron – see II.5, II.59), prior to an attempted attack on England in July of the same year (compare VII.10). His enemy's 'redness', with which line 3 makes great play, no doubt refers to the red crosses universally displayed by the uniforms and banners of his Imperial adversaries. The prophetic context is presumably the *Mirabilis Liber*'s predicted Western counter-invasion of the Middle East (see I.55)

2. Original 1555 text

Le divin verbe donrra à la sustance
Comprins ciel terre, or occult au fait mystique

Corps, ame, esprit aiant toute puissance,
Tant sous ses pieds, comme au siege celique.

Read as modern French:

donnera à la substance
Y compris; caché [sans 'or' dans l'éd. de Vienne]

ayant
céleste

> **The Word Divine to substance crude shall grant**
> **In heaven and earth, 'neath mystic act concealed,**
> **Its body, soul and sprite omnipotent**
> **As underfoot, so, too, in heaven revealed.**

Source: The contemporary doctrine of the transubstantiation of Christ's body and blood into physical bread and wine in the Catholic Mass, possibly restated in response to the notorious *Affaire des placards* of 1534, when posters attacking it were famously put up by the Reformers in Paris – not least on the door of the King's own bedroom.

3. Original 1555 text

Read as modern French:

Mars & Mercure & l'argent joint ensemble *et la lune; joints*
Vers le midi extreme siccité: *sécheresse*
Au fond d'Asie on dira terre tremble, *de l'Asie Mineure*
Corinthe, Ephese lors en perplexité.

> **Mars, moon and Mercury conjunction make:**
> **Towards the south a great and mighty drought.**
> **In central Turkey earth, they'll say, 's aquake:**
> **In Ephesus and Corinth fear and doubt.**

Source: The *Mirabilis Liber*, supplemented by a variety of earthquake omens from Julius Obsequens's *On Omens* and reports of droughts from Livy's *History of Rome* (such as at IV.30 for 428 BC). See I.20, I.46. I.69, I.87, II.43, and compare II.52 on the same topic. The triple conjunction mentioned is far too frequent to permit the pinpointing of the original year in question, but all three 'planets' were in Aquarius on 5–6 January 1554, for example, and again at the beginning of February, as well as in Aries at the beginning of March and in Taurus at the beginning of May – any one of which might thus well indicate the date when Nostradamus reached this particular verse.

4. Original 1555 text

Read as modern French:

Quand seront proches le defaut des lunaires, *l'éclipse/la faillite; luminaires [voir Gen. 1:16*
             et quatrain suivant]
De l'un a l'autre ne distant grandement,
Ftoid, siccité, danger vers les frontieres, *Froid, sécheresse*
Mesmes ou l'oracle a prins commencement. *pris*

> **When sun and moon shall shortly cease to shine**
> **When from each other scarcely far away,**
> **Cold, peril, drought near th' borders shall combine,**
> **There where the oracle first saw the day.**

Source: The *Mirabilis Liber*'s description of the end of the world: 'Thus it was that the Sibyl predicted to the Romans what must happen . . . Then shall commence the desolation and the anguish. The sun and the stars shall lose their brightness, and the moon its light. The hills shall be laid low, and the valleys raised up. There shall no longer be on earth any eminence or unevenness, for the azure waters of the sea shall roll in level with the mountaintops. All shall cease to be; the shattered earth shall perish' (Prophecy of the Tiburtine Sibyl). The last line presumably refers back to the same Sibyl's origins in Asia Minor, as described in the same source. Compare III.3.

5. Original 1555 text

Pres, loin defaut de deux grand luminaires
Qui surviendra entre l'Avril & Mars.
O quel cherté! mais deux grands debonaires
Par terre & mer secourront toutes pars.

Read as modern French:

Longtemps après l'éclipse/la faillite

> **Not long after both lights afar go out**
> **('Twixt March and April shall that time befall),**
> **What prices! But two gentle lords, no doubt,**
> **By land and sea shall succor bring to all.**

Source: Possibly the *Mirabilis Liber*'s references to Elias and Enoch in the context of its dramatic end-of-the-world scenario: 'Then the Antichrist shall reveal himself publicly; he shall seat himself in the house of the Lord in Jerusalem. During his reign, there shall appear two illustrious men, Elias and Enoch, to announce the coming of the Lord. The Antichrist shall put them to death, and two days later the Lord shall revive them' (Prophecy of the Tiburtine Sibyl). Brind'Amour suggests a specific back-reference to consecutive lunar and solar eclipses that were visible over distant eastern Europe in the spring of 1540. François I's new *gabelle*, or salt-tax, was imposed the following year, while freezing weather in 1541 and especially 1542 brought about steep rises in the price of food.

6. Original 1555 text

Dans temples clos le foudre y entrera,
Les citadins dedans leurs forts grevés:
Chevaux, beufs, hommes, l'onde mur touchera,
.Par faim, soif sous les plus foibles arnés

Read as modern French:

la foudre
accablés

sales [lat. sucidus]⁹; épuisés

> **The lightning deep within closed churches falls,**
> **Citizens overcome in each redoubt –**
> **Men, horses, cows – as water laps the walls.**
> **No food or drink; filthy, the weak worn out.**

Source: Julius Obsequens's *On Omens* (44) for 102 BC: 'The enclosure of the temple of Jupiter was struck by lightning'; and (54) for 91 BC: 'The enclosure of the temple of Piety in the circus Flaminius was struck by lightning' – both as slightly misconstrued by Nostradamus; for floods, see I.69.

7. Original 1555 text   **Read as modern French:**

Les fuitifs, feu du ciel sus les piques: fugitifs
Conflit prochain des courbeaux s'esbatans,
De terre on crie aide secour celiques,   célestes
Quand pres des murs seront les combatans

> **Fire from the sky strikes spear-points as they fly,**
> **Of fighting crows the conflict seen quite near:**
> **From earth to heaven for help goes up the cry**
> **When near the walls the combatants appear.**

Source: Among many other possible classical references for the first line,[9] Julius Obsequens's *On Omens* (47) for 98 BC: 'In the circus, fire flashed [*fulsus*] among the spears of the soldiers' – all possibly assimilated to the *Mirabilis Liber*'s forecasts of future war and invasion (see I.9, I.75, II.24).

8. Original 1555 text   **Read as modern French:**

Les Cimbres joints avecques leurs voisins,
Depopuler viendront presque l'Hespaigne:
Gents amassés Guienne & Limosins
Seront en ligue, & leur feront compaignie.

> **The Cimbrians, joined by their neighbors, too,**
> **Shall near depopulate the bulk of Spain:**
> **From Guyenne, Limousin come many who**
> **Shall join them as companions in their train.**

Source: Plutarch's brief account in his *Parallel Lives* of the invasion of Spain by the Cimbri, who, having incorporated a whole variety of tribes *en route*, were eventually defeated near Aix-en-Provence in 102 BC by the Roman general Gaius Marius (a favorite character of Nostradamus's, no doubt because of his local associations): '. . . a great deal of luck seemed to attend Marius, for as a result of the enemy's changing course, as it were, and descending first upon Spain, he had time to exercise his soldiers . . . The Cimbri . . . plundered and depopulated all the country round about . . .'; but specifically Julius Obsequens's *On Omens* (43) for 104 BC: 'The Cimbri, having crossed the Alps after devastating Spain, joined up with the Teutons.'

9. Original 1555 text   **Read as modern French:**

Bourdeaux, Rouen, & la Rochele joints
Tiendront autour la grand mer oceane:
Anglois, Bretons, & les Flamans conjoints
Les chasseront jusques au-pres de Roane

> **Bordeaux, Rouen and la Rochelle shall hold**
> **Firmly together round the ocean sea.**

But English, Bretons, Flemings shall make bold
T' unite and force them to Roanne to flee.

Source: Unknown, but evidently referred to the *Mirabilis Liber*'s predictions of a Western counter-invasion against the future Muslim occupiers of Europe (see I.55). Roanne stands on the upper river Loire, not far from Lyon.

10. Original 1555 text   Read as modern French:

De sang & faim plus grande calamité
Sept fois s'apreste à la marine plage,
Monech de faim, lieu prins, captivité,   *Monaco; pris*
Le grand mené croc en ferrée caige.   *par un crochet*

> Seven times of blood and famine they shall see
> E'en greater woes along the ocean shore:
> Monaco starved, the place shall captured be,
> Their lord hooked, dragged in iron cage and more.

Source: The *Mirabilis Liber*'s account either of a future invasion of Europe by the Muslims, or of the continent's subsequent liberation. The verse's general description fits the former (see I.9, I.75, II.24), but the expression 'seven times' is more reminiscent of the latter: 'Then shall emerge in Gaul a king of the Greeks, Francs, and Romans, of lofty stature and handsome appearance; his body and limbs shall have the most beautiful proportions; he shall reign a hundred and twelve years; he shall carry written on his forehead: "This man, verily, is destined to avenge Christendom, snatch it away from the yoke of Ishmael [i.e. the Arabs], conquer it from the Saracens; none of the Saracens shall thereafter be able to reign." Seven times over, he shall cause them the greatest ill, shall ruin their whole empire, shall strike them; after that, peace shall reign for Christians up until the time of the Antichrist' (Prophecy of the Tiburtine Sibyl). For iron cages, see I.10.

11. Original 1555 text   Read as modern French:

Les armes batre au ciel longue saison,
L'arbre au milieu de la cité tumbé: *tombé*
Vermine, rongne, glaive en face tyson,   *ronge; devant le visage*
Lors le Monarque d'Hadrie succombé.   *de Venise*

> Long time aloft the sky shall battle churn,
> Once at the city's heart shall fall the tree.
> Swords; vermin gnaw; a torch the face shall burn.
> Venice's Monarch then shall worsted be.

Source: One of a number of reported visions – both ancient and contemporary (see II.85) – of armies fighting in the sky, recalled, perhaps, by the very recent case of the summer of 1554 reported by Job Fincelius in his *De miraculis sui temporis*, later collected and illustrated by Conrad Lycosthenes in his *Prodigiorum ac ostentorum chronicon* of 1557[44] and duly translated into the English of the day by Dr Stephen Batman:[5] *On the fifth of Auguste at nine a clocke at nighte neare to Stolpen, in the south-part of the Element there was seene armies of souldiours, makying a great shoute and running togither with dreadfull weapons.* 'Element' is Batman's standard word for 'sky' (here *coelo* in the Latin). Whichever case is referred to in this verse – taken to portend the imminent fall of Venice's ruler – is related by

Nostradamus to an incident in 1521 (a year of grasshopper-plagues and epidemics), in which King François I was seriously burned in the face by a burning torch during war-games on the feast of Epiphany, and Pope Leo X died in the city of Rome.[60] The 'falling tree' reference, though, appears to be to the death of a different pope entirely – namely that of Pope Julius II in 1513 (an ally of Venice whose family name of Della Rovere, duly reflected in his coat of arms, identified him with an oak tree). Whether Nostradamus's evident confusion of papal families (Leo X was a Medici) is accidental or deliberate (i.e. allegorical) is not known, though the former would not be untypical.

12. Original 1555 text

	Read as modern French:
Par la tumeur de Heb. Po, Tag. Timbre & Rosne,	*de l'Ébre, du Po, du Tage, du Tibre et du Rhône*
Et par l'estang Leman & Aretin,	*d'Arezzo*
Les deux grans chefs & cites de Garonne	*des [ès]*
Prins, morts, noies. Partir humain butin.	*Pris; noyés*

By swoll'n Po, Tagus, Tiber, Rhône, Ebro
And by Geneva's and Arezzo's waters,
From Bordeaux and Toulouse two great lords go.
The human booty leaves – drowned, captives, slaughters.

Source: Presumably the *Mirabilis Liber*'s scenario of a future invasion of Europe by the Arabs. See I.9, I.75, II.24.

13. Original 1555 text

	Read as modern French:
Par foudre en l'arche or & argent fondu:	*dans le coffre à argent*
Des deux captifs l'un l'autre mangera,	
De la cité le plus grand estendu,	*tué*
Quand submergée la classe nagera.	*la flotte*

Lightning shall in the chest gold, silver melt.

Of captives twain shall one the other eat.
The city's lord shall th' hand of death have felt,
When 'neath the waves shall sink the mighty fleet.

Source: Julius Obsequens's *On Omens* (41) for 106 BC: 'The shut up silver was melted by a bolt of lightning'– a phenomenon also discussed by Cardano in his *On Subtlety* of 1547;[9] assimilated to the various omens reported as accompanying the death of Lorenzo de' Medici, Lord of Florence, in 1492, as reported by Lycosthenes[44] and translated into English by Batman[5]: *Before that the worthie Laurence Medices, a prince never ynough to be praised for ye manifold qualities of his minde, died at Florence: these things in a maner went before his death, although other things also were commonly spoken of . . . when the Skie uppon the sodayne was overcast with clowdes, the toppe* [i.e. the dome] *of that great Cathedrall Churche which hath the excellentest roofe (for the wonderfull workemanship) in all the world, was stricken with lightning, so that certain great shivers were thrown down . . . and with a certaine horrible force & violence great Marble Stones were flong down, and ye same night ye Laurence died . . . a couple of the Noblest Lyons didde so fiercely fighte together in the Denne where they were commonlye kepte, that the one was verye sore hurte, the other slayn: at Aretam also upon the Castle there were sayd two flames to have burned like Castor and Pollux....* And then, two years later, the allied Neapolitan fleet was sunk off Rapallo.[60]

14. Original 1555 text   **Read as modern French:**

Par le rameau du vaillant personage   *Par le descendant*
De France infime: par le pere infelice
Honneurs, richesses travail en son viel aage   *souffrance*
Pour avoir creu le conseil d'homme nice.   *sot/ignorant*

> For one so slight who from brave personage
> Of France descends, of wretched sire the son,
> Honors and wealth, but woe in his old age
> For crediting th' advice of a simpleton.

Source: Unknown.

15. Original 1555 text   **Read as modern French:**

Cueur, vigueur, gloire le regne changera,
De tous points contre aiant son adversaire.
Lors France enfance par mort subjuguera.
Le grand regent sera lors plus contraire.

> From courage, glory, strength the realm shall stray,
> Having grim foes on every side opposed:
> Then infancy through death shall France betray,
> The mighty regent being less well-disposed.

Source: Current worries about the French succession should King Henri II die or be killed and the Dauphin Francois, then eleven or twelve, have to take over responsibility for defending the kingdom against the encircling armies of Charles V, albeit under the regency of his formidable mother, Queen Catherine de Médicis.[9]

16. Original 1555 text   Read as modern French:

Le prince Anglois Mars à son cueur de ciel   *au Milieu du Ciel*
Vouldra poursuivre sa fortune prospere,
Des deux duelles l'un percera le fiel:
Hay de lui, bien aymé de sa mere.

> **The English Prince, Mars in his Mid-Heaven seen,**
> **Shall wish to seek his fortune and his hoard.**
> **One dueller shall pierce the other's spleen:**
> **Hated by him, by mother still adored.**

Source: Two subjects – first, the deeds of the warlike Henry VIII of England, who had died only recently, in 1547; and second, duelling, which was a common problem at the time.

17. Original 1555 text   Read as modern French:

Mont Aventine brusler nuict sera veu: *vu*
Le ciel obscur tout à un coup en Flandres,
Quand le Monarque chassera son nepveu:
Leurs gens d'eglise commetront les esclandres.   *[A]lors*

> **Th' Aventine Hill at night is seen to burn:**
> **In Flanders suddenly the sky's unlit,**
> **When the King shall his nephew chase and spurn:**
> **Then Church officials scandals shall commit.**

Source: Probably a vague memory of the story of the Great Fire of Rome of AD 64, assimilated to the solar eclipse of January 1544, which did indeed cross Flanders. For Church depravities, see the *Mirabilis Liber*'s predictions at II.12 above.

18. Original 1555 text   Read as modern French:

Apres la pluie laict assés longuete,   *de lait*
En plusieurs lieux de Reins le ciel touché   *de Reims*
Helas quel meurtre de seng pres d'eux s'apreste.
Peres & filz rois n'oseront aprocher.

> **After of milky rain a longish shower**
> **Shall Reims in parts be shattered from th' sky.**

What bloody murder o'er the place shall lour!
Nor royal sires nor sons dare venture nigh.

Source: Julius Obsequens's *On Omens* (14) for 163 BC: 'At Gabii it rained milk'; (28) for 130 BC: 'At Rome it rained milk at the Graecostasis'; (30) for 125 BC: 'At Veii it rained oil and milk'; (31) for 124 BC: 'It rained milk at the Graecostasis'; (35) for 118 BC: 'It rained milk'; (36) for 117 BC: 'At Praeneste it rained milk'; (39) for 111 BC: 'It rained milk for three days'; (40) for 108 BC: 'It rained milk twice'; (41) for 106 BC: 'At Perusinum and various places in Rome it rained milk'; (43) for 104 BC: 'At Lucani it rained milk, at Luna blood . . . It rained milk at the assembly'; (50) for 95 BC: 'At Caere it rained milk'; (53) for 92 BC: 'At Rome it rained milk'; plus the various lightning-omens listed under II.70 above – presumably with reference to the *Mirabilis Liber*'s anticipated Muslim invasion of Europe, and particularly of a site as sacred as Reims to French royalty, who seem to be referred to in the last line.

19. Original 1555 text

En Luques sang & laict viendra plouvoir:
Un peu devant changement de preteur,
Grand peste & guerre, faim & soif fera voyr
Loing, ou mourra leur prince recteur.

Read as modern French:

À Lucca; il viendra pleuvoir
avant; magistrat principal

leur prince et leur recteur [chef dirigeant]

In Lucca it both blood and milk shall rain
Shortly before the change of magistrate:
Great plague and thirst, famine and war again,
Far, far from where their prince and lord shall die.

Source: Julius Obsequens's *On Omens* (see previous verse and II.32), possibly assimilated to the *Mirabilis Liber*'s predicted invasion of Europe via Italy (see I.9, I.47, II.9, II.24, and especially I.75).

20. Original 1555 text

Par les contrées du grand fleuve Bethique
Loing d'Ibere, au regne de Granade:
Croix repoussées par gens Mahumetiques
Un de Cordube trahira la contrade.

Read as modern French:

du Guadalquivir
Loin du nord de l'Espagne
Les chrétiens
le pays

Through all the lands of great Guadalquivir,
Far from the Ebro, 'neath Granada's sway,
Muslims the Christians shall repulse, I fear:
Of Cordoba shall one the land betray.

Source: The *Mirabilis Liber*'s grisly scenario of future invasion of Europe by Muslim forces from North Africa. See I.47, I.75, II.9, II.24, and especially I.9.

21. Original 1555 text

Au crustamin par mer Hadriatique
Apparoistra un horride poisson,
De face humaine, & la fin aquatique,
Qui se prendra dehors de l'ameçon.

Read as modern French:

à Crustumerium/Crustumium; Adriatique

et la queue
sans hameçon

At Adriatic Crustumerium
There shall appear a fish of fearful look
That, fishy-tailed and human-faced, shall come
And let itself be caught without a hook.

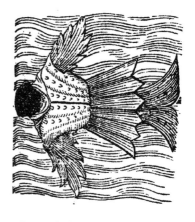

Source: A familiar tale of washed-up sea-monsters, in this case probably the one reported by Gaspar Peucerus to have been stranded on the shores of the Baltic in 1550 (in which case Nostradamus not uncharacteristically gets the wrong sea and port!) as collected and illustrated by Lycosthenes in 1557[44] and translated by Batman in 1581:[5] *In the Sea Baltgicum not far from Hafnia, Gaspar Pucerus in his booke of Teratoscopia affirmeth, a fishe was taken with a mans face, his heade shaven about like a Monkes crown, having scales on his body, like unto a Friers cowle.*

Lycosthenes' complete gallery of sea-monsters is shown below.

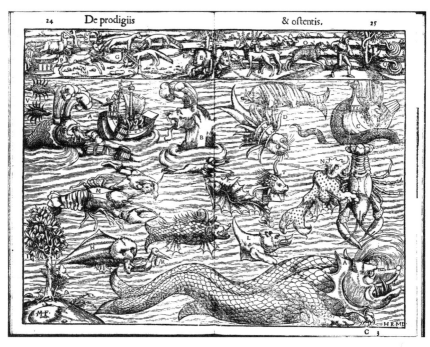

22. Original 1555 text

Read as modern French:

Six jours l'assaut devant cité donné:
Livrée sera forte & aspre bataille:
Trois la rendront & à eux pardonné:
Le reste a feu & sang tranche traille.   *l'on tranche et taille [?]*

Six days before the town th' assault is given,
Surrendered after battle strong and grim.
Three who surrender it shall be forgiven,
The rest 'midst blood and fire cut limb from limb.

Source: An unknown historical siege, presumably assimilated to the *Mirabilis Liber*'s predictions of a massive Arab invasion of Europe. See I.9, I.75, II.24.

23. Original 1555 text

Read as modern French:

Si France passes outre mer lygustique,   *Ligurienne*
Tu te verras en isles & mers enclos:
Mahommet contraire: plus mer Hadriatique: *Les Musulmans; Adriatique*
Chevaulx & d'asnes tu rougeras les os.   *rongeras*

If, France, beyond th' Ligurian sea you go,
You'll see yourself by isles and seas hemmed in.
E'en more the Adria with its Muslim foe:
Of horse and ass you'll gnaw the bones and skin.

Source: Past French military disasters in Italy under Louis XII, François I, and Henri II, assimilated to the *Mirabilis Liber*'s scenario of future Muslim invasion and French counter-invasion. See I.9, I.47, I.55, I.75, II.9, II.24.

24. Original 1555 text

Read as modern French:

De l'entreprinse grande confusion,   *entreprise*
Perte de gens, thresor innumerable:
Tu ny dois faire encor extension
France a mon dire fais que sois recordable.   *à ce que je dis; d'accord*

The undertaking chaos would portend,
Great loss of men and treasure beyond price.
Thither not yet your fight you must extend.
France, be content to follow my advice.

Source: As per the companion verse above (III.23).

25. Original 1555 text   Read as modern French:

Qui au royaume Navarrois parviendra
Quand de Secile & naples seront joints: *Sicile*
Bigorre & Landes par Foyx Loron tiendra,   *Foix; Oloron*
D'un qui d'Hespaigne sera par trop conjoint   *de l'Espagne*

> **He who the kingdom of Navarre reigns o'er**
> **When Sicily and Naples are allied,**
> **Through Foix, Oloron the Landes holds and Bigorre**
> **From one who'll be too much on th' Spanish side.**

Source: Contemporary politics.

26. Original 1555 text   Read as modern French:

Des rois & princes dresseront simulacres,   *images*
Augures, creuz [/] eslevez aruspices: *Augures crus; devinateurs*
Corne, victime d'orée, & d'azur, d'acre: *dorée; de lapis lazuli; de nacre*
Interpretés seront les extispices.   *les signes des entrailles*

> **Of kings and princes images they'll raise,**
> **Believe the augurs, the diviners praise:**
> **Gilt, pearly, azure-tipped the victim's horn.**
> **The entrails they'll interpret every morn.**

Source: The well-known divinatory practices of the classical world.

27. Original 1555 text   Read as modern French:

Prince Libyque puissant en Occident   *Libyen*
Francois d'Arabe viendra tant enflammer:
Scavans aux letres fera condescendent,
La langue Arabe en Francois translater.   *traduire*

> **A Libyan leader puissant in the West**
> **The French for Arabic shall so impassion**
> **That certain scholars shall at his behest**
> **French into Arabic translate after their fashion.**

Source: King *François* I's inauguration of a chair of Arabic at the Collège de France in the 1540s, though the 'Libyan prince' is unidentified.

28. Original 1555 text   Read as modern French:

De terre foible & pauvre parentele,   *parenté*
Par bout & paix parviendra dans l'empire.   *par moment et discrètement*
Long temps regner une jeune femele,
Qu'oncq en regne n'en survint un si pire.   *Que jamais*

From country weak and poor of ancestry,
By quiet steps to Empire she'll attain:
Long time her ruler shall a young girl be,
Than whom no worse shall e'er have come to reign.

Source: The remarkable reign of the Byzantine Empress Theodora (527–548), daughter of a bear-keeper, and herself a former actress and wool-spinner, who eventually came to rule her husband, Justinian I – to say nothing of the Empire itself – with a rod of iron, and was a vigorous promoter of women's rights.[60] Whether this novelty is the reason for Nostradamus's rather harsh judgment on her in the last line is not entirely clear.

29. Original 1555 text

Read as modern French:

Les deux nepveus en divers lieux nourris:
Navale pugne, terre, peres tumbés *Bataille navale; tombés*
Viendront si haut eslevés enguerris *aguerris*
Venger l'injure: ennemis succombés.

 Brought up in different spots, the nephews twain –
 Their lands and sires fallen in naval fight –
 As warriors fully trained such power shall gain,
 As th' injury to avenge: foes beaten quite.

Source: Unidentified.

30. Original 1555 text

Read as modern French:

Celuy qu'en luite & fer au fait bellique, *lutte; épée; en guerre*
Aura porté plus grand que lui le pris,
De nuit au lit six luy feront la pique, *l'attaqueront*
Nud sans harnois subit sera surpris.

 He who by armèd bout and martial act
 From greater man than he shall take the prize
 Shall be by six at night in bed attacked:
 Naked, unarmed, how sudden his surprise!

Source: Either the assassination in 1547, on the orders of the Emperor Charles V, of Pierluigi Farnese, Duke of Parma, while in bed in his castle at Piacenza;[9] or that of the Byzantine Emperor Nicephorus Phocas, a doughty warrior and military commander, by a group of friends at the behest of his wife Theophano in AD 969.[60] He was famously buried in a sarcophagus that consequently bore the legend, 'You conquered all, except a woman.'

31. Original 1555 text

Aux champs de Mede, d'Arabe & d'Armenie,
Deux grands copies trois foys s'assembleront:
Pres du rivage d'Araxes la mesnie,
Du grand Solman en terre tomberont.

Read as modern French:

Deux grandes armées
le ménage
Soliman

> **On Median, Arab and Armenian plains,**
> **Shall two great hosts three times together clash:**
> **Near to Araxes' banks the mighty thanes**
> **Of Soliman down to the ground shall crash.**

Source: Three unidentified battles, probably from classical times, used as omens of the defeat of a future 'Suleiman the Magnificent' on the borders of Iran and/or Armenia, under the terms of the future re-invasion of the Middle East by Western Christian forces anticipated by the *Mirabilis Liber*.

32. Original 1555 text

Le grand sepulcre du peuple Aquitanique
S'aprochera aupres de la Tousquane,
Quand Mars sera pres du coing Germanique,
Et au terroir de la gent Mantuane.

Read as modern French:

enterreur [sépulteur]

la guerre

> **The mighty burier of Aquitaine**
> **T'wards Tuscany shall shortly make his way,**
> **When war not far from Germany shall reign**
> **And o'er the Mantuan country shall hold sway.**

Source: The Italian campaigns of High Constable Anne de Montmorency between 1536 and 1538, who would later mercilessly quell the salt-tax revolt in Aquitaine in 1548, possibly assimilated to the *Mirabilis Liber*'s prediction of the future liberation of Europe from its expected Arab occupiers (see I.55). The evident inversion of the original chronology seems entirely par for the course.

33. Original 1555 text

En la cité ou le loup entrera,
Bien pres de là les ennemis seront:
Copie estrange grand païs gastera.
Aux murs & Alpes les amis passeront.

Read as modern French:

Une armée étrangère; pays
des Alpes

> **When the wolf shall the city enter, then**
> **The enemies shall be quite close at hand.**
> **An alien army shall lay waste the land:**
> **O'er Alpine walls shall allies send their men.**

Source: Julius Obsequens's *On Omens*: (43) for 104 BC: 'A wolf entered the city'; (49) for 96 BC: 'A wolf that had entered the city was killed in a private house'; (52) for 93 BC: 'Wolves entered the city'; (63) for 53 BC: 'Wolves were seen in the city' – assimilated to the *Mirabilis Liber*'s predicted Muslim invasion of Europe via Italy (see I.9, I.75, II.24).

34. Original 1555 text

Quand le defaut du Soleil lors sera,
Sus le plain jour le monstre sera veu:
Tout autrement on l'interpretera.
Cherté n'a garde: nul ny aura pourveu.

Read as modern French:

l'éclipse

When heavenly sun eclipsed no beams shall shed,
In broad daylight the omen shall appear.
But being mistakenly interpreted,
None shall foresee how things will cost them dear.

Source: Numerous classical reports of solar eclipses and deformed births seen as omens of disaster (in this case severe inflation), such as Julius Obsequens's *On Omens* (43) for 104 BC: 'At the third hour of the day the eclipsed sun hid its light' – but especially those of Nostradamus's own day such as that of 1540, as later collected, reported and illustrated by Lycosthenes[44] and translated into English by Batman:[5] *Thys yeare a childe was borne at Hassia with two heads turned towards the backe, whose faces standing one against the other, behelde eache other with a threatning countenaunce . . . The Sommer of this yeare was parching and dry, more than many Sommers were before, there was greate scarcitie of Hay and Pot hearbes and other things growing, by reason of great heate*

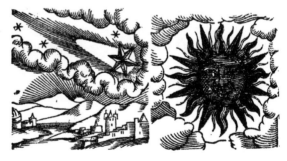

. . . Many judged the comet seene that yeare was the cause of the heate and drought, as also the greate eclypse of the Sunne whiche happened at the beginning of Sommer, the seaventh daye of Aprill, whose beginning was before the Sunnes rising, and lasted two whole houres after the Sun was up.

35. Original 1555 text

Du plus profond de l'Occident d'Europe,
De pauvres gens un jeune enfant naistra,
Qui par sa langue seduira grande troupe:
Son bruit au regne d'Orient plus croistra.

Read as modern French:

une grande foule
son renom grandira

> In occidental Europe's furthest part
> To poorest folk a little child is sent
> Who shall whole throngs beguile by speaker's art:
> His fame shall spread unto the orient.

Source: Given that Nostradamus on several occasions links the term *profonds Occidentaux* with the British Isles, possibly the doings of 27–year-old John Dee, Queen Elizabeth of England's future court astrologer, who had already been attracting attention in France by drawing crowds of enthusiastic students to his mathematical lectures at the Universities of Louvain and Paris – and the fame of whose deeds at the English court would indeed spread to eastern Europe, where Dee in person would some thirty years later attain great notoriety with his public magical séances.

36. Original 1555 text   Read as modern French:

Enseveli non mort apopletique
Sera trouve avoir les mains mangées: *trouvé*
Quand la cité damnera l'heretique,
Qu'avoit leur loys si leur sembloit changées.   *Qui avait*

> Buried alive, and apoplectic too,
> He shall be found to 've gnawed his hands right through
> When th' city shall the heretic condemn
> Who had their laws debased, as seemed to them.

Source: The condemnation of Savonarola in 1498, within a few days of the death of the sickly King Charles VIII of France, whose nails were subsequently found (it was said) to have grown clean through the gauntlets in which he was buried – as recalled in this characteristically garbled version of the story.[60] Nostradamus's hint of skepticism in the last line is understandable, given that he himself borrows extensively from Savonarola in his own *Preface* (see Appendix A below).

37. Original 1555 text   Read as modern French:

Avant l'assaut oraison prononcée:
Milan prins d'aigle par embusches deceuz: *pris par l'Empire*
Muraille antique par canons enfoncée,
Par feu & sang à mercy peu receuz.

> Before th' attack a great speech shall be made,
> Milan through trickery by Eagle ta'en:
> The ancient wall knocked down by cannonade,
> 'Midst blood and fire few mercy shall obtain.

Source: Unidentified incident from the campaigns of Charles V and the Holy Roman Empire (whose symbol was the eagle) in Italy, probably assimilated to the *Mirabilis Liber*'s predictions of a future Muslim invasion of Europe via Italy. See I.9, I.75, II.24.

38. Original 1555 text   **Read as modern French:**

La gent Gauloise & nation estrange
Outre les monts, mors prins & profligés: *morts, captifs ou abattus*
Au mois contraire & proche de vendange
Par les seigneurs en accord rediges.   *rappelés*

> Both armies French and alien people, too,
> Beyond the mounts dead, overthrown or ta'en.
> Six months from thence, ere harvest shall be through,
> Their lords a new agreement shall attain.

Source: Unidentified six-month military campaign, probably in Italy, presumably assimilated to the *Mirabilis Liber*'s scenario of future invasion and counter-invasion. See I.9, I.75, II.24 and I.55.

39. Original 1555 text   **Read as modern French:**

Les sept en trois mis en concorde   *seront en trois mois [?]*
Pour subjuguer des alpes Apennines:
Mais la tempeste & Ligure couarde
Les profligent [//] en subites ruines.

> For three months shall the seven ally together
> The Apennines to conquer and o'erthrow.
> Ligurian cowardice and stormy weather
> Shall quickly ruin them and lay them low.

Source: Unidentified account of recent campaigns in Italy, presumably assimilated to the *Mirabilis Liber*'s forecast of an eventual Western counter-attack against the future Arab occupiers of Europe. See I.55.

40. Original 1555 text   **Read as modern French:**

Le grand theatre se viendra redresser:
Le dez getés & les rets ja tendus.   *le dais; déjà*
Trop le premier en glaz viendra lasser,   *le premier à être annoncé par la sonnerie [?]*
Par arcz prostraits de log temps ja fendus.   *prostré; longtemps; déjà*

> The mighty theatre shall rise up again,
> The dais be raised, the nets be stretched about.
> The first announced by fanfare feels the strain,
> Worn out by bows long, long ago cut out.

Source: Contemporary efforts to revive the ancient classical games. Compare I.45, IX.83.

41. Original 1555 text

Bosseu sera esleu par le conseil,
Plus hideux monstre en terre n'aperceu.
Le coup volant prelat crevera l'œil:
Le traistre au roy pour fidele receu.

Read as modern French:

Bossu; élu

> **Hunchback shall by the Council be elected:**
> **None e'er on earth more hideous freak shall see.**
> **The bishop's eye by flying blow extracted:**
> **The king's betrayer as loyal they shall see.**

Source: The first two lines are evidently based on Louis de Bourbon, First Prince of Condé, the leader-in-waiting of the contemporary Protestant faction – which may explain the devoutly Catholic Nostradamus's clearly-expressed detestation.

42. Original 1555 text

L'enfant naistra à deux dents à la gorge
Pierres en Tuscie par pluie tomberont:
Peu d'ans apres ne sera bled, ne orge,
Pour saouler ceux qui de faim failliront.

Read as modern French:

en Toscane; pour/au lieu de
blé; ni

> **With two teeth in its craw the child is born:**
> **Stones 'stead of rain shall fall in Tuscany.**
> **Within few years they'll barley lack and corn**
> **To satisfy those who shall starving be.**

Source: Julius Obsequens's *On Omens* and Livy's *History of Rome*, as detailed under II.7 and II.18 above, together with numerous contemporary reports of unusual births and violent hailstorms – together with their inevitable effects – as later collected and illustrated by Conrad Lycosthenes[44] and then translated into English by Dr Stephen Batman[5] for 1544: *At Nissa a towne of Silecia, there fell Hayle of wonderful greatnesse, whereby the fieldes of that Countrey were spoyled everye where. So also the sixteenth day of June, after a blacke cloudie weather, there arose a tempest and such aboundance of Hayle, that in Suntgoia from the Towne of Brudtrut as farre as the Rhene, it so beate downe the Corne in the Fields, and the Grapes in the Vineyardes, that the Vines were quite marred, and in the Fieldes there was no straw lefte for the cattell: the next day it didde no lesse harme at Brigoria and in the dominyon of the Marques of Baden, and the third daye in the miery valley. There followed a great dearth of al things . . .* See woodcuts attached to I.58 above.

43. Original 1555 text

Gents d'alentour de Tarn, Loth, & Garonne,
Gardés les monts Apennines passer,
Vostre tombeau pres de Rome & d'Anconne
Le noir poil crespe fera trophée dresser.

Read as modern French:

Lot
Gardez-vous de

votre cénotaphe

You folk from round the Tarn, Garonne and Lot,
Take care not o'er the Apennines to pass.
Near Rome, Ancona lie your graves, alas!
Black curly-beard your tombstone shall allot.

Source: France's huge losses in the Italian wars to date, assimilated to the *Mirabilis Liber's* predictions of a future invasion and counter-invasion of Europe via Italy. See I.9, I.75, II.24, I.55.

44. Original 1555 text

Quand l'animal à l'homme domestique
Apres grans peines & saults viendra parler:
Le fouldre à vierge sera si maleficque,
De terre prinse, & suspendue en l'air.

Read as modern French:

Qu'elle sera enlevée

When the domestic animal at last
After great toils and strides shall find its tongue,
The bolt the virgin shall so deadly blast,
She'll be caught up and in the air be hung.

Source: Julius Obsequens's familiar tales of talking oxen (see I.64), combined with a presumably recent incident when lightning was alleged to have blasted a girl clean off the ground. If this seems improbable, it needs to be remembered that among the various recent prodigies collected by Lycosthenes[44] would be several cases of lightning striking gunpowder-stores – as for example, in the case of Mechlin in 1545, subsequently translated into the English of the day by Batman:[5]

The seventh day of August about eleven of the Clock at afternoone, a fearefull tempest hapned over the Citie of Machlin, the like whereof was never scarsely heard of, for by reason of a Thunder the Citie was in such a feare, that moste men thoughte that the latter judgement was at hande, or that the Citie should be destroyed, for there followed that fearefull cracking of the Cloudes, a cloudye lightning, and an intollerable sulpherous stinke . . . untill at length a rumour ranne in the Cittie, that the Lightning had stricken the Sand Gate, where there were layde up eightie Vessels of Gunpouder, whose sodayne setting on fyre made so greate a confusion in the Citie, that no man didde ever see a more wonderfull sighte: The Sandegate was destroyed in the twinkling of an eye, and beaten into smal pieces, and not only the Foundations of the Towre, but also the Stones of the Walles neare too were pulled up from the Foundation, and scattered over all the Citie . . . wherefore the next daye in the morning there were founde all about that place as it was thoughte three hundred deade Carcasses, and one hundred and fiftie sore hurt: there was also found a woman in that Tempest who going to shut her chamber windowe loste her heade upon the sodayne . . . .

45. Original 1555 text   **Read as modern French:**

Les cinq estranges entrés dedans le temple,   *étrangers*
Leur sang viendra la terre prophaner:
Aux Thoulosains sera bien dur exemple
D'un qui viendra ses loys exterminer.   *De quiconque*

> **Five foreigners into their temple come**
> **Shall cause their blood to soil its holy ground –**
> **To all Toulouse an earnest grim, in sum,**
> **Of one who would its ancient laws confound.**

Source: The arrival in Toulouse of five monks – two Franciscans and three Augustinians, one of them Italian – in 1531, intent on preaching religious reform; severe religious repression followed.[60]

46. Original 1555 text   **Read as modern French:**

Le ciel (de Plancus la cité) nous presaige   *de Lyon*
Par clairs insignes & par estoiles fixes,   *signes*
Que de son change subit s'aproche l'aage,
Ne pour son bien, ne pour ses malefices.   *ni... ni...*

> **The chart of Lyon doth to us foretell**
> **By fixèd stars and signs both bright and clear**
> **That of its sudden change the age draws near,**
> **Nor for its ill, nor yet for good and well.**

Source: The celebrated Lyon meteor of 1528,[9] taken as an omen of the 'change of era' expected in 1525 by Trithemius,[68] between 1530 and 1535 by Luca Gaurico, and in 1532 by Richard Roussat[67] – a change that was supposed to inaugurate what was assumed by many to be the world's final, lunar, 'seventh age' of 354 years and three months. Often referred to by Nostradamus (see I.25, I.48, and I.56, for example), this was expected to come to an end at some point between 1800 and 1887, though Roussat himself (and evidently Nostradamus too) expected the world to last at least one further 'solar' age that would bring it to the year 2242. In the last line Nostradamus seemingly admits that, during the intervening twenty years or so, nothing of note seems in fact to have changed, for Lyon at least.

47. Original 1555 text   **Read as modern French:**

Le vieux monarque deschassé de son regne
Aux Orients son secours ira querre: *chercher*
Pour peur des croix pliera son enseigne: *des chrétiens*
En Mitilene ira pour port et terre.

> **The aged monarch hounded out from power**
> **Shall from the Orient seek a helping hand.**

For fear of Christian might his flag he'll lower.
At Mitilini seek a port and land.

Source: The *Mirabilis Liber*'s prediction of a final Western counter-attack against the future Muslim occupiers of Europe. See I.55.

48. Original 1555 text

Read as modern French:

Sept cens captifs estaches rudement   *attachés/liés*
Pour la moitie meurtrir, donné le sort,   *le sort échu*
Le proche espoir viendra si promptement,
Mais non si tost qu'une quinzieme mort.   *quinzaine*

> Seven hundred captives they shall crudely tie,
> Lots thrown to murder half of them alive:
> Good hope of safety quickly shall arrive,
> But not before some fifteen of them die.

Source: Unknown incident, possibly recent.

49. Original 1555 text

Read as modern French:

Regne Gauloys tu seras bien changé:
En lieu estrange est translaté l'Empire   *transféré*
En autres meurs, & loys seras rangé:
Rouan & Chartres te feront bien du pire.

> O Gallic realm, you'll changed be for the worse!
> To foreign lands your rulership shall pass.
> New laws and customs shall your country curse:
> Rouen and Chartres shall treat you worst, alas!

Source: The *Mirabilis Liber*'s forecast of a huge and devastating Arab invasion and occupation of Europe, and of France in particular. See I.9, I.75, II.24. Whether Rouen and Chartres are foreseen as sites of future battles or as centers of occupation – or even of pure maladministration – is not clear, however.

50. Original 1555 text

Read as modern French:

La republicque de la grande cité   *Le gouvernement*
A grand rigeur ne voudra consentir:
Roy sortir hors par trompete cité   *par héraut*
L'eschele au mur, la cité repentir.

> The rulers of the mighty city shall
> Most stubbornly to give it up refuse.

To quit it shall the king the herald call:
The wall once scaled, the town shall change its views.

Source: Unidentified siege, possibly quite recent.

51. Original 1555 text   Read as modern French:

PARIS conjure un grand meurtre commetre,
Bloys le fera sortir en plain effet:
Ceulx d'Orleans voudront leur chef remetre,
Angiers, Troye, langres leur feront grand forfait.   *Angers*

Paris conspires grand murder to commit:
Blois shall arrange to bring the deed to pass.
Orléans would restore its leader's writ.
Angers, Troyes, Langres shall harm them much, alas!

Source: For the first two lines, possibly the death in 1550 of Claude de Guise, First Duke of Lorraine, who had aroused King François I's distrust, and was believed at the time to have been poisoned for suspected complicity in the death in 1546 of François de Bourbon, Lord of Enghien.

52. Original 1555 text   Read as modern French:

En la Campaigne sera si longue pluie,   *En Campanie*
Et en la Pouile si grande siccité.   *la Pouille [Apulia]; sécheresse*
Coq verra l'aigle, l'aesle mal accomplie:
Par Lyon mise sera en extremité.

Across Campania it shall rain and rain:
Apulia, though, a mighty drought shall see.
Cock th' Eagle sees, its wing deformed, in pain,
By Lion placed in sore extremity.

Source: For rains and floods, see I.69. For droughts, possibly Livy's *History of Rome* (IV.30) for 429 BC (though for Latium, not Apulia): 'The year was marked by much drought: not only was there not enough rainfall, but the moisture in the ground was barely capable of supplying the perennial streams.' For the last two lines, the *Mirabilis Liber*: 'Now the lion shall arise, and the black eagle, flapping its shining wings above its eyrie, shall take to the air: then shall commence the tribulations and battles by land and sea' (Prophecy of St Severus); 'The lily, partner of the great eagle, shall sweep from the West to the East against the lion; the lion, defenseless, shall be overcome by the lily, which shall spread its perfume over Germany, while the eagle, in its flight, shall carry its fame afar' (Prophecy of St Brigid of Sweden).

53. Original 1555 text

Read as modern French:

Quand le plus grand emportera le pris
De Nuremberg d'Auspurg, & ceux de Basle
Par Aggripine chef Francqfort repris
Transverseront par Flamans jusques en Gale.

prix
d'Augsburg
par Cologne [lat: Colonia Agrippina]
au Pays de Galles [?]

> **When he who's greatest shall the victory gain**
> **O'er Nürnberg's folk, o'er Augsburg's and o'er Basle's,**
> **Shall Frankfurt by Cologne's lord be re ta'en:**
> **With Flemish help they'll cross the seas to Wales.**[9]

Source: Unknown, but possibly a reference to the occasional elections for Holy Roman Emperor.

54. Original 1555 text

Read as modern French:

L'un des plus grands fuira aux Hespaignes,
Qu'en longue plaie apres viendra saigner:
Passant copies par les hautes montaignes
Devastant tout & puis en paix regner.

se rendra en toute hâte en Espagne

armées

> **One of the noblest lords shall speed to Spain,**
> **Which he'll then bleed with wound so long, so sore:**
> **Passing his hosts the lofty mountains o'er,**
> **He'll lay waste all, then he in peace shall reign.**

Source: Possibly Froissart's account in his *Chroniques* (Luce I:238–245) of the powerful military incursion of Edward the Black Prince across the Pyrenees and into Spain during 1367, in his campaign to restore Don Pedro the Cruel of Castile to his throne. See III.80, IV.99, VI.88, VIII.48.

55. Original 1555 text

Read as modern French:

En l'an qu'un oeil en France regnera,
La court sera à un bien fascheux trouble:
Le grand de Bloys son ami tuera:
Le regne mis en mal & doute double.

> **The year when One-Eye power in France shall gain**
> **The Court shall undergo vexatious trouble:**
> **By Blois's great lord his bosom-friend is slain,**
> **The kingdom placed in doubt and trouble double.**

Source: In the case of the first two lines, the rise to power of the swashbuckling François de Lorraine, 2nd Duke of Guise, who had famously lost an eye at the siege of Boulogne in 1545 and become Lord Great Chamberlain in 1547 on the death of François I. The last two lines seem to be unconnected, but in his *Pronostication* *nouvelle* for 1562 Nostradamus would claim in an open letter to Jean de Vauzelles, the Prior of Montrotier, that it was in this verse that he had predicted the accidental death in a tournament of Henri II in the summer of 1559 at the hands of his young adversary, Gabriel de Lorge, Count de Montgomery – even though in order to do so he would retrospectively have to change the word *grand* in line 3 to read *grain*, of which *l'orge* (barley) is of course a particular type!

56. Original 1555 text

56. Original 1555 text	Read as modern French:
Montauban, Nismes, Avignon, & Besier,	*Béziers*
Peste, tonnerre & gresle à fin de Mars:	
De Paris pont, Lyon mur, Montpellier,	
Depuis six cent & sept. xxiii. pars.	

> On Montauban, Nîmes, Avignon, Béziers
> Plague, thunder, hail fall at the end of March,
> In Paris th' bridge, wall Lyon, Montpellier:
> From year 1607 twenty-three parts.

Source: The various 'falling' omens that accompanied the death of King François I in 1547. The almost impenetrable last line could conceivably refer to the contemporary proliferation of religious sects and parties.

57. Original 1555 text

57. Original 1555 text	Read as modern French:
Sept foys changer verrés gent Britannique	*vous verrez*
Taintz en sang en deux cent nonante an:	
Franche non point par apui Germanique.	
Aries doute son pole Bastarnan.	*redoute; la latitude/région de Bastarnie*

> Seven times you'll see the British change their lord,
> In years two hundred ninety stained with gore,
> But France not so, through Germany's support.
> Aries shall fear its Czech and Slovak shore.

Source: The violent deaths (according to Prévost[60]) of seven prominent British leaders between 1265 and 1555 (the date of the current composition), namely Simon de Montfort, Edward II, Richard II, Henry VI, Edward V, Richard III, and Lady Jane Grey) – which, if correct, is a clear demonstration that Nostradamus is basing himself on previous, not future history. The last line refers back to Claudius Ptolemy via Albumasar's *De magnis conjunctionibus*, which assigned France, Germany, and England to the sign Aries; the 'fear' is evidently directed towards the invading Turks, currently being fought off in Transylvania by Ferdinand, the brother of the Emperor Charles V, in apparent accordance with the *Mirabilis Liber's* scenario of future massive Muslim invasion (see I.9, I.75, II.24).

58. Original 1555 text   **Read as modern French:**

Aupres du Rin des montaignes Noriques   *Rhin; Autrichiennes*
Naistra un grand de gents trop tart venu,   *tard*
Qui defendra SAUROME & Pannoniques,   *les Sauromates/Sarmates*
Qu'on ne saura qu'il sera devenu.

> **Near Rhine and Alps Norician, fate shall send**
> **A lordly child to parents lately come,**
> **Who'll eastern Europe, Hungary defend,**
> **Such that none knows what shall of him become.**

Source: Surprisingly, perhaps, unidentified.

59. Original 1555 text   **Read as modern French:**

Barbare empire par le tiers usurpé
La plus grand part de son sang metra à mort:
Par mort senile par luy le quart frapé,
Pour peur que sang par le sang ne soit mort.

> **The Muslim empire by the third is seized**
> **Who'll promptly kill the best part of his folk,**
> **To strike the fourth in his old age well pleased,**
> **For fear that kin on kin should death invoke.**

Source: The bloody struggles of succession, real or imagined, that were *de rigueur* in the former Ottoman empire.

60. Original 1555 text   **Read as modern French:**

Par toute Asie grande proscription,   *Asie Mineure*
Mesmes en Mysie, Lysie & Pamphylie:
Sang versera par absolution
D'un jeune noir rempli de felonnie.

> **Many shall be outlawed throughout all Turkey,**
> **E'en in the southwest regions of the nation.**
> **He'll shed the blood, as in propitiation,**
> **Of a young Moor replete with crime most murky.**

Source: Presumably a further, unidentified incident from the history of the Ottomans, as per the previous verse. One has the impression that the verse-order is sometimes dictated by Nostradamus's tendency to compose whole rafts of verses under the influence of each source-reference in turn.

61. Original 1555 text

La grande bande & secte crucigere
Se dressera en Mesopotamie:
Du proche fleuve compaignie legiere,
Que telle loy tiendra pour ennemie.

Read as modern French:

croisée/chrétienne
se dressera contre

dispensation

The mighty Christian sect and its alliance
Upon Mesopotamia shall fall:
A lighter force beyond the river shall
Its tenets hold as matter for defiance.

Source: The *Mirabilis Liber*'s forecast of an eventual counter-invasion of the Middle East by the forces of Christendom. See I.55.

62. Original 1555 text

Proche del duero par mer Tyrrene close
Viendra percer les grans monts Pyrenées.
La main plus courte & sa percée gloze,
A Carcassonne conduira ses menées

Read as modern French:

Douro; Tyrrhénienne

Ayant peu de temps; expliquée de façon spécieuse

By Duero (closed the great Tyrrhenian Sea)
He'll penetrate the Pyrenees so high.
Time short, his penetration masked, shall he
To Carcassonne his followers lead by.

Source: The future invasion of Europe anticipated by the *Mirabilis Liber*, with a sideways glance at the famous campaign of the Carthaginian general Hannibal, as described in Livy's *History of Rome*.

63. Original 1555 text

Romain pouvoir sera du tout abas,
Son grand voysin imiter ses vestiges:
Occultes haines civiles, & debats
Retarderont aux bouffons leurs folligges,

Read as modern French:

Empire Romain [lat: Imperium Romanum]; abaissé

Cachées
folies

The Roman power shall be quite overthrown,
Its mighty neighbor following in its track,
While hidden hatreds, civil feuds alone
The stupid fools from folly shall hold back.

Source: The *Mirabilis Liber*'s predictions of a future Islamic invasion of Europe, and particularly of Italy and France, aided and abetted by general collapse and decay from within. See I.9, I.75, II.24.

64. Original 1555 text

Le chef de Perse remplira grande OLX???S
Classe trireme contre gent Mahumetique
De Parthe, & Mede: & piller les Cyclades:
Repos long temps au grand port Ionique.

Read as modern French:

[anciens] vaisseaux de transport [gr.] perses

The Persian chief great cargo-hulks shall pack,
A fleet of triremes 'gainst his Muslim foes.
From Persia then the Cyclades he'll sack
And in Ionian port take long repose.

Source: Apparently, once again, the *Mirabilis Liber*'s predictions of a future Islamic invasion of Europe. See I.9, I.75, II.24.

65. Original 1555 text

Quand le sepulcre du grand Romain trouvé,
Le jour apres sera esleu pontife,
Du senat gueres il ne sera prouvé
Empoisonné son sang au sacré scyphe.

Read as modern French:

approuvé
et son parent; par la coupe sacrée/le calice

One day the mighty Roman's tomb is found:
The next, a new-elected pope in th' palace.
The Council shall have found the first unsound.
Poisoned, his blood within the sacred chalice.

Source: Bandini's *Dell'obelisco de Cesare Augusto* of 1549, which recounted the discovery of what appeared to be the tomb of Augustus Caesar in 1521, the year in which Pope Leo X, having allegedly been poisoned, died after being bled into the very chalice in which votes were collected at the traditional conclaves convened to elect new popes.[60] Compare V.7.

66. Original 1555 text

Le grand baillif d'Orleans mis à mort
Sera par un de sang vindicatif:
De mort merite ne mourra, ne par sort:
Des pieds & mains mal le faisoit captif.

Read as modern French:

parenté/famille
digne/mérité

Of Orleans the bailiff great laid low
Shall surely be by one of vengeful clan.
Neither by death deserved nor fate he'll go,
But tied by hands and feet, a captive man.

Source: Unknown incident, but line 3 borrowed in familiar topsy-turvy fashion from Virgil's *Aeneid* (IV.696): 'For since nor by fate deserved nor death she died . . .'

67. Original 1555 text   **Read as modern French:**

Une nouvele secte de Philosophes
Meprisant mort, or, honneurs & richesses,
Des monts Germains ne seront limitrophes: *voisins/limités*
A les ensuivre auront apui & presses.

> Of new philosophers a sect refined,
> Scornful of honors, wealth, or death, or gold,
> Shall not to German mountains be confined:
> To follow them shall many folk make bold.

Source: The Anabaptists of southern Germany who took refuge in Moravia during the 1530s following the Peasants' Revolt of 1525 and were known as 'Moravian Brethren' or 'Brethren of Bohemia'.[9] See also IV.32.

68. Original 1555 text   **Read as modern French:**

Peuple sans chef d'Espagne & d'Italie
Morts, profligés dedans le Cherronnesse: *la Chersonèse/la péninsule*
Leur duyct trahy par legiere folie,   *conduite; sotte*
Le sang nager par tout à la traverse.   *en empêchant leur opération [?]*

> Leaderless folk from Spain and Italy,
> Shall die in mainland Greece, torn limb from limb,
> Their acts betrayed by crass stupidity,
> And every crossroads with their blood shall swim.

Source: Apparently a hiccup to the *Mirabilis Liber*'s predicted counter-invasion of the Middle East by the forces of western Christendom. See I.55.

69. Original 1555 text   **Read as modern French:**

Grand exercite conduict par jouvenceau,   *armée*
Se viendra rendre aux mains des ennemis:
Mais le viellard nay au demi pourceau,   *à Milan*
Fera Chalon & Mascon estre amis.

> A mighty host with stripling at its head
> Shall be delivered into hostile hand:
> But the old man born in Milan abed
> Shall bring Chalon and Mâcon hand-in-hand.

Source: Unknown historical incident. The *demi pourceau* reference in line 3 is from the section on Milan in Andrea Alciato's absolutely seminal *Emblamata* of 1531:

> 'The sign of sheepish pig is o'er the door
> Which half with hair, half wool is covered o'er.

'Such is the etymology of the name of Milan, which is said to have been so called because when it was originally founded a biform pig was discovered, half-pig and half sheep, covered half with hair and half with wool – whence its name Milan in French [i.e. *mi-laine*: 'half-wool'] and Mediolanum in Latin.'

70. Original 1555 text

Read as modern French:

La grand Bretagne comprinse l'Angleterre	*y comprise*
Viendra par eaux si hault à inunder	*à être inondée*
La ligue neufve d'Ausonne fera guerre,	*d'Italie*
Que contre eux mesmes il se viendront bander	*si bien que*

> **Great Britain, in which England then shall count,**
> **Shall be by waters flooded deep and high.**
> **The new Italian league a war shall mount,**
> **Such that against each other they'll ally.**

Source: For the first two lines, presumably the *Mirabilis Liber*'s forecasts of general floods, as per I.69: for the last two lines, contemporary struggles in Italy.

71. Original 1555 text

Read as modern French:

Ceux dans les isles de long temps assiegés	
Prendront vigueur force contre ennemis:	*et force*
Ceux par dehors morts de faim profligés,	
En plus grand faim que jamais seront mis.	

> **Those long besieged in th' isles shall by and by**
> **Build up their force and strength against the foe.**
> **'Tis those outside, all hunger-struck, who'll die,**
> **And famine worse than ever they shall know.**

Source: Apparently a setback in the *Mirabilis Liber*'s prophetic scenario of Muslim invasion via the Mediterranean islands. See I.9, I.75, II.24.

72. Original 1555 text

Read as modern French:

Le bon viellard tout vif enseveli,	
Pres du grand fleuve par fauce souspeçon	*par faux soupçon*
Le nouveau vieux de richesse ennobli	
Prins au chemin tout l'or de la rançon.	

> **The good old man alive shall buried be**
> **Near the great river through suspicion vain:**
> **Of new old man enriched in high degree**
> **The golden ransom shall *en route* be ta'en.**

Source: Unidentified historical incidents.

73. Original 1555 text   **Read as modern French:**

Quand dans le regne parviendra le boiteux
Competiteur aura proche bastard:
Luy & le regne viendront si fort rogneux,   *deviendront; galeux*
Qu'ains qu'il guerisse son fait sera bien tard.   *Qu'à moins qu'il ne guérisse*

> **When to the throne the limping one shall come,**
> **Shall bastard kinsman be competitor.**
> **So rotten shall he and the realm become**
> **That, but it heal, his prospects shall be poor.**

Source: Plutarch's *Parallel Lives* ('Agesilaus') (3): 'It was during Agis' reign that Alcibiades . . . was accused of having an affair with Timaea, the king's wife. When she bore a child, Agis refused to recognise it and claimed that Alcibiades was the father . . . The boy . . . was never recognized as a king's legitimate son should be . . . However, after the death of Agis, Lysander . . . started to put forward Agesilaus's claim to the throne, using Leotychidas's illegitimacy to argue that he should not become king . . . However, there was in Sparta a soothsayer called Diopithes . . . and he said that it was wrong for anyone who was lame to become king of Lacedaemon . . . Lysander argued in reply that, if the Spartans were truly concerned about the oracle, Leotychidas was the one that they ought to beware of. The god, he said, was concerned not that a person with a bad foot might become king, but that a person who was illegitimate and not a descendant of Heracles might come to the throne . . .'

74. Original 1555 text   **Read as modern French:**

Naples, Florence, Favence & Imole,   *Faenza*
Seront en termes de telle facherie,   *sur le point de*
Que pour complaire aux malheureux de Nolle,
Plainct d'avoir fait à son chef moquerie.

> **Naples, Faenza, Florence, Imola**
> **Shall at the very point of rage soon be**
> **Because, to please the wretches of Nola,**
> **Of their own head was made a mockery.**

Source: Unknown, but Nostradamus appears to be referring to a list of towns, possibly astrologically arranged, to which he also refers more or less verbatim in his *Almanachs* for 1562 and 1567.[9]

75. Original 1555 text   **Read as modern French:**

PAU. Veronne, Vicence, Sarragousse   *Pavie*
De glaifves loings [/] terroirs de sang humides: *Par glaives venus de loin/étrangers*
Peste si grande viendra à la grand gousse
Proche secours, & bien loing les remedes.

Vicenza, Saragossa, Verona, Pavia –
Through alien swords, bloodsoaked their lands shall be.
Such great disease shall pods make heavier.
Help's near at hand, yet far the remedy.

Source: The *Mirabilis Liber*'s predictions of a grisly Muslim invasion of Europe accompanied by disease, in this case of the crops (a choice of target presumably dictated purely by Nostradamus's need to rhyme!). See I.9, I.75, II.24.

76. Original 1555 text   Read as modern French:

En Germanie naistront diverses sectes,
S'approchans fort de l'heureux paganisme,
Le cueur captif & petites receptes,
Feront retour à payer le vray disme.

In Germany strange sects shall come to be
That almost shall the blissful pagan play.
As they gain hearts, but little money, see
How folk return their proper tithes to pay.

Source: Contemporary groups of German Protestant Reformers who were intent on reviving the simple economics of the early Church. Compare the prophecies on the Angelic Pastor at VI.21.

77. Original 1555 text   Read as modern French:

Le tiers climat soubz Aries comprins   sous; compris
L'an mil sept cens vingt & sept en Octobre,
Le roy de Perse par ceux d'Egypte prins: pris
Conflict, mort, pte: à la croix grand opprobre.   perte

In climate third, subject to Aries placed,
October seventeen hundred, seven and twenty,
Is Persia's king by Egypt ta'en, 'midst plenty
Of war, death, and destruction: cross disgraced.

Source: An attempted – and, in the event, failed – astrological prediction, somewhat confusedly based, according to Prévost,[60] on the Byzantine Emperor Heraclius's attack on Persia in the year 627. This had resulted in the capture of Egypt and the death of King Chosroes II, whose successor Siroes then demanded the return both of Egypt and of the 'Holy Cross' that had been removed from Jerusalem in 614.

78. Original 1555 text   **Read as modern French:**

Le chef d'Escosse avec six d'Alemagne
Par gens de mer Orientaux captifs,   *captif [accord habituel de proximité]*
Transverseront le Calpre & Hespagne   *le détroit de Gibraltar par l'Espagne*
Present en Perse au nouveau roy craintif.

> **The Scottish chief, with six from Germany,**
> **By Easterners shall captured be at sea:**
> **They'll pass Gibraltar's Spanish strait, and bring**
> **Him to Iran, a gift for the new king.**

Source: Unknown, but presumably assimilated to the *Mirabilis Liber*'s forecast of a Muslim invasion of Europe. See I.9, I.75, II.24.

79. Original 1555 text   **Read as modern French:**

L'ordre fatal sempiternel par chaisne
Viendra tourner par ordre consequent:
Du port Phocen sera rompue la chaisne: *De Marseille*
La cité prinse, l'ennemy quand & quand.   *en même temps*

> **The chain of fate, from age to age ordained,**
> **Returns, to later orders giving rise:**
> **The mouth of Marseille's port shall be unchained,**
> **The city taken, foes as thick as flies.**

Source: A well-known phrase from the *Attic Nights* of Aulus Gellius (VII.2.1–3), quoting Chrysippus, and referred to again by Nostradamus in his *Preface*: 'Destiny is a certain eternal and immutable series of events that both constantly revolves in a chain and brings with it those unending sequences of consequences to which it is appropriate and attached.' This is then used as the basis for a wordplay on the capture of Marseille by Alphonso of Aragon in 1425, which in turn is assimilated to the vast Muslim invasion of Europe from the Mediterranean confidently predicted by the *Mirabilis Liber*. See I.9, I.75, II.24.

80. Original 1555 text   **Read as modern French:**

Du regne Anglois l'indigne deschassé,   *Par le regne*
Le conseillier par ire mis à feu:
Ses adherans iront si bas tracer,
Que le bastard sera demi receu.

> **Th' unworthy one removed by English power,**
> **Through wrath the councilor's burnt at the stake:**
> **Yet his adherents, stooping lower and lower,**
> **Shall soon the Bastard half accepted make.**

Source: Froissart's stirring account in his *Chroniques* (Luce I.231–244) of the seizure of the throne of Castile by Henry of Trastámara, better known as Henry the Bastard, from his younger half-brother Don Pedro the Cruel, followed by his defeat and removal with huge military losses by Edward the Black Prince at the Battle of Najera or Navarette in April 1367 and his eventual regaining of power with the aid of numerous adherents whom he suitably rewarded. See III.54, IV.99, VI.88.

81. Original 1555 text

Read as modern French:

Le grand criard sans honte audacieux,
Sera esleu gouverneur de l'armée:
La hardiesse de son contentieux,   *de son aggressivité*
Le pont rompu, cité de peur pasmée:

> **The great loud-mouth, shameless and just as daring,**
> **Shall of the army be appointed head.**
> **So bold his fight is, and so fierce his bearing,**
> **The bridge once downed, the city faints with dread.**

Source: Possibly the story of the celebrated third Roman slave revolt of 73–71 BC under the former gladiator Spartacus. The unqualified term 'the city' often refers, in Nostradamus as in most classical writings, to Rome.

82. Original 1555 text

Read as modern French:

Freins, Antibol, villes au tour de Nice,   *Fréjus, Antibes*
Seront vastées fer, par mer & par terre:
Les sauterelles terre & mer vent propice,
Prins, morts, troussés, pilles sans loy de guerre.

> *Fréjus, Antibes and towns near Nice shall be*
> **By land and sea laid waste, put to the sword.**
> **Locusts by wind blown in o'er land and sea,**
> **Captives trussed up, raped, killed, war-rules ignored.**

Source: A logical extension towards the French Riviera of the scenario painted by the *Mirabilis Liber*: 'The children of Agar shall seize Tarento, and spreading through Apulia, shall sack a host of towns. They shall be determined to enter Rome, and nobody in the world shall be able to resist them, unless it be the Lord God himself. The Armenians, pursuing their depredations, shall advance from the East, shall fight the Romans, and shall achieve peace for a short time . . . Swarms of grasshoppers and an immense host of caterpillars shall devour all

the trees and their fruits in Cappadocia and Sicily, and the people shall starve to death, without a doubt' (Prophecy of the Tiburtine Sibyl). As though in fulfillment of it, Lycosthenes[44] would record at least half a dozen sixteenth-century accounts of plagues of locusts: the one reported and illustrated for 1536, and duly translated into English by Batman,[5] reflects Nostradamus's verse almost exactly: *In that part of Sarmatia which they of later time cal at this day Podolia, so great a number of Grasshoppers* [in the Latin, *locustarum*] *was broughte a lande with the greate violence of Winde from the sea Euxinus* [the Black Sea], *that they eate uppe all the Corne in every place. There ensued a greate plague and Morraine of menne and beastes.*

83. Original 1555 text   **Read as modern French:**

Les lons cheveux de la Gaule Celtique   *longs*
Accompagnés d'estranges nations,
Metront captif la gent Aquitanique,
Pour succomber à internitions.   *massacres*

The long-haired warriors of Celtic Gaul
Accompanied by nations overseas
In Aquitaine shall capture one and all,
And then shall massacre them by degrees.

Source: The ancient invasions of the Vandals and Visigoths, assimilated to the *Mirabilis Liber*'s prediction of an eventual liberation of Europe from its future Muslim invaders (see I.55). The Romans applied the term 'Celtic Gaul' to mid-Gaul (from the Seine to the Garonne), in contradistinction to 'Hairy Gaul' (*Gallia comata*) to the north and 'Be-toga-ed Gaul' (*Gallia togata*) to the south.[9]

84. Original 1555 text   **Read as modern French:**

La grand cité sera bien desolée   *rendue déserte*
Des habitans un seul ny demeurra:
Mur, sexe, temple, & vierge violée   *sectes*
Par fer, feu, peste, canon peuple mourra.

The mighty city shall be desolated,
Of its inhabitants not one remain.
Church walls and orders, virgins violated,
By sword, fire, plague and gun the people slain.

Source: The *Mirabilis Liber*'s gruesome description of the destruction of Rome and the persecution of the Church by the expected Arab invaders of Europe. See I.9, I.75, II.24, and especially I.15.

85. Original 1555 text

La cité prinse par tromperie & fraude,
Par le moyen d'un beau jeune atrapé:
Lassaut donné [/] Roubine pres de l'AUDE
Luy & touts morts pour avoir bien trompé.

Read as modern French:

[Narbonne] prise

L'assaut

> **The city shall be ta'en by ruse and fraud**
> **Through one young beau who shall deluded be:**
> **Once battle's giv'n by Robine, near the Aude,**
> **Shall he and his die for their treachery.**

Source: Probably the *Mirabilis Liber*'s anticipated Arab invasion of France in particular. See I.9, I.75, II.24.

86. Original 1555 text

Le chef d'Ausonne aux Hespagnes ira
Par mer fera arrest dedans Marseille:
Avant sa mort un long temps languira:
Apres sa mort on verra grand merveille:

Read as modern French:

d'Italie en Espagne
fera escale à

> **From Italy the lord shall sail to Spain**
> **By sea: at Marseille he en route shall call:**
> **Before his death he'll linger long in pain:**
> **After his death a wonder seen by all.**

Source: Unknown.

87. Original 1555 text

Classe Gauloyse n'aproches de Corseigne
Moins de sardaigne, tu t'en repentiras
Trestous mourres frustrés de laide Grogne:
Sang nagera: captifs ne me croyras.

Read as modern French:

de la Corse
Encore moins
Tous; de l'aide au groin

> **Sail not near Corsica, O fleet from Gaul,**
> **Still less Sardinia, lest you regret:**
> **All aid denied, you'll perish one and all,**
> **Beasts, captives – scarce shall you believe me yet.**

Source: The French expedition to Corsica of 1553 which, while partially successful, resulted in its being blockaded and starved out there by the Italian admiral Andrea Doria – a case, in other words, of good advice after the event, to say nothing of 'retrodiction'!

88. Original 1555 text   **Read as modern French:**

De Barcelonne par mer si grand armée,
Toute Marseille de frayeur tremblera:
Isles saisies de mer aide fermée,
Ton traditeur en terre nagera.   *naviguera*

> **From Barcelona such a mighty host**
> **Shall come by sea that all Marseille shall quake:**
> **All aid cut off by sea, the Isles all lost,**
> **Your traitor shall by land his passage make.**

Source: The invasion of Provence (and of Marseille in particular) by land in 1524 by the renegade former Chancellor Charles de Bourbon on behalf of the Emperor Charles V, supported by Spanish vessels at sea – all assimilated to the *Mirabilis Liber*'s scenario of future Arab invasion. See I.9, I.75, II.24.

89. Original 1555 text   **Read as modern French:**

En ce temps la sera frustré Cypres   *Chypre*
De son secours, de ceux de mer Egée:
Vieux trucidés: mais par masles & lyphres   *tués; débauchés [galyphres[9]]*
Seduict leur roy, royne plus outragée.

> **And in that time shall Cyprus be from aid**
> **Cut off by those from the Aegean Sea,**
> **Their old be killed, their king seduced, betrayed,**
> **By males depraved: their queen outraged shall be.**

Source: Either the *Mirabilis Liber*'s predictions of a future Arab invasion (see I.9, I.75, II.24) or its sequel, the expected counter-invasion by the Western powers (see I.55).

90. Original 1555 text   **Read as modern French:**

Le grand Satyre & Tigre de Hyrcanie,
Don presente à ceux de l'Ocean: *presenté*
Un chef de classe istra de Carmanie   *sortira*
Qui prendra terre au Tyrren Phocean.   *au tyrant/chef Marseillais*

> **The satyr and Hyrcanian tiger they'll**
> **As gifts to those of th' ocean sea award:**
> **Carmania shall produce an admiral**
> **Who'll take the land from Marseille's overlord.**

Source: The wild animals sent as gifts to François I via the Ottoman pirate Barbarossa in 1533 by Suleiman the Magnificent, who was currently campaigning in Carmania (Persia), preparatory to the forging of their brief but extraordinary alliance against the Holy Roman Empire (see II.5) during which Marseille was virtually occupied for a while by the Ottoman fleet. The details offered in Pliny's *Natural History* (V.7, V.46, VI.197, VII.24) suggest that the word 'satyr' was applied in antiquity to various types of ape or monkey, while the Hyrcanian tiger was a variety of what is known today as the Bengal tiger (Pliny, VIII.66). The prophetic reference is presumably to the *Mirabilis Liber*'s projected Muslim invasion of Europe via the Mediterranean. See I.9, I.75, II.24.

91. Original 1555 text

L'arbre qu'avoit par long temps mort seché,
Dans une nuit viendra a reverdir:
Cron. roy malade, prince pied estaché
Craint d'ennemis fera voile bondir.

Read as modern French:

Chroniquement; détaché[9]

The tree which for so long was dry and dead
Shall in one night burst forth all green again:
The king long ill, the prince's feet are freed:
Foe-feared, he'll set his sails upon the main.

Source: Suetonius, *The Twelve Caesars* (Augustus: 92): 'On the isle of Capri the fallen branches of an extremely old oak, already drooping to the ground, sprang to life again at his [Augustus's] advent'; no doubt assimilated to the death of François I in 1547 and the accession of the young Henri II.

92. Original 1555 text

Le monde proche du dernier periode,
Saturne encor tard sera de retour:
Translat empire devers nation Brodde:
L'œil arraché à Narbon par Autour.

Read as modern French:

Transféré; à la nation alpine
par un vautour/par Milan [?]

As the world's final age draws on apace
Saturn 'turns slow his influence to wreak.
Empire shall pass to Savoy's mountain race;
Narbonne's bright eye plucked out by goshawk's beak.

Source: Richard Roussat's *Livre de l'estat et mutations des temps*, subtitled *Proving by authority of Sacred Scripture and by astrological reasons that the end of the world is nigh*, assimilated to the *Mirabilis Liber*'s prophecies for this event, as summed up particularly at II.13 above, and notably those for the anticipated Muslim invasion of Europe around which it was expected to revolve (see I.9, I.75, II.24). This in turn is evoked in terms of the end of the former Roman Empire in the west and the arrival of the invading Arabs at Narbonne.[60]

93. Original 1555 text   **Read as modern French:**

Dans Avignon tout le chef de l'Empire
Fera arrest pour Paris desole: *désolé*
Tricast tiendra l'Annibalique ire: *Le bas Dauphiné*
Lyon par change sera mal consolé.

> **In Avignon shall all th' Imperial lords**
> **Come to a stop, Paris being desolate:**
> **While Tricastin resists Tunisian swords,**
> **Lyon shall at the change bewail its fate.**

Source: The *Mirabilis Liber*'s grim forecast of the destruction of Paris as a result of the expected Muslim invasion of Europe (see I.9, I.75, II.24): 'Before the world arrives at the year of our Lord 1525, the Catholic Church and the entire world shall mourn the capture, despoliation, and devastation of the most illustrious and famous city, capital and mistress of the Kingdom of all the French' (Prophecy of Jean de Vatiguerro), with special reference to Livy's account of Hannibal's invasion of Europe in his *History of Rome*. Compare V.30.

94. Original 1555 text   **Read as modern French:**

De cinq cents ans plus compte lon tiendra   *l'on*
Celuy qu'estoit l'ornement de son temps: *De celui qui*
Puis à un coup grande clarté donrra
Que par ce siecle les rendra trescontens.   *Qui à cette époque-là/pendant cet âge-là*

> **After five hundred years more heed they'll take**
> **Of him who was th' adornment of his age.**
> **Then light effulgent suddenly shall break**
> **Such as that time's great pleasure to engage.**

Source: Probably Nostradamus's own original estimate of his own fame in ages to come, or perhaps a re-evocation of the reign of the charismatic Hohenstaufen emperor Frederick II.[60]

95. Original 1555 text   **Read as modern French:**

La loy Moricque on verra defaillir:
Apres une autre beaucoup plus seductive,
Boristhenes premier viendra faillir: *le Dniepr*
Pardons & langue une plus attractive.   *Par dons*

> **The Moorish dispensation shall collapse**
> **In favour of another more seductive:**
> **Those from Bohemia shall fall first, perhaps,**
> **Finding its gifts and words much more attractive.**

Source: The *Mirabilis Liber*'s prediction that Western Christendom would eventually defeat Islam in the Middle East – and even convert its adherents to Christianity (see I.55) – bundled together with the expectation that Protestantism, which could be traced back in continental Europe to the Bohemian (Czech) John Hus, would likewise bite the dust at around the same time.

96. Original 1555 text   Read as modern French:

Chef de FOUSSAN aura gorge couper	*coupée*
Par le ducteur du limier & levrier:	*conducteur; chien de chasse*
Le faict patré par ceux du mont TARPEE	*perpétré; par la justice*
Saturne en Leo xiii. de Fevrier.	

Fossano's lord's throat promptly cut shall be
By his own master of the dog and hound
At the behest of the Tarpeian mount.
Saturn in Leo, fifteenth of February.

Source: A historical incident dating, on the basis of the astrology, from 1536, and possibly based on François I's recent hunting trip at Pagny, and to an incident related by the celebrated contemporary surgeon Ambroise Paré in which three soldiers had their throats cut by an older colleague in order to put them out of their misery.[60]

97. Original 1555 text   Read as modern French:

Nouvelle loy terre neufve occuper	
Vers la Syrie, Judee, & Palestine:	
Le grand empire barbare corruer,	*barbarique/arabe; s'écroulera*
Avant que Phebés son siecle determine.	*Avant que le soleil ne termine son âge*

A new law in a new land shall hold sway
Near Syria's, Palestine's, Judea's shore,
The Arab empire, crumbling, melt away
Ere solar Phoebus' age is fully o'er.

Source: The *Mirabilis Liber*'s confident prediction of the eventual defeat of Islam by Christendom (see I.55) within the timescale of ages specified by Richard Roussat in his *Livre de l'estat et mutations des temps*[67] – i.e. by 2242 AD (the next 'age of the sun' of 354 years and four months having theoretically started in 1887).

98. Original 1555 text   Read as modern French:

Deux royals freres si fort guerroyeront	
Qu'entre eux sera la guerre si mortelle,	
Qu'un chacun places fortes occuperont:	
De regne & vie sera leur grand querele.	

Two brothers royal fiercely shall make war:
So mortal shall that war between them be,
That each of them shall take great strongpoints o'er.
O'er power and life shall their great dispute be.

Source: Any one of a host of possible recent precedents, possibly with religious overtones.

99. Original 1555 text	Read as modern French:
Aux champs herbeux d'Alein & du Varneigne,	*Alleins; Vernègues^P [près de Salon-de-Provence]*
Du mont Lebron proche de la Durance,	*Lubéron*
Camp de deux pars conflict sera sy aigre:	*Sur le champ de bataille*
Mesopotamie deffallira en la France.	

From Vernègues' fields and Alleins's pastures green
To Lubéron's mount quite near to the Durance,
Bitter on both sides shall the fight have been –
But Babylon shall fail right here in France!

Source: The *Mirabilis Liber*'s prediction of the final liberation of Europe from its expected future Islamic invaders, narrowed down to a purely local context involving local villages. See I.55.

100. Original 1555 text	Read as modern French:
Entre Gaulois le dernier honoré.	
D'homme ennemi sera victorieux:	*Sur*
Force & terroir en moment exploré,	*territoire/pays*
D'un coup de trait quand mourra l'envieux.	

Among the Gauls the last who'll honors wrest
O'er him who was his foe shall victory cry,
His forces and the land's lie once assessed,
When, arrow-shot, the envious one shall die.

Source: Evidently the remarkable victory of Vercingetorix the Gaul over Julius Caesar at Gergovia in 52 BC, as somewhat grudgingly recounted by Caesar himself in Book VII of his *Gallic War*, possibly assimilated to the eventual victory by the French over their future Muslim occupiers confidently predicted by the *Mirabilis Liber* (see I.55).

Century IIII

1. Original 1555 text

Cela du reste de sang non espandu:
Venise quiert secours estre donné:
Apres avoir bien long temps attendu.
Cité livrée au premier corn sonné.

Read as modern French:

À *cela*

cor

> **For what of blood shall not yet have been shed,**
> **Venice demands that aid be sent at last:**
> **But after having waited long unfed**
> **The city's yielded at first trumpet blast.**

Source: Unidentified historical siege, possibly assimilated to the *Mirabilis Liber*'s promised Muslim invasion of Europe via Italy. See I.9, I.75.

2. Original 1555 text

Par mort la France prendra voyage à faire
Classe par mer, marcher monts Pyrenées,
Hespagne en trouble, marcher gent militaire:
Des plus grand dames en France emmenées.

Read as modern French:

de la France il prendra [?]
En flotte

> **From France through death he'll expedition make,**
> **By fleet at sea, o'er Pyrenees on foot.**
> **The army's march shall shake Spain to the root:**
> **Their greatest ladies into France they'll take.**

Source: Possibly Froissart's account in his *Chroniques* (Luce I:238–245) of the expedition into Spain of Edward the Black Prince (then in control of much of western France) in 1367, following the death of Alphonso XI of Castile in 1350 and the assumption of power by his illegitimate son known as Henry the Bastard – see III.54, III.80 – presumably assimilated to the *Mirabilis Liber*'s predictions of the eventual liberation of Europe from its invaders (see I.55).

3. Original 1555 text   **Read as modern French:**

D'Arras & Bourges, de Brodes grans enseignes   *Allobroges; compagnies*
Un plus grand nombre de Gascons batre à pied,
Ceulx long du Rosne saigneront les Espaignes:
Proche du mont ou Sagonte s'assied.

> **From Bourges and Arras and the Alps they'll flood:**
> **Of Gascons even more on foot shall fight,**
> **Those from along the Rhône spill Spanish blood**
> **Near to Sagunto's lofty mountain height.**

Source: Evidently as per IV.2 above, though the mention of Sagunto makes the Black Prince's expedition less likely as a source.

4. Original 1555 text   **Read as modern French:**

L'impotent prince faché, plainctz & quereles.
De rapts & pilles par coqz & par libyques: *enlèvements; pillages; Français; Barbaresques*
Grand est par terre, par mer infinies voiles,   *armée [ost]*
Seure Italie sera chassant Celtiques.   *Sûre; Celtes*

> **The powerless prince shall fret while all complain**
> **Of French and Afric troops that sack and loot.**
> **On land great hosts; ships countless ply the main;**
> **Italy safe, the French in hot pursuit.**

Source: The frustrations of the Emperor Charles V when, in 1536, the French and the Turks allied to attack his possessions in Italy and Savoy. See II.5, II.59.

5. Original 1555 text   **Read as modern French:**

Croix, paix, sous un accompli divin verbe,   *Paix pour les chrétiens*
L'Hespaigne & Gaule seront unis ensemble.
Grand clade proche, & combat tresacerbe: *désastre/défaite*
Cueur si hardi ne sera qui ne tremble.   *coeur*

> **Christians at peace, and Holy Writ fulfilled,**
> **Under one king shall France and Spain unite.**
> **Disaster looms, fierce combat, many killed:**
> **No heart so bold as not to quake with fright.**

Source: The *Mirabilis Liber*'s forecast of the future liberation of Christian Europe from its Muslim invaders and its subsequent bloody invasion of the Middle East. See I.55.

6. Original 1555 text

Read as modern French:

D'habits nouveaux apres faicte la treuve,   *la découverte*
Malice tramme & machination: *piège*
Premier mourra qui en fera la preuve
Couleur venise insidiation.

> **In guise all new after discovery**
> **Of deadly plot and fiendish machination,**
> **The first to try it killed shall duly be,**
> **Tainted with guile of the Venetian nation.**

Source: Unknown 'cloak-and-dagger' incident from internal Italian history.

7. Original 1555 text

Read as modern French:

Le mineur filz du grand & hay prince,
De lepre aura à vingt ans grande tache:
De dueil sa mere mourra bien triste & mince.
Et il mourra la ou toumbe chet lasche.   *où sera enseveli [son] chef*

> **The younger son of prince both great and hated**
> **At twenty shall show signs of leprosy:**
> **His grieving mother shall die sad and wasted –**
> **As, where his cowardly leader lies, shall he.**

Source: Unidentified.

8. Original 1555 text

Read as modern French:

La grand cité d'assaut prompt repentin   *vite et soudain*
Surprins de nuict, gardes interrompus   *Surprise; interceptés*
Les excubies & veilles sainct Quintin,   *Pendant la vigile et la veille de*
Trucidés, gardes & les pourtails rompus.   *Les gardes tués*

> **By quick assault the city, in its might,**
> **The guards o'erwhelmed, shall be surprised at night**
> **Upon St Quentin's vigil and his eve.**
> **The guards all killed, the gates down they shall heave.**

Source: An unidentified military operation on 30 March.

9. Original 1555 text

Read as modern French:

Le chef du camp au milieu de la presse   *de la bataille*
D'un coup de fleche sera blessé aux cuisses,
Lors que Geneve en larmes & detresse
Sera trahie par Lozan & Souysses.   *par Lausanne et les Suisses allemands*

> The warlord in the middle of the press
> By arrow shot in th' thighs is wounded laid
> When shall Geneva, tearful, in distress,
> By German Swiss and Lausanne be betrayed.

Source: Unknown.

10. Original 1555 text

Read as modern French:

Le jeune prince accusé faulsement
Metra en trouble le camp & en querelles:
Meurtri le chef pour le soustenement: *pour l'avoir soutenu*
Sceptre apaiser: puis guerir escroueles.   *[puis il deviendra roi lui-même]*

> The youthful prince accused right falsely, he'll
> The troops disturb, set at each other's throat,
> The leader killed for giving him his vote.
> He'll swage the Crown: then scrofula he'll heal.

Source: Possibly the story of Henry V of England and the attempted coup on behalf of the Earl of Cambridge just before his departure for Harfleur in 1415. At this point in his narrative Nostradamus appears to be working from a history that has not so far been recovered – possibly one of those on which the contemporary English chronicler Raphael Holinshed also drew. Charles Duke of Orleans (captured as a young man at Agincourt, and father of Louis XII, king of France during Nostradamus's childhood) is a possible literary source.

11. Original 1555 text

Read as modern French:

Celuy qu'aura gouvert de la grand cappe   *gouvernement; de la papauté*
Sera induict a quelque cas patrer: *à perpétrer quelque crime*
Les XII. rouges viendront souiller la nappe   *cardinaux*
Sous meurtre, meutre se viendra perpetrer   *meurtre sur meurtre*

> He who rules o'er the mighty papacy
> Shall be induced a crime to perpetrate.
> Twelve cardinals their cloth shall sullied see:
> Murder on murder shall the world await.

Source: Unknown.

12. Original 1555 text

Read as modern French:

Le camp plus grand de route mis en fuite,   *mis en déroute*
Gueres plus outre ne sera pourchassé:
Ost recampé, & legion reducte
Puis hors des Gaules du tout sera chassé.

Routed, the greater army put to flight,
They'll not much further be pursued at all.
Their host unhosted, and reduced their might,
They shall be chased completely out of Gaul.

Source: The *Mirabilis Liber*'s triumphant prophecy of the eventual expulsion of the future Muslim occupiers from France. See I.55.

13. Original 1555 text

Read as modern French:

De plus grand perte nouvelles raportées,
Le raport fait [/] le camp s'estonnera: *l'armée*
Bandes unies encontre revoltées:
Double phalange grand abandonnera.   *le noble*

When of the greater loss the news they'll tell,
That news received, the host shall gape at it.
As one, the troops against him shall rebel:
The double force the lord shall promptly quit.

Source: Unidentified.

14. Original 1555 text

Read as modern French:

La mort subite du premier personnaige
Aura changé & mis un autre au regne:
Tost, tard venu à si haut & bas aage,
Que terre & mer faudra que lon le craigne.   *l'on*

The First Man's sudden death shall change the state
And place another in the seat of power,
So young to be so high, or soon or late,
Who o'er both land and sea shall fearful lour.

Source: Evidently the *Mirabilis Liber*'s forecast that a magnificent young ruler will arise in France to expel the invader and save the world. See I.4, I.92, and especially 'Then shall emerge in Gaul a king of the Greeks, Francs, and Romans, of lofty stature and handsome appearance; his body and limbs shall have the most beautiful proportions; he shall reign a hundred and twelve years . . . after that, peace shall reign for Christians up until the time of the Antichrist . . .' (Prophecy of the Tiburtine Sibyl).

15. Original 1555 text

Read as modern French:

D'ou pensera faire venir famine,
De la viendra le ressasiement:
L'œil de la mer par avare canine   *Le roi/La cité la plus splendide [?]*
Pour de l'un l'autre donrra huyle, froment.

From thence whence famine they'll be thought to bring
Shall be instead replenishment at hand:
With avaricious fang, the ocean king
Shall barter oil and flour from land to land.

Source: Possibly the Turkish alliance with France of 1536, projected into the future in connection with the *Mirabilis Liber*'s scenario of future Arab invasion and counter-invasion. See I.9, I.75, II.24 and I.55.

16. Original 1555 text	Read as modern French:
La cité franche de liberté fait serve:	esclave
Des profligés & resveurs faict asyle.	
Le roy changé à eux non si proterve:	insolent
De cent seront devenus plus de mille.	

To freedom now enslaved, the city free
To thinkers and oppressed shall refuge show:
The king, now changed, no foe to them shall be:
From a mere hundred shall a thousand grow.

Source: The recent history of the port of La Rochelle, and notably the unexpected pardoning by King François I in person of its citizens in 1544 after their revolt against the salt-tax of the previous year. Compare V.35.[9]

17. Original 1555 text	Read as modern French:
Changer à Beaune, Nuy, Chalons & Digeon	Nuits-Saint-Georges; Dijon
Le duc voulant amander la Barrée	le Barrois
Marchant pres fleuve, poisson, bec de plongeon	
Verra la queue: porte sera serrée.	

At Beaune, to scourge Chalon, Dijon and Nuits,
Wishing the Barrois to chastise, the Duke
Marching beside the Saône shall see the fluke
Of fish in diver's beak: gates shut shall be.

Source: The story of a local omen associated with an unidentified military incident.

18. Original 1555 text	Read as modern French:
Des plus letrés dessus les faits celestes	
Seront par princes ignorants reprouvés:	
Punis d'Edit, chassés, commes scelestes,	
Et mis à mort la ou seront trouvés.	

Of those most learn'd of facts celestial
Shall some by princes ignorant be slated,
By edict banned, hounded as criminal
And put to death where'er they are located.

Source: An unidentified persecution of astrologers.

19. Original 1555 text

Read as modern French:

Devant ROUAN d'Insubres mis le siege,   *Rouen; combattants venus de Milan*
Par terre & mer enfermés les passages:
D'Haynault, & Flandres, de Gand & ceux de Liege,
Par dons laenees raviront les rivages.   *de Bacchus [Lenaeus]*

Troops from Milan to Rouen shall lay siege:
By land and sea all passage they shall foil.
Of Hainaut, Flanders, Gent and of Liège
Like drunken men the borders they'll despoil.

Source: Probably the *Mirabilis Liber*'s forecast of a massive Muslim of Europe via Italy. See I.9, I.75.

20. Original 1555 text

Read as modern French:

Paix uberté long temps lieu louera   *et fécondité*
Par tout son regne desert la fleur de lis:
Corps morts d'eau, terre la lon apportera,   *jusque là l'on*
Sperants vain heur d'estre la ensevelis.   *Souhaitant en vain la chance d'y être*

Long time the place shall plenty reap, and peace:
Through all its empty realm shall lilies blow.
Thither the dead they'll bring o'er land and seas
In empty hope there to their graves to go.

Source: Nostradamus's own first-hand knowledge of the vast ancient necropolis at nearby Arles[P] known as *les Alyscamps* – a local version of the *Champs Élysées* or Elysian Fields, the classical Abode of the Dead – a name which of course bears buried within it the very words *à lys camps* ('fields for lilies'). The last two lines refer to the former practice of bringing the dead there from far and wide for burial – often ferried across the Rhône with coins in their eyes for the ferryman, exactly as per the legend of Charon, who in classical mythology ferried the dead across the river Styx. The whole is seemingly assimilated to the *Mirabilis Liber*'s promise of France's eventual liberation from its future Muslim oppressors after its virtual desolation by the occupiers. See I.55.

21. Original 1555 text   **Read as modern French:**

Le changement sera fort difficile:
Cité, province au change gain fera:
Cueur haut, prudent mis, chassé lui habile.   *l'inhabile*
Mer, terre, peuple son estat changera.

> Most difficult the change is bound to be,
> Yet town and country both by it shall gain.
> Heart high and wise, banished the bungler, he,
> Installed, shall change their state by land and main.

Source: The *Mirabilis Liber*'s confident prediction of the future French *Grand Monarque*'s expulsion of all Islamic invaders from France. See I.4, I.55, I.92.

22. Original 1555 text   **Read as modern French:**

La grand copie qui sera deschassée,
Dans un moment fera besoing au roy:
La foy promise de loing sera fauscée
Nud se verra en piteux desarroy.

> Of th' mighty host that shall be sent away
> The king shall all at once have need of th' aid,
> The promise made be grievously betrayed:
> Exposed he'll be, in piteous disarray.

Source: The famous defeat of King François I at the Battle of Pavia in 1525, betrayed by the sudden withdrawal from the battle of his brother-in-law the Duke of Alençon, who commanded the rearguard – possibly assimilated to the expected French defeat in the course of the *Mirabilis Liber*'s predicted Arab invasion of Europe via Italy. See I.9, I.75.

23. Original 1555 text   **Read as modern French:**

La legion dans la marine classe   *dans la flotte*
Calcine, Magnes soulphre, & poix bruslera: *[du 'feu grec']*
Le long repos de l'asseurée place:
Port Selyn, Hercle feu les consumera.   *Port Selyn [?] et Port'Ercole*

> The warriors of th' armada maritime
> Shall burn pitch, lime, sulfur, magnesium.
> O strongpoint sure, and safe so long a time!
> Fire Genoa, Port'Ercole shall consume.

Source: The *Mirabilis Liber*'s prophecies of a forthcoming Arab invasion of Europe via Italy. See I.9, I.75. In the first two lines it is the 'Greek fire' that burns the invading forces, not the reverse, since it was essentially a defensive weapon.[9]

24. Original 1555 text

Ouy sous terre [/] saincte d'ame voix fainte,
Humaine flamme pour divine voyr luire,
Fera des seuls de leur sang terre tainte
Et les saints temples pour les impurs destruire.

Read as modern French:

Entendu; dame

des moines [<gr. monachos = 'solitaire']
par

Heard underground, the Virgin's voice is faint –
'Man's fire shall shine, while light Divine shall wane':
Thus shall the earth with monkish blood be stained
And holy churches wrecked by the profane.

Source: A contemporary 'aural apparition', possibly experienced in local mine- or quarry-workings such as those of ancient Glanum, just south of St-Rémy, and taken to prefigure the destruction of the Church, in accordance both with growing contemporary religious troubles and with the *Mirabilis Liber*'s prediction of religious atrocities under a future Muslim occupation of Europe. See I.15.

25. Original 1555 text

Corps sublimes [/] sans fin à l'œil visibles
Obnubiler viendront par ses raisons:
Corps, front comprins, sens, chief & invisibles,
Diminuant les sacrées oraisons.

Read as modern French:

sublimés

compris; sans tête [sans chef]

Substances sublimate that once were seen
Shall for that reason come to fade from view:
Bodies made headless, browless and unseen,
And holy prayers soon fading like the dew.

Source: Alchemical experiments, probably by Nostradamus himself, but suspected by him of being essentially inimical to religion.

26. Original 1555 text

Lou grand eyssame se levera d'abelhos,
Que non sauran don te siegen venguddos
De nuech l'embousq;, lou gach dessous las
   treilhos,
Cieutad trahido p cinq lengos non nudos.

Read as modern French:

Le grand essaim se levera d'abeilles
Qu'on ne saura d'où elles seront venues.
De nuit l'embuscade, le guet sous les
   treilles,
Cité trahie par cinq bavards non nus.

The mighty swarm of bees shall climb on high,
But where they came from nobody can say.
A trap at night, 'neath vines the watch shall spy:
Five hidden tongues shall give the town away.

Source: Julius Obsequens's *On Omens* (65a) for 48 BC: 'A swarm of bees on the standards portended calamity'; Livy's *History of Rome* (XXI, 46) for 218 BC: 'The

Romans, on their part, were by no means so keen to engage [with Hannibal, who subsequently defeated them near the Ticino] . . . [since] a swarm of bees had settled on a tree over the commander's tent'; evidently assimilated to a manuscript account *in Provençal* by Nostradamus's younger brother Jehan (and subsequently quoted by the latter's nephew César in his *Histoire et chronique de Provence*[47]) of the Emperor Charlemagne's victory over the Saracens at the foot of the Mont Gaussier that overlooks the ancient city of Glanum just south of Nostradamus's birthplace of St-Rémy: 'Charlemagne turned up, together with all his host that looked like a swarm of bees on the move.'[60] Thus, yet another reference to the *Mirabilis Liber*'s expected liberation of France from its future Arab occupiers. See I.55.

27. Original 1555 text	**Read as modern French:**
Salon, Mansol, Tarascon de SEX. l'arc,	*St-Paul-de-Mausole*
Ou est debout encor la piramide,	
Viendront livrer le prince Dannemarc	*libérer*
Rachat honni au temple d'Artemide.	

> **At Salon, Mausole, Tarascon,[P] arch of SEX,**
> **Where yet the lofty 'Pyramide' doth rise**
> **The hostage prince of Denmark he collects –**
> **Shameful to Artemisia's fane the price!**

Source: Still at St-Rémy, the so-called *Antiques* just south of Nostradamus's birthplace – i.e. the municipal gate and lofty mausoleum that marked the entrance to the now-ruined Graeco-Roman city of Glanum.[P] These stood – and still stand – just across the road from the former abbey of St-Paul-de-Mausole (now a psychiatric clinic that once housed the painter Vincent van Gogh),[P] which itself adjoins an ancient Roman stone quarry in the middle of which still stands the extraordinary pinnacle of stone known locally as *la Pyramide* (presumably from *la pierre-en-mi*, 'the rock in the middle')[P] that was a typical feature of ancient stone quarries – as, for example, at Syracuse in Sicily. The world's original *Mausoleum* having been the huge tomb (one of the original Seven Wonders of the World) formerly erected for her husband King Mausolus of Caria by his wife Artemisia, the *temple d'Artemide* has to refer to the mausoleum at Glanum, now known as the Mausoleum of the Julii, which bears the legend:

SEX.L.M.IULIEI C.F. PARENTIBUS SUEIS

('Sextus, Lucius, Marcus, sons of Caius Julius, to their parents').[P] The 'Danish prince' reference is once again to Charlemagne's nearby defeat of the Saracens (see previous verse), after which Godfrey of Denmark was knighted by the Emperor for his sheer cheek in sending his son Ogier as hostage in order to free himself from the tribute he owed him.[60]

28. Original 1555 text

Lors que Venus du sol sera couvert,
Souz l'esplendeur sera forme occulte,
Mercure au feu les aura descouvert
Par bruit bellique sera mis à l'insulte.

Read as modern French:

le cuivre; de l'or [?]

le mercure [?]
par Mars [le fer] [?]

> **When Venus by the sun is blotted out,**
> **Forth from its light a form occult shall rise.**
> **Then Mercury through fire shall find them out,**
> **Though strife's loud rumor do him sore surprise.**

Source: Possibly some untoward domestic incident in Nostradamus's own household, somewhat along the lines of *The Sorcerer's Apprentice,* disguised in alchemical language purporting to describe the transmutation of copper to gold with the aid of mercury.[9]

29. Original 1555 text

Le Sol caché eclipse par Mercure
Ne sera mis que pour le ciel second.
De Vulcan Hermes sera faite pasture:
Sol sera veu pur rutilant & blond.

Read as modern French:

l'or; le mercure [?]
que pour la deuxième planète [que pour du mercure?]
du feu; le mercure [?]

> **The hidden Sun, eclipsed by Mercury,**
> **Shall come to rank but second in the sky.**
> **By Vulcan Mercury shall foddered be,**
> **Then shall the pale, pure, bright Sun rise on high.**

Source: As per the previous verse: what seems to be mere Mercury will turn into pure gold.

30. Original 1555 text

Plus xi. fois ☽.☉. ne voudra,
Tous augmentés & baissés de degré:
Et si bas mis que peu or lon coudra:
Qu'apres faim peste descouvert le secret.

Read as modern French:

l'argent; l'or [?]

l'on recherchera

> **Eleven more times the moon the sun shall shun,**
> **Each raised or lowered in its own degree,**
> **And so abased that no gold shall be spun –**
> **Then, after dearth and plague, the secret see!**

Source: Possibly the same incident as above, but expressed in terms of the fluctuations in the value of gold and silver with which Nostradamus is so often concerned, though evidently expecting the eventual discovery of the transmutation of base metals into gold finally to solve the problem.

31. Original 1555 text   **Read as modern French:**

La lune au plain de nuit sus le haut mont,
Le nouveau sophe d'un seul cerveau la veu: *l'a vue*
Par ses disciples estre immortel semond   *invité/appelé*
Yeux au mydi. En seins mains, corps au feu.   *en feu*

The moon at midnight o'er the lofty mount
The new-found sage's mind alone can claim.
Him for immortal his disciples count,
Eyes southward, hands in lap, body aflame.

Source: Possibly the resolution of the same incident alluded to in the three previous quatrains, with the restoration of domestic calm and the recognition of Nostradamus himself as the master of his occult, prophetic element.

32. Original 1555 text   **Read as modern French:**

Es lieux & temps chair au poiss. donra lieu.   *poisson*
La loy commune sera faicte au contraire:
Vieux tiendra fort, puis oste du milieu   *ôté*
Le πάντα χοινα φιλωμ mis fort arriere.   *pánta choìna philòm [gr. 'tout partagé entre*
                                           amis']

Some time, some place shall meat to fish give way,
The common law be turned upon its head,
The old hold firm, but then be cast away,
And common ownership be left for dead.

Source: Froissart's report in his *Chroniques* (NY, Pierpoint: II.49) of the incendiary speech of the revolutionary firebrand John Ball during the failed English Peasants' Revolt of 1381: 'My friends, things cannot go well in England until all possessions are held in common, and until there is neither serf nor gentleman, and all of us are one', presumably applied to the contemporary German Anabaptist sects of which Nostradamus disapproved so heartily. The last line is based on Erasmus's phrase *amicorum communia omnia* ('all things in common among friends') in his *Adages* of 1500 (I.1).

33. Original 1555 text   **Read as modern French:**

Juppiter joint plus Venus qu'à la Lune   *L'étain; au cuivre; qu'à l'argent [?]*
Apparoissant de plenitude blanche:
Venus cachée soubs la blancheur Neptune,   *Le cuivre; de l'eau [?]*
De Mars frappé par la granée branche.   *De fer [?]; gravée [alourdie]*

Then copper-coated more than silvered tin,
Appearing full of brightness shining white,

> Copper 'neath water white all covered in,
> With iron-weighted pestle they shall smite.

Source: An alchemical operation designed to transmute base metals into silver. The mention of Neptune is sufficient to dispel any idea that the verse is actually about planets, since the planet subsequently so-named after the Roman god of the sea was not discovered until 1846.

34. Original 1555 text

Read as modern French:

Le grand mené captif d'estrange terre,
D'or enchainé au roy CHYREN offert,   *Henri [anagramme d'Henryc]*
Qui dans Ausonne, Millan perdra la guerre,   *Italie*
Et tout son ost mis à feu & à fer.

> The noble lord's dragged captive from abroad
> Before King Henry chained with gold embossed,
> Italy's war, Milan's great battle lost,
> And all his host put to the flames and sword.

Source: The transfer in 1495 by Pope Alexander Borgia VI to Charles VIII of France of Prince Zimzim, the brother of the Turkish Sultan Bajazet, just before Charles had to retreat from Naples to Lombardy, finally losing his current Italian war[60] – assimilated to the standard Roman triumph-ritual for victorious returning generals that involved parading their prisoners through the city in chains; and applied (apparently in reverse) to the *Mirabilis Liber*'s anticipated final defeat by Christendom of its future Middle Eastern invaders, attributed successively by Nostradamus and his various successors first to Henri II, then to Henri IV, and finally to some future 'Henri V'. See I.4, I.55, I.92.

35. Original 1555 text

Read as modern French:

Le feu estaint, les vierges trahiront
La plus grand part de la bande nouvelle:
Fouldre à fer, lance [//] les seulz roy garderont: *les moines [gr. monachos < monos]*
Etrusque & Corse, de nuit gorge allumelle.   *Étrurie; à lamelle/épée*

> The fire once out, the nuns shall soon betray
> The greater section of the sect so new:
> Bolts strike sword, lance: monks guard the king, they say:
> In Corsica, Etruria, throats at night run through.

Source: Unknown betrayal of a semi-magical sect (compare I.42). Line 3 recalls Livy's *History of Rome* (XXII.1): 'In Sicily a number of spear-points caught fire'; and Julius Obsequens's *On Omens* (47) for 98 BC: 'In the circus, fire flashed [*fulsus*] among the spears of the soldiers.'

36. Original 1555 text   **Read as modern French:**

Les jeux nouveaux en Gaule redressés,
Apres victoire de l'Insubre champaigne: *du Milanais et de la Campanie [?]*
Monts d'Esperie, les grands liés, troussés: *de l'Espagne*
De peur trembler la Romaigne & l'Espaigne.   *les États Papaux*

> Once more the games in France they shall re-found,
> Victory o'er Milan and Naples won.
> On western mountains leaders trussed and bound:
> In Rome and Spain they'll tremble, every one.

Source: The *Mirabilis Liber*'s prediction of the expulsion of the future Arab invaders from Italy and Spain. See I.55.

37. Original 1555 text   **Read as modern French:**

Gaulois par saults, monts viendra penetrer: *par détroits/défilés/assauts*
Occupera le grand lieu de l'Insubre: *Attaqueront ; du Milanais*
Au plus profond son ost fera entrer: *son armée*
Gennes, Monech pousseront classe rubre.   *Gênes et Monaco repousseront la flotte rouge*

> The attacking Frenchman shall the mountains breach,
> The mighty Milanais assault and beat.
> His mighty host its furthest shore shall reach,
> From Genoa, Monaco chase the bloody fleet.

Source: Once again the *Mirabilis Liber*'s prophecy of an eventual liberation of Europe from its future Muslim invaders under a future *Grand Monarque* of France. See I.55 and compare the previous verse.

38. Original 1555 text   **Read as modern French:**

Pendant que duc, roy, royne occupera
Chef Bizant dn captif en Samothrace: *Byzantin; un*
Avant l'assauit l'un l'autre mangera: *assaut*
Rebours ferré suyvra du sang la trasse.   *Hérissé, cruel; trace*

> While the duke shall the king and queen distract,
> The Turkish chief is held in Samothrace.
> Before th' assault as cannibals they'll act:
> Cruel, angry, he of blood the trail shall trace.

Source: Unknown, but possibly related to the *Mirabilis Liber*'s expected Western counter-attack on the Middle East. See I.55.

39. Original 1555 text

Les Rodiens demanderont secours
Par le neglet de ses hoyrs delaissée.
L'empire Arabe revalera son cours
Par Hesperies la cause redressée.

Read as modern French:

retracera/redescendra
Par l'Ouest

> **For urgent help the folk of Rhodes entreat,**
> **By its heirs long left to ruin and to rack.**
> **The Arab empire beats a swift retreat,**
> **By Westerners things soon to rights put back.**

Source: Once again the *Mirabilis Liber*'s prediction of a successful Western invasion of the Middle East, following its occupation by Islamic forces. See I.55.

40. Original 1555 text

Les forteresses des assieges sarrés
Par pouldre à feu profondés en abysme:
Les proditeurs seront tous vifs serrés
Onc aux sacristes n'avint si piteux scisme.

Read as modern French:

serrés
profondées [?]
Les traîtres; sciés [lat. serratus]
Jamais; n'advint

> **The fortresses of the besieged, shut up,**
> **Reduced by gunpowder to ruins shall be.**
> **The traitors they'll alive with saws cut up.**
> **Never was priesthood split more piteously!**

Source: Probably the *Mirabilis Liber*'s account either of the future invasion of Europe (see I.9, I.75, II.24) or of the Christian re-invasion of the Middle East (see I.55), with a particularly grim religious joke in the last line.

41. Original 1555 text

Gymnique sexe captive par hostaige
Viendra de nuit custodes decevoyr:
Le chef du camp deceu par son langaige
Lairra à la gente, fera piteux à voyr.

Read as modern French:

Sexe feminin
les gardes
de l'armée
cédera à la jolie; sera; à la voir

> **Of woman's sex the captive, hostage led,**
> **At night shall trick her guards deceitfully:**
> **The commandant, by what she says misled,**
> **Shall to her charms defer, so sad to see.**

Source: Plutarch's *Parallel Lives* (Romulus, 29: Camilla, 33), describing the trick played by the Romans on their enemies under the command of Livius Postumius in 390 BC, when they used female hostages to set a trap for them.[9]

42. Original 1555 text

Geneve & Langres par ceux de Chartres & Dolle,
Et par Grenoble captif au Montlimard:
Seysset, Losanne par fraudulente dole,
Les trahiront par or soyxante marc.

Read as modern French:

Seyssel; ruse

Geneva, Langres, Grenoble by Chartres and Dole
All taken captive to Montélimar,
By Seyssel, Lausanne they by ruse soon are
Betrayed for a mere sixty marks in gold.

Source: Unknown.

43. Original 1555 text

Seront oys au ciel les armes batre:
Celuy an mesme les divins ennemis
Voudront loix sainctes injustement debatre
Par foudre & guerre bien croyans à mort mis.

Read as modern French:

entendus

Par anathème

The clash of arms shall sound aloft the skies:
That same year shall religious foes dispute
The sacred laws unjustly to refute.
They'll kill the faithful, anathematize.

Source: One of the various celestial prodigies from Julius Obsequens's *On Omens* (see II.85), or from the various contemporary omen-reports later collected and illustrated by Lycosthenes,[44] projected into the future as an omen of contemporary religious conflicts on earth. For 1520 Lycosthenes would report (as translated by Batman[5]): *At Wissenburgh by the river of Rhene at noone dayes the Citizens hard a great and horrible noyse, and a meeting togither of weapons sounding in the ayre, wherupon manye being astonyed with feare, taking also their*  *weapons in hand, drew togither, supposing that enimies hadde besieged the Citie,* while recording that a similar occurrence was reported in 1527 by Pamphilus Gengenbachius.

44. Original 1555 text

Lous gros de Mende, de Roudés & Milhau
Cahours, Limoges, Castres malo sepmano

De nuech l'intrado, de Bourdeaux un cailhau
Par Perigort au toc de la campano.

Read as modern French:

Pour les grands de Mende, de Rodez et Millau
Cahors, Limoges, Castres, une mauvaise
*   semaine:*
Irruption de nuit à Bordeaux par un apostat[60]
Par le Périgord au son du tocsin.

> **For those who lead Mende, Rodez, Millau,**
> **Cahors, Limoges and Castres the week bodes ill.**
> **By apostate a night-raid on Bordeaux:**
> **Through Perigord the tocsin's sound shall thrill.**

Source: Contemporary religious conflicts in the south-west of France.

45. Original 1555 text

Par conflit roy, regne abandonera:
Le plus grand chef faillira au besoing:
Mors profligés peu en rechapera,
Tous destranchés, un en sera tesmoing.

Read as modern French:

taillés en morceaux

> **On field of battle king and realm shall he,**
> **The greatest chief, let down in hour of need.**
> **All dead and fallen, few of them shall flee:**
> **All cut apart: one witness to the deed.**

Source: The disastrous Battle of Pavia in 1525, during which King François, having been deserted at the critical moment by his brother-in-law the Duke of Alençon, commander of his rearguard, was captured, and almost the whole of the flower of French chivalry slain – presumably assimilated to the *Mirabilis Liber*'s prophecies of an overwhelming future Islamic invasion of Europe. See IV.22.

46. Original 1555 text

Bien defendu le faict par excelence,
Garde toy Tours de ta proche ruine.
Londres & Nantes par Reims fera defense
Ne passés outre au temps de la bruine.

Read as modern French:

Ne sortez pas

> **So well defended though you surely are,**
> **Beware, O Tours – your ruin is at hand!**
> **London and Nantes through Reims shall travel bar.**
> **Do not pass forth when mist shall veil the land!**

Source: Evidently the *Mirabilis Liber*'s prediction of a massive Arab invasion of Europe (see I.9, I.75, II.24) advancing at length across the Loire into northern France (see V.84).

47. Original 1555 text   **Read as modern French:**

Le noir farouche quand aura essayé
Sa main sanguine par feu, fer, arcs tendus:
Trestout le peuple sera tant effraie,   *Tout; effrayé*
Voyr les plus grads par col & pieds pendus.   *grands/nobles; cou*

> **Once the fierce Moor his bloody hand has tried**
> **And everyone to fire, sword, bow has put,**
> **The common folk shall soon be terrified**
> **To see their noblest hanged by neck and foot.**

Source: The *Mirabilis Liber*'s grim prediction of the invasion and occupation of France by Islamic invaders. See I.9, I.75, II.24.

48. Original 1555 text   **Read as modern French:**

Plannure Ausonne fertile, spacieuse   *La plaine italienne*
Produira taons si trestant sauterelles:
Clarté solaire deviendra nubileuse,
Ronger le tout, grand peste venir d'elles.

> **Those Latin plains so fertile and so vast**
> **So many flies and locusts shall produce**
> **That the sun's light shall be quite overcast**
> **And, eating all, great plagues they shall induce.**

Source: Julius Obsequens's *On Omens* (30) for 125 BC: 'Immense swarms of locusts appeared in North Africa, which, blown out to sea by the wind, then pushed back again by the waves, caused a severe cattle-plague at Cyrene through their intolerable smell and deadly vapors: it was reported that 80,000 people [too] were consumed by the pestilence'; assimilated to the great plague of locusts that invaded the region of Milan in 1542, the year of a solar eclipse,[60] and presumably taken as a vivid symbol for the swarms of future Arab invaders confidently expected by the

Mirabilis Liber (see I.9, I.75, II.24). In Lycosthenes' words,[44] as translated into the English of the day by Dr Stephen Batman:[5] *At the ende of September there was seene in manye places a great number of Grashoppers* [in the Latin, *locustarum*] *as it were a cloude, which at the beginning lacking wings, had afterward foure, who eating up one fielde immediately flying from thence went to another, consuming all that grew upon the ground, saving that they could not so much hurt the vines: the territorie of Milan felt this*

miserie. In like sort that kind of Grashhoppers breaking into Silesia out of Poland, in the moneth of November, did the like or also greater harme to the ground, which at the beginning of October making a gret spoyle not far from Torga in Misnia, and at a Towne called Oschewitz or Ossitium, left behinde them a foule stincke, which greater foule could not abide. At length in the colde of Autumne they pyned awaye and were foode for swine. Historians write that such plagues do light on mens grounds trimmed and untrymmed, but yet never without the betokening of evil, & judgement of Gods wrath. For later in the same year Batman notes additionally, on the basis of Fincelius, that: *A greate number of Grashoppers driven into Misnia and Marchia did much harme to ye fields on every side. That same came to passe also at that time in the countrey aboute Luca, where so great a number was found, that in some places, Job Fincelius hath noted, they being clustered togither lay more than a Cubit high.*

49. Original 1555 text

Devant le peuple sang sera respandu
Que du haut ciel ne viendra eslogner:
Mais d'un long temps ne sera entendu
L'esprit d'un seul le viendra tesmoigner.

Read as modern French:

éloigner

d'un moine [?]

> **Before the people blood shall then be shed**
> **Which shall not from high heaven too far appear.**
> **Long shall it be by none interpreted:**
> **The mind of one alone shall make it clear.**

Source: Unknown, but apparently an attack on a high Church dignitary, taken as an omen that only Nostradamus himself reckons he can interpret satisfactorily.

50. Original 1555 text

Libra verra regner les Hesperies,
De ciel, & terre tenir la monarchie:
D'Asie forces nul ne verra peries
Que sept ne tiennent par rang la hierarchie.

Read as modern French:

l'Ouest

De l'Asie Mineure
la hiérarchie ecclésiastique

> **Libra shall see the West's full power deployed**
> **Dominion wielding over earth and heaven:**
> **Yet none shall see the Turkish power destroyed**
> **Till th' papacy in turn is held by seven.**

Source: Manilius's *Astronomica* (IV.773–5), in one of Nostradamus's favorite Manilian passages praising the Emperor Augustus:[9]

> His Libra rules the West, whereby great Rome
> And her world-empire once did come to be,
> Disposes what shall hap, and doth the nations
> Raise up and dash . . .

assimilated to the *Mirabilis Liber*'s anticipated Western re-invasion of the Middle East. See I.55.

51. Original 1555 text

Read as modern French:

Le duc cupide son ennemi ensuivre
Dans entrera empeschant la phalange:
Astes à pied si pres viendront poursuivre,　　　*Hastés/Empressés*
Que la journee conflite pres de Gange　　　*Ganges [près de Montpellier]*

> **The duke, his foe desirous to pursue,**
> **Shall enter in and keep the army back:**
> **The foot-escapers they'll so close pursue,**
> **Near Ganges the self-same day they'll them attack.**

Source: Unidentified. Ganges is not the river, but a village near Montpellier.

52. Original 1555 text

Read as modern French:

La cité obsesse [/] aux murs hommes & femmes　　　*assiégée*
Ennemis hors [/] le chef prestz à soy rendres　　　*se rendre*
Vent sera fort encontre les gens-darmes:
Chassés seront par chaux, poussiere & cendre.

> **Besieged the town, before the walls the foe,**
> **On them men, women, chief to cede about,**
> **The wind shall in th' troops faces strongly blow:**
> **With quicklime, dust and ash they shall them rout.**

Source: Unidentified historical siege, successfully resisted with the aid of the essentially defensive technique described in the last line. See IX.99.

53. Original 1555 text

Read as modern French:

Les fuitifs & bannis revoqués:　　　*rappelés*
Peres & filz grand garnisent les hauts puids:　　　*tenant garnison; tertres/collines*
Le cruel pere & les siens suffoqués:
Son filz plus pire submergé dans le puis.　　　*puits*

> **The refugees and exiles gathered in,**
> **Father and noble sons the heights shall keep:**
> **The cruel father smothered, and his kin;**
> **His son, e'en worse, drowned in the well so deep.**

Source: Unknown. This is the last verse of the original edition dated 4 May 1555.

54. Original September 1557 text

Du nom qui onques ne fut au Roy gaulois,
Jamais ne fut un fouldre si craintif:
Tremblant l'Italie, l'Espagne, & les Anglois,
De femme estrangiers grandement attentif.

Read as modern French:

jamais
à craindre

de femmes étrangères/d'une femme étrangère

> **Named by a name no French king ever bore,**
> **Never was bolt of Jove so feared by all:**
> **Italy, England, Spain shall quake the more.**
> **For foreign women he shall greatly fall.**

Source: King François I, the terror of Italy, Spain and England and a passionate womanizer, who in 1530 married the Emperor Charles V's sister, Eleanor of Spain, and who, in 1515, became the first French king ever to bear the name 'François'.

55. Original September 1557 text

Quant la corneille sur tour de brique joincte,
Durant sept heures ne fera que crier:
Mort presagée [/] de sang statue taincte,
Tyran meurtri, au Dieux peuple prier.

Read as modern French:

aux Dieux/à Dieu

> **When sits the crow atop the bricky tower,**
> **For seven hours it shall caw and caw away:**
> **A death foreshadowed: statue bloodied o'er.**
> **The Tyrant killed, folk to the gods shall pray.**

Source: Apparently a half-remembered version of Suetonius's description, in his *The Twelve Caesars*, of the omens accompanying the death of the tyrannical Emperor Domitian (XII.15, 23): 'The temple of Jupiter Capitolinus, the temple of the Flaviae, the Palace and his own room were all struck by lightning, and even the plaque at the base of a triumphal statue was wrenched off by a tempest and fell into a nearby tomb . . . and turning around, he assured those nearest to him that on the following day the moon would be bloody in Aquarius . . . A few months before he was killed, a crow [obviously an educated one!] perched on the Capitol and called out the [Greek] words: *Estai panta kalos*: nor was there lacking a wag who [given that Roman crows were supposed to call 'Cras! Cras!' – 'Tomorrow! Tomorrow!'] would celebrate the omen thus:

> Of late on Capitol there spoke
> A crow that, sitting there, did croak,
> 'All shall be well' (in its defense,
> It had to use the future tense!).

56. Original September 1557 text   Read as modern French:

Apres victoire de rabieuse langue,
L'esprit tempté en tranquil & repos: *tranquillité*
Victeur sanguin par conflict faict harangue,
Roustir la langue & la chair & les os.   *À rôtir*

When once the Rabid-Tongue has won the battle
The mind is tempted peace and quiet to seek:
The bloody victor of the war shall prattle
Enough to roast flesh, bones *and* tongue (in-cheek!).

Source: Unidentified historical 'Great Prattler', no doubt projected into the future as a leader of the forthcoming Islamic invasion expected by the *Mirabilis Liber*. See I.9, I.75, II.24.

57. Original September 1557 text   Read as modern French:

Ignare envie du grand Roy supportée,
Tiendra propos deffendre les escriptz:
Sa femme non femme par un autre tentée,
Plus double deux ne fort ne crys.   *ne f[eront ni brui]t ni cris*

Ignorant envy by the King supported,
He shall propose all writings to forbid:
His wife – no wife – by other shall be courted.
More than twice two their loud cries shall have hid.

Source: Once again Suetonius's *Twelve Caesars* on the Emperor Domitian (XII.1, 10): 'He carried off Domitia Longina, although she was the wife of Aelius Lamia, and married her . . . he likewise killed Hermogenes of Tarsus on account of one or two allusions in a *History* of his, and even crucified the scribes who had copied them out . . . he banished all philosophers from the city and from Italy.'

58. Original September 1557 text   Read as modern French:

Soleil ardant dans le gosier coller,
De sang humain arrouser terre Etrusque:
Chef seille d'eaue mener son filz filer,
Captive dame conduicte en terre turque.

With human throats parched by the burning sun,
'Tis human blood shall o'er Etruria rain.
Water in pail, the chief leads off her son
To Turkish lands, the lady captive ta'en.

Source: The landing on the Italian coast of the Turkish pirate Barbarossa in 1543 in search of water, during which he married Doña Maria, daughter of the governor of Gaeta, who subsequently converted to Islam and followed him to Turkey;[60] presumably assimilated to the *Mirabilis Liber*'s prophecies of an Islamic invasion of Europe via Italy. See I.9, I.75.

59. Original September 1557 text   **Read as modern French:**

Deux assiegés en ardante ferveur,
De soif estainctz pour deux plainnes tasses:
Le fort limé, & un viellart resveur,
Aux Genevois de Nira monstra trasse.

      Two towns besieged in burning fever rage
      For want of water to assuage their thirst:
      The fort stripped down, a dreamer old in age
      To Genoa shows what he in Nice did first.

Source: The attack on Nice by the Turkish pirate Barbarossa (now 80) in 1544, assimilated to the *Mirabilis Liber*'s constant warnings of an eventual Islamic invasion of Europe via Italy. See I.9, I.75.

60. Original September 1557 text   **Read as modern French:**

Les sept enfans en hostaige laissés,
Le tiers viendra son enfant trucider:
Deux par son filz seront d'estoc percés,
Gennes, Florence lors viendra encunder.   *percer/pénétrer*

      Of seven children who are hostage left
      The third shall kill his child, and of the six
      Two shall with dagger by his son be cleft.
      Then he Genoa, Florence shall transfix.

Source: Unknown historical incident, possibly projected into the future in connection with the *Mirabilis Liber*'s familiar warnings of Arab invasion from the Mediterranean. See I.9, I.75.

61. Original September 1557 text   **Read as modern French:**

Le vieulz mocqué, & privé de sa place,
Par l'estrangier qui le subornera:
Mains de son filz mangees devant sa face
Le frere à Chartres, Orl. Rouan trahyra.

      The old man mocked, shorn of his rightful place
      By foreigner who shall him straight suborn,
      His offspring's hands devoured before his face,
      Brother at Chartres, betrays Orleans, Rouen.

Source: Leoni[41] suggests the deposition from power of the High Constable Anne de Montmorency in favor of the 'foreign' Guises of Lorraine in 1541 – though Montmorency was only 48 at the time. Certainly an episode from French history – one of many during the course of the next few verses.

62. Original September 1557 text   Read as modern French:

Un coronnel machine ambition,   colonel
Se saisira de la plus grande armee:
Contre son prince faincte invention,
Et descouvert sera soubz la ramee.   sous les ramifications [?]

> **A colonel to advance himself shall plot**
> **And of the greater army seize command:**
> **Against his prince he'll feign to find a plot,**
> **But he beneath the tangle shall be found.**

Source: The essentially baronial machinations of Gaspard de Coligny, appointed the first Colonel General of the French Infantry in the late 1540s and, in 1552, Admiral of France, who from 1555 was making clear his support of the Huguenot (Protestant) cause and later became a prominent Huguenot leader.

63. Original September 1557 text   Read as modern French:

L'armee Celtique contre les montaignars,
Qui seront sceuz & prins à la lipee: connus; en plein repas
Paysans fresz poulseront tost faugnars,   repousseront; presseurs de raisins[41]
Precipitez tous au fil de l'espee.

> **The army French the mountain-folk attack,**
> **Who shall be found and taken while they sup:**
> **Fresh peasants shall the grape-treaders push back,**
> **And all of them by sword-blade be cut up.**

Source: Unidentified military campaign.

64. Original September 1557 text   Read as modern French:

Le deffaillant en habit de bourgois,
Viendra le Roy tempter de son offence:
Quinze souldartz la pluspart Ustagois,   hors-la-loi
Vie derniere & chef de sa chevance.   de son bien-fonds

> **The weak-willed one in garb of citizen**
> **Shall try the King with doings reprobate:**
> **Soldiers fifteen, most of them outlaws then.**
> **A final life as head of his estate.**

Source: Unidentified.

65. Original September 1557 text   Read as modern French:

Au deserteur de la grand forteresse,
Apres qu'aura son lieu abandonné:
Son adversaire fera si grand prouesse,
L'Empereur tost mort sera condemné.   *Par l'Empereur [?]*

> Against th' deserter of the mighty fort,
> After he shall have given it up to them,
> His foe shall fight with prowess of such sort,
> That th' Emperor to death him shall condemn.

Source: Unknown, but probably (in view of the use of the term 'Emperor') an incident in the recent history of the Holy Roman Empire.

66. Original September 1557 text   Read as modern French:

Soubz couleur faincte de sept testes rasees
Seront semés divers explorateurs: *espions*
Puys & fontaines de poyson arrousees,
Au fort de Gennes humains devorateurs.

> Various spies, disguised from toe to top,
> Shall be sent forth by seven with shaven pates.
> In wells and fountains they shall poison drop:
> Man shall eat man within Genoa's gates.

Source: Unknown siege-account, presumably referring to the *Mirabilis Liber*'s predicted Arab invasion of Europe (see I.9, I.75, II.24) or the later counter-invasion (see I.55).

67. Original September 1557 text   Read as modern French:

L'an que Saturne & Mars esgaulx combust,   *à proximité égale du soleil*
L'air fort seiché, longue trajection:
Par feux secretz, d'ardenr grand lieu adust,   *d'ardeur/de flammes; brûlé*
Peu pluye, vent chault, guerres, incursions.

> The year Saturn and Mars near th' sun shall burn,
> Th' air dry, a long-tailed meteor shall pass o'er.
> To ashes hidden fires great swathes shall turn.
> Scarce rain, hot winds there'll be, and raids and war.

Source: The conjunction of Mars and Saturn in Aries close to the sun of mid-March 1556, the comet of the same spring and the severe heat and drought of the following summer, all well-attested in annals of the time,[8] possibly amplified with the aid of François de Guise's expedition to conquer Naples in May of 1557, Mary of England's declaration of war on France in June, and the Imperial general

Emmanuel Philibert of Savoy's devastating attack on St-Quentin in August, or at least the preparations for it; the events, in other words, were almost contemporaneous with the writing of the verse.

68. Original September 1557 text   Read as modern French:

En l'an bien proche non esloigné de Venus,   *de Venise*
Les deux plus grans le l'Asie & d'Affrique   *de l'Asie Mineure et de l'Afrique du nord*
Du Ryn & hister qu'on dira sont venus,
Crys, pleurs à Malte & coste ligustique.   *et sur la côte ligurienne [la Riviera]*

> **From Venice (some year soon) not far away,**
> **Shall Turkish and North Afric heads and hosts**
> **Meet those from Rhine and Danube, as they say.**
> **In Malta tears; screams on Ligurian coasts.**

Source: The *Mirabilis Liber*'s prophecies of a bloody invasion of Europe from the Middle East and North Africa via the Mediterranean islands and Italy, as already outlined at I.9, I.75, II.24, with a backward glance at the former Roman Empire's traditional definition of its north-eastern frontier against the barbarian invaders in terms of the Rhine and the Danube (the latter being the meaning of the name *Hister*, as Nostradamus himself explains in his almanac for 1554).

69. Original September 1557 text   Read as modern French:

La cité grande les exilés tiendront,
Les citadins mors, meurtris, & chassés: *Meurtris; ou*
Ceulx d'Aquilee à Parme promettront,
Monstrer l'entree par les lieux non trassés   *tracés*

> **The mighty town holds many a refugee,**
> **The townsfolk dead, dying, wounded or in flight.**
> **With Parma Aquileians then agree**
> **To guide them in by trackways out of sight.**

Source: Unidentified incident from the contemporary Italian wars.

70. Original September 1557 text   Read as modern French:

Bien contigue des grans monts Pyrenees,
Un contre l'aigle grand copie adresser: *dressera*
Ouvertes veines, forces exterminees,   *veines*
Que jusque à Pau le chef viendra chasser.

> **The mighty Pyrenees quite close about**
> **Shall one his army 'gainst the Eagle throw.**
> **He'll ope their veins, their forces all wipe out,**
> **And shall pursue their chief as far as Pau.**

Source: Possibly Froissart's account in his *Chroniques* (Luce I:238–245) of the expedition into Spain of Edward the Black Prince in 1367, following the death of Alfonso XI of Castile in 1350 and the assumption of power by his illegitimate son known as Henry the Bastard – see III.54, III.80 – assimilated to the *Mirabilis Liber's* prediction of an eventual counter-invasion by the Western powers against Europe's future Arab invaders, as summarized at I.55 above. For the 'Eagle' reference – presumably to the contemporary Holy Roman Empire – see St Brigid's prophecies at III.52.

71. Original September 1557 text

Read as modern French:

En lieu d'espouse les filles trucidees,
Meurtre à grand faulte ne sera supestile:
Dedans le puys vestules inondees,
L'espouse estaincte par hauste d'Aconile.

survivante [superstite]
vierges [vestales] noyées
par une potion d'aconite

> **In place of wife, the daughters they shall kill:**
> **Yet this foul murder she shall not survive.**
> **The virgins they shall drown down in the well,**
> **Snuffed out by draft of aconite the wife.**

Source: Unknown episode of family murder.

72. Original September 1557 text

Read as modern French:

Les Artoniques par Agen & l'Estore,
A sainct Felix feront leur parlement:
Ceulx de Basas viendront à la mal'heure,
Saisir Condon & Marsan promptement.

Arécomiques [peuple de la Narbonnaise]

> **Through Agen and Lectoure shall Narbonne's men**
> **At St-Félix their parliament convoke.**
> **Those from Bazas at the wrong time shall then**
> **Take both Condom and Marsan at a stroke.**

Source: An unidentified historical conflict in the south-west of France, possibly connected with the thirteenth-century Albigensian crusade.

73. Original September 1557 text

Read as modern French:

Le nepveu grand par forces prouvera,
Le pache faict du cœur pusillanime:
Ferrare & Ast le Duc esprouvera,
Par lors qu'au soir sera le pantomime.

Le pacte

> **The noble nephew to the proof shall put**
> **The pact agreed with heart so faint and wan:**

The Duke shall feel Asti's, Ferrara's foot
One evening when the pantomime is on.

Source: Possibly Suetonius's *Twelve Caesars* (Augustus, 45): 'At the request of the praetor, he had a pantomimer [comedian] called Hylas publicly flogged in the hall of his own residence', related to political and military conflicts between the contemporary Italian city states.

74. Original September 1557 text   Read as modern French:

Du lac lyman & ceulx de Brannonices,
Tous assemblez contre ceulx d'Aquitaine
Germains beaucoup encor plus Souisses,   *et encore*
Seront deffaictz avec ceulx d'Humaine.   *[avecques]; de Maine*

From Lake Geneva and the Eure and Sarthe
Shall all united be 'gainst Aquitaine.
Germans galore, and more Swiss, shall take part:
They'll beaten be, along with those from Maine.

Source: The contemporary religious conflicts between the Protestants of northern France, Switzerland, and Germany and the surviving Catholics of southern and western France.

75. Original September 1557 text   Read as modern French:

Prest a combatre fera defection,
Chef adversaire obtiendra la victoire:
Larriere garde fera defention,   *L'arrière-garde; défense*
Les deffaillans mort au blanc territoire.   *morts*

As battle's set to join, he shall defect:
Th' opposing chief the victory shall gain.
The rearguard shall resist to some effect,
The weak ones dead in no-man's-land remain.

Source: Once again the catastrophic defeat of King François I – and the slaying of the cream of French chivalry – at the Battle of Pavia in 1525, betrayed by the sudden withdrawal from the battle of his brother-in-law the Duke of Alençon who commanded the rearguard, possibly assimilated to the expected French defeat in the course of the *Mirabilis Liber*'s predicted Arab invasion of Europe via Italy. See I.9, I.75. Compare IV.22, IV.45.

76. Original September 1557 text   **Read as modern French:**

Les Nictobriges par ceulx de Perigort,   *Les Agenois*
Seront vexez tenant jusques au Rosne:
Lassotie de Gascons & Begorn,   *L'associé*
Trahir le temple, le prebstre estant au prosne.

> **The Agenais by those from Perigord**
> **Shall harried be as far as th' river Rhône.**
> **A henchman of the Gascons and Bigorre**
> **Betrays the church ere yet the sermon's done.**

Source: Evidently one of the interminable contemporary religious conflicts in the south-west of France.

77. Original September 1557 text   **Read as modern French:**

SELIN monarque l'Italie pacifique,   *Le monarque à bannière lunaire [Henri II]*
Regnes unis Roy chrestien du monde:
Mourant vouldra coucher en terre blesique   *blésoise*
Apres pyrates avoir chasse de l'onde.   *chassés de la mer*

> **Lunar the Monarch, Italy at peace,**
> **This Christian king a world at one shall rule.**
> **At Blois he would repose on his decease,**
> **Once having freed the seas from pirates cruel.**

Source: The *Mirabilis Liber*'s confident forecast of an eventual triumphant re-invasion of the Middle East by Western Christendom (see I.55) under a future French *Grand Monarque* (see I.4, I.55, I.92), here apparently identified with the contemporary Henri II and his lunar banner.

78. Original September 1557 text   **Read as modern French:**

La grand armee de la pugne civille,
Pour de nuict Parme à l'estrange trouvee   *à l'étranger*
Septante neuf meurtris dedans la ville,
Les estrangiers passez tous à l'espee.

> **The mighty army in the civil strife**
> **Found around Parma in the night abroad:**
> **Within shall seventy-nine soon lose their life,**
> **The foreigners be all put to the sword.**

Source: More reports of the various contemporary wars in Italy.

79. Original September 1557 text   **Read as modern French:**

Sang Royal fuis Monthurt, Mas, Eguillon,   *Aiguillon*
Remplis seront de Bourdelois les landes,
Navarre, Bygorre, poinctes & eguillons,   *aiguillons*
Profondz de faim vorer de liege glandes.   *ils dévoreront*

Flee Aiguillon, Mas, Montheurt, royal kin!
The Landes shall be with Bordelais replete,
Navarre, Bigorre with swords and spurs, so thin
And famished that cork acorns they shall eat.

Source: Yet again the various contemporary conflicts in the south-west of France.

80. Original September 1557 text   **Read as modern French:**

Pres du grand fleuve grand fosse terre egeste,   *par conduit/canalisation; arrosée*
En quinze pars sera l'eau divisee:
La cité prinse, feu, sang, crys, conflict mestre,   *un conflit y sera infligé [mettre]*
Et la plus part concerne au collisee.   *dans l'amphithéatre/aux arènes*

Great river near, great conduit feeds the land:
In fifteen parts the water is split up.
The city taken, fire, blood, screams at hand:
Most in the ancient theatre are holed up.

Source: More contemporary fighting, this time in southern France around Nîmes, whose mighty Pont du Gard aqueduct[P] and amphitheatre[P] are well described; presumably assimilated to the *Mirabilis Liber*'s prophecy of a huge Muslim invasion of the area (see I.9, I.75, II.24). The local amphitheater was traditionally used as a refuge by the citizens in times of crisis (compare X.6). The aqueduct's distribution-point, however, high on the hill to the north-west, and close to the ancient *Tour Magne* dating from pre-Roman times, in fact had ten, not fifteen leaden exit-pipes.[P]

81. Original September 1557 text   **Read as modern French:**

Pont on fera promptement de nacelles,
Passer l'armee du grand prince Belgique:
Dans profondrés & non loing de Brucelles,   *Sombrés dedans*
Oultre passés detrenchés sept à picque.   *Au-delà; tranchés en morceaux*

A pontoon-bridge they'll make, in haste withal
To bear the army of the Belgian prince:
Not far from Brussels city, in they'll fall,
Save seven whom, once across, they'll promptly mince.

Source: Presumably an incident in the contemporary wars between France and the

Holy Roman Empire: an attempted Imperial crossing of the Scheldt seems to be indicated.

82. Original September 1557 text   Read as modern French:

Amas s'approche venant d'Esclavonie,
L'Olestant vieulx cité ruynera: *Le destructeur ancien*
Fort desolee verra la Romanie,
Puis la grand flamme estaindre ne scaura.

> **Out of Slavonia the horde draws nigh:**
> **The Old Destroyer shall destroy the city.**
> **A desolate Roman Empire he'll espy,**
> **Nor know the flames t'extinguish, more's the pity.**

Source: The *Mirabilis Liber*'s warning of a massive Muslim invasion of Europe culminating in the destruction of Rome, in this case assimilated to the contemporary invasion of the Balkans by the Ottomans. See I.9, I.75, II.24, and particularly 'These [i.e. the Arabs] shall, however, renew their enterprise, they shall destroy the land, shall invade the globe from the East unto the West, from the South to the North, as far as Rome' (Prophecy of Pseudo-Methodius); 'The children of Agar shall seize Tarento, and spreading through Apulia, shall sack a host of towns. They shall be determined to enter Rome, and nobody in the world shall be able to resist them, unless it be the Lord God himself. The Armenians, pursuing their depredations, shall advance from the East, shall fight the Romans, and shall achieve peace for a short time . . . The Romans shall be beaten, and the Roman city shall be destroyed. The earth shall be covered in ruins: never shall monarch have done such a thing. This city [i.e. Rome] shall be called Babylon; this kingdom shall be of iron, and Rome shall be prey to persecution and the sword' (Prophecy of the Tiburtine Sibyl); 'Rome and Florence shall perish, delivered by him into the flames' (Anonymous prophecy).

83. Original September 1557 text   Read as modern French:

Combat nocturne le vaillant capitaine,
Vaincu fuyra, peu de gens profligé:
Son peuple esmeu sedition non vaine,
Son propre filz le tiendra assiegé.

> **From night-combat the doughty captain then**
> **With casualties but few shall, beaten, flee.**
> **His folk stirred up by schemings far from vain,**
> **By his own son he shall besiegèd be.**

Source: A so-far unidentified incident from sixteenth-century French history – which should nevertheless not be too difficult to identify once the facts are unearthed.

84. Original September 1557 text   Read as modern French:

Un grand d'Auserre mourra bien miserable,
Chassé de ceulx qui soubz luy ont esté: *sous*
Serré de chaisnes, apres d'un rude cable,
En l'an que Mars, Venus, & Sol mis en esté   *été*

> A noble from Auxerre a wretch shall die,
> Hunted by those who were his underlings:
> In rough chains, then crude cable, they'll him tie,
> The year when summer Mars, Sun, Venus brings.

Source: Unidentified incident, linked to a frequently recurring astronomical conjunction, which is therefore not very helpful for pinning down the year in question.

85. Original September 1557 text   Read as modern French:

Le charbon blanc du noir sera chassé,
Prisonnier faict mené au tombereau:
More Chameau sus piedz entrelassez,   *maure; entrelacés*
Lors le puisné sillera l'auberau.   *cillera*

> The black plague follows on the white plague's heels,
> The captive's dragged in execution-cart.
> His legs the Moorish camel hobbled feels:
> The younger son the hawk shall hood apart.

Source: The events of 1546–7, when the 'pestilence of Naples' gave way to the Plague, Protestant heretics were being dragged to the stake, the Dauphin (the future Henri II) withdrew from Court quarrels with his dying father François I to devote himself to falconry, and François himself bequeathed to him (his younger son) a camel, a lion, and a panther that he had had brought from Africa in 1533. The camel was still there three years later, when Henri II and Catherine de Médicis made their ceremonial entry as King and Queen into Rouen.[60]

86. Original September 1557 text   Read as modern French:

L'an que Saturne en eaue sera conjoinct,
Avecques Sol, le Roy fort & puissant:
A Reims & Aix sera receu & oingt,
Apres conquestes meurtrira innocens.   *l'innocent*

> When sun in th' water-sign with Saturn makes
> Conjunction, is the mighty king and great
> Anointed and received at Reims and Aix:
> War won, the innocent he'll immolate.

Source: Apparently the coronation of Charles VIII of France in 1483 under Scorpio (a water-sign), cleverly projected into the future as a prophecy of the future *Grand Monarque* after the fashion of Charlemagne, in line with the *Mirabilis Liber* (see I.4, I.55, I.92). From 1486, when Provence was subsumed into France, French kings were routinely crowned not only at Reims, but at Aix-en-Provence too. The innocent who is murdered is presumably the Turkish prince Zimzim, who was poisoned in 1495 while held prisoner by Charles, following the latter's successful Italian campaign of 1494–5.[60]

87. Original September 1557 text   **Read as modern French:**

Un filz du Roy tant de langues aprins,   *ayant appris*
A son aisné au regne different: *son supérieur*
Son pere beau au plus grand filz comprins   *Son beau-père*
Fera perir principal adherant.

> A royal son who's learned so many a tongue,
> Shall o'er his senior in the realm excel:
> Yet father-in-law, urged by the greater son,
> Shall have his leading henchman killed pell-mell.

Source: Unknown.

88. Original September 1557 text   **Read as modern French:**

Le grand Antoine du nom de faict sordide
De Phthyriase à son dernier rongé: *phtyriase*
Un qui de plomb vouldra estre cupide,
Passant le port d'esleu sera plonge.   *sera déposé de sa poste déléguée*

> The great Antoine, who by that filthy thing,
> Phtyriasis, is eaten to the bone,
> Who to mere lead would covetousness bring,
> Th' appointed post shall lose, his refuge gone.

Source: The demise of Chancellor Antoine Duprat, Cardinal Archbishop of Sens and papal legate, suspected in 1530 of having debased and misappropriated gold from the huge ransom collected for handing over to the Empire for the release of François I. Duprat would die of phtyriasis (lice) and gangrene in 1535.

89. Original September 1557 text   **Read as modern French:**

Ttente de Londres secret conjureront,   *Trente*
Contre leur roy sur le pont l'entreprise: *sur la mer [lat. pontus]*
Luy, satalites la mort degousteront,   *Lui et ses acolytes: dégusteront*
Un Roy esleu blonde, natif de Frize.

Thirty from London secretly lay schemes
By sea to act against their king anointed.
He, his supporters death shall taste, it seems:
A Frieslander, a blond king is appointed.

Source: Presumably the death of Edmund Ironside and the accession to the English throne of King Canute of Denmark in 1016. See VI.41.

90. Original September 1557 text   Read as modern French:

Les deux copies aux murs ne pourront joindre
Dans cest instant trembler Milan, Ticin: cet; Pavie
Faim, soif, doubtance, si fort les viendra poindre,   doute
Chair, pain, ne vivres n'auront un seul boncin.   ni; [boucin] morceau

The walls shall both the armies keep apart:
Milan, Pavia shall trembling overcome.
Hunger, thirst, doubt shall pierce them to the heart.
No bread, no food: of rations not a crumb.

Source: Accounts of a contemporary siege in northern Italy, assimilated to the *Mirabilis Liber*'s prediction of a future Islamic invasion of Europe via that country. See I.9, I.75.

91. Original September 1557 text   Read as modern French:

Au duc Gaulois contraint battre au duelle,   en
La nef Mellele monech n'aprochera,   le navire de Mélille [Melilla]
Tort accusé, prison perpetuelle,
Son filz regner avant mort taschera.

The Gallic Duke is forced to fight a duel;
From Monaco Mellila's ship far plies:
Wrongly accused, condemned to life-long jail,
His son shall try to rule before he dies.

Source: Unknown.

92. Original September 1557 text   Read as modern French:

Teste tranchee du vaillant capitaine,
Sera gettée devant son adversaire:
Son corps pendu de sa classe à l'antenne,
Confus fuira par rames à vent contraire.

The valiant captain's head, split all asunder,
They shall before his adversary throw.

His body hanged his navy's yard-arm under,
Confused, 'gainst headwinds, it away shall row.

Source: Unidentified.

93. Original September 1557 text   Read as modern French:

Un serpent veu proche du lict royal,
Sera par dame nuict chiens n'abayeront: n'aboyeront pas
Lors naistra en France un prince tant royal,
Du ciel venu tous les princes verront.

Beside the royal bed a serpent's coil
Is seen by lady: that night no dog cries.
Then shall in France be born a prince so royal,
Heaven-sent, as every Prince shall realize.

Source: Plutarch's account in his *Parallel Lives* (Alexander, 2) of an omen preceding the birth of Alexander the Great: 'Moreover, a serpent was once seen lying beside the sleeping body of Olympias [Alexander's mother]'; assimilated to the *Mirabilis Liber*'s prediction of the coming of a future *Grand Monarque* to save France and all of Europe from its enemies (see I.4, I.55, I.92).

94. Original September 1557 text   Read as modern French:

Deux grans freres seront chassés d'Espaigne,
L'aisné vaincu soubz les monts Pyrenees:
Rougir mer, rosne, sang leman d'Alemaigne,   Rhône
Narbon, Bliterre, D'Agath. contaminees.   Narbonne, Béziers; d'Agde [gr. Agatha]

Two brothers out of Spain expelled shall be,
The elder vanquished 'neath the Pyrenees.
From Agde, Narbonne, Béziers; from Germany,
Léman infected; red the Rhône and seas.

Source: The *Mirabilis Liber*'s grim predictions of a huge Muslim invasion of Europe. See I.9, I.75, II.24. For the projected landing at Agde, see VIII.21.

95. Original September 1557 text   Read as modern French:

Le regne à deux laissé bien peu tiendront,
Trois ans sept mois passés feront la guerre
Les deux vestales contre rebeleront,   [terres] vassales [?]
Victor puis nay en Armonique terre.   en Bretagne [en Armorique terre]

Not long the realm bequeathed they'll rule, that pair.
After three years seven months at war they'll be

Till both the vassal lands revolt declare.
The younger'll win the war in Brittany.

Source: Charles V's division of his empire between his son Philip and his brother Ferdinand in 1555–6 – with two or three injudicious predictions thrown in for good measure!

96. Original September 1557 text   Read as modern French:

La soeur aisnee de l'isle Britannique,
Quinze ans devant le frere aura naissance:
Par son promis moyennant verrifique,   *vérification*
Succedera au regne de balance.

The elder sister of the British Isle
Fifteen years ere her brother'll have her birth:
Through her fiancé, if confirmed the while,
She shall succeed to Libra's realm on earth.

Source: Contemporary English dynastic politics, apparently referring (with a not untypical degree of confusion) to Queen Mary, Philip II of Spain (whom she had in fact married in 1554) and Mary's half-brother Edward (in fact born 21 years after her). Nostradamus evidently had no inkling that Mary, far from inheriting the 'Libran' kingdom of Spain, was about to die and be succeeded by Elizabeth, and so, inevitably, he projected an inaccurate picture into the future.

97. Original September 1557 text   Read as modern French:

L'an que Mercure, Mars, Venus retrograde,
Du grand Monarque la ligne ne faillir:
Esleu du peuple l'usitant pres de Gagdole,   *Lusitain; Gaddes [Cadiz] ou Almade [Almada]*
Qu'en paix & regne viendra fort envieillir.

Retrograde Venus, Mars and Mercury,
That year the great King's line shall sure not fail:
By Portuguese near Cadiz chosen, he
In peace and power to great age shall prevail.

Source: The birth in 1502 of John II of Portugal, who reigned for 36 years. Unfortunately, by the time Nostradamus was incautious enough to add the prediction in the last line, John had no more than a year or so to live, thus rather invalidating the prophecy's future application.

98. Original September 1557 text   Read as modern French:

Les Albanois passeront dedans Rome,
Moyennant Langres demiples affublés,   *à mi-drisse [?]*
Marquis & Duc ne pardonner à homme,
Feu, sang morbilles, point d'eau, faillir les bledz.

> Duke Alba's troops straight into Rome shall fare,
> In view of Langres at half-mast flags hung out:
> Marquis and Duke no living soul shall spare.
> Fire, smallpox, blood, crop-failures, widespread drought.

Source: More unidentified contemporary Italian regional squabbles.

99. Original September 1557 text   Read as modern French:

L'aisné vaillant de la fille du Roy,
Repoulsera si profond les Celtiques:
Qu'il mettra fouldres, combien en tel arroy
Peu & loing puis profond es Hesperiques   *dans l'Ouest/en Espagne*

> Of the king's 'daughter' valiant eldest son
> So far shall chase the fleeing Celts hard-pressed,
> That he'll send thunders flashing gun on gun
> First near, then far, deep into t' Spanish west.

Source: Once again Froissart's account in his *Chroniques* of the famous victories of Edward the Black Prince, grandson of Edward I of England and eldest son of the effeminate Edward II, first over the French – notably at Poitiers in 1356 (Luce I:158–165) – then over Henry of Trastámara, better known as Henry the Bastard, on behalf of the ousted Don Pedro the Cruel of Castile at the Battle of Navarette in 1367 (Luce I:238–241).

100. Original September 1557 text   Read as modern French:

De feu celeste au Royal edifice,
Quant la lumiere de Mars deffaillira:
Sept mois grand guerre, mort gent de malefice,
Rouan, Evreux au Roy ne faillira.

> Upon the palace fire falls from the sky
> When Mars's light dims, fades and grows more pale.
> Seven months, then grisly war, and folk shall die:
> But Rouen, Evreux the Monarch shall not fail.

Source: Julius Obsequens's *On Omens* (14) for 163 BC: 'There were a large number of lightning strikes on the Palatine Hill' (*in Palatio*, incorrectly taken by Nostradamus to mean 'on the palace'), combined with Richard Roussat's hint in his *Livre de l'estat et mutations des temps*[67] that the 'Age of Mars' allegedly just ended (in 1533, as per I.48) might be repeated again in the future (theoretically, in 3569), with calamitous consequences in terms of the *Mirabilis Liber*'s forecast of a massive Islamic invasion of Europe signaling the imminent End of the World. For the role of Rouen and Évreux in this, see V.84.

Century V

1. Original September 1557 text

Avant venue de ruïne Celtique,
Dedans le temple deux parlamenteront:
Poignard cueur, d'un monté au coursier & picque,
Sans faire bruit le grand enterreront.

Read as modern French:

chefs [ducs ?]
au coeur

> Before the ruin of the Celts shall start
> Shall chiefs inside the church talk head to head.
> Dagger shall one on charger stab in th' heart:
> Without a word the noble's burièd.

Source: A cloak-and-dagger incident from one of many contemporary conflicts, probably religious, presumably assimilated to the *Mirabilis Liber*'s forecast of an imminent Muslim invasion of Europe. See I.9, I.75, II.24.

2. Original September 1557 text

Sept conjurés au banquet feront luyre,
Contre les trois le fer hors de navire:
L'un les deux classes au grand fera conduire,
Quant par le mail Denier au front luy tire.

Read as modern French:

flottes/armées
Quand; pour un denier comptant [maille]

> Seven plotters while there at the feast the sword
> Shall draw against the three while they're ashore:
> One of two fleets to lead they'll give the lord
> When he'll be shot in th' head for pence, no more.

Source: Unknown incident, probably contemporary. This is the only verse containing a quadruple rhyme, though I have not attempted to reproduce it in English.

3. Original September 1557 text

Le successeur de la duché viendra,
Beaucoup plus oultre que la mer de Tosquane,
Gauloise branche la Florence tiendra,
Dans son giron d'accord nautique Rane.

Read as modern French:

plus loin [lat. plus ultra]

poisson de mer [lat. Rana marina]

173

The duchy's next successor shall head out
Far, far beyond the little Tuscan sea.
The Gallic branch within its lap, no doubt,
Shall Florence hold: the Sea-Fish shall agree.

Source: The maritime exploits of the Emperor Charles V, Duke of Burgundy (whose motto's expression *Plus ultra* Nostradamus could never resist playing with), and not least the extension of his empire to Central and South America. The 'sea-fish', 'frog-fish' or 'angler' looks to be the Ottoman pirate-admiral Barbarossa, who was actually welcomed by the French king François I as a temporary ally against Charles's forces in Italy during 1533. See III.90.

4. Original September 1557 text   **Read as modern French:**

Le gros mastin de cité deschassé,
Sera fasché de l'estrange alliance.
Apres aux champs avoir le cerf chassé,
Le loup & l'Ours se donront deffiance.

The mighty Hound out of the city chased
Shall angered be th' alliance foreign by:
Then after they the Stag in fields have chased
The Wolf and Bear each other shall defy.

Source: The expulsion of Pandolfo Malatesta, the Tyrant of Rimini who was known as the 'Great Hound', by Pope Clement VII in 1528.[60] The *gros mâtin* was traditionally the three-headed Cerberus, guardian of the underworld. The other symbolic animals in this verse seem to refer merely to the various factions in a contemporary war, apparently in imitation of the Prophecies of St Brigid in the *Mirabilis Liber*.

5. Original September 1557 text   **Read as modern French:**

Soubz umbre faincte d'oster de servitude,
Peuple & cité, l'usurpera luy mesmes: lui-même
Pire fera par fraulx de jeune pute,
Livré au champ lisant le faulx proesme.   la fausse introduction

'Neath vain pretense to save from serfdom sore
City and folk, himself shall it decree:
Worse he shall do than e'en the falsest whore,
Run out of town for false publicity.

Source: Another episode from contemporary politics, probably in Italy, unidentifiable because applicable to innumerable power-hungry politicians throughout the ages!

6. Original September 1557 text

Read as modern French:

Au roy l'Augur sus le chef la main mettre.   *sur la tête*
Viendra prier pour la paix Italique:
A la main gauche viendra changer le sceptre
De Roy viendra Empereur pacifique.

> **On the king's head laying his priestly hand,**
> **The augur'll pray for peace in Italy.**
> **The scepter changing then to his left hand,**
> **From King an Emperor of peace he'll be.**

Source: A garbled version of Livy's account in his *History of Rome* (I.18) of the coronation of the semi-legendary King Numa in around 710 BC, presumably assimilated to the *Mirabilis Liber*'s prediction of the eventual liberation of Europe by a glorious young future king of France (see I.4, I.55, I.92): 'Then, having been led by an augur to the citadel, [Numa] sat down on a stone facing southwards. The augur sat on his left with his head covered, holding in his right hand the crooked staff without knots that they call the *lituus*. Then, glancing out over the city and the country beyond, he prayed to the gods . . . Then, having transferred the staff to his left hand, and having placed his right upon Numa's head, he prayed thus: "Father Jupiter, if it be Heaven's will that this man, Numa Pompilius, whose head I am holding, should reign over Rome, give us clear and certain signs . . .".' Compare II.99, V.75.

7. Original September 1557 text

Read as modern French:

Du Triumvir seront trouvez les os,
Cherchant profond tresor aenigmatique,
Ceulx d'alentour ne seront en repos,
De concaver mabre & plomb metalique.   *D'excaver*

> **The bones of the Triumvir shall be found**
> **While seeking buried treasure most mysterious:**
> **The peace shall be disturbed of those around,**
> **Digging out lead-and-marble vaults imperious.**

Source: Contemporary excavations of the ancient Gallo-Roman *oppidum* of Constantine, near Lançon, just south of Salon. A note of a consultation with Nostradamus on the topic was recorded by the humanist Nicolas Fabri de Peiresc: 'At the time of Mark Antony... [the crack in the rock] was filled up precisely because of the chasm, and the re-excavators shall be assured of finding the said bones of the head of the Triumvirate. People in the past have searched for treasure there and found marble and metallic lead under the white clay that supports the rock...'[63] See I.21.

8. Original September 1557 text   Read as modern French:

Sera laissé le feu vif, mort caché,
Dedans les globes horrible espouventable   *foules/amas [de corps]*
De nuict à classe cité en pouldre lasché,   *le fait attribué à l'armée/à la flotte*
La cité à feu l'ennemy favorable.

> The lately living are hid, dead, away
> In heaps galore: a horror, dread to know:
> By night reduced to ash by troops, they say,
> Th' burnt city shall support the former foe.

Source: An unidentified vengeance-attack on a renegade city (probably contemporary), with full play made with the dual meanings of *feu* ('fire'/'late') and *cité* ('city'/'cited').

9. Original September 1557 text   Read as modern French:

Jusques aux fondz la grand arq demolue,   *la grande prison*
Par chef captif l'amy anticipé:
Naistra de dame front face chevelue,   *visage*
Lors par astuce duc à mort attrape.   *attrapé*

> The mighty prison to the ground they'll raze,
> By captive chief his friend anticipated.
> Of dame child born with hair on brow and face:
> Then shall the duke be tricked, trapped, extirpated.

Source: Another contemporary politico-military incident, with a contemporary omen thrown in for good measure.

10. Original September 1557 text   Read as modern French:

Un chef Celtique dans le conflict blessé,
Aupres de cave voyant siens mort abatre:
De sang & playes & d'ennemis pressé,
Et secourus par incognuz de quatre.

> A Celtic chief who's wounded in the war,
> Seeing his folk dead near the vault struck down
> Shall be hard-pressed by foes and wounds and gore
> And saved by four who to him are unknown.

Source: Unidentified.

11. Original September 1557 text   **Read as modern French:**

Mer par Solaires seure ne passera,   *par les chrétiens; en sécurité; ne sera pas passée*
Ceulx de Venus tiendront toute l'Affrique: *Les Musulmans; l'Afrique du Nord*
Leur regne plus Sol, Saturne n'occupera,   *les chrétiens et les Juifs*
Et changera la part Asiatique.   *abîmera; l'Asie Mineure/le moyen orient*

> **No longer sure shall Christians cross the main,**
> **North Africa shall Islam hold in fee,**
> **Nor Jew nor Christian in their realm remain,**
> **And Asia Minor sorely changed shall be.**

Source: The contemporary world inter-religious situation, identified with the *Mirabilis Liber*'s predictions for the run-up to the coming Islamic invasion of Europe. See I.9, I.75, II.24.

12. Original September 1557 text   **Read as modern French:**

Aupres du lac Leman sera conduite,
Par garse estrange cité voulant trahir:
Avant son meurtre à Auspurg la grand fuitte   *Augsbourg*
Et ceulx du Ryn la viendront invahir.   *là*

> **Beside Geneva's lake she shall be led**
> **By foreign girl who'd have the town betrayed:**
> **Before her murder all to Augsburg fled,**
> **And from the Rhineland shall they it invade.**

Source: The religious conflicts between the Calvinists based in Geneva and other sects, made unidentifiable here by a grand confusion of pronouns.

13. Original September 1557 text   **Read as modern French:**

Par grand fureur le roy Romain Belgique,
Vexer vouldra par phalange barbare:
Fureur grinsseant chassera gent lybique,
Despuis Pannons jusques Hercules la hare.   *la Hongrie; Gibraltar; la chasse*

> **The Roman Belgian king in fury black**
> **Shall wish to harry the Barbarian host:**
> **With fury grim he'll chase the Libyans back**
> **From Hungary to stern Gibraltar's coast.**

Source: The recent military campaigns of the Holy Roman Emperor Charles V (who was born at Ghent in East Flanders) to repulse the invading Ottomans, assimilated to the *Mirabilis Liber*'s prophecy of the eventual liberation of Europe from its future Arab invaders (see I.9, I.75, II.24) by a future *Grand Monarque* (see I.4, I.55, I.92).

14. Original September 1557 text   Read as modern French:

Saturne & Mars en leo Espaigne captifve,
Par chef lybique au conflict attrapé:
Proche de Malthe, Heredde prinse vive,   *héritière [lat. heres?]/ [Don Juan] de Heredia[8] [?]*
Et Romain sceptre sera par coq frappé.   *par la France*

> **Saturn and Mars in Leo, captive Spain.**
> **Trapped by the Libyan chief in time of war,**
> **Near Malta shall Heredia live be ta'en**
> **While Cock shall strike the Roman Empire sore.**

Source: The imprisonment at Trabzon of Don Juan de Heredia, head of the Knights Hospitallers, or Knights of St John of Jerusalem, after Suleiman the Magnificent captured Rhodes in 1522, following which the Order retired in the face of Ottoman pressure first to Crete and then (in 1530) to Malta – assimilated to the *Mirabilis Liber*'s prediction of Arab invasion. See I.9, I.75. The astrological configuration is for 1535–6 – as well as, looking ahead, for July 1564, when Mars and Saturn would be joined in Leo by Jupiter, Mercury, and the sun. This gives some idea of the immediacy that Nostradamus attached to the fulfillment of the prophecies regarding the expected Muslim threat.

15. Original September 1557 text   Read as modern French:

En navigant captif prins grand pontife,   *En Nef [la 'barque' de l'Église]; pris*
Grans apretz faillir les clercz tumultuez:
Second esleu absent son bien debife,
Son favory bastard à mort tue.   *tué*

> **The Pope's made captive whilst abroad a-wander.**
> **Arrangements fail: priests, outraged, waste their breath.**
> **Absent, the next-elected's wealth he'll squander,**
> **His bastard favorite be done to death.**

Source: The sack of Rome by Imperial forces in May 1527, with Pope Clement VII fleeing the Vatican to become a virtual prisoner in the Castel Sant' Angelo until December, assimilated to the *Mirabilis Liber*'s prophecy of the flight of the Pope from Rome in the face of its expected Muslim invasion, augmented with a few details taken from the unedifying story of the contemporary papacy: 'The barque of Peter is the Roman Church . . . Peter shall doubt so much that God shall not have appeared; and the pastors shall be amidst affliction until the Lord has spoken' (Prophecy of Joachim of Fiore); '. . . and then the barque of Peter, attacked by powerful enemies, shall be shaken. Terrified, Peter shall be forced to flee, in order not to incur the infamy of servitude' (Prophecy of St Brigid of Sweden). The second pope mentioned is evidently Clement's successor, the vastly self-indulgent and nepotistic Paul III, who had reigned from 1534 to 1549.

16. Original September 1557 text

Read as modern French:

A son hault pris plus la lerme sabee,   *l'encens mâle*
D'humaine chair par mort en cendre mettre,
A l'isle Pharos par croisars perturbee,   *Paros [?]*
Alors qu'a Rodes paroistra dur espectre.   *à Rhodes*

The price of frankincense shall all but double
For embalming human flesh when it has died:
Crusaders shall the Isle of Paros trouble,
While there at Rhodes a grisly sight's espied.

Source: The grisly Turkish assault mounted on Rhodes from 1522, assimilated to the Muslim assault on Europe via the Mediterranean islands predicted by the *Mirabilis Liber.* See I.9, I.75, II.24. Frankincense was obtained exclusively from Ottoman-controlled Somalia and southern Arabia, though Nostradamus may be confusing it with myrrh.

17. Original September 1557 text

Read as modern French:

De nuict passant le roy pres d'une Andronne,
Celuy de Cipres & principal guette: *Chypre; le guette*
Le roy failli, [/] la main fuict long du Rosne   *l'armée s'empresse*
Les conjurés l'iront à mort mettre.

As he pursues by night a narrow track,
The king the princely Cypriot shall spy.
King fallen, down the Rhône the soldiers fly:
The plotters then shall kill him in th' attack.

Source: Unknown.

18. Original September 1557 text

Read as modern French:

De dueil mourra l'infelix proflige,
Celebrera son vitrix l'heccatombe: *sa conquérante; les obsèques*
Pristine loy [/] franc edict redigé,
Le mur & Prince au septiesme jour tombe.

The wretch laid low, out of sheer grief he'll die:
His conqueress shall celebrate his fall.
A brand-new law drawn up, and edict high,
The seventh day shall fall both Prince and wall.

Source: Unidentified.

19. Original September 1557 text　　　Read as modern French:

Le grand Royal d'or, d'aerain augmenté,
Rompu la pache, par jeune ouverte guerre:　　*la trève*
Peuple affligé par un chef lamenté,
De sang barbare sera couverte terre.

> **Royals of gold with bronze debased galore,**
> **Broken the truce, to war the youth shall go.**
> **By chief lamented folk afflicted sore:**
> **With Muslim blood the earth again shall flow.**

Source: The *Mirabilis Liber*'s prediction of a glorious young *Grand Monarque* who will finally expel the future Muslim occupiers of Europe, with current concerns about the debasement of the currency thrown in for good measure. See I.4, I.55, I.92.

20. Original September 1557 text　　　Read as modern French:

Dela les Alpes grand armee passera,　　　*Au-delà des Alpes*
Un peu devant naistra monstre vapin:　　　*avant; rapineur [rapin]*
Prodigieux & subit tornera,
Le grand Tosquan à son lieu plus propin.　　*proche/chez lui*

> **A mighty army o'er the Alps shall climb**
> **Shortly before a greedy monster's born:**
> **Suddenly, miraculously he'll turn,**
> **That mighty Tuscan, back to his native clime.**

Source: The expulsion of the Medici from Florence in 1512 by the French under Gaston de Foix, Duke of Nemours, shortly before the alleged discovery of the famous Ravenna monster of 1513 (see II.32, and note especially the phrase in the contemporary chronicle of Joannes Multivallis: 'In its horns, pride was evident, in its wings fickleness, greed, usury and all forms of avarice . . .').

21. Original September 1557 text　　　Read as modern French:

Par le trespas du monarque latin,
Ceulx qu'il aura par regne secouruz:
Le feu luyra, divisé le butin,
La mort publique aux hardis incoruz.　　　*incorrompus*

> **Upon the Roman monarch's death, to those**
> **For whom throughout the realm he aid provided**
> **'Midst burning fires the plunder is divided.**
> **To public death each honest, brave man goes.**

Source: Events surrounding the death of almost any Roman emperor, as reported by Livy or Suetonius.

22. Original September 1557 text   **Read as modern French:**

Avant qu'a Rome grand aye rendu l'ame   *ait*
Effrayeur grande à l'armée estrangiere:
Par Esquadrons, l'embusche pres de Parme,
Puis les deux roges ensemble feront chere.   *rouges*

> **Before the lord of Rome gives up the ghost**
> **Terror shall reign among the foreign host.**
> **Squadrons at Parma'll set an ambush up,**
> **Then the two red ones shall together sup.**

Source: Military and political developments involving two cardinals, marking the imminent death of an unidentified pope.

23. Original September 1557 text   **Read as modern French:**

Les deux contens seront unis ensemble,   *contentieux [lat. contendere]*
Quant la pluspart à Mars seront conjoinct:
Le grand d'Affrique en effraieur & tremble,   *de l'Afrique du Nord*
DUUMVIRAT par la classe desjoinct.   *par la flotte/armée divisé*

> **The rivals twain as one shall be united**
> **When most of th' planets are with Mars conjoined:**
> **The Afric lord shall tremble, sore affrighted,**
> **When the duumvirate by sea's disjoined.**

Source: The brief alliance struck up between François I and the Emperor Charles V in 1538, marked by a conjunction of Mars, Jupiter, Venus, and Mercury in Cancer during July 1539, and discontinued at around the time of the projected Spanish naval expedition against Algiers of 1541;[60] possibly assimilated to the *Mirabilis Liber*'s prophecy of a coming Arab invasion of Europe (see I.9, I.75, II.24) – a two-pronged one from North Africa and from the Middle East, as Nostradamus sees it – and the counter-invasion that eventually is set to throw it back again (see I.55).

24. Original September 1557 text   **Read as modern French:**

Le regne & loy soubz Venus eslevé,   *sous l'Islam*
Saturne aura sus Jupiter empire: *les Juifs; sur les jovialistes [les princes et le clergé]*
La loy & regne par le Soleil levé,   *par la chrétienté*
Par Saturnins endurera le pire.   *par les Juifs*

> **When power and law 'neath Islam are exalted**
> **The Jews o'er prince and clergy shall hold sway:**
> **When law and power by Christians are exalted,**
> **Through Jews they shall endure the worst, they say.**

Source: Unknown, but the sense seems to be garbled: Nostradamus is evidently making a contrast (as he often does) between the first half of the verse and the second, which suggests that the last line should really read *Les Saturnins endureront le pire*, or

The Jews shall then endure the worst, they say.

The contrast, in other words, (duly projected into the future) seems to be between the relatively tolerant attitude of former Arab rulers towards the Jews, especially in Moorish Spain, and the intolerance of Christian rulers from which Nostradamus's own family had no doubt suffered in the past.

25. Original September 1557 text   **Read as modern French:**

Le prince Arabe, Mars, Sol, Venus, Lyon,   *au Lion*
Regne d'Eglise par mer succombera:
Devers la Perse bien pres d'un million,   *De vers [?]*
Bisance, Egipte ver. serp. invadera.   *le serpent lové [lat. serpens versus]*

> **Mars, Venus, sun in Leo: to Arab Khan**
> **The Church's kingdom shall by sea succumb.**
> **Some million men from over by Iran –**
> **To Nile, Byzantium shall the coiled snake come.**

Source: The *Mirabilis Liber*'s description of a coming invasion of Europe by Arab forces from the Middle East via the Mediterranean (see I.9, I.75), coupled with Virgil's description, in his *Aeneid* (XI.753), of a serpent (*serpens*) that twists and turns (*versat*) as it is snatched up by an eagle:

> Yet doth the wounded serpent twist its coils
> Abundantly, bristling with scales erect,
> And hissing as it rears its angry head.

The astrology, as in V.14 above, is for 1535–6, as well as, looking ahead, for July 1564, when Mars and Saturn would be joined in Leo by Jupiter – another possible indication of the imminence that Nostradamus attaches to the projected invasion.

26. Original September 1557 text   **Read as modern French:**

La gent esclave par un heur martial,
Viendra en hault degré tant eslevee:
Changeront prince, naistre un provincial,
Passer la mer copie aux monts levee.   *armée*

> **By warlike fortune shall the slavish race**
> **Become raised up to such a high degree.**
> **One rustic-born their monarch shall replace.**
> **His army, mountain-raised, shall cross the sea.**

Source: Possibly the *Mirabilis Liber*'s prediction of an eventual Arab invasion of Europe via the Mediterranean, in this case conceivably from the area of the Atlas Mountains. See I.9, I.75, II.24.

27. Original September 1557 text   **Read as modern French:**

Par feu & armes non loing de la marnegro,   *de la Mer Noire*
Viendra de Perse occuper Trebisonde: *Trabzon*
Trembler Phatos Methelin, Sol alegro,   *Paros; Mitilène; les Solaires [chrétiens] joyeux*
De sang Arabe d'Adrie couvert unde.   *l'eau*

> **Near the Black Sea, by fire and weapons gained,**
> **Soon Persia's town of Trebizond he'll take.**
> **Christians rejoice, Paros and Lesbos quake:**
> **With Arab blood the Adriatic's stained.**

Source: The *Mirabilis Liber*'s prophecy of a massive eventual counter-invasion by the Western powers of the Muslim heartlands in the Middle East (see I.55) by a future *Grand Monarque* of France (see I.4, I.92). Compare VII.36 below.

28. Original September 1557 text   **Read as modern French:**

Le bras pendu & la jambe liee,
Visaige pasle au seing poignard caché: *pâle; au sein; plongé [?]*
Trois qui seront jurés de la meslee,
Au grand de Gennes sera le fer lasché.

> **Hung by the arms, and hobbled with a thong,**
> **Their faces pale, daggers in breasts concealed,**
> **Because three sworn to act by milling throng**
> **The sword against Genoa's lord did wield.**

Source: Another obscure incident drawn from the recent history of local Italian political conflict.

29. Original September 1557 text   **Read as modern French:**

La liberté ne sera recouvree,
L'occupera noir fier vilain inique:
Quant la matiere du pont sera ouvree,
D'Hister, Venise fachee la republique.   *du Danube*

> **Freedom shall not recovered be, the whiles**
> **The proud, black, evil villain's in possession:**
> **When the bridge-question occupies their session**
> **O'er Danube, this the state of Venice riles.**

Source: The contemporary advance of the Ottomans into the Balkans and Hungary, assimilated to the *Mirabilis Liber*'s expected Muslim invasion of Europe. See I.9, I.75, II.24.

30. Original September 1557 text   **Read as modern French:**

Tout à l'entour de la grande cité,
Seront soldartz logés par champs & ville:
Donner l'assault Paris, Rome incité,   *par Rome*
Sur le pont lors sera faicte grand pille.   *par mer [lat. pontus]*

> **All round the mighty city there shall roam**
> **Troops billeted in every field and town**
> **Urged on to strike at Paris and at Rome.**
> **Upon the sea great pillage shall abound.**

Source: The *Mirabilis Liber's* anticipated invasion of Italy and France by Arab forces via the Mediterranean. See I.9, I.75.

31. Original September 1557 text   **Read as modern French:**

Par terre Attique chef de la sapience,   *de la sagesse/de la science*
Qui de present est la rose du monde:
Pont ruyné & sa grand preeminence,   *Par mer [lat. pontus]*
Sera subditte & naufragé des undes.   *submergée*

> **That Attic land, foremost in wisdom's lore,**
> **Which still remains the rose-bloom of the world,**
> **The sea shall ruin, tumbled its fame of yore,**
> **By waves sucked down and to destruction hurled.**

Source: The *Mirabilis Liber's* forecast of worldwide floods in the run-up to the end of the world. See I.69.

32. Original September 1557 text   **Read as modern French:**

Ou tout bon est, tout bien Soleil & lune,   *en or et en argent*
Est abondant sa ruyne s'approche:
Du ciel s'advance vaner ta fortune,   *vanner/disperser*
En mesme estat que la septiesme roche.   *que la pierre alchimique de la septième planète*
                                                  [?]

> **Where bonds abound, and gold and silver are**
> **Richly abundant, comes wealth's ruin near.**
> **To waste your fortune comes a distant star:**
> **Like the seventh rock – like lead – it shall appear.**

Source: Directly or indirectly (the explanatory phrase 'like lead', relating to contemporary alchemy, is mine), Matthew 6:19: 'Do not store up for yourselves treasure on earth . . .', taken as a warning of economic disaster in the run-up to the supposedly imminent end of the world.

33. Original September 1557 text   **Read as modern French:**

Des principaulx de cité rebellee,   *rebelle/en rébellion*
Qui tiendront fort pour liberté ravoir: *recouvrir*
Detrencher masles infelice meslee,
Crys urlemens à Nantes piteux voir.

> **Among the city's chiefs that shall rebel,**
> **Their freedom to recover holding fast,**
> **The stern the wretched mob shall cut down, fell.**
> **Shouts, screams at Nantes: one can but be aghast.**

Source: Unidentified historical incident in Brittany.

34. Original September 1557 text   **Read as modern French:**

Du plus profond de l'occident Anglois,
Ou est le chef de l'isle britannique:
Entrera classe dans Gyronde par Blois,   *une flotte; pour*
Par vin & sel, feuz cachés aux barriques. *Pour [au lieu de]*

> **From England and from out the furthest west**
> **Where of the British Isle the chief's residing**
> **Ships shall Gironde invade at Blois's behest,**
> **Dread fire, not wine or salt, in barrels hiding.**

Source: Presumably an incident from the Hundred Years' War, when the English held much of western France, as recounted by Froissart in his *Chronicles*.

35. Original September 1557 text   **Read as modern French:**

Par cité franche de la grand mer Seline,   *saline [?]*
Qui porte encores à l'estomach la pierre:
Angloise classe viendra soubz la bruine,
Un rameau prendre [/] du grand ouverte guerre. *rameau de palmier [voir I.30]*

> **Off the free city of the salty ocean**
> **Which at its heart still bears of 'Rock' the name,**
> **Shall English ships inward through drizzle aim**
> **To seize the palm: the lord sets war in motion.**

Source: Another incident from Froissart's *Chronicles* (Luce II:1–11), in which the Earl of Pembroke's returning fleet was defeated by a Spanish fleet summoned by the King of France on 23 June 1372 as it approached what in Nostradamus's day was the 'free city' of La Rochelle (a name which of course has the word *roche* at its heart).

36. Original September 1557 text **Read as modern French:**

De soeur le frere par simulte faintise, *par déception*
Viendra mesler rosee en myneral:
Sur la placente donne à vieille tardifve, *Sur le gâteau; donné*
Meurt. le goustant sera simple & rural.

> His sister duping, shall her brother make
> Mixture of laurel rose in mineral:
> Given too late to crone upon a cake,
> She'll die. Some yokel they shall taster call.

Source: Totally unknown, but probably very local!

37. Original September 1557 text **Read as modern French:**

Trois cens feront d'un vouloir & accord,
Que pour venir au bout de leur attainte:
Vingtz moys apres tous & recordz, *en s'en souvenant tous*
Leur roy trahir simulant haine faincte.

> Three hundred of one mind and will shall be
> To bring their rising to its final end
> Twenty months later, by (as they agree)
> Their king betraying while they hate pretend.

Source: Once again unidentified.

38. Original September 1557 text **Read as modern French:**

Ce grand monarque qu'au mort succedera
Donnera vie illicite & lubrique:
Par nonchalance à tous concedera,
Qu'à la parfin fauldra la loy Salique.

> That mighty king, the dead duly succeeding,
> Shall live a life illicit and impure,
> And yet through nonchalance to all conceding
> That Salic law must in the end endure.

Source: Unknown, but French history offers several possible royal candidates, all under the power of the women around them, yet all deferring in practice to the Salic law's insistence that the succession could pass only through the male line.

39. Original September 1557 text   **Read as modern French:**

Du vray rameau de fleur de lys issu,   sorti
Mis & logé heritier d'Hetrurie:
Son sang antique de longue main tissu,
Fera Florence florir en l'armoirie.

> **Born of the true stock of the *fleur-de-lys*,**
> **Then set in place as heir to Tuscany,**
> **His ancient lineage wov'n on age-old loom,**
> **He'll see upon his crest fair Florence bloom.**

Source: King Henri II – whose queen, Catherine de Médicis, was the pre-eminent daughter of the ruling Medici of Florence – identified with the *Mirabilis Liber's* future *Grand Monarque*. See I.4, I.55, I.92.

40. Original September 1557 text   **Read as modern French:**

Le sang royal sera si tresmeslé,
Constraint seront Gaulois de l'Hesperie: Boutés!poussés; de l'Italie
On attendra que terme soit coulé,
Et que memoire de la voix soit perie.

> **The royal blood shall mingle with the dust,**
> **The French be forced to quit all Italy:**
> **Then the long wait until the time has passed**
> **And of his voice vanished all memory.**

Source: The catastrophic French defeat by Imperial forces at Pavia in 1525, the capture of King François I, and his subsequent near-fatal imprisonment in Madrid until March 1526.

41. Original September 1557 text   **Read as modern French:**

Nay soubz les umbres & jornee nocturne,
Sera en regne & bonté souveraine:
Fera renaistre son sang de l'antique urne,
Renouvelant siecle d'or pour l'aerain.

> **Born in the shadows where day never grew,**
> **With sovereign goodness he'll the scepter hold.**
> **From th' ancient source he shall his line renew,**
> **Replacing th' age of bronze with one of gold.**

Source: The *Mirabilis Liber's* predictions of a future French *Grand Monarque* who would go on to rule the world. See I.4, I.55, I.92.

42. Original September 1557 text   **Read as modern French:**

Mars eslevé en son plus hault beffroy,   *à son plus haut degré*
Fera retraire les Allobrox de France: *les gens de l'Est*
La gent Lombarde fera si grand effroy,
A ceux de l'Aigle comprins soubz la balance.   *À l'Empire*

> **Mars once ascended to his apogee**
> **Shall drive the Easterners from France again:**
> **Such fears they'll raise, shall those of Lombardy**
> **Where lands Imperial under Scales remain!**

Source: The *Mirabilis Liber*'s prophecy of the eventual liberation of France and Italy from their future Arab occupiers. See I.55. The lands referred to in the last line conventionally included both Tuscany and Savoy.[8]

43. Original September 1557 text   **Read as modern French:**

La grand ruyne des sacrés ne s'esloigne,
Provence, Naples, Secile, seez & Ponce: *Sicile, Sées et Pons*
En Germanie, au Ryn & à Cologne,
Vexés à mort par tous ceulx de Magonce.   *de Mayence*

> **The priesthood's ruin is not far ahead**
> **Throughout Provence, Spain, Italy and France.**
> **On Rhine and at Cologne the Germans dead,**
> **Harried to death as Mainz's hordes advance.**

Source: The *Mirabilis Liber*'s grim forecast of the destruction of the Church throughout Europe by future Islamic invaders (see I.15), as they advance across the continent both via the Mediterranean and via Germany (see I.9, I.75, II.24).

44. Original September 1557 text   **Read as modern French:**

Par mer le rouge sera prins des pyrates,   *le cardinal*
La paix sera par son moyen troublee:
L'ire & l'avare commettra par fainct acte,
Au grand Pontife sera l'armee doublee.

> **At sea the cardinal's by pirates ta'en,**
> **And peace thereby placed in horrendous trouble:**
> **Anger and avarice make gestures vain,**
> **But the great Pontiff shall his army double.**

Source: Unidentified incident affecting the distinctly martial sixteenth-century Vatican.

45. Original September 1557 text   Read as modern French:

Le grand Empire sera tost desollé,
Et translaté pres d'ardue ne silve: *de la forêt des Ardennes [d'arduenne silve]*
Les deux bastardz par l'aisné deco lé,   *décapités [décollés]*
Et regnera Aenobarb. nez de milve.   *de milan*

> **The mighty Empire shall be desolate,**
> **Power transferred to Ardennes' forest cool.**
> **Two bastards th' elder shall decapitate:**
> **Hawk-nosed Ahenobarbus then shall rule.**

Source: The troubles inaccurately anticipated by Nostradamus for the contemporary Holy Roman Empire, probably assimilated to the *Mirabilis Liber*'s forecast either of a future Islamic invasion of Europe (see I.9, I.75, II.24) or of the expulsion of the invaders from Europe again (see I.55), with a backward glance either (in the first case) at the Emperor Nero or (in the second case) at his near namesake, the doughty Lucius Domitius Ahenobarbus, who conducted a spirited resistance against the perceived usurper Julius Caesar from his base in Marseille until he was finally killed in battle.

46. Original September 1557 text   Read as modern French:

Par chapeaux rouges querelles & nouveaux scismes,
Quant on aura esleu le Sabinois: *élu*
On produira contre luy grans sophismes,
Et sera Rome lesee par Albanois.   *par ceux d'Alba*

> **The cardinals shall feud and disagree**
> **When Sabine candidate shall be elected.**
> **Great theses shall against him be directed**
> **And Rome by those of Alba injured be.**

Source: The Great Western Church Schism of 1378 when, under pressure from the local Roman mob (Alba, just to the south-east, was Rome's original mother-city), a breakaway 'alternative papacy' was instituted by a group of cardinals in Avignon.

47. Original September 1557 text   Read as modern French:

Le grand Arabe marchera bien avant,
Trahy sera par les Bisantinois:
L'antique Rodes luy viendra au devant,
Et plus grand mal par austre Pannonois.   *austère*

> **The mighty Arab on and on shall go,**
> **Yet be by Byzantines betrayed and tricked.**
> **Then ancient Rhodes shall face him, while worse woe**
> **Shall th' stern Hungarian on him inflict.**

Source: The *Mirabilis Liber's* scenario of Arab invasion, modified by a series of expected setbacks that appear to be Nostradamus's own copyright. See I.9, I.75, II.24.

48. Original September 1557 text Read as modern French:

Apres la grande affliction de sceptre,   *renversement [lat.]; du roi/de par le roi*
Deux ennemis par eulx seront deffaictz:
Classe d'Affrique aux Pannons viendra naistre, *Une flotte de l'Afrique du Nord; aux Hongrois*
Par mer & terre seront horribles faictz.

> **After the mighty kingly overthrow**
> **Shall two great foes by them defeated fall.**
> **To Hungary shall Afric vessels row:**
> **By land and sea shall awful things befall.**

Source: The *Mirabilis Liber*, as per the previous verse, to which it appears to be a direct sequel.

49. Original September 1557 text Read as modern French:

Nul de l'Espagne mais de l'antique France,
Ne sera esleu pour le tremblant nacelle, *pour l'église troublée*
A l'ennemy sera faicte fiance,
Qui dans son regne sera peste cruelle.

> **From ancient France, but never one from Spain,**
> **He'll chosen be o'er th' trembling Barque to rule:**
> **In th' enemy they'll place their trust in vain**
> **Who to his realm shall prove a plague so cruel.**

Source: Once again the Avignon papacy of the Great Western Church Schism between 1378 and 1417, presumably with a sideways glance at the North African pirates who continually ravaged the Mediterranean coasts during this period. Once again, in other words, Nostradamus is basing a whole raft of verses on a single, recently consulted source.

50. Original September 1557 text Read as modern French:

L'an que les freres du lys seront en aage, *les frères français*
L'un d'eulx tiendra la grande Romanie: *l'Empire Romain*
Trembler les monts, ouvert latin passaige,
Pache marcher contre fort d'Armenie.   *Ayant formé un pacte pour*

> **The year when brothers French shall be of age**
> **Shall one of them Rome's Empire hold as fief:**
> **Hills quake as th' road to Rome he shall engage,**

Full pledged to march against Armenia's chief.

Source: The *Mirabilis Liber*'s forecast of the advent of a future *Grand Monarque* who would push the occupying Arabs all the way back to the Middle East (see I.55), assimilated to the same book's evident expectation that François I (duly adjusted by Nostradamus to fit his son Henri II, and thus *his* sons in their turn, who were still young at the time) would be elected Holy Roman Emperor.

51. Original September 1557 text

	Read as modern French:
La gent de Dace, d'Angleterre & Polonne	*de la Roumanie*
Et de Bohesme feront nouvelle ligue:	
Pour passer oultre d'Hercules la colonne,	*au delà de Gibraltar*
Barcins, Tyrrens dresser cruelle brigue.	*Ceux de Barcelone et de Tyr [les Carthaginois]*

> **Romanians, English, Poles and Czechs shall all**
> **A new alliance then together knot**
> **To pass Gibraltar's narrow strait withal:**
> **Tunis and Spain cook up a fiendish plot.**

Source: The *Mirabilis Liber*'s forecast of a huge invasion of Europe from North Africa and the Middle East (see I.9, I.75, II.24), and of an equally huge eventual European counter-invasion (see I.55).

52. Original September 1557 text

	Read as modern French:
Un Roy sera qui donra l'opposite,	*qui mettra tout à l'envers*
Les exilés eslevés sur le regne:	
De sang nager la gent caste hyppolite,	*les prêtres*
Et florira long temps soubz telle enseigne.	

> **A King there'll be who'll turn all upside down,**
> **To power the exiles raising, and esteem.**
> **The priestly caste, once used in blood to drown,**
> **Long time shall flourish under such regime.**

Source: The *Mirabilis Liber*'s prophecy of the advent of a *Grand Monarque* who would restore everything to rights after the predicted Muslim invasion of Europe. See I.4, I.55, I.92.

53. Original September 1557 text

	Read as modern French:
La loy du Sol, & Venus contendens,	*De la chrétienté et de l'islam*
Appropriant l'esprit de propheties	*prophétie*
Ne lun ne lautre ne seront entendens,	*ne sera d'accord avec l'autre*
Par Sol tiendra la loy du grand Messie.	*Par/Pour la chrétienté*

Islam and Christendom shall disagree
Over which shall true prophecy inspire:
Never the twain shall in agreement be.
To Christendom adheres the great Messiah.

Source: Nostradamus's own personal religious convictions, assimilated to the *Mirabilis Liber*'s end-of-the-world scenario. See II.13.

54. Original September 1557 text   Read as modern French:

Du pont Euxine, & la grand Tartarie,   *De la Mer Noire et de l'Asie Centrale*
Un roy sera qui viendra voir la Gaule:
Transpercera Alane & l'Armenie,
Et dans Bisance lairra sanglante Gaule.

From Black Sea's shores and greater Tartary
To see our France a monarch westward goes.
Alania and Armenia pierced, shall he
On Istanbul his bloody rod impose.

Source: The *Mirabilis Liber*'s grim prediction of a Muslim invasion of Europe, in this case from the region of the Caspian Sea, directly after the model of the invasions of the Huns and Mongols. Compare I.9, I.75, II.24.

55. Original September 1557 text   Read as modern French:

De la felice Arabie contrade,   *contrée*
Naistra puissant de loy Mahometique:
Vexer l'Espaigne conquester la Grenade,   *conquérir*
Et plus par mer à la gent lygustique.   *au peuple ligurien [de l'Italie du nord-ouest]*

A mighty man and lord shall come to birth
In Araby the Blest – a Muslim, he.
He'll take Granada, harrow Spanish earth
And worse do to th' Italians from the sea.

Source: The *Mirabilis Liber*'s prediction of a coming Antichrist (see I.47, I.76, II.9) who is destined to lead a massive invasion of Europe (see I.9, I.75, II.24).

56. Original September 1557 text   Read as modern French:

Par le trespas de tresvieillart pontife,   *Par la mort*
Sera esleu Romain de bon aage:
Qu'il sera dict que le siege debiffe,
Et long tiendra & de picquant ouvraige.

When dies the Pope who is so full of years
They shall a Roman fairly old elect:

Of him they'll say the throne quite out he wears,
So long he'll reign, and to such fierce effect.

Source: The death of Pope Paul III in 1549 at the age of 81, to be succeeded by Julius III, then aged 63. Although he in fact only reigned until 1555 (as Nostradamus must have known when he wrote the verse, unless he had already written much of the second edition before publication of the first edition in that same year), he certainly made an impression, having presided over the opening session of the fiercely reactionary Council of Trent, as well as siding with the Holy Roman Emperor against France, until forced by the latter's success to make peace in 1552.

57. Original September 1557 text **Read as modern French:**

Istra du mont Gaulsier & Aventin,
Qui par le trou advertira l'armee:
Entre deux rocz sera prins le butin, *roches; pris*
De SEXT mansol faillir la renommee. *Du mausolée de Sextus*

Down from the Aventine (from Mont Gaussier!),
He'll warn the host who spied out through the hole.
Between two rocks they'll fall upon their prey:
So fades the fame of Saint-Paul-de-Mausole.

Source: The waylaying, during the Imperial invasion of Provence in 1536, of Charles V's scouts just south of St-Rémy (Nostradamus's birthplace), thanks to a lookout posted high on the Mont Gaussier that overlooks the ruins of ancient Graeco-Roman Glanum, where two extraordinary holes through the rock-crest (well-known to all the local inhabitants) afford the unseen observer magnificent views over all the country to the north.[P]

58. Original September 1557 text **Read as modern French:**

De laqueduct d'Uticense, Gardoing, *de Castrum Uteciense [Uzès] et du Gard*
Par la forest & mont Inaccessible:
En my du pont sera tasché au poing,
Le chef Nemans qui tant sera terrible. *Nîmois*

On th' aqueduct from Uzès to the Gard
That's so remote through forest and o'er hill,
On mid-bridge he'll receive a blow so hard,
That chief from Nîmes who is so terrible!

Source: A known set-to atop the huge and celebrated Roman aqueduct near Avignon known as the Pont du Gard,[P] between the twin gang-leaders the Baron des Adrets, Lord of Pompignan near Nîmes, and his rival Charles du Puy, Lord of Montbrun.[60]

59. Original September 1557 text   **Read as modern French:**

Au chef Anglois à Nymes trop sejour,
Devers l'Espaigne au secours Aenobarbe: *d'Ahénobarbe*
Plusieurs mourront par Mars ouvert ce jour,   *Beaucoup; par guerre*
Quant en Artoys faillir estoille en barbe.   *tombera*

> **Too long at Nîmes the English chief shall stay**
> **En route to help Ahenobarbe in Spain:**
> **Many shall die through war that starts that day**
> **When o'er Artois a bearded star shall rain.**

Source: Unidentified military campaign.

60. Original September 1557 text   **Read as modern French:**

Par teste rase viendra bien mal eslire,   *Par un moine/évêque/pape [?]*
Plus que sa charge ne porte passera:
Si grand fureur & raige fera dire,
Qu'a feu & sang tout sexe trenchera.   *toute secte/toutes sectes*

> **For shaven head they'll make a lousy choice:**
> **Any more weight and he'd not pass the door.**
> **Such angry, raging sentiments he'll voice:**
> **In fire and blood he'll cut sects to the floor.**

Source: Probably the contemporary Pope Paul IV (1476–1559), a former monk who, on becoming Pope in 1555 at the age of 79, proceeded to enrich his worthless nephews and add a good deal of fire to the Inquisition, even having prominent clerics dragged before it on the merest suspicion of heresy.

61. Original September 1557 text   **Read as modern French:**

L'enfant du grand n'estant à sa naissance,
Subjuguera les haultz mont Apennis: *Apennins*
Fera trembler tous ceulx de la balance,
Et des monts feux jusques à mont Senis.

> **Child of the lord who was not at his birth**
> **The Apennines shall conquer, and not stop:**
> **He'll force to quake the Libran lands of earth,**
> **And fire the mountains up to Cenis' top.**

Source: The *Mirabilis Liber*'s prediction of a huge Arab invasion of Europe (see I.9, I.75) led by the Antichrist in person (see I.47, I.76, II.9). The 'Libran lands' traditionally included Tuscany, Savoy, the Dauphiné, Alsace, and Austria.[8]

62. Original September 1557 text

Sur les rochers sang on verra plouvoir,
Sol Orient, Saturne Occidental:
Pres d'Orgon guerre, à Rome grand mal voir,
Nefz parfondrees & prins le Tridental.

Read as modern French:

pleuvoir
se levant

pris; la galère[8]/ le siège de Neptune [le Vatican]

> **Blood falls like rain the very rocks upon:**
> **Sun rising, Saturn in the west shall stand.**
> **Great woes in Rome are seen, war near Orgon,**
> **Ships sunk, the fisher's barque in hostile hand.**

Source: The *Mirabilis Liber*'s forecast of a coming Islamic invasion of southern Europe (see I.9, I.75), including the town of Orgon, a regional administrative center on the Durance commanding an important pass through the Alpilles just north of Nostradamus's home-town of Salon. The reference to blood raining could be either purely figurative or a reference to any one of the many occasions when such meteorological phenomena were reported as omens during Nostradamus's own lifetime. In the words of Lycosthenes' report for 1553,[44] as translated into contemporary English by Dr Stephen Batman:[5] *The fift of June it rayned blood at Erforde.*

63. Original September 1557 text

De vaine emprise l'honneur indue plaincte
Gallotz errans par latins froit, faim, vagues
Non loing du Tymbre de sang terre taincte,
Et sur humains seront diverses plagues.

Read as modern French:

entreprise
Gaulois [Français]; froid
Tibre
pestilences

> **Too much they'll plead vain enterprise's glory:**
> **The French astray, Italians cold, starved, wet.**
> **Not far from Tiber all the land is gory:**
> **All kinds of plagues poor humans shall beset.**

Source: Once again, the *Mirabilis Liber*'s grim prophecy of an Islamic invasion of Europe via Italy. See I.9, I.75. Once again, too, Nostradamus is devoting several verses to a single theme.

64. Original September 1557 text   Read as modern French:

Les assemblés par repoz du grand nombre,
Par terre & mer conseil contremandé:
Pres d l'Automne Gennes, Nice de l'ombre,   *Près de l'Ausonne [l'Italie] [?]*
Par champs & villes le chef contrebandé.

> **To calm most of those present there, in fact,**
> **They'll countermand advice by sea and land.**
> **In Italy Nice, Genoa shall darkly act:**
> **In fields and towns against their chief they'll band.**

Source: Unidentified politico-military machinations.

65. Original September 1557 text   Read as modern French:

Subit venu l'effrayeur sera grande,
Des principaulx de l'affaire cachés:
Et dame en braise plus ne sera en veue,
De peu à peu seront les grans faschés.

> **Upon his prompt arrival, major fright:**
> **Of the affair the ringleaders unknown:**
> **The more the flaming lady fades from sight**
> **The more the lords are angered at what's done.**

Source: Unknown. The 'flaming lady' could be the planet Venus.

66. Original September 1557 text   Read as modern French:

Soubz les antiques edifices vestaulx,
Non esloignez d'aqueduct ruyne: *ruiné*
De Sol & Luna sont les luisans metaulx.   *D'or et d'argent*
Ardante lampe Traian d'or burine.   *Troyenne [?]; buriné*

> **Buried 'neath ancient vestal buildings deep**
> **Not far from ruined aqueduct so old**
> **Sun's and moon's metals still all shiny sleep**
> **And burning lamp of Trajan 'graved in gold.**

Source: The severe floods of 1403 (a repetition of those of 1309), in whose wake various ritual objects of gold and silver were apparently discovered in and around the Sacred Lake at Nîmes, having been dumped there during the earlier desecration of the temple of Diana (originally of Vesta), whose crumbling ruins still stand beside it today.[P] The prediction would, as it happened, be re-fulfilled again virtually to the letter when equally devastating floods struck on 9 September 1557, just three days after its original publication! Compare also IX.9, IX.12, X.6.

67. Original September 1557 text   Read as modern French:

Quant chef Perouse n'osera sa tunique
Sens au couvert tout nud s'expolier: *Sans; s'exposer*
Seront prins sept faict Aristocratique,
Le pere & filz mors par poincte au colier.

> **When shall the Lord Perouse in no wise dare**
> **To strip off tunic, save in private wrapped,**
> **Shall seven by lordly act be captured there,**
> **Father and son both killed, in carcan clapped.**

Source: Unidentified incident, probably contemporary, involving torture by spiked collar.

68. Original September 1557 text   Read as modern French:

Dans le Dannube & du Rin viendra boire,
Le grand Chameau ne s'en repentira:
Trembler du Rosne & plus fort ceulx de loire
Et pres des Alpes coq le ruïnera.

> **He'll come to drink by Rhine's and Danube's shore –**
> **That mighty Camel no remorse shall show.**
> **The folk of Rhône shall quake, of Loire e'en more.**
> **Yet near the Alps the Cock shall lay him low.**

Source: The *Mirabilis Liber*'s prediction of a coming Arab invasion of Europe, flooding in across the traditional borders of the ancient Roman Empire (the Rhine and the Danube), and across the major rivers of France (see I.9, I.75, II.24), as well as of its eventual defeat by a future *Grand Monarque* of France (see I.4, I.55, I.92), with a nod in the direction of the same book's animal symbolism in its prophecy of St Brigid of Sweden (see III.52). The trigger for line 1 may well have been the report by Gasparus Peucerus in his *Teratoscopia* of a vision in the clouds seen in 1534, as subsequently collected by Lycosthenes[44] and translated into English by Batman:[5] *Afterward there appeared the platforme of a verye greate Cittie standing by a greate water, besieged with an armye by Sea and by Lande, and over this was a crosse of a bloody colour turning by little and little into blacke . . . Afterwarde in a large playne there appeared two burning Castels neare to a high hill, to the whiche stoocke a greate Eagle hiding the halfe of his body behind the side of the hill: there appeared also certayne yong Eagles of a brighte white coloure, likewise the heade of a Lyon lying upright, having a Crowne upon his heade, a Cocke striking and digging the heade with his Bill untill it was loose and fell from the body . . . In that place where before the greate Citie was seene, at the Bankes of the greate Water stoode a Camell, as if he hadde dronke.*

69. Original September 1557 text   Read as modern French:

Plus ne sera le grand en faulx sommeil,
L'inquietude viendra prendre repoz:
Dresser phalange d'or, azur, & vermeil,
Subjuguer Affrique la ronger jusques aux oz.   l'Afrique du Nord

> No longer shall the great lord dream away,
> No longer troubled thoughts the people harrow:
> In gold, blue, red he shall his troops array
> Africa conquer, crunch it to the marrow.

Source: The Emperor Charles V's triumphant raid of 1535 on the forces of the pirate Barbarossa at Tunis, assimilated to the *Mirabilis Liber's* forecast of the future *Grand Monarque's* equally triumphant expected counter-attack against the former Muslim occupiers of Europe. See I.4, I.55, I.92.

70. Original September 1557 text   Read as modern French:

Des regions subjectes à la Balance,
Feront troubler les monts par grande guerre
Captif tout sexe deu, & tout bisance,   toute secte de Dieu, partout les Turcs
Qu'on criera à l'aulbe terre à terre.

> In lands that are of Libra subjects true
> With mighty war the mountains they'll assail.
> Captive all holy sects, Byzantium too:
> From land to land each dawn they'll mourn and wail.

Source: Once again the *Mirabilis Liber's* forecast of a Muslim invasion of Europe (see I.9, I.75, II.24) that will destroy the Church (see I.15). Compare V.61; as in that case, the 'Libran lands' traditionally included Tuscany, Savoy, the Dauphiné, Alsace, and Austria.[8]

71. Original September 1557 text   Read as modern French:

Par la fureur d'un qui attendra l'eau,
Par la grand raige tout l'exercite esmeu: toute l'armée
Chargé des nobles à dixsept bateulx,   bateaux
Au long du Rosne tard messagier venu.

> With the great rage of those of thirst who die,
> With such great rage is the whole army stirred,
> Loaded on seventeen boats the nobles by:
> Too late along the Rhône the word is heard.

Source: An unidentified occasion when a military expedition was frustrated by communications delays.

72. Original September 1557 text   **Read as modern French:**

Pour le plaisir d'edict voluptueux,
On meslera la poyson dans l'aloy: *dans la foi [?]*
Venus sera en cours si vertueux,   *l'Islam*
Qu'obfusquera du Soleil tout aloy.   *de la chrétienté*

> **For pleasure of an edict too indulgent**
> **Shall poison mixed into the faith become:**
> **Islam shall in its course be so effulgent,**
> **It shall outshine all types of Christendom.**

Source: The Edict of Coucy of 1535, which granted an amnesty to Protestants and pardoned returning religious exiles who recanted. Nostradamus, using an analogy drawn from the field of alchemical metallurgy, evidently feels, on the basis of what happened subsequently, that this and other efforts to reconcile Protestantism with traditional Catholicism merely weakened Christendom in the face of the growing power of Islam.

73. Original September 1557 text   **Read as modern French:**

Persecutee sera de Dieu l'Eglise,
Et les sainctz temples seront expoliez:
L'enfant la mere mettra nud en chemise,
Seront Arabes aux Polons raliez.   *Polois/ceux de Saint-Paul-de-Mausole [?]*

> **The Church of God shall sorely be oppressed,**
> **Of holy churches plundered all the treasure,**
> **The naked child by mother but half-dressed,**
> **Saint-Rémois, Arabs joined in ample measure.**

Source: The *Mirabilis Liber*'s forecast of dire persecution of the Church throughout Europe – and particularly of the abbey of St-Paul just south of his own birthplace of St-Rémy-de-Provence – in the wake of a future Muslim invasion. See I.15.

74. Original September 1557 text   **Read as modern French:**

De sang Troyen naistra coeur Germanique   *De sang royal français*
Qu'il deviendra en si haulte puissance:
Hors chassera gent estrange Arabique,
Tournant l'eglise en pristine preeminence.

> **From Trojan blood a heart shall grow apace**
> **That is Germanic, mighty power attaining.**
> **He'll chase away the alien Arab race,**
> **The Church's former eminence regaining.**

Source: The *Mirabilis Liber*'s confident prediction that a future *Grand Monarque* of

France, a natural successor of Charlemagne and somewhat after the model of the Holy Roman Emperor Charles V, would liberate Europe from its expected Islamic invaders and become the savior of Christendom. See I.4, I.55, I.92.

75. Original September 1557 text   **Read as modern French:**

Montera hault sur le bien plus à dextre,   *à droite*
Demouura assis sur la pierre quarree: *carrée*
Vers le midy posé à la senestre,   *à gauche*
Baston tortu en main, bouche serree.   *tordu*

> **High o'er the realm, towards the right inclining,**
> **Upon the square-shaped stone he'll sit and look**
> **Towards the south, now on the left reclining,**
> **His mouth clamped shut, grasping his twisted crook.**

Source: The ceremonial coronation of the somewhat taciturn Emperor Charles V in Rome in 1536, which was deliberately devised, as its original at Aix-la-Chapelle had been in 1520, in direct imitation of that of the semi-legendary King Numa of Rome in around 710 bc, who was (rightly) equally silent on that occasion;[60] compare Livy's original text as translated at II.99 and V.6, which Nostradamus has, as ever, slightly garbled.

76. Original September 1557 text   **Read as modern French:**

En lieu libere tendra son pavillon,   *Dans la campagne*
Et ne vouldra en cités prendre place:
Aix, Carpen l'isle volce, mont Cavaillon,   *Carpentras; l'Isle-sur-la-Sorgue; Vaucluse*
Par tous les lieux abolira sa trasse.   *trace*

> **In open land he his encampment makes,**
> **Nor will in any city take his place:**
> **Carpentras, Cavaillon, Vaucluse or Aix –**
> **Where'er he goes he'll raze his every trace.**

Source: The itinerant marauding expedition of the Emperor Charles V and his forces into Provence during 1536, possibly assimilated to the *Mirabilis Liber*'s prediction of a future invasion by his Muslim equivalent. See I.9, I.75, II.24.

77. Original September 1557 text   **Read as modern French:**

Tous les degréz d'honneur ecclesiastique,
Seront changez en dial. quirinal: *en Jupiter Quirinus*
En Martial quirinal flaminique,   *en Mars Quirinus*
Puis un roy de France le rendre vulcanal.

> **Of honor all the ranks ecclesiastic**
> **For Jupiter Quirinus they'll revise,**

For Mars Quirinal priests enthusiastic:
Then France's monarch shall them Vulcanize.

Source: The increasing contemporary tendency towards religious militancy, even among the priesthood, currently being discouraged by the French Court, and here satirized in classical religious terms.

78. Original September 1557 text   Read as modern French:

Les deux unyz ne tiendront longuement,
Et dans treze ans au Barbare satrappe:
Aux deux costés feront tel perdement,
Qu'on benyra le barque & sa cappe.   *Que l'un d'eux[?]*

    The duo shall not long allied remain –
    'Gainst th' Arab lord – some thirteen years or less.
    On either side such losses they'll sustain
    That one the Barque (and in his cope) shall bless.

Source: The thirteen-year alliance (1534–47) between the Emperor Charles V and Pope Paul III against the Ottomans' client pirate-admiral Barbarossa, who constantly harried the coasts and shipping of the Mediterranean on their behalf to the point where Charles felt moved to mount his celebrated raid on Tunis of 1535, with the fleet solemnly blessed on its departure by the Pope in person, arrayed in his ceremonial robes.[60] This allows Nostradamus to play unmercifully on the word *barque*, which of course he also constantly uses to refer to the Vatican itself, as per the *Mirabilis Liber's* prophecies of Joachim of Fiore and St Brigid of Sweden. Compare I.15.

79. Original September 1557 text   Read as modern French:

La sacree pompe viendra baisser les aesles,
Par la venue du grand legislateur:
Humble haulsera vexera les rebelles,   *relèvera*
Naistra sur terre aucuu aemulateur.   *aucun*

    All sacred pomp its wings shall soon abase
    Once the great legislator comes to reign:
    He'll raise the lowly, every rebel chase.
    None like him shall be born on earth again.

Source: The *Mirabilis Liber's* prophecy of the expected *Grand Monarque* who would eventually restore all the world to rights after the expected Muslim invasion of Europe. See I.4, I.55, I.92. Note the reformist Nostradamus's evident aversion to the more flamboyant aspects of the reigning Catholic religion.

80. Original September 1557 text   **Read as modern French:**

Logmion grand bisance aprouchera,   *L'Ogmion*
Chassé sera la barbarique ligne: *ligue [voir rime]*
Des deux loix l'une l'estinique lachera,   *l'une (l'ethnique [la païenne])*
Barbare & franche en perpetuelle brigue.

> **Ogmion shall Byzantium draw nigh:**
> **Routed shall be the pagan federation.**
> **Of the two creeds in constant confrontation,**
> **Arab and French, the heathen one shall die.**

Source: The *Mirabilis Liber*'s confident prophecy that a future *Grand Monarque*, here assimilated to the Gallic version of Hercules (the actual first name of King Henri II's youngest son), would not only drive the invading Muslims back to their Middle Eastern heartlands, but convert them to Christianity into the bargain. See I.4, I.55, I.92, and compare II.22, VI.85, VI.21, VIII.83, IX.43, and VII.36.

81. Original September 1557 text   **Read as modern French:**

L'oyseau royal sur la cité solaire,   *la cité chrétienne [Rome]*
Sept moys devant fera nocturne augure: *dès sept mois auparavant*
Mur d'Orient cherra tonnairre, esclaire,   *tombera*
Sept jours aux portes les ennemis à l'heure

> **Seven months before, o'er solar city's walls,**
> **The royals' bird its nightly omen shows.**
> **Midst thunderbolts the eastern bastion falls:**
> **Seven days to th' hour, then 'fore the gates the foes.**

Source: The sacking of Rome by Imperial forces after seven days of siege on 6 May 1527, linked to the omens surrounding the assassination of Julius Caesar in 44 BC – and in particular the 'royals' bird' (*avem regaliolum*) reported by Suetonius (I.81) as having flown into the Hall of Pompey the previous day with a laurel-twig in its beak before being torn to pieces by other birds – and presumably assimilated to the *Mirabilis Liber*'s prediction of the destruction of Rome by Arab forces from the Mediterranean. See I.9, I.75. Suetonius's 'a few months before', though, had in fact referred to a quite different omen in the same passage; Nostradamus has evidently introduced the notion of 'seven months' simply in order to act as a suitable presage for the 'seven days' in the last line.

82. Original September 1557 text   **Read as modern French:**

Au conclud pache hors de la forteresse,   *Le pacte ayant été conclu,*
Ne sortira celuy en desespoir mys:
Quant ceulx d'Arbois, de Langres, contre Bresse,   *quand*
Auront monts Dolle bouscade d'ennemis.   *[buscadé] dressé l'embuscade contre*

The pact once signed, forth from the great fortrèss
Despairing, he'll not deign or dare to go
When those from Langres and Arbois against Bresse
On hills near Dole shall ambush every foe.

Source: Unknown incident, probably from the French Wars of Religion.

83. Original September 1557 text   Read as modern French:

Ceulx qui auront entreprins subvertir,   *entrepris de*
Nompareil regne puissant & invincible:
Feront par fraulde, nuictz trois advertir,   *nuiseurs [lat. nocentes]*
Quant le plus grand à table lira Bible.   *Pendant que*

> Those who have undertaken to subvert
> That matchless realm puissant, unconquerable
> Deceitfully three villains shall alert
> While their chief plotter reads at board his Bible.

Source: Unknown incident in the contemporary French religious conflicts, here featuring one of the Protestant factions. Catholic laymen were not supposed to read the Bible at the time!

84. Original September 1557 text   Read as modern French:

Naistra du goulphre & cité immesuree,
Nay de parents obscurs & tenebreux:
Qui la puissance du grand roy reveree,
Vouldra destruire par Rouan & Evreux.   *Rouen*

> Forth from the gulf and city without end
> He'll come, his parents dark and quite obscure,
> Who would that Prince's power most reverend
> Destroy through Rouen and Evreux, 'tis most sure.

Source: The *Mirabilis Liber*'s gruesome scenario of Muslim invasion of Europe (see I.9, I.75, II.24) and destruction of the Church (see I.15), led by the Antichrist in person (see I.47, I.76, II.9).

85. Original September 1557 text   Read as modern French:

Par les Sueves & lieux circonvoisins,   *les Souabes*
Seront en guerre pour cause des nuees: *nouveautés [prov.]*
Camp marins locustes & cousins,   *Armée; moustiques/excommuniés[60] [?]*
Du Leman faultes seront bien desnuees.   *révélées*

> Among the Swabians and the Swiss shall they
> Against the new ideas prepare to fight:

Against sea-locusts, hordes of flies the fray.
Geneva's faults are soon exposed to light.

Source: The contemporary conflict between Catholicism and Calvin's Protestants based in Geneva, which (for Nostradamus) pale into significance beside the coming threat from the Mediterranean.

86. Original September 1557 text   Read as modern French:

Par les deux testes & trois bras separés,
La cité grande par eaues sera vexee:
Des grans d'entre eulx par exil esgarés,
Par teste perse Bisance fort pressee.   *Par la tête bleue [?]*

By two capes and three sea-arms separate
The city they by sea shall sorely fret:
Its leaders banished, incommunicate,
Byzantium by blue-head is beset.

Source: The *Mirabilis Liber*'s prediction of a massive Middle-Eastern invasion of Europe via Constantinople, assimilated to the Turkish capture of Constantinople in 1453, and cunningly disguised to suggest that it is referring to one of the prodigies from Julius Obsequens's *On Omens* describing the births of infants with multiple heads and arms. The 'blue-heads' of the day were Persian Shi'ites.

87. Original September 1557 text   Read as modern French:

L'an que Saturne sera hors de servaige,
Au franc terroir sera d'eaue inundé:
De sang Troyen, sera son mariage,
Et sera seur d'Espaignolz circonder.   *sûr; entouré [circondé]*

The year that Saturn shall withdraw his writ
Shall mighty floods afflict the Frankish land.
With Trojan blood he shall a marriage knit,
As Spanish guards for safety round him stand.

Source: The *Mirabilis Liber*'s predictions of major floods (see I.69), as well as of the expected *Grand Monarque* of France who will eventually come to rule the world and set everything to rights (see I.4, I.55, I.92), linked with the ancient tradition (likewise taken up by Ronsard) that the kings of France were descended from Francus, son of Hector of Troy.

88. Original September 1557 text **Read as modern French:**

Sur le sablon par un hideux deluge,
Des autres mers trouvé monstre marin:
Proche du lieu sera faict un refuge,
Tenant Savone esclave de Turin.

> **Upon the sand after a hideous storm**
> **From other seas a sea-monster is found:**
> **Near to that place a refuge they shall form**
> **That holds Savona slave to Turin bound.**

Source: An unidentified event presaged by an omen in the form of a sea-monster, such as the various ones reported by Lycosthenes,[44] and especially that reported for 1553. See I.29.

89. Original September 1557 text **Read as modern French:**

Dedans Hongrie par Boheme, Navarre,
Et par banniere fainctes seditions:
Par fleurs de lys pays pourtant la barre,   *portant*
Contre Orleans fera esmotions.

> **In Hungary through Czechs and Navarrois**
> **And that device there'll be seditions fake**
> **Which bears the fleur de lys crossed by a bar:**
> **'Gainst Orleans he'll people restless make.**

Source: Unidentified political schemings, apparently involving the Bourbons, whose crest is actually described.

90. Original September 1557 text **Read as modern French:**

Dans les cyclades, en perinthe & larisse,
Dedans l' Sparte tout le Pelloponnesse:
Si grand famine, peste, par faulx connisse,   *imposés avec énergie [lat. connisus]*
Neuf moys tiendra & tout le cherrouesse.

> **On Corinth, Larissa and Cyclades**
> **Along with Sparta and Peloponnese**
> **Shall famine, plague by traitors be inflicted,**
> **Nine months the whole peninsula afflicted.**

Source: The *Mirabilis Liber's* prophecy of an Arab invasion of Greece and all of Europe. See I.9, I.75, II.24.

91. Original September 1557 text   **Read as modern French:**

Au grand marché qu'on dict des mensongiers,
Du bout Torrent & camp Athenien: *et champ*
Seront surprins par les chevaulx legiers,
Par Albanois Mars, Leo, Sat. un versien.   *en Verseau*

> **At the great forum that 'of liars' they call**
> **By the Athenian torrent and its plain**
> **Shall horse Albanian upon them fall.**
> **Saturn Aquarius, Mars in Leo shall reign.**

Source: Unknown. The reference in the first line is an expression used by both Hippocrates and Galen to describe the 'swindlers' market' of Athens; the 'torrent' is the river Cephissus, which flows across the plain of Attica.[8] The reference seems once again to be to the *Mirabilis Liber*'s invasion of Europe. See I.9, I.75, II.24.

92. Original September 1557 text   **Read as modern French:**

Apres le siege tenu dixsept ans,
Cinq changeront en tel revolu terme.:
Puis sera l'un esleu de mesme temps,
Qui des Romains ne sera trop conforme.

> **Once he for seventeen years has held the see**
> **Five shall be changed in time equivalent,**
> **What time another shall elected be**
> **Who from the Romans shall somewhat dissent.**

Source: A slightly confused account of the Great Western Church schism (possibly picked up initially from Froissart's *Chroniques*), when rival popes reigned for a time in Rome and Avignon, starting with the reign of the Avignon Pope Clement VII between 1378 and 1394 (seventeen years by the traditional French 'inclusive reckoning', which counts the individual calendar years involved rather than the actual period elapsed, just as it counts a week as *huit jours* ['eight days'] and a fortnight as *une quinzaine* ['fifteen']).

93. Original September 1557 text   **Read as modern French:**

Soubz le terroir du rond globe lunayre,
Lors que sera dominateur Mercure:
L'isle d'Escosse fera un luminaire,
Qui les Anglois mettra à desconfiture.

> **Beneath the realm of the round lunar globe**
> **When Mercury at height of power shall reign**
> **Shall Scotland a great luminant enrobe**
> **Who'll cause the English much defeat and pain.**

Source: At first sight, apparently the account by Froissart in his *Chroniques* (Luce I:17–20) of how the forces of King Robert the Bruce freed Scotland from the English, notably at the Battle of Bannockburn of 1314, and thereafter made constant inroads into England itself. The apparent astrological reference is rather inaccurate, however, if it is to the 'planetary ages' listed by Richard Roussat in his *Livre de l'estat et des mutations des temps*,[67] which dated the 'age of Mercury' to the period between 824 and 1179. A more satisfactory chronological match might be with William the Lion, who raided England in the 1170s, only to be taken prisoner and forced to do homage to England's King Henry II in 1174 – though in this case it is difficult to imagine where Nostradamus could have found the requisite information.

94. Original September 1557 text

Translatera en la grand Germanie,

Brabant & Flandres, Gand, Bruges & Bologne:
La tresve faincte le grand duc d'Armenie,
Assaillira Vienne & la Coloigne.

Read as modern French:

Il transférera/changera; grande [forme invariable]

Into Great Germany he shall absorb
Brabant and Flanders, Gent, Bruges and Boulogne.
Feigning a truce, Armenia's mighty lord
Vienna shall attack, and then Cologne.

Source: The imperial activities of the contemporary Holy Roman Emperor Charles V, as also of the equally contemporary Turkish Suleiman the Magnificent, who indeed besieged Vienna in 1529 – though he never in fact made it to Cologne!

95. Original September 1557 text

Nautique rame invitera les umbres,
Du grand Empire [/] lors viendra conciter:
La mer Aegée des lignes les encombres,
Empeschant l'onde Tyrrene desflotez.

Read as modern French:

rane [poisson de mer]

du bois [lat. lignum]
de flotter [?]

The Ocean Fish shall summon up the shade
Of the great Empire, then shall stir the sea
Of the Aegean with wreckage driftwood made,
Impeding passage of th' Tyrrhenian sea.

Source: Evidently the ancient sea-battle between Octavian and Mark Antony at Actium in 31 BC (reported by Suetonius at *Augustus*, 17), or the much more recent Battle of Preveza of 1538 in the same area, assimilated to the contemporary raids on coastal shipping by the Turkish pirate Barbarossa off the Mediterranean coasts, and thus eventually to the *Mirabilis Liber*'s expected future invasion of Europe via the Mediterranean (see I.9, I.75, II.24). Compare V.3 above.

96. Original September 1557 text   **Read as modern French:**

Sur le millieu du grand monde la rose,
Pour nouveaux faictz sang public espandu:
A dire vray on aura bouche close,
Lors au besoing viendra tard l'attendu.

> At the world's center rules the mighty rose:
> For projects new the state and folk shall bleed.
> If truth were told, t'were best one's mouth to close,
> Till comes th' awaited one in hour of need.

Source: Presumably the *Mirabilis Liber*'s prediction of a brutal occupation of Europe by foreign powers (see I.9, I.75, II.24), followed by its eventual liberation by the expected *Grand Monarque* (see I.4, I.55, I.92).

97. Original September 1557 text   **Read as modern French:**

Le nay difforme par horreur suffoqué,   *né*
Dans la cité du grand Roy habitable: *habitant*
L'edict severe des captifz revoqué,
Gresle & tonnerre, Condom inestimable.

> For horror they shall smother child deformed
> Born live in th' city of the mighty King:
> The law severe on captives is reformed:
> Prodigious hail at Condom, thundering.

Source: Recent events reported in France.

98. Original September 1557 text   **Read as modern French:**

A quarante huict degré climaterique,   *de latitude*
A fin de Cancer si grande seicheresse:
Poisson en mer fleuve, lac cuit hectique,
Bearn, Bigorre par feu ciel en detresse.

> At forty-eight degrees of latitude
> In mid-July there'll be a drought so dry
> That fish in sea, rivers and lakes are stewed,
> Béarn, Bigorre with fire seared from the sky.

Source: The *Mirabilis Liber*'s forecast of major droughts and heat waves, and in particular of fishes being cooked alive by the heat. See II.3.

99. Original September 1557 text   **Read as modern French:**

Milan, Ferrare, Turin, & Aquilleye,   *Aquilée*
Capne, Brundis vexés par gent Celtique: *Capoue, Brindisi*
Par le Lyon & phalange aquilee,
Quant Rome aura le chef vieulx Britannique.

> **Milan, Turin, Ferrara, Aquilei',**
> **Brindisi, Capua by Celts brought to grief,**
> **By Lion and by Imperial Eagle's sway,**
> **When Rome shall have an old Britannic chief.**

Source: The unique pontificate of the English Pope Adrian IV between 1154 and 1159, covering a rebellion in Milan, a major incursion by the Emperor Frederick Barbarossa into northern Italy, the great fire of Capua in November 1557 and the capture of Brindisi by the Norman King William I of Sicily.[60]

100. Original September 1557 text   **Read as modern French:**

Le boutefeu par son feu attrapé,
De feu du ciel à Carcas & Cominge: *Carcassonne*
Foix, Aux, Mazeres, haut vieillart eschapé,
Par ceulx de Hasse, des Saxons & Turinge.   *Hesse*

> **The firebrand shall be trapped by his own fire,**
> **Carcassonne and Comminges, Foix, Auch, Mazères**
> **Seared from the sky: then 'scapes the old grandsire**
> **Who through west Germans then away shall fare.**

Source: The *Mirabilis Liber*'s predictions of fire from the sky (see I.46, II.16), taken as omens for unidentified contemporary events within the Holy Roman Empire.

Century VI

1. Original September 1557 text

Read as modern French:

Autour des monts Pyrenees grand amas
De gent estrange, secourir roy nouveau:
Pres de Garonne du grand temple du Mas,   *du Mas d'Agenais*
Un Romain chef le caindra dedans l'eau.   *craindra*

Around the Pyrenees a mighty throng
Of foreign folk come to the new king's aid:
By church of Mas d'Agenais near the Garonne
Shall Roman chief fearful in water wade.

Source: Plutarch's account in his *Parallel Lives* of the flight of the old Roman general Gaius Marius from the pursuing forces of Sulla, the new commander-in-chief: 'At Marius's wish, he bore him into the marshes and bade him hide himself in a hollow by the riverside, where he laid upon him many reeds . . . But within a short time he was disturbed . . . Whereupon Marius, arising and stripping himself, plunged into a pool full of thick muddy water . . . ' – possibly assimilated to the *Mirabilis Liber*'s prediction of a coming invasion of Europe by forces from North Africa. See I.9, I.75.

2. Original September 1557 text

Read as modern French:

En l'an cinq cens octante plus & moins,   *mil cinq cent quatre-vingts plus ou moins*
On attendra le siecle bien estrange: *un âge*
En l'an sept cens, & trois cieulx en tesmoings,   *mil sept cent*
Que plusieurs regnes un à cinq feront change.   *beaucoup de*

In the year 1580, more or less,
We should expect an age that's passing strange:
While in 1703, the heavens confess
That many realms – from one to five – shall change.

Source: A slightly garbled version of the predictions of Richard Roussat's *Livre de l'estat et mutations des temps* of 1549–50 for what, under his terms, was the 'age of the moon' (1533–1887): 'Now let us come to the leadership, reign, and government of the Moon which is currently in full sway: we affirm that under this latter there shall occur things truly wondrous, unheard of, and unusual . . . it likewise signifies wondrous variety, inconstancy, diversity, instability, splittings of the Faith, violence, and deformity . . . for our Astrologers and natural Theologians state that throughout the whole duration of the world there shall be only six major sects . . .' The dates may seem purely arbitrary (Nostradamus seems to have taken the last statement as referring to the age of the Moon, rather than to the duration of the world itself) but, as the third line suggests, are probably based on astrological conjunctions – in this case those of Saturn and Jupiter in Aries of both 1584 and 1703.[8]

3. Original September 1557 text   Read as modern French:

Fleuve qu'esprove le nouveau nay Celtique,
Sera en grande de l'Empire discorde:
Le jeune prince par gent ecclesiastique,
Ostera le sceptre coronal de concorde.

> **That stream that tests the newborn Celtic king**
> **Shall be by th' Empire placed in disarray:**
> **The new-come prince through Churches' bickering**
> **Shall Concord's regal scepter take away.**

Source: The religious problems that beset the Holy Roman Emperor Charles V right from his coronation in 1520, and that were probably the main reason for his eventual despairing abdication in 1556. Leoni[41] quotes Garencières (1672) as stating that the ordeal described in the first line was one that was imposed on newborn French kings on the River Rhine – the theoretical border between France and the Empire – to test their legitimacy.

4. Original September 1557 text   Read as modern French:

Le Celtiq fleuve changera de rivaige,   Le Rhin
Plus ne tiendra la cité d'Agripine: de Colonia Agrippinensis [Cologne]
Tout transmué ormis le vieil langaige,   hormis
Saturne, Leo, Mars, Cancer en rapine.

> **The Celtic stream shall shore exchange for shore:**
> **Cologne's great city shall, alas, go under.**
> **All but the former tongue shall be changed o'er:**
> **Saturn in Leo, Mars shall Cancer plunder.**

Source: The invasion of France across the Rhine by the Emperor Charles V in July 1536, as presaged by the astrology of the last line, which had applied until just three months previously. The invasion did not stop until the Imperial forces reached the Somme the following year.

5. Original September 1557 text

Read as modern French:

Si grand famine par unde pestifere,
Par pluye longue le long du polle arctique: *de la région septentrionale*
Samarobryn cent lieux de l'hemispere,   *Amiens [gall. Samarobriva]*
Vivront sans loy, exempt de pollitique.

> **Such famine reigns, so great a wave of peste,**
> **While ceaseless rains the northern world shall rake:**
> **A hundred leagues from where meet east and west**
> **Amiens shall know no law and no side take.**

Source: Continuing from the previous verse, the new situation of Amiens (the Gallic *Samarobriva*) after the Imperial invasion, standing as it were in no-man's-land between the Holy Roman Empire to the east and France to the west, whereas it had previously been some 91 French leagues as the crow flies from the former border with the Empire on the Rhine (Nostradamus's 'hundred leagues' is an approximation, but probably reflects the likely traveling distance at the time). Once again, in other words, Nostradamus has just composed a whole raft of prophecies on a single theme – in this case the continuing wars with the Empire in the north-east, while the plagues, floods, and famines of Europe's developing Little Ice Age continued to rack the continent.

6. Original September 1557 text

Read as modern French:

Apparoistra vers le Septentrion,   *vers le nord/Ursa Major*
Non loing de Cancer l'estoille chevelue: *la comète*
Suze, Sienne, Boece, Eretrion,   *Érétrie de Béotie*
Mourra de Rome grand, la nuict disperue.   *de sa disparition*

> **Near Cancer's claws, tending towards the north,**
> **O'er Susa, Siena th' bearded star appears,**
> **And over Thebes, Eretrion goes forth.**
> **Rome's lord shall die the night it disappears.**

Source: Reports of the comet of 1530, as subsequently recorded by Lycosthenes[44] and translated into English by Batman:[5] *The same yere a Comet was seene in Germany, Italy, and Fraunce, the sixte day of August, and first he appeared certayne dayes in the morning before the Sunnes rising, afterwarde he followed the Sunne, and was seene about three weekes in the Evening after the Sunnes going downe untill the thirde daye of September, his course was through Cancer, Virgo and Libra, where he ceased to be seene, neyther did he appeare any more afterward.* Possibly this is

assimilated to Julius Obsequens's *On Omens* (68) for the death of Julius Caesar in 44 BC, which, translated literally, read: 'At the games of Venus the Generatrix . . . at the eleventh hour a hairy star appearing beneath the constellation of the Great Bear drew all eyes.' The list of place names appears to be little more than poetic padding, but may be connected with the predations of the pirate Barbarossa in the eastern Mediterranean in 1533, a year that was similarly marked by a notable comet and followed not only by a royal death in 1534, but also by that of Pope Clement VII of Rome.[60] In Batman's translation: *On the 17. day of July and somewhat after, a Comet with a long taile was seene at Lubeck, and the yeare following that vertuous and peaceable king Frederick ended his life.*

7. Original September 1557 text   Read as modern French:

Norneigre & Dace, & l'isle Britannique,	*Norvège et Roumanie/Hongrie*
Par les unis freres seront vexees:	
Le chef Romain issu de sang Gallique,	
Et les copies aux forestz repoulsees.	*Les armées*

> **Norway, Pannonia and the Isle of Britain**
> **Shall by the pair of brothers harried be.**
> **Rome's chief, of French blood, shall be backward smitten,**
> **With all his troops, 'midst forest, bush and tree.**

Source: Tacitus's *Annals of Imperial Rome* concerning Germanicus Caesar (brother of the Emperor Claudius who was born at Lyon and invaded Britain in AD 43) – a commander who had distinguished himself in the east against the Pannonians and who, though victorious over the German tribes in the wake of the immense earlier Roman defeat in the depths of the Teutoburger Wald of AD 9 (when three whole legions literally disappeared), was forced finally to withdraw from Germany.

8. Original September 1557 text   Read as modern French:

Ceulx qui estoient en regne pour scavoir,	*tenus pour savants*
Au Royal change deviendront apouvris:	*appauvris*
Uns exilés sans appuy, or n'avoir,	
Lettrés & lettres ne seront à grans pris.	*prix*

> **Those in the realm whose knowledge once did count**
> **Shall with the change of King quite poor become,**
> **Some banished without gold or bank account,**
> **Learning and learned count for no great sum.**

Source: A familiar complaint of Nostradamus about the contemporary undervaluing of scholars and scholarship under Henri II, by contrast with the situation under his father François I.

9. Original September 1557 text   Read as modern French:

Aux sacrés temples seront faictz escandales
Comptés seront par honneurs & louanges   *pour*
D'un que on grave d'argent, d'or les medalles,   *D'un dont*
La fin sera en tormens bien estranges.

> **In holy churches scandals truly grave**
> **Shall soon be counted honors fit for praising.**
> **For whom gold, silver medals they'll engrave**
> **The end shall come 'midst torments most amazing.**

Source: The *Mirabilis Liber*'s predictions of Church degeneracy (see I.44, II.10, II.12), coupled with the grisly fate of the money-laundering Chancellor Antoine Duprat (see IV.88), Papal Legate and Cardinal Archbishop of Sens, who died of phtyriasis (lice) and gangrene in 1535.

10. Original September 1557 text   Read as modern French:

Un peu de temps les temples des couleurs
De blanc & noir des deux entremeslee: *entremêlés*
Roges & jaunes leur embleront les leurs
Sang, terre, peste, faim, feu, d'eaue affollee.

> **A little while shall Christian churches stay**
> **A mixture of both colors – white and black.**
> **Reds, yellows then from them shall steal away**
> **Blood, land: fire, plague, flood, famine them shall rack.**

Source: The *Journal* of Louise de Savoie, regent during the imprisonment of King François I in Spain: 'In the year 1522 my son and I began to be aware of the hypocrites – white, black, murky and of sundry colors, from whom may God by his infinite goodness and mercy preserve and defend us,'[60] combined with the various 'end-of-the-world' phenomena that were proliferating at the time. The implication is that Catholics and Reformers, originally co-existing uneasily within the Church, were destined eventually to be split apart by growing factionalism – as indeed was already happening by 1557 – as conditions generally went from bad to worse.

11. Original September 1557 text   Read as modern French:

Des sept rameaulx à trois seront reduictz   *enfants*
Les plus aisnés [/] seront surprins par mort:
Fratricider les deux seront seduictz,   *les chefs [lat. duces]*
Les conjurés en dormant seront mors.

> **Of offspring seven, to three shall be reduced**
> **The eldest males: that death shall them surprise.**

By fratricide the leaders are seduced:
Each plotter, though, while sleeping surely dies.

Source: Evidently the contemporary French royal family, with Nostradamus anticipating the early death of the sickly young Dauphin who would shortly become
King François II, leaving his brothers Charles (later to become Charles IX), Henri
(the future Henri III) and Hercule-François (Duke of Alençon), while the Catholic
Guises and the Protestant Condé and his supporters would continue to vie mur-
derously for power behind the throne. If so, a genuine, if short-term, prophecy.

12. Original September 1557 text	**Read as modern French:**
Dresser copies pour monter à l'Empire,	*armées*
Du Vatican le sang Royal tiendra:	
Flamans, Anglois, Espaigne avec Aspire,	*y sera favorable*
Contre l'Italie & France contendra.	

The royal prince shall raise great armies and
'Gainst th' Empire of the Vatican advance
With Belgium, England. Spain with them shall stand,
And shall contend 'gainst Italy and France.

Source: Contemporary geopolitical and military events involving King Henri II of
France.

13. Original September 1557 text	**Read as modern French:**
Un dubieux ne viendra loing du regne,	
La plus grand part le vouldra soustenir:	
Un capitole ne vouldra point qu'il regne,	
Sa grande charge ne pourra maintenir.	

A dubious one the throne shall nearly gain,
The greater number wish him to sustain.
The council, though, shall want him not to reign,
His office great unable to maintain.

Source: The story of the mentally ill Pope Urban VI, elected in 1378, but then
reneged on by the formerly supportive cardinals in favor of Pope Clement VII, who
duly became the first Avignon 'Antipope' of the Great Western Church Schism that
was to split the Catholic Church down the middle for almost forty years.

14. Original September 1557 text	**Read as modern French:**
Loing de sa tetre Roy perdra la bataille,	*terre*
Prompt eschappé poursuivy suivant prins	*pris*
Ignare prins soubz la doree maille,	*Ignorant; prince*
Soubz fainct habit & l'ennemy surprins.	*surpris*

Far from his land, the King's defeated there.
Escaped, pursued, he'll captured be again.
Of prince beneath the gold mail unaware
The foes by his disguise aback are ta'en.

Source: A slightly garbled version of the capture and imprisonment of King Richard I of England in Vienna in 1192, while making his way back in disguise from the largely unsuccessful Third Crusade to Jerusalem.

15. Original September 1557 text   Read as modern French:

Dessoubz la tombe sera trouvé le prince,
Qu'aura le pris par dessus Nuremberg:
L'Espaignol Roy en Capricorne mince,
Fainct & trahy par le grand Vvitemberg.

Beneath the tombstone shall the prince be found
Who shall have gained the prize o'er Nuremberg.
The King of Spain, just within Capricorn,
Shall be betrayed by th' lord of Wittenberg.

Source: An unidentified discovery presaging the spiriting away of Martin Luther to the castle of Wartburg after the celebrated Diet of Worms of 1521 by his patron and protector, the Elector Prince Frederick.

16. Original September 1557 text   Read as modern French:

Ce que ravy sera du jeune Milve,   *du Milan*
Par les Normans de France & Picardie:
Les noirs du temple du lieu de Negresilve   *les bénédictins; de la Forêt Noire*
Feront aulberge & feu de Lombardie.

What from the youthful Hawk is put to sack
By French from Normandy and Picardy
The black monks of the church of Forest Black
Shall make the inn and hearth of Lombardy.

Source: The expulsion of the Emperor Frederick Barbarossa from northern Italy by the Norman regime in Sicily in 1176, leaving only his Benedictine entourage behind.

17. Original September 1557 text   Read as modern French:

Apres les limes bruslez les asiniers,   *livres; assignés*
Constrainctz seront changer habitz divers:
Les Saturnins bruslez par les meusniers,   *Les Juifs; moines [mot déguisé par précaution?]*
Hors la pluspart qui ne sera couvers.   *qui sera converti [convers]*

After the books, they'll burn th' accused as well,
Or make them change their clothes in many a way,
The Jews burnt at the stake by monkish knell
Apart from most who shall converted stay.

Source: The history of Nostradamus's own Jewish forebears, first persecuted and expelled from Spain, then oppressed all over again in France.

18. Original September 1557 text   Read as modern French:

Par les phisiques le grand Roy delaissé,   médicaments
Par sort non art de l'Ebrieu est en vie:
Luy & son genre au regne hault poulsé,
Grace donnee à gent qui Christ envie.

For th' mighty King all medicines being waived,
By luck, not Hebrew's art, his life is saved,
He and his kin then in the realm raised high
Preferment given to th' folk that Christ deny.

Source: Pursuing the Jewish theme of the previous verse, presumably the story of one of the contemporary Jewish doctors at the Court in Paris – if not of Nostradamus himself.

19. Original September 1557 text   Read as modern French:

La vraye flamme engloutira la dame,
Que vouldra mettre les Innocens à feu: Qui
Pres de l'assault l'exercite s'enflamme,   l'armée
Quant dans Seville monstre en boeuf sera veu.   en Taurus [?]

The flame of truth her ladyship shall roast
Who would the Innocents burn to a toast:
Before the attack the army burns with zeal
When in a bull a sign's seen at Seville.

Source: Unknown events linked to an omen seen at a Spanish bullfight, with the theme of 'burning' played by Nostradamus for all he is worth.

20. Original September 1557 text   Read as modern French:

L'union faincte sera peu de duree,   sainte
Des uns changés reformés la pluspart:
Dans les vaisseaux sera gent enduree,   endurcie
Lors aura Rome un nouveau liepart.   Alors; un nouveau pape

The Holy League shall not too long endure:

Of those who change most shall change back again.
Within the fleet a hard race fights for sure,
But then o'er Rome a lion new shall reign.

Source: The Holy League of 1537, drawn up between Pope Paul III, the Emperor Charles V, and the republic of Venice to oppose the Ottoman Emperor Suleiman the Magnificent – a confederacy that collapsed the following year despite the determined efforts of the admiral Andrea Doria up until his defeat at Preveza.[60] The 'new lion' who was Julius III did not ascend the papal throne until 1550, however, so the reference is presumably to a reformed and somewhat chastened Paul III himself.

21. Original September 1557 text   Read as modern French:

Quant ceulx du polle artiq unis ensemble,   *du nord*
En Orient grand effraieur & crainte:
Esleu nouveau, sustenu le grand temple,   *l'Église*
Rode Bisance de sang Barbare taincte.   *Musulman/Arabe*

Once most of th' northern hemisphere unites
Shall in the East great fear and terror reign.
A new pope chosen, Church restored to rights,
While Arab blood Byzantium, Rhodes shall stain.

Source: The *Mirabilis Liber*'s predictions of a mighty Western counter-attack against the Muslim invaders and occupiers of Europe, and the restoration of the Church under a new 'Angelic Pastor' and/or Holy Roman Emperor. See I.4, I.55, I.92, and especially 'There shall be battles, and mortality such as has not been seen since the beginning of the world, nor shall ever be seen again. Among the kings of the nations, there shall be one who shall triumph. He shall be borne on an elephant and shall come to establish his empire in these places. From those days onwards there shall be only one shepherd in the Lord's Church, by whose efforts peace and unity of doctrine shall be reborn . . . The king in question shall reign for a long time. All the tyrants who oppressed the Church shall be suddenly put down; all the scepters shall be collected into the hand of the pastor announced by the predictions' (Prophecy of St Severus); 'Then shall appear a hermit of great saintliness. As [the Abbot] Joachim says, a man of remarkable holiness shall be elevated to the papal see. The Lord shall use him to perform so many miracles that all men shall revere him, and no one shall dare to challenge his teachings. He shall forbid the conferring of several benefices on a single person, and he shall take measures to ensure that the clergy live [only] on the tithes and offerings of the faithful. He shall forbid all pompous vestments and everything that is dishonest, as well as dancing and hymn singing; he shall preach the gospel, and shall encourage honest women to appear in public without gold or jewelry. After he has occupied the papacy for a long time, he shall happily rejoin the Lord' (Prophecy of St Cyril on the Angelic Pastor); '. . . after the still distant sufferings of the Christians, and after too great a shedding of innocent blood, the prosperity of the Lord shall descend upon the devastated nation; a remarkable pastor shall take his seat upon the papal throne, under the protection of the angels. Pure and full of grace, he shall annul everything [untoward that has taken place hitherto], and shall redeem with his amiable virtues the State of the Church and the dispersed temporal powers. He shall revere the stars and shall fear the sun, because his conscience shall be in the hand of the Lord. He shall overcome every other power and re conquer the kingdom of Jerusalem. A single pastor shall lead both the Eastern and Western churches at the same time. One single faith shall be in force. Such shall be the virtue of the benevolent pastor that the peaks of the mountains shall bow in his presence. This saintly man shall break the pride of the religious, who shall all return to the fold of the primitive Church; that is to say, there shall henceforth be only a single pastor, a single law, a single master, modest, humble, fearing God' (Prophecy on the Angelic Pastor attributed to Merlin).

22. Original September 1557 text   Read as modern French:

Dedans la terre du grand temple celique,
Nepveu à Londres par paix faincte meurtry:
La barque alors deviendra scismatique,   *L'Église*
Liberté faincte sera au corn & cry.   *à cor et à cri*

> **Where stands the church of God in land apart**
> **At London, 'neath sham truce, a nephew's maimed:**
> **Then shall the Holy Barque be split apart,**
> **Sham liberty be everywhere proclaimed.**

Source: An unidentified incident in England taken as an omen for the rise of Protestantism in the name of liberty of belief, which was leading in France inexorably towards the gruesome Wars of Religion. See also the *Mirabilis Liber*'s predictions of the destruction of the 'barque' that is the Church, as listed at I.15.

23. Original September 1557 text   Read as modern French:

D'esprit de regne munismes descriees,   *monnaies [numismes: lat. numisma]*
Et seront peuples esmeuz contre leur Roy:
Faix, faict nouveau, sainctes loix empirees,   *Paix*
Rapis onc fut en si tresdur arroy.   *Paris [anagr.] ne fut jamais*

> **Wits shall the kingdom's currency talk down**
> **And folk against their King they shall incite.**
> **Pacts, novelties, laws sacred watered down:**
> **Never was Paris in such parlous plight.**

Source: Current developments, colored by Nostradamus's horror at the dangerous 'new ideas' (and especially the religious ones) that were threatening to adulterate traditional religious values and destroy the existing social order, as well as by the *Mirabilis Liber*'s predictions of fatal religious decay. See I.44, II.10, II.12.

24. Original September 1557 text   Read as modern French:

Mars & le sceptre se trouvera conioinct,   *et Jupiter*
Dessoubz Cancer calamiteuse guerre:
Un peu apres sera nouveau Roy oingt,
Qui par long temps pacifiera la terre.

> **When Mars and Jupiter are in conjunction,**
> **'Neath Cancer ghastly war shall be unfurled.**
> **Later they shall anoint with royal unction**
> **A new king who'll long pacify the world.**

Source: The *Mirabilis Liber's* predictions of the advent of a future *Grand Monarque* (see I.4, I.55, I.92), timed astrologically by Nostradamus to follow a summer war.

25. Original September 1557 text   Read as modern French:

Par Mars contraire sera la monarchie.   *À cause d'une guerre hostile*
Du grand pescheur en trouble ruyneux:
Jeune noir, rouge prendra la hierarchie,   *un nouveau cardinal*
Les prodieteurs iront jour bruyneux.   *Les traîtres*

> **Mars being opposed, the sacred monarchy**
> **Of th' Fisher shall into dire trouble fall.**
> **A new, dark red-hat takes the hierarchy.**
> **Traitors shall act that day 'neath misty pall.**

Source: The *Mirabilis Liber's* predictions of an invasion of Europe by vast Muslim forces (see I.9, I.75, II.24) and the consequent betrayal and destruction of the Church and Papacy (see I.15).

26. Original September 1557 text   Read as modern French:

Quatre ans le siege quelque peu bien tiendra,
Un survien ra libidineux de vie: *surviendra*
Ravenna & Pyse, Veronne soustiendront,
Pour eslever la croix de Pape envie.

> **Four years the see he'll fairly well maintain:**
> **One shall succeed who'll live a life of lust,**
> **Ravenna, Pisa, Verona him sustain.**
> **The Pope to mount a great Crusade shall thrust.**

Source: Apparently Pope Julius III, who reigned for four years, and Gregory VIII, who presided over preparations for the Third Crusade – but was not noted for his lewd lifestyle!

27. Original September 1557 text   **Read as modern French:**

Dedans les isles de cinq fleuves à un,   *Du milieu des Indes*
Par le croissant du grand Chyren Selin: *Pour; Henri Lunaire*
Par les bruynes de l'aër fureur de l'un,
Six eschapés cachés fardeaux de lyn.

> **From Indic land where five streams join in one**
> **For crescent he'll 'gainst lunar Henry bid.**
> **In misty air in fury rages one:.**
> **Six shall escape, in flaxen bundles hid.**

Source: Plutarch's account, in his *Parallel Lives*, of Alexander the Great's conquest of the Punjab (which literally means 'five rivers'), transferred to the context of the *Mirabilis Liber*'s expected Western counter-attack against the future Muslim invaders of Europe (see I.55), with a few other details added for good measure.

28. Original September 1557 text   **Read as modern French:**

Le grand Celtique entrera dedans Rome,
Menant amas d'exilés & bannis:
La grand pasteur mettra à mort tout homme,   *à port [?]*
Qui pour le coq estoient aux Alpes unys.

> **The mighty Celt into great Rome then goes**
> **Leading many an exile and outcast:**
> **The mighty Pope shall shelter all of those**
> **Who with the Cock over the Alps have passed.**

Source: Possibly the Italian campaign of Duke François de Guise in May 1557 – though in this case line 3 would be extremely dubious unless *mort* should be read as *port*, as I have transcribed it here.

29. Original September 1557 text   **Read as modern French:**

La vefve saincte entendant les nouvelles,   *veuve*
De ses rameaux mis en perplex & trouble: *enfants; perplexité*
Qui sera duict appaiser les querelles,   *induite à*
Par son pourchas des razes fera comble.   *poursuite; moines*

> **The holy widow, once the news she gets**
> **About her children placed in trouble sore,**
> **Induced to calm the quarrels and the frets,**
> **Through doggedness the monks shall triumph o'er.**

Source: Unknown story of a mother who manages to save her sons from the Inquisition.

30. Original September 1557 text   **Read as modern French:**

Par l'apparence de faincte saincteté,   *prétendue*
Sera trahy aux ennemis le siege:
Nuict qu'on cuidoit dormir en seureté,   *pensait; sureté*
Pres de Braban marcheront ceulx du Liege.   *de Liège*

> **By one who shall feign sanctity to keep**
> **The see shall be betrayed to foes most arch,**
> **E'en on that night when they thought safe to sleep.**
> **Near Brabant, those from Liège are on the march.**

Source: The *Mirabilis Liber*'s prophecy of the destruction of the Church in the course of an invasion of Europe by Arab forces. See I.9, I.15, I.75.

31. Original September 1557 text   **Read as modern French:**

Roy trouvera ce qu'il desiroit tant,
Quant le Prelat sera reprins à tort: *repris*
Responce au duc le rendra mal content,
Qui dans Milan mettre plusieurs à mort.   *beaucoup de gens*

> **The King shall what he most desired find out**
> **When th' Bishop they recapture by mistake:**
> **His answer to the Duke his wish shall flout**
> **Who in Milan shall many corpses make.**

Source: Unidentified.

32. Original September 1557 text   **Read as modern French:**

Par trabysons [//] de verges gens à mort battu,   *Pour trahisons*
Prins surmonté sera par son desordre:
Conseil frivole au grand captif sentu,
Nez par fureur quant Begich viendra mordre.   *Belgique [?]; se mangera le nez*

> **For treasons folk to death are beaten sore,**
> **The prince o'erwhelmed by chaos consequent,**
> **Stupid advice to th' captive handed o'er,**
> **While Belgians quarrel furiously at Ghent.**

Source: Unknown, failing any certain identification of 'Begich', but if the word should read 'Belgique' the reference would be to the contemporary troubles of Charles V within the Low Countries. 'At Ghent' is purely my own contextual, rhyme-induced insertion.

33. Original September 1557 text   **Read as modern French:**

Sa main derniere par Alus sanguinaire,   *bataille; Halus [ancienne ville de Babylonie]*
Ne se pourra par la mer guarantir:
Entre deux fleuves caindre main militaire,   *craindre; une armée [lat. manus]*
Le noir l'ireux le fera repentir.

> Bloody from Halus, his remaining force
> Fails to ensure his safety o'er the ocean.
> 'Twixt rivers twain he'll fear an armèd force.
> The angry Black shall make him rue the notion.

Source: Tacitus's account, in his *Annals of Imperial Rome* (VI.41–4), of the deposing of the Roman puppet Tiridates III by the Scythian Artabanus III in Mesopotamia, the 'land between two rivers', in AD 37, after he had occupied Halus and Artemita; 'And now that he [Artabanus] was rapidly approaching Seleucia with a large host [*manu*], Tiridates, unnerved by the fame and very presence of Artabanus, was in two minds as to whether to engage him or commit himself to a guerilla campaign . . . At length Tiridates spared [his allies] the dishonor of treacherous desertion by returning to Syria with a few followers' – all of it presumably assimilated to the *Mirabilis Liber*'s expected invasion of Europe via the Middle East. See I.9, I.75, II.24.

34. Original September 1557 text   **Read as modern French:**

De feu vloant la machination.   *volant*
Viendra troubler au grand chef assiegés:
Dedans sera telle sedition,
Qu'en desespoir seront les profligés.

> Of flying fire th' ingenious machine
> Shall trouble those by the great chief beset:
> Within, there shall be such sedition seen
> That the poor wretches shall all hope forget.

Source: Unidentified use of a catapult that fired flaming objects, possibly assimilated to the celestial vision reported by Lycosthenes[44] for 1550, and subsequently translated into English by Dr Stephen Batman:[5] *The 12th of the Kalends of July, at Wittenberg there was seene a bloodye sworde and an engine of Warre layde upon wheeles in the Element, as writeth Job Fincelius.* The accompanying woodcut, though, appears merely to show soldiers bearing shields.

35. Original September 1557 text   Read as modern French:

Pres de Rion, & proche à blanche laine,   *d'Orion; d'Aries*
Aries, Taurus, Cancer, Leo la Vierge:
Mars, Jupiter, le Sol ardra grand plaine,   *incendiera*
Boys & cités, lettres cachés au cierge.   *cachetées*

> **Near white-wooled Ram, and quite close to Orion,**
> **With Mars and Jupiter in Bull, Crab, Lion**
> **And Virgin, shall the sun the plains ignite,**
> **Forests and cities. Letters with wax sealed tight.**

Source: Unidentified spring and early summer drought, fire, and other events, apparently during 1551–3.

36. Original September 1557 text   Read as modern French:

Ne bien ne mal par bataille terrestre,   *Ni . . . ni . . .*
Ne parviendra aux confins de Perouse:
Rebeller Pise, Florence voir mal estre,
Roy nuict blessé sur mulet à noire house.

> **Nor good nor ill the land-fight shall bestow**
> **The limits of Perugia's town inside.**
> **Pisa rebels: Florence shall know much woe.**
> **King hurt at night shall mule all muddy ride.**

Source: Plutarch's account in his *Parallel Lives* of the flight of the aged general Marius from the pursuing troops of Sulla some eighty years before Christ: 'Thus, deserted by everybody, he pressed forward with pain and difficulty over pathless ground until, wading through deep marshes and ditches full of muddy water, he came upon the hut of an old man . . . Whereupon Marius, standing up and stripping himself, plunged into a pool of thick, muddy water . . . ', somewhat confusedly assimilated to the same book's explanation of the term 'Marius's mules' in terms of the tradition that the soldiery, 'when jokingly praising a man who was a laborious drudge, called him "Marius's mule"' – all possibly assimilated to the *Mirabilis Liber*'s expected Muslim invasion of Europe via Italy. See I.9, I.75.

37. Original September 1557 text   Read as modern French:

L'oeuvre ancienne se parachevera,
Du toict cherra sur le grand mal ruyne: tombera
Innocent faict mort on accusera: de l'acte mortel
Nocent caiché, taillis à la bruyne.   Le coupable

The ancient work shall be fulfilled in time:
Down from the roof on th' lord disaster drops.
An innocent they'll blame for th' mortal crime,
The guilty hiding in a misty copse.

Source: Unidentified fulfillment of an equally unidentified ancient prophecy, probably from classical times.

38. Original September 1557 text   Read as modern French:

Aux profligés de paix les ennemis,
Apres avoir l'Italie supperee: vaincue
Noir sanguinaire, rouge sera commis,
Feu, sang verser, eaue de sang couloree.

The beaten shall the foes of peace behold,
Once they have Italy full vanquishèd.
The bloody Moor and red shall then make bold
Fires to light, blood to spill, till streams run red.

Source: The *Mirabilis Liber*'s grim prophecies of a gruesome invasion by forces from Africa and the Middle East. See I.9, I.75, II.24.

39. Original September 1557 text   Read as modern French:

L'enfant du regne par paternelle prinse,   prise/enlèvement
Expolié sera pour delivrer: exposé [exposié?]
Aupres du lac Trasimen l'azur prinse,
La troupe hostaige pour trop fort s'enyvrer

The royal child, once by his father taken,
In order to claim ransom he'll expose:
Near Trasimen the Blue shall then be taken
The whole troop hostage, drunk as heaven knows.

Source: Unknown incident from contemporary Italian conflicts.

40. Original September 1557 text   **Read as modern French:**

Grand de Magonce pour grande soif estaindre,   *De Mayence*
Sera privé de sa grand dignité:
Ceux de Cologne si fort le viendront plaindre
Que le grand groppe au Ryn sera getté.   *groupe*

> **For slaking of his thirst shall Mainz's lord's**
> **Great office be removed from him at last:**
> **Those of Cologne shall 'plain with such harsh words**
> **That his whole crew shall in the Rhine be cast.**

Source: Unknown incident from contemporary German politics, probably concerning the Elector Archbishop of Mainz.

41. Original September 1557 text   **Read as modern French:**

Le second chef du regne Dannemarc,
Par ceulx de Frise & l'isle Britannique,
Fera despendre plus de cent mille marc,   *dépenser*
Vain exploicter voyage en Italique.   *effectuer*

> **The second chief who Denmark's realm has graced**
> **The lord of Frisia and of Britain too,**
> **More than a hundred thousand marks shall waste**
> **To make a trip to Italy he'll rue.**

Source: The pilgrimage of King Canute (Knut II of Denmark) to Rome in 1027, timed to coincide with the coronation of the Holy Roman Emperor Conrad II. See IV.89.

42. Original September 1557 text   **Read as modern French:**

A logmyon sera laissé le regne,   *À l'Ogmion [l'Hercule gallois]*
Du grand Selin qui plus fera de faict: *Lunaire; défait [deffaict]*
Par les Italies estendra son enseigne,
Regi sera par prudent contrefaict.

> **To Ogmion the kingdom they shall hand**
> **Of the great Muslim, who'll defeated be:**
> **His banner he'll extend o'er Latin land,**
> **Being ruled by guile and prudent subtlety.**

Source: The *Mirabilis Liber*'s prediction of the advent of a future *Grand Monarque* who will liberate first France, then the rest of Europe, from its future Muslim invaders. See I.4, I.55, I.92.

43. Original September 1557 text   **Read as modern French:**

Long temps sera sans estre habitee,
Ou Seine & Marne autour vient arrouser:
De la Tamise & martiaulx temptee,   *affligée*
Deceuz les gardes en cuidant repouser.   *pensant/croyant*

Long time unpeopled shall the country stay
That's watered by the rivers Marne and Seine,
By English hosts subjected to affray:
Such guards who think to rest shall think in vain.

Source: The long struggle between France and England, especially in northern France, during the Hundred Years' War of roughly 1337 to 1453, as recounted in particular by Froissart in his *Chroniques*.

44. Original September 1557 text   **Read as modern French:**

De nuict par Nantes Lyris apparoistra,   *l'Iris/l'arc-en-ciel*
Des artz marins susciteront la pluye:
Arabiq goulfre grand classe parfondra,   *flotte*
Un monstre en Saxe naistra d'ours & truye.

By night near Nantes the rainbow shall be seen,
Maritime arts raise rain out of thin air.
Fleet sunk in Arab Gulf, and monster seen
In Saxony, born of a sow and bear.

Source: A series of reported contemporary omens, linked to a notable maritime sinking. The first omen is of a type also reported by Lycosthenes[44] for 1520 and later translated into English by Batman[5]: *The seaventh daye aboute the breake of daye there were seene* [in Vienna] *three Sunnes. Philosophers call them* Parahelios: *from sixe untill seaven a clocke, there was seene a Rainebowe with a three double Moone, which prodigies with their images were sent by Pamphilus Gengenbach to King Charles and published through Germanie.*

45. Original September 1557 text Read as modern French:

Le gouverneur du regne bien scavant,
Ne consentir voulant au faict Royal:
Mellile classe par le contraire vent, *Malte [?] [Mellite]*
Le remettra à son plus desloyal.

> **The governor right learned of the realm**
> **Shall not assent to th' King's command because**
> **Mellila's fleet against the wind shall helm,**
> **And make him as disloyal as e'er he was.**

Source: Unknown act of disloyalty by an erudite but suspect regional governor who is over-impressed by the approach of a fleet from Melilla in Morocco (Spanish from 1490 onwards).

46. Original September 1557 text Read as modern French:

Un juste sera en exil renvoyé,
Par pestilence aux confins de Nonseggle: *nom-de-sceau [lat: sigilla; donc la Sigillaria*
                (le marché des sceaux) à Rome

Responce au rouge le fera desvoyé,
Roy retirant à la Rane & à l'aigle. *devant le Poisson de Mer et l'Empire*

> **The just one into exile shall be sent**
> **With Plague around the 'Market of the Sigil':**
> **His answer to the Red means banishment,**
> **While King retreats before Sea Fish and Eagle.**

Source: Unidentified incident involving the disgrace of a noble on account of an ill-advised response to a cardinal in Rome, while the French king is on the defensive against the pirate Barbarossa and the Emperor Charles V. Compare V.3.

47. Original September 1557 text Read as modern French:

Entre deux monts les deux grands assemblés
Delaisseront leur simulte secrete: *hostilité*
Brucelle & Dolle par Langres acablés,
Pour à Malignes executer leur peste.

> **Between two mounts the two lords, duly met,**
> **Shall leave aside their hatred well-concealed –**
> **Brussels and Dole by Langres quite beset –**
> **Their plague t' inflict on Malines in the field.**

Source: Unidentified incident from the contemporary wars in the Netherlands.

48. Original September 1557 text   **Read as modern French:**

La saincteté trop faincte & seductive,
Accompaigné d'une langue diserte: *claire/courante*
La cité vieille & Parme trop hastive,   *hâtive*
Florence & Sienne rendront plus desertes.

> **Despite sham holiness that shall seduce,**
> **Accompanied by clever language-use,**
> **The ancient town and Parma prone to haste**
> **Shall Florence, Siena both the more lay waste.**

Source: Unidentified.

49. Original September 1557 text   **Read as modern French:**

De la partie de Mammer grand Pontife,   *de Mamers [Mars]*
Subjuguera les confins du Dannube:
Chasser les croix par fer raffe ne riffe,   *coûte que coûte [prov. de rifla ou de raffa]*
Captifz, or, bagues plus de cent mille rubes. *rubis*

> **On Mars's part, a great religious lord**
> **The Danube and its lands shall soon suppress:**
> **By hook or crook Christ's flock put to the sword,**
> **Captives, gold rings, and rubies numberless.**

Source: The *Mirabilis Liber*'s prediction of a massive Muslim invasion of Europe (see I.9, I.75, II.24), including a Hungarian component (presumably derived from the contemporary Ottoman occupation) which it will subsequently take Hungarians to redress: 'The pride of the Turks shall be cast down; the kingdoms and the principalities shall be joined with the Church because the children of Sagittarius, Spaniards, and Hungarians, shall exceed all Catholics in valor, and shaking off the shame of the original disasters, shall put to flight the Turkish perversity' (Prophecy of Reynard Lolhardus, quoted in chapter 26 of Part 2 of Lichtenberger's 'Prognosticatio' of 1488).

50. Original September 1557 text   **Read as modern French:**

Dedans le puys seront trouvés les oz,
Sera l'incest commis par la maratre:
L'estat changé on querra bruit & loz,   *on cherchera renom et louanges*
Et aura Mars ascndant pour son astre.   *ascendant*

> **Out of the ditch the ancient bones they'll raise:**
> **Stepmother then shall incest perpetrate.**
> **Her state once changed, they'll seek renown and praise,**
> **And Mars ascending shall rule o'er his fate.**

Source: The recovery from the Tiber of the body of the Duke of Gandia, murdered on the orders of Cesare Borgia in 1497, together with the sinister activities of his sister Lucretia and his subsequent translation from being a cardinal to life as a soldier.[60]

51. Original September 1557 text **Read as modern French:**

Peuple assemblé, voir nouveau expectacle, *spectacle*
Princes & Roys par plusieurs assistans: *beaucoup*
Pilliers faillir, murs, mais comme miracle
Le Roy sauvé & trente des instans. *assistants*

>**The folk shall gather for the novel view,**
>**Princes and Kings among the many there.**
>**Pillars and walls shall crumble but Pardieu!**
>**The King is saved, and thirty there at prayer.**

Source: The coronation of Pope Clement V at Lyon on 14 November 1305, attended by King Philip the Fair, the Kings of Aragon and Majorca and a crowd of other royals and nobles, during which a collapsing wall killed many of the spectators standing on it, as well as the Duke of Brittany. Compare II.97.[60]

52. Original September 1557 text **Read as modern French:**

En lieu du grand qui sera condemné,
De prison hors [/] son amy en sa place:
L'espoir Troyen en six moys joinct, mort nay, *de la famille royale française*
Le Sol à l'urne [/] seront prins fleuves en glace. *en Aquarius; pris*

>**In place of th' lord condemned e'en though high-born,**
>**From jail instead his friend they shall release:**
>**The royal hope after six months stillborn.**
>**Sun in Aquarius, all the rivers freeze.**

Source: Among other events, possibly one of Queen Catherine de Médicis's miscarriages, on this occasion in the depths of winter.

53. Original September 1557 text **Read as modern French:**

Le grand Prelat Celtique à Roy suspect,
De nuict par cours sortira hors du regne: *Au cours de la nuit*
Par duc fertile à son grand Roy, Bretaigne,
Bisance à Cipres & Tunes insuspect.

>**The Celtic prelate suspect to the King**
>**Shall quit the realm by night all undetected,**
>**Helped by a duke serving his British king.**
>**Turkey by Cyprus, Tunis unsuspected.**

Source: An unidentified cloak-and-dagger incident serving as an omen for a Turkish attack in the Mediterranean, possibly assimilated to the *Mirabilis Liber's* prediction of a Middle Eastern invasion of Europe. See I.9, I.75, II.24.

54. Original September 1557 text   Read as modern French:

Au poinct du jour au second chant du coq,
Ceulx de Tunes, de Fez, & de Bugie:
Par les Arabes captif le Roy Maroq,
L'an mil six cens & sept, de Liturgie.   *de l'Ityrie [l'Ityrée, au Liban]/de l'ère*
                                                    chrétienne[8][?]

> **At daybreak, when the cock shall call again,**
> **From Tunis, Fez and Bougie they'll appear.**
> **Morocco's King by Arabs shall be ta'en**
> **From Lebanon, 1607 the year.**

Source: Apparently the assassination of King Mohammed al-Mahdi by the Pasha of Algiers in 1557, following raids by the Turks on Fez and Bougie, simply projected (not for the first time!) fifty years into the future and assimilated to the *Mirabilis Liber's* dire predictions of Arab invasion (see I.9, I.75). On the other hand, St Ambrose's *Canon of the Mass*, the core of the Roman Catholic *liturgy*, was officially promulgated by the then Emperor Theodosius I in AD 392, which could possibly make this not merely an actual dated prediction of marauders from the Middle East, but one for 1999 (392 + 1607), when King Hassan II of Morocco, while not actually being captured . . . *died!*

55. Original September 1557 text   Read as modern French:

Au chalmé Duc en arrachant l'esponce,   *Sous la chaleur de midi*
Voille arabesque voir, subit descouverte:
Tripolis Chio, & ceulx de Trapesonce,   *de Trabzon*
Duc prins Marnegro, & sa cité deserte.

> **Diving for sponges, Duke 'neath noonday sun**
> **Suddenly sees the Arab fleet sail past.**
> **Tripolis, Chios, Trebizond o'errun:**
> **Emptied his city: by Black Sea held fast.**

Source: The *Mirabilis Liber's* prophecy of a huge Arab invasion via the Middle East. See I.9, I.75, II.24.

56. Original September 1557 text   Read as modern French:

La crainte armee de l'ennemy Narbon,   *Narbonnais*
Effrayera si fort les Hesperiques: *les Espagnols [?]*
Parpignan vuide par l'aveuglé darbon,   *Perpignan vidé par la taupe aveugle [prov.]*
Lors Barcelon par mer donra les piques.   *Barcelone*

The dreaded hostile army from Narbonne
The Spaniards so shall daunt! Emptied shall be
Perpignan by the mole that blind runs on.
Then Barcelona shall attack by sea.

Source: The *Rozier historial de France* (1522), speaking of the Spaniards who 'all took to the fields and came and took up position before the French camp . . . The King of Spain, by dint of payments (as has been established since) blinded the eyes of various of them, in such wise that the loyal French were sore astonished when they became aware of such great and evident treason.'[60]

57. Original September 1557 text   Read as modern French:

Celuy qu'estoit bien avant dans le regne,
Ayant chet rouge proche à la hierarchie: *Tête [chapeau] rouge*
Aspre & cruel, & se fera tant craindre,
Succedera à sacré monarchie.

He who within the realm was close to power,
With Cardinal close to the hierarchy,
So feared, so harsh, so cruel shall come to lour.
He shall take o'er the sacred monarchy.

Source: The enthronement in 1503 of Pope Julius II, known as *Uomo terribile*.[60]

58. Original September 1557 text   Read as modern French:

Entre les deux monarques esloignés,
Lors que le Sol par Selin clair perdue: *éclipsé par la lune*
Simulte grande entre deux indignés,   *Dispute*
Qu'aux Isles & Sienne la liberté rendue.

Between the somewhat distanced monarchs twain,
When the sun's light Selene shall impede,
Great argument and great affront shall reign
Such that Siena and the Isles are freed.

Source: The solar eclipse of the summer of 1551, marking the beginning of a new conflict between King Henri II and the Emperor Charles V, leading to the French-inspired rebellion of Siena of 1552 and a pact between Henri and the Turkish pirate Turgut which enabled French forces to land in Corsica in 1553, liberating the island from the Genoans.[60]

59. Original September 1557 text   **Read as modern French:**

Dame en fureur par raige d'adultere,
Viendra à son prince conjurer non de dire:
Mais bref cogneu sera le vitupere,   *les injures/invectives*
Que seront mis dixsept à martire.

> **The lady furious at th' adultery**
> **Her prince beseeches firmly 'No' to say,**
> **But soon the quarrel widely known shall be**
> **And seventeen shall go the martyr's way.**

Source: The discovery *en flagrant délit* of Henri II with his lover Lady Fleming by his mistress Diane de Poitiers, and the King's vain efforts to hush up the incident, torpedoed by her subsequent pregnancy and confinement in 1551, the year of the Edict of Châteaubriant, which prescribed burning at the stake as the punishment for heresy.

60. Original September 1557 text   **Read as modern French:**

Le prince hors de son terroir Celtique,
Sera trahy, deceu par interprete:
Rouan, Rochelle, par ceulx de l'Armorique   *Rouen; de la Bretagne*
Au port de Blaue deceuz par moine & prebstre.   *Blaye*

> **The Prince out of his Celtic lands shall be**
> **By an interpreter right roundly fleeced:**
> **Rouen, Rochelle by those from Brittany**
> **At Blaye shall be deceived by monk and priest.**

Source: Recriminations between Charles V and Philip of Hesse in 1547 as a result of a bad translation of a communiqué, and the Aquitaine salt-tax revolt of 1548.[60]

61. Original September 1557 text   **Read as modern French:**

Le grand tappis plié ne monstrera,
Fors qu'à demy la pluspart de l'histoire: *Pas plus qu'*
Chassé du regne loing aspre apparoistra,
Qu'au fait bellique chascun le viendra croire.

> **The tapestry still folded shall but show**
> **The half of what the tale is famous for:**
> **From th' realm chased far away, so fierce he'll grow**
> **That all shall think him quite a warrior.**

Source: The successful breaking by the brilliant Duke of Guise of the Emperor Charles V's siege of Metz in 1552 (thanks not least to the remarkable efforts of Nostradamus's young friend and colleague, the architect and engineer Adam de

Craponne), and the virtual routing of his vastly superior army. The first two lines relate to the six great tapestries depicting the life of the archetypal fifth- to sixth-century Frankish King Clovis, which the Emperor (about whom Nostradamus is suitably ironic) had to leave behind in his abandoned tent that had in any case been too small to display them all at once.[60]

62. Original September 1557 text   **Read as modern French:**

Trop tard tous deux, les fleurs seront perdues,   *Firenze [Florence], Firenzuola [?]*
Contre la loy serpent ne vouldra faire: *foi [?]*
Des ligueurs forces par gallotz confondues
Savone, Albingne par monech grand martyre.   *Albenga*

> **The Flowers are lost through being both too late.**
> **'Gainst holy law no act the snake shall try.**
> **The French stave off the force confederate.**
> **Through Monaco, Savonan martyrs die.**

Source: The *Mirabilis Liber's* forecast of a massive invasion of southern Europe via Italy (including Florence and Firenzuola) and the Mediterranean. See I.9, I.75. For the *serpent,* see V.25.

63. Original September 1557 text   **Read as modern French:**

La dame seule au regne demoureee,
L'unic estaint premier au lict d'honneur:
Sept ans sera de douleur exploree,
Puis longue vie au regne par grand heur.

> **The lady left alone upon the throne,**
> **The first within the bed of honor dead,**
> **Seven years shall be by grief tried to the bone,**
> **Then a long reign most fortunate instead.**

Source: Apparently the story of the contemporary Queen Catherine de Médicis, following the death of her husband Henri II while jousting in 1559. If so, a notably successful prophecy.

64. Original September 1557 text   **Read as modern French:**

On ne tiendra pache aucune arresté,
Tous recevans iront par tromperie:
De paix & tresve terre & mer proteste,   *protesté [déclaré/réclamé]*
Par Barcelone classe prins d'industrie.   *la flotte prise par assiduité*

> **They shall not hold to what they shall agree:**
> **All who accept them shall be duped the while.**

Of pact and truce loud claims by land and sea:
The fleet shall Barcelona take by guile.

Source: Possibly the *Mirabilis Liber*'s predictions of an Arab invasion of Europe, in part via Spain. See I.9, I.75.

65. Original September 1557 text **Read as modern French:**

Gris & bureau, demie ouverte guerre,
De nuict seront assaillis & pillés:
Le bureau prins passera par la serre,
Son temple ouvert deux au plastre grillés. *à deux en plâtre cuit*

'Twixt gray and brown shall war half-opened be:
Each ravaged and attacked amid the night.
The brown once captured, into prison he,
His church oped to two plaster saints in white.

Source: Unidentified religious quarrel apparently between Franciscans, eventually settled by the white-robed Dominicans of the Inquisition.

66. Original September 1557 text **Read as modern French:**

Au fondement de la nouvelle secte,
Seront les oz du grand Romain trouvés,
Sepulcre en marbre apparoistra couverte,
Terre trembler en Avril, mal enfouetz. *enfoui*

When they shall come to found the sect quite new
The bones of the great Roman shall be found.
Covered in marble springs the tomb to view
When earth in April quakes, half-underground.

Source: Possibly the discovery in 1502 – the year in which Pietro Bernardino was burned alive for founding a new sect of 'primitive Christians' called the *unti* – of the half-buried obelisk of Augustus Caesar, following an earthquake in the area of Coni in 1500.[60] Compare V.7.

67. Original September 1557 text **Read as modern French:**

Au grand empire parviendra tout un autre
Bonté distant plus de felicité:
Regi par un issu non loing du peaultre,
Corruer regnes grande infelicité.

Imperial power another shall suborn,
Further from goodness than felicity.

One shall bear rule who's near the brothel born,
And realms condemn to mighty misery.

Source: The *Mirabilis Liber*'s prophecies of the coming Antichrist (see I.47, I.76, II.9), supplemented with a detail from the smaller *Liber mirabilis* by Telesphorus of Cosenza: 'He shall be born of a filthy adulterous woman.'

69. Original September 1557 text   Read as modern French:

La pitié grande sera sans loing tarder,
Ceulx qui donnoient seront constrains de prendre:
Nudz affamez de froit, soif, soy bander,
Les monts passer commettant grand esclandre.

> Their pity great shall not survive too long:
> Those who once gave shall be to take constrained.
> Naked, starved, thirsty, cold, they'll form a throng
> And cross the mountains, with great scandals stained.

Source: Possibly the desertion of Marshal Brissac in 1556 by his troops, who made their way to join the army of the more generous Duke of Guise instead, plundering Piedmont on the way.

70. Original September 1557 text   Read as modern French:

Au chef du monde le grand Chyren sera,   Henri[c] [anagr.]
Plus oultre apres aymé craint redoubté: Beaucoup plus [lat: Plus ultra]
Son bruit & loz les cieulx surpassera,   Son renom et ses louanges
Et du seul tiltre victeur fort contenté.

> Lord over all great Chyren is acclaimed,
> 'Further beyond' they'll fear him and shall love.
> His fame and praise shall soar all heaven above,
> Well pleased the only victor to be named.

Source: The Emperor Charles V's triumphant raid on the pirate Barbarossa's headquarters at Tunis in June 1535 – the verse even quotes in translation part of his Latin motto *PLUS ULTRA* – assimilated to the *Mirabilis Liber*'s prediction of the final defeat of Europe's future Muslim invaders by a *Grand Monarque* whom Nostradamus here associates with Henri II, just as his successors would associate him with Henri IV in his turn. See I.4, I.55, I.92, and compare II.79.

71. Original September 1557 text   Read as modern French:

Quand on viendra le grand roy parenter
Avant qu'il ait du tout l'ame rendue:
Celuy qui moins le viendra lamenter,
Par lyons, d'aigles, croix, couronne vendue.

> When of the King they'll come to take their leave,
> Even before he shall his soul lay down,
> To him who has least cause to mourn and grieve
> Shall Lion, Eagle sell the cross and crown.

Source: The abdication of the increasingly old and ailing Emperor Charles V in 1555, in which Nostradamus evidently sees a golden opportunity for his own king Henri II to take over the Imperial crown, sanctioned by Rome and the Electors of the Holy Roman Empire.

72. Original September 1557 text   Read as modern French:

Par fureur faincte d'esmotion divine,
Sera la femme du grand fort violee:
Juges voulans damner telle doctrine,
Victime au peuple ignorant imolee.

> In frenzy feigned of influence Divine
> The woman by the lord is violated:
> While judges try th' idea to undermine,
> The victim by the mob is immolated.

Source: An unidentified, but not unfamiliar case of sexual misconduct involving a high cleric.

73. Original September 1557 text   Read as modern French:

En cité grande un moyne & artisan,
Pres de la porte logés & aux murailles:
Contre Modene secret, cave disant,   disant 'Prenez garde!'
Trahys, pour faire soubz couleur d'espousailles.

> In the great city, monk and worker come
> To take up lodgings near the wall and gate,
> Plotting against Modena, keeping mum,
> Betrayed for feigning a betrothal date.

Source: Totally unknown incident in Italy.

74. Original September 1557 text   Read as modern French:

La deschassee au regne tournera,   retournera
Ses ennemis trouvés des conjurés:
Plus que jamais son temps triomphera,
Trois & septante à mort trop asseurés.

> One hounded out shall then return to power,
> Her foes revealed conspirators to be.

More than before above her age she'll tower:
Of death all too assured are seventy-three.

Source: Unidentified female ruler.

75. Original September 1557 text   Read as modern French:

Le grand pilot par Roy sera mandé,   *pilier [lat. pila]*
Laisser la classe pour plus hault lieu attaindre: *la flotte/armée*
Sept ans apres sera contrebandé,   *contremandé [?]*
Barbare armee viendra Venise caindre.   *faire peur à*

'Lord Pillar' by the King shall ordered be
To leave the army for a higher post:
Seven years thereafter, in rebellion, he.
Venice shall fear the great Barbarian host.

Source: The promotion of Gaspard de Coligny (Nostradamus plays here on the resemblance between his name and the word *colonne*, 'pillar', by way of the similarly-spelt *Cologne*) to the purely terrestrial post of 'Admiral of France' in 1552, at a time of continued Ottoman occupation of the Balkans as well as of military expansion in North Africa. If so, there is an attempted prophetic element in line 3. The last line reflects the usual invasion-fears of the *Mirabilis Liber*. See I.9, I.75, II.24.

76. Original September 1557 text   Read as modern French:

La cité antique d'antenoree forge,   *Padoue; construction*
Plus ne pouvant le tyran supporter:
Le manchet fainct au temple couper gorge,   *manchot [?]*
Les siens le peuple à mort viendra bouter.

That ancient town that Antenor did build
No longer can the mighty tyrant stand.
In church, throat cut, by sham one-armed one killed,
The folk shall kill his henchmen out of hand.

Source: The unidentified historical disposal of an unloved and probably Venetian tyrant of Padua.

77. Original September 1557 text   Read as modern French:

Par la victoire du deceu fraudulente,
Deux classes une, la revolte Germaine: *armées*
Un chef murtry, & son filz dans la tente,
Florence, Imole pourchassés dans romaine.   *Romagna*

Through victory deceitful, fraudulent

Two forces one, revolt in Germany.
One leader killed, his son, too, in the tent:
Florence, Imola to Romagna flee.

Source: Absolutely unidentifiable.

78. Original September 1557 text   Read as modern French:

Crier victoire du grand Selin croissant,
Par les Romains sera l'Aigle clamé:
Ticcin, Milan, & Gennes n'y consent,
Puis par eulx mesmes Basil grand reclamé.   *Empereur*

To vaunt o'er lunar crescent victory
The folk of Rome the Eagle shall proclaim.
Pavia, Milan and Genoa disagree,
Then later shall themselves the great King name.

Source: The triumphant return of the Emperor Charles V in 1536 first to Rome, then to northern Italy, after his resounding victory over the pirate Barbarossa at Tunis the previous year, when he was acclaimed as the hero of all Europe. The Eagle was the Imperial symbol *par excellence,* as well as forming part of Charles's personal device. See II.79 and VI.70 above.

79. Original September 1557 text   Read as modern French:

Pres du Tesin les habitans de Loyre,   *Tessin*
Garonne & Saone Seine, Tain & Gironde:
Oultre les monts dresseront promontoire,   *Au-delà; s'imposeront/avanceront*
Conflict donné, Pau granci, submergé onde.   *Po; grandi/saisi [tusc. grancito?]*

Near the Ticino, people from the Seine,
From Loire, Tain and Gironde, Garonne and Saône,
Beyond the mountains shall a bridgehead gain.
Fight joined, the floods shall come, the Po much grown.

Source: Contemporary wars between France and the Empire in northern Italy, assimilated to the *Mirabilis Liber*'s prophecy of an eventual counter-attack against the future Muslim occupiers of Europe. See I.55. For floods, see I.69.

80. Original September 1557 text   Read as modern French:

De Fez le regne parviendra à ceulx d'Europe,
Feu leur cité, & lame trenchera:
Le grand d'Asie terre & mer à grand troupe,   *de l'Asie Mineure*
Que bleux, pers, croix, à mort deschassera.

From Fez shall rulership to Europe spread,
Burning their cities, slashing with the sword.
By land and sea shall Asia's kingly horde,
Blue-green, hound Christians till they drop down dead.

Source: The *Mirabilis Liber*'s prediction of a mighty Arab invasion of Europe, in part via North Africa, assimilated to the contemporary Ottoman invasions. See I.9, I.75, II.24. The 'blue-green' reference seems to be to the Shi'ites of contemporary Persia.

81. Original September 1557 text

Read as modern French:

Pleurs, crys & plaintz, hurlement effraieur,   *hurlements d'*
Coeur inhumain, cruel noir, & transy:
Leman, les isles de Gennes les maieurs,
Sang espancher, frofaim à nul mercy.   *froid, faim*

Tears, wailing, cries of fear and screams of woe,
Hearts cold as ice, cruel, black and hard as stone,
Léman and Genoa's greater isles shall know,
Famine and bloodshed, mercy never shown.

Source: The *Mirabilis Liber*'s prophecies of a horrific Arab invasion of Europe via the Mediterranean that will at least have the merit, as Nostradamus sees it, of wiping out Calvin's Protestants at Geneva. See I.9, I.75.

82. Original September 1557 text

Read as modern French:

Par les desertz de lieu, libre, & farouche,
Viendra errer nepveu du grand Pontife:
Assomé à sept avecques lourde souche,
Par ceulx qu'apres occuperont le cyphe.   *saisiront; le calice [le Vatican]*

Through deserts wild and open fen and field
Shall roam the great Pope's nephew by degrees,
Murdered by seven who candlestick shall wield,
And who shall afterwards the chalice seize.

Source: Unidentified, but the mention of 'nephews' or 'grandsons' suggests some connection with Pope Paul III (reigned 1534–49).

83. Original September 1557 text

Read as modern French:

Celuy qu'aura tant d'honneurs & caresses,   *qui*
A son entree de la gaule Belgique:
Un temps apres fera tant de rudesses,
Et sera contre à la fleur tant bellique.   *à la fleur de lys; belliqueux*

He who shall so much love and honor know
When into Belgic Gaul he first shall go
Shall soon thereafter so ungracious be,
As well as warlike towards the fleur-de-lys.

Source: The accession of Philip II to the Imperial throne in 1556, and his subsequent tactlessness towards the Spanish Netherlands, as well as his initially bellicose attitude to France.

84. Original September 1557 text   Read as modern French:

Celuy qu'en Sparte claude ne peult regner,
Il fera tant par voye seductive:
Que du court, long, le fera araigner,
Que contre Roy fera sa perspective.

He who's too lame o'er Spartan land to reign
Shall take seduction's sleazy road instead.
Sooner or later, then, they'll him arraign,
Because he shall the King have targeted.

Source: Apparently a somewhat misremembered version of the celebrated story of Oedipus of Thebes.

85. Original September 1557 text   Read as modern French:

La grand cité de Tharse par Gaulois,
Sera destruicte, captifz tous à Turban:
Secours par mer du grand Portugalois,
Premier d'esté le jour du sacré Urban.

Tarsus' great city shall by Frenchmen be
Destroyed, all those in turbans led away –
Helped by the mighty Portuguese at sea –
When summer starts, on good Saint Urban's day.

Source: The *Mirabilis Liber*'s prediction of a great Western counter-invasion against the future Muslim occupiers of Europe that will pursue them all the way to the Middle East. See I.55. The precise dating suggests the application of comparative horoscopy[37, 38] to an earlier event. My own research[35] suggests that this was Charles V's triumphant expedition against the pirate Barbarossa in Tunis in 1535, transferred geographically to Tarsus in Asia Minor and projected forwards astrologically to any one of a series of future dates (of which 25 May 2036 is one!). Compare VI.70 and VI.78 above.

86. Original September 1557 text   Read as modern French:

Le grand Prelat un jour apres son songe,
Interpreté au rebours de son sens:
De la Gascoigne luy surviendra un monge,   *un moine*
Qui fera eslire le grand Prelat de sens.   *Sens*

> **The day after the Prelate dreams a dream,**
> **It shall be read as saying the opposite:**
> **A Gascon monk to encounter him shall seem**
> **Who as Sens' chosen Bishop him shall cite.**

Source: Unidentified report citing a popular approach to dream interpretation.

87. Original September 1557 text   Read as modern French:

L'eslection faicte dans Frankfort,   *[dedans?]*
N'aura nul lieu Milan s'opposera:
Le sien plus proche semblera si grand fort
Que oultre le Ryn es mareschz chassera.   *au-delà; dans les marais*

> **The election past, in Frankfurt it shall not**
> **Be carried out: Milan shall it decline.**
> **His nearest kin so great and strong has got**
> **He'll chase him into marshes o'er the Rhine.**

Source: The nominal election in 1531 of Ferdinand of Hapsburg as the successor of his brother Charles V, with his Imperial coronation planned for 1558 in Frankfurt. Nostradamus wrongly expects that the plan will be scuppered by a last-minute dispute between him and his nephew Philip II of Spain, by then lord of Milan. Another example of the short-term 'window-forecasts' that the seer was sometimes unwise enough to indulge in.

88. Original September 1557 text   Read as modern French:

Un regne grand demourra desolé,   *demeurera*
Aupres del Hebro se feront assemblees:
Monts Pyrenees le rendront consolé,
Lors que dans May seront terres tremblees.

> **A mighty kingdom desolate shall stay:**
> **Near to the Ebro they shall all assemble.**
> **The Pyrenees him shall console that day,**
> **When in the month of May the earth shall tremble.**

Source: Froissart's account in his *Chroniques* of the rescue and reinstatement of Don Pedro the Cruel of Castile to his throne by the Black Prince at the Battle of Navarrette in 1367 with the aid of heavy cannon fire, first used in war by the Prince and his father at the Battle of Crécy some twenty years before. See III.54, III.80, IV.99, VIII.48.

89. Original September 1557 text   Read as modern French:

Entre deux cymbes piedz & mains estachés,   bateaux [lat. cimba]
De miel face oingt & de laict substanté: visage; soutenu
Guespes & mouches, fitine amour faschés,   de l'amour paternel [gr. phitos]
Poccilateur faulcer, Cyphe temptee.   L'échanson; rendront faux; Calice

**Between two boats both hand and foot staked out,
Face smeared with honey mixed with milk about,
Shall wasps and flies, by father's love stirred up,
Warp the cup-bearer tempted by the Cup.**

Source: Totally unfathomable.

90. Original September 1557 text   Read as modern French:

L'honnissement puant abhominable,
Apres le faict sera felicité:
Grand excusé pour n'estre favorable,
Qu'a paix Neptune ne sera incité.   l'amiral [terme habituel chez Nostradamus]

**Stinking, outrageous, and a rank disgrace:
Yet after it they'll him congratulate –
The lord excused who turned away his face
Lest th' admiral be moved peace to create.**

Source: Unidentified.

91. Original September 1557 text   Read as modern French:

Du conducteur de la guerre navalle,
Rouge effrené severe horrible grippe,   griffe/querelle
Captif eschappé de l'aisné dans la basle: balle
Quant il naistra du grand un filz Agrippe.

**The leader of the naval war shall skipper,
Frantic and red, a fierce and grim attack.
Captive shall 'scape the elder in a pack
When to the lord is born a son Agrippa.**

Source: Unidentified. For line 3, compare VI.27 above.

92. Original September 1557 text

Prince de beauté tant venuste,
Au chef menee, le second faict trahy:
La cité au glaifve de pouldre, face aduste,
Par trop grand meurtre le chef du roy hay.

Read as modern French:

[Prince sera]; gracieuse
la seconde fois
visage brûlé

> **The Prince shall be by beauty full of grace**
> **Brought to the chief the second time betrayed.**
> **Town put to th' sword, by powder burned the face:**
> **By too much blood to King chief hateful made.**

Source: Unidentified, not least because virtually impenetrable.

93. Original September 1557 text

Prelat avare d'ambition trompé,
Rien ne sera que trop viendra cuider:
Ses messagiers & luy bien attrapé,
Tout au rebours voir, qui le bois fendroit

Read as modern French:

croira/pensera

fendra [?]

> **Ambitious bishop shall be sore mistaken:**
> **Nought happens but too much of it he'll make.**
> **His messengers and he shall all be taken:**
> **A woodsman would have quite a different take!**

Source: Unidentified story of a high cleric who fails to keep his feet on the ground.

94. Original September 1557 text

Un roy iré sera aux sedifragues,
Quant interdictz seront harnois de guerre:
La poison taincte au sucre par les fragues
Par eaux meurtris, mors, disant terre, terre

Read as modern French:

aux destructeurs du [saint] Siège

fraises

> **A king shall rage at breakers of the See**
> **When arms and armor disallowed shall be:**
> **With sugared poison on each berried hand**
> **He'll drown them as they shout 'More land! More Land!'**

Source: The continuing backstage efforts of King François I to suppress Protestants while persecution of them was officially banned, possibly in the wake of the relatively permissive Edict of Coucy of 1535. Dunking heretics upside-down in barrels of liquid was one of the Inquisition's favorite methods of unofficial disposal a little later in the century.

95. Original September 1557 text   Read as modern French:

Par detracteur calumnié à puis nay,
Quant istront faictz enormes & martiaulx: *Tellement paraîtront*
La moindre part dubieuse à l'aisnay,   *l'aisné*
Et tost au regne seront faictz partiaulx.

> The younger prince a slanderer shall blast,
> When he such warlike deeds and great commits.
> The lesser part on th' elder doubt shall cast,
> And soon the whole realm shall be torn to bits.

Source: Unidentified.

96. Original September 1557 text   Read as modern French:

Grande cité à souldartz habandonnee,   *soldats*
Onques ny eust mortel tumult si proche,   *Il n'y eut jamais*
O quel hideuse calamité s'approche,
Fors une offence n'y sera pardonnee.   *Sauf*

> The mighty town to soldiers is abandoned:
> Never was mortal tumult closer by.
> What hideous disaster shall come nigh,
> Save one offense that never shall be pardoned!

Source: The *Mirabilis Liber*'s forecast of the destruction of Rome (habitually referred to by Nostradamus and the Romans alike as 'the city') by foreign invaders from the Mediterranean. See I.9, I.75, II.24.

97. Original September 1557 text   Read as modern French:

Cinq & quarante degrés ciel bruslera,
Feu approucher de la grand cité neufve,
Instant grand flamme esparse saultera,   *Avec violence/véhémence [lat. instanter]*
Quant on voudra des Normans faire preuve:

> Latitude forty-five, the sky shall burn:
> To great 'New City' shall the fire draw nigh.
> With vehemence the flames shall spread and churn
> When with the Normans they conclusions try.

Source: Once again, on the face of it, the *Mirabilis Liber*'s gruesome invasion-scenario. See I.9, I.75, II.24. The given latitude suggests either Villanova d'Asti in northern Italy or Villeneuve-sur-Lot in south-western France. On the other hand, the last line is more reminiscent of the Norman invasions of southern Italy and Muslim Sicily in the eleventh century (see II.16) – but this would make Nostradamus's latitude incorrect, since the 'New City' would be Naples (Greek

Neapolis, 'New City'), which lies at 40º 50′ North, rather than 45º 00′ North. However, line 1 could conceivably be intended to read *Cinq- & quarante degrés* (i.e. fif [ty minutes] and forty degrees), which would be correct. Meanwhile the subject would instead be the *Mirabilis Liber*'s promised Western *counter*-invasion (see I.55), rather than the original Muslim invasion itself, and the 'fire from the sky' would inevitably be an eruption of nearby Vesuvius that, in Nostradamus's view, is destined to mark it. Compare I.87.

98. Original September 1557 text   Read as modern French:

Ruyné aux Volsques de peur si fort terribles,	*Ruine*
Leur grand cité taincte, faict pestilent:	
Piller Sol, Lune & violer leurs temples:	*or, argent*
Et les deux fleuves rougir de sang coulant.	

> **Ruin to the Volcae, fearsome to behold,**
> **Who'll have their chief town by the plague o'errun!**
> **They'll sack their churches, seize their silver, gold,**
> **And both their rivers red with blood shall run.**

Source: Strabo's account of the sacking of Toulouse, sacred city of the Volcae, by the Roman consul Quintus Servilius Caepio (a colleague of the general Marius, one of Nostradamus's favorite classical characters) in 106 BC. The story of Caepio's alleged hiding of the resulting treasure is retold at I.27 above. The 'two rivers' are of course the twin branches of the river Garonne that both flow through the city.

99. Original September 1557 text   Read as modern French:

L'ennemy docte se tournera confus,	
Grand camp malade, & deffaict par embusches,	
Montz Pyrenees & Poenus luy seront fait refus,	*et Carthage [au moins 2 syllabes de trop!]*
Proche du fleuve descouvrant antiques oruches.	*cruches*

> **The learned foe shall turn about, confused,**
> **By ambushes undone, his army ailing:**
> **Both Pyrenees and Carthage him refused,**
> **Near to the river ancient jugs unveiling.**

Source: Livy's account in his *History of Rome* (books XXI-XXX) of the invasion of Italy by the brilliant Carthaginian general Hannibal between 218 and 203 BC, in the course of which he became cut off in southern Italy. The detail of the unearthing of the amphorae seems to refer to an unrelated incident taken from Livy at XXXI-II.29.

[100.] Original September 1557 text Read as:

LEGIS CANTIO CONTRA INEPTOS   *CAUTIO [avertissement]*
   CRITICOS

Quos legent hosce versus mature censunto,
Profanum vulgus & inscium ne attrestato:
Omnesque Astrologi Blenni, Barbari procul
   sunto,
Qui aliter facit, is rite, sacer esto.

LEGAL WARNING AGAINST INEPT CRITICS

Who reads these lines, let him read sagely on,
But shun my verse, you mob profane and shallow.
Astrologers, fools, barbarians, begone!
Or else yourselves to rites satanic hallow.

Source: Petrus Crinitus's Latin warning *to lawyers* in his *De honesta disciplina* of 1504, as reprinted by Gryphius of Lyon in 1543:

> **Legis cautio contra ineptos criticos.**
> *Quoi legent hosce libros, maturè censunto:*
> *Profanum volgus & inscium, ne attrectato:*
> *Omensque legulei, blenni, barbari procul sunto:*
> *Qui aliter faxit, is ritè sacer esto.*[8]

but re-directed by Nostradamus against the professional *astrologers* of the day, who were always lambasting the mere 'astrophile' for his astrological incompetence. The fact that Nostradamus has directly, if inaccurately, plagiarized the verse without acknowledgment is not, perhaps, quite as shocking as it may seem to us today. Such things were much more normal at the time, as the example of Shakespeare and his contemporaries should possibly remind us. The term *profanum vulgus* ('the common crowd') is taken from the Roman poet Horace (*Odes*, 3,1,1).

Century VII

1. Original September 1557 text **Read as modern French:**

L'ARC du tresor par Achiles deceu,
Aux procrees sceu la quadrangulaire: *connu*
Au faict Royal le comment sera sceu, *command*
Corps veu pendu au veu du populaire

> **The treasure-chest Achilles shall conceal:**
> **Descendants shall the panel recognize.**
> **The kingly act the total shall reveal –**
> **Corpses are hung before the public's eyes.**

Source: Nostradamus's 'local knowledge' to the effect that the treasure of the Golden Fleece was allegedly hidden behind the western panel (showing in carved relief the death of Achilles) on the base of the ancient Roman Mausoleum of the Julii just south of his birthplace at St-Rémy-de-Provence, linked with the contemporary hanging of Protestants by royal command, which Nostradamus takes as an omen for its rediscovery.[60] He was always fascinated with the rediscovery of such buried treasure, as well as of ancient classical artifacts of any kind. Compare IV.27.

2. Original September 1557 text **Read as modern French:**

Par Mars ouvert Arles ne donra guerre,
De nuict seront les souldartz estonnés:
Noir, blanc à l'inde dissimulés en terre,
Soubz la faincte umbre traitres verez & sonnés. *verrez*

> **War once declared, Arles shall refuse to fight.**
> **The soldiers all shall be surprised at night.**
> **Black, white, like Indians hidden in the ground,**
> **Traitors disguised you'll see, once they are found.**

Source: Unknown.

3. Original September 1557 text   **Read as modern French:**

Apres de France la victoire navale,
Les Barchinons, Saillinons, les Phocens: Barcelonois, Saliens [Saliques/Francs];
                                               Marseillais
Lierre d'or, l'enclume serré dedans la basle [Au] lieu d'or/Lièvre d'or [?]; balle
Ceulx de Ptolon au fraud seront consens.   Toulon [?]

> **After the victory of France at sea**
> **O'er Franks and Spaniards by the Marseillais,**
> **Instead of gold an anvil wrapped shall be.**
> **Toulon conspires to aid the fraud that day.**

Source: Unidentified incident, possibly involving the transfer of the spoils of war.

4. Original September 1557 text   **Read as modern French:**

Le duc de Langres assiegé dedans Dolle,
Accompaigné d'Ostun & Lyonnois: Autun
Geneve, Auspurg, joinct ceulx de Mirandole, Augsbourg
Passer les monts contre les Anconnois.

> **The Duke of Langres shall be at Dole beset –**
> **With folk from Autun and the Lyon region –**
> **Geneva, Augsburg, Mirandola set**
> **To cross the mounts against Ancona's legion.**

Source: The *Mirabilis Liber*'s account of an expected future counter-attack by Christian forces against the Muslim occupiers of Europe, for whom the Marches of Ancona in Italy will previously have served as one of the main landing-beaches. See I.15.

5. Original September 1557 text   **Read as modern French:**

Vin sur la table en sera espandu,
Le tiers n'aura celle qu'il pretendoit:
Deux fois du noir de Parme descendu,
Perouse à Pize fera ce qu'il cuidoit.   pensait

> **Wine they shall spill the common table o'er:**
> **The third the woman claimed shall not have still.**
> **Descended (twice) from Parma's famous Moor,**
> **Perouse at Pisa does whate'er he will.**

Source: Unidentified political or military disagreements in Italy.

6. Original September 1557 text   Read as modern French:

Naples, Palerme, & toute la Secille,   *Sicile*
Par main Barbare sera inhabitee,
Corsicque, Salerne & de Sardeigne l'isle,
Faim peste, guerre fin de maulx intemptee.   *guère; instituée*

Palermo, Sicily and Naples are
Depopulated by the heathen might.
Salerno, Corsica, Sardinia –
Famine and plague; no end of ills in sight.

Source: The Saracen invasion and occupation of Sicily and southern Italy from the sixth century onwards, assimilated to the *Mirabilis Liber*'s prophecy of an Arab invasion of Europe via the Mediterranean. See I.9, I.75.

7. Original September 1557 text   Read as modern French:

Sur le combat des grans chevaulx legiers,
On criera le grand croissant confond: *confondu*
De nuict ruer monts, habitz de bergiers,
Abismes rouges dans le fossé profond.   *Abîmés*

Upon the combat of the horses light
Great Islam they shall claim confused to keep.
Death, shepherd-dressed, shall storm the hills at night:
Cardinals all undone in ditch so deep.

Source: The *Mirabilis Liber*'s predictions of a huge and grisly Muslim invasion of Europe, and the consequent destruction of the Church and persecution of the clergy. See I.9, I.15, I.75, II.24.

8. Original September 1557 text   Read as modern French:

Flora fuis, fuis le plus proche Romain,
Au Fesulan sera conflict donné: *Fiesole*
Sang espandu les plus grans prins à main,   *pris*
Temple ne sexe ne sera pardonné.   *secte*

Flee, Florence! Flee the nearest one from Rome!
At Fiesole shall battle be declared.
Blood shall be shed, the mighty overcome,
Nor church nor any sect at all be spared.

Source: An unidentified military campaign – probably papal – no doubt assimilated to the *Mirabilis Liber*'s forecast of an Arab invasion of Rome and all of Italy. See I.9, I.75.

9. Original September 1557 text   **Read as modern French:**

Dame à l'absence de son grand capitaine,
Sera priee d'amours du Viceroy:
Faincte promesse & malheureuse estraine,   *étrenne*
Entre les mains du grand prince Barroys.   *de Bar [de Lorraine]*

> **A lady in the absence of her lord**
> **By Viceroy's courted, as great ladies are:**
> **A promise feigned and lover's gift abhorred**
> **Between the hands of the great prince from Bar.**

Source: Apparently a thinly veiled suggestion of an illicit affair between Diane de Poitiers, mistress of Henri II, and the Duke de Guise, born at the castle of Bar.[41]

10. Original September 1557 text   **Read as modern French:**

Par le grand prince l'imitrophe du Mans,   *limitrophe*
Preux & vaillant chef de grand exercite: *armée*
Par mer & terre de Gallotz & Normans,   *Gaulois*
Caspre passer Barcelone pillé isle.   *Gibraltar*

> **For the great Prince who near Le Mans resides,**
> **Of army great a bold and valiant chief**
> **On land and sea of French, Normans besides,**
> **Gibraltar'll pass, Majorca plundered leave.**

Source: The successful and almost unprecedented passage of the Strait of Gibraltar by Nostradamus's friend the Baron de la Garde, Admiral of the Eastern Mediterranean, with 25 galleys in 1545, in the face of Spanish and Imperial opposition, prior to an attempted attack on England in July of the same year. Compare III.1.

11. Original September 1557 text   **Read as modern French:**

L'enfant Royal contemnera la mere,
Oeil, piedz blessés, rude, inhobeissant:
Nouvelle à dame estrange & bien amere,
Seront tués des siens plus de cinq cens.

> **The royal child his mother shall despise,**
> **Crude, disobedient, halt of foot, bad eyes.**
> **News shall the lady reach both strange and dread:**
> **More than five hundred of her men are dead.**

Source: Possibly the relationship between Queen Catherine de Médicis and one of her sickly sons.

12. Original September 1557 text   **Read as modern French:**

Le grand puisné fera fin de la guerre,
Aux Dieux assemble les excusés: assemblera
Cahors, Moissac iront long de la serre,   loin
Reffus Lestore, les Agennois razés.

> The junior lord shall put an end to war,
> And shall the pardoned to the gods commend.
> Moissac his grasp shall flee; so shall Cahors:
> Lectoure shall he repulse, Agen he'll rend.

Source: Unidentified military campaign in the south-west of France.

13. Original September 1557 text   **Read as modern French:**

De la cité marine & tributaire,
La teste raze prendra la satrapie: Le moine/L'évêque
Chasser sordide qui puis sera contraire,
Par quatorze ans tiendra la tyrannie.

> Of city maritime that tribute owes
> Shall shaven-head acquire the satrapy:
> The villain he expels, who hostile grows.
> Fourteen full years he shall the 'Tyrant' be.

Source: The take-over over in the name of France of the government of Genoa between 1508 and 1522 by the cleric Thomas de Grailly de Foix-Lautrec, Viscount of Lescun and former Prothonotary at the Vatican Chancery.[60]

14. Original September 1557 text   **Read as modern French:**

Faulx exposer viendra topographie,
Seront les cruches des monuments ouvertes:
Pulluler secte, faincte philosophie,   sectes
Pour blanches, noires, & pour antiques vertes. nouveaux

> The scythe shall of the land reveal the lie:
> Vases discovered at the ancient site.
> Of sham philosophy sects multiply:
> New shall be ta'en for old, and black for white.

Source: Discoveries of ancient artifacts, possibly at the site of Glanum (near St-Rémy), taken as an omen for the emergence of the latest religious ideas (especially of Protestantism), which Nostradamus, like many contemporary Catholics, regarded as new-fangled and therefore of the Devil.

15. Original September 1557 text   **Read as modern French:**

Devant cité de l'insubre contree,   *du Milanais*
Sept ans sera le siege devant mis:
Le tresgrand Roy y fera son entree,
Cité, puis libre hors de ses ennemis.

> **The mighty city of Milan about**
> **For seven long years that dreadful siege they'll lay.**
> **The mighty King shall enter it one day**
> **So freeing it from enemies without.**

Source: The domination of Lombardy by François I between 1515 and 1522, when the military defeat of La Bicoque lost him most of the Milanais.[60]

16. Original September 1557 text   **Read as modern French:**

Entree profonde par la grand Royne faicte   *Reine*
Rendra le lieu puissant inaccessible:
L'armee des trois lyons sera deffaicte,
Faisant dedans cas hideux & terrible.

> **The mighty gate erected by the Queen**
> **Shall fortify the place, keep foes at bay.**
> **The English soon shall have defeated been:**
> **Within shall hideous deeds be done that day.**

Source: The fortification of Calais by the forces of England's Queen Mary, with her banner bearing three lions *passant guardant,* and what was expected to be its imminent defeat by the French under the Duke of Guise. Since this actually occurred in January 1558, this has to be accounted a successful prophecy, albeit made only a few months in advance.

17. Original September 1557 text   **Read as modern French:**

Le prince rare de pitié & clemence,
Viendra changer par mort grand cognoissance:
Par grand repos le regne travaillé,   *troublé*
Lors que le grand tost sera estrillé.   *étrillé*

> **The prince of pity and of mercy rare**
> **Shall change ere death much that his people knows**
> **In time of mighty peace: the realm he'll scare**
> **When the lord a quick drubbing undergoes.**

Source: The reign of the late King François I, with his love and promotion of learning, rudely interrupted by his defeat and capture at the disastrous Battle of Pavia in 1525.

18. Original September 1557 text   Read as modern French:

Les assiegés couloureront leurs paches,
Sept jours apres feront cruelle issue:
Dans repoussés feu, sang, sept mis à l'hache
Dame captive qu'avoit la paix tissue.

> Those long besieged 'neath truce their plans disguise.
> Seven days therefrom they'll cruelly storm outside:
> Fire, blood, seven hacked to death, driven back inside,
> The lady captured who'll the truce devise.

Source: Unidentified.

19. Original September 1557 text   Read as modern French:

Le fort Nicene ne sera combatu,   Niçois
Vaincu sera par rutilant metal:
Son faict sera un long temps debatu,
Aux citadins estrange espouvental.

> No combat o'er the fort at Nice shall rage,
> But it shall fall to gleaming gold instead.
> Long time its fate shall great debate engage:
> The citizens shall find it strange and dread.

Source: Possibly the fall of Nice to a combined force of French and Turks in 1543, on the basis of a pact that actually permitted the latter to pillage the city.[41]

20. Original September 1557 text   Read as modern French:

Ambassadeurs de la Tosquane langue,
Avril & May Alpes & mer passer:
Celuy de veau expousera l'harangue,   Vaud [Suisse]
Vie Gauloise ne venant effacer.

> Ambassadors who speak the Tuscan tongue
> In April, May shall pass the Alps and sea:
> He of Lausanne reveals the talks still young
> So that French life might not effacèd be.

Source: What is believed to have been an intervention by Théodore de Bèze, Professor of Greek at Lausanne between 1549 and 1558 and Calvin's eventual successor at Geneva, to expose Imperial plans to attack France from the south-east.[41]

21. Original September 1557 text   Read as modern French:

Par pestilente inimitié Volsicque,
Dissimulee chassera le tyran:
Au pont de Sorgues se fera la traffique,
De mettre à mort luy & son adherant.

> While rabid hatred Languedoc shall o'errun,
> In secret it the tyrant shall pursue:
> At bridge of Sorgues the bargain shall be done
> To put the man to death – his henchman too.

Source: Unidentified.

22. Original September 1557 text   Read as modern French:

Les citoyens de Mesopotamie,
Yrés encontre amis de Tarraconne: *Fâchés envers; Tarragone*
Geux, ritz, banquetz, toute gent endormie   *Jeux, rites*
Vicaire au rosne, prins cité, ceux d'Ausone. *d'Italie*

> The people of Iraq shall fury heap
> Upon the friends of Spanish Catalonia.
> With games, rites, feasts, all of them are asleep:
> Pope by the Rhône; Rome taken, and Ausonia.

Source: The *Mirabilis Liber*'s forecast of a huge Middle Eastern invasion of Europe via Spain and Italy, assimilated to the Great Western Church Schism of the fourteenth century, when a series of Antipopes ruled from Avignon. See I.9, I.75, V.16. Compare the beginning of line 3 with II.16.

23. Original September 1557 text   Read as modern French:

Le Royal sceptre sera contrainct de prendre,   *il sera*
Ce que ses predecesseurs avoient engaigé,
Puis par l'aneau on fera mal entendre,   *l'anneau papal*
Lors qu'on viendra le palays saccager.

> The royal scepter he'll be forced to take,
> As those before him had agreed to do.
> Then with the Pope they'll understanding break
> When to the palace comes that plundering crew.

Source: Once again the Great Western Church Schism of 1378 when, under pressure from the local Roman mob who sacked the Vatican, the chosen Pope (the mentally ill Pope Urban VI) was discarded by the formerly supportive cardinals in favor of Pope Clement VII, who duly became the first Avignon 'Antipope' of the Great Western Church Schism that was to split the Catholic Church down the middle for almost forty years. See V.46, VI.13.

24. Original September 1557 text

L'ensevely sortira du tombeau,
Fera de chaines lier le fort du pont:
Empoysoné avec oeufz de barbeau,
Grand de Lorraine par le Marquis du Pont.

Read as modern French:

il sortira

> The buried one out of the tomb he'll mount,
> And have the strong part of the bridge chained fast:
> By the Marquis du Pont Lorraine's great Count
> Shall poisoned be with barbel roe at last.

Source: Unidentified incident involving the House of Lorraine and its traditional heir who was also the heir to the Duchy of Bar, the Marquis de Pont-à-Mousson.[41] Compare VII.9 above.

25. Original September 1557 text

Par guerre longue tout l'exercité expuise,
Que pour souldartz ne trouveront pecune:
Lieu d'or, d'argent, cuir on viendra cuser,
Gaulois aerain, signe croissant de Lune.

Read as modern French:

l'armée épuisée
de l'argent [lat. pecunia]; frapper

> Long drawn-out war the army's strength so saps,
> To pay the soldiers shall no funds be found.
> Instead of coins they'll issue leather scraps.
> Bronze Gallic, bearing crescent moon, is found.

Source: The historical issuing of substitute money, marked by an omen in the form of an archaeological discovery. To judge by the Latinate word *pecune* and the traditionally associated words for gold and silver, the so-far unidentified antecedent is almost certainly some desperate monetary expedient from Roman military history.

26. Original September 1557 text

Fustes & galees autour de sept navires,
Sera livree une mortelle guerre:
Chef de Madric recevra coup de vires,
Deux eschapees & cinq menees à terre.

Read as modern French:

Madrid; d'évirage

> Galleys and other craft seven ships beset
> And wage on them dread war on every hand:
> The Spanish chief they shall emasculate:
> Two shall be captured, five towed in to land.

Source: Slightly garbled version of an attack by French privateers from Dieppe on a group of Spanish galleons in the English Channel during November 1555, in the course of which the Spanish admiral and four other nobles were captured.[41]

27. Original September 1557 text   **Read as modern French:**

Au cainct de Vast le grand cavalerie,   *Aux alentours de Vasto*
Proche à Ferrare empeschee au bagaige,
Prompt à Turin feront tel volerie,
Que dans le fort raviront leur hostaige.

> In Vasto's train shall the great cavalry,
> Ferrara near, the baggage-train delay:
> Soon at Turin such plunderings there'll be,
> They'll from the fort their hostage snatch away.

Source: Unidentified Italian campaign, apparently by the Imperial general Alfonso II of Avalos, Marquis of Vasto.[41]

28. Original September 1557 text   **Read as modern French:**

Le capitaine conduira grande proye,
Sur la montaigne des ennemis plus proche:
Environné, par feu fera tel voye,
Tous eschapez or trente mis en broche.   *hormis*

> The captain shall his many captives drive
> Over the mountains near the enemy:
> Surrounded, he by fire-power through shall flee:
> All shall escape, save thirty burned alive.

Source: Unidentified.

29. Original September 1557 text   **Read as modern French:**

Le grand duc d'Albe se viendra rebeller,
A ses grans peres fera le tradiment: *grandpères [?]; la trahison*
Le grand de Guise le viendra debeller,   *défaire*
Captif mené & dressé monument.   *tombeau*

> The Duke of Alba shall rebellion raise:
> Betraying all his forefathers before him.
> The Duke of Guise shall him defeat, abase,
> Lead captive and a tombstone set up o'er him.

Source: Entirely unknown incident: possibly another of Nostradamus's ill-advised 'window-forecasts'.

30. Original September 1557 text

Le sac s'approche, feu grand, sang espandu
Po grana fleuves, aux bouviers l'entreprinse:
De Gennes, Nice, apres long attendu,
Foussan, Turin, à Savillan la prinse.

Read as modern French:

grands

Fossano; Savigliano; prise

> Shortly shall many drovers sack and harry
> Po's burning lands as rivers bloody course:
> Nice and Genoa long shall wait and tarry,
> Then from Savigliano Turin, Fossano force.

Source: Unknown, but possibly assimilated to the *Mirabilis Liber*'s forecast of an Arab invasion of Europe via Italy. See I.9, I.75.

31. Original September 1557 text

De Languedoc, & Guienne plus de dix,
Mille voudront les Alpes repasser:
Grans Allobroges marcher contre Brundis
Aquin & Bresse les viendront recasser.

Read as modern French:

Savoyards; Brindisi
Aquino; Bréscia; rechasser

> Ten thousand come from Languedoc, Guyenne
> Once more across the Alps to trace their track.
> 'Gainst Brindisi lords from Savoy shall then
> March on; Aquino, Bréscia chase them back.

Source: The *Mirabilis Liber*'s prediction of an eventual Western counter-attack against the Muslim occupiers of Europe. See I.55.

32. Original September 1557 text

Du mont Royal naistra d'une casane,
Qui cave, & comte viendra tyranniser,
Dresser copie de la marche Millane,
Favene, Florence d'or & gents expuiser.

Read as modern French:

case
cave et compte
armée
épuisera

> In Montereale shall be born, I fear,
> One who shall rule o'er bank account and vault:
> He'll raise an army from Milan's frontier,
> Favena and Florence drain of men and gold.

Source: Unidentified member of the powerful Medici banking family of Florence.

33. Original September 1557 text   Read as modern French:

Par fraulde regne, forces expolier,
La classe obsesse, passaiges à l'espie:
Deux fainctz amys se viendront rallier,
Esveiller hayne de long temps assoupie.   *réveiller*

> Fraud's reign shall sap the kingdom of its strength,
> The fleet blockaded, passes 'neath surveillance.
> Two friends pretended shall combine at length
> To awaken hatreds long time in abeyance.

Source: Unknown, but possibly a reference to the contemporary Wars of Religion.

34. Original September 1557 text   Read as modern French:

En grand regret sera la gent Gauloise,
Coeur vain, legier, croira temerité:
Pain, sel, ne vin, eaue, venim ne cervoise,   *médecine*
Plus grand captif, faim, froit, necessité.

> In great regret the French shall mope and pine.
> Light-heartedness for foolishness they'll hold.
> No bread, salt, water, beer, nor drugs, nor wine:
> Their noblest captive: hunger, need and cold.

Source: The *Mirabilis Liber's* prophecy of the invasion of Europe by a particularly grim Muslim occupation regime. See I.9, I.75, II.24.

35. Original September 1557 text   Read as modern French:

La grande pesche viendra plaindre, plorer   *Le grand Poisson; déplorer*
D'avoir esleu, trompés seront en l'aage:
Guiere avec eulx ne vouldra demourer,
Deceu sera par ceulx de son langaige.

> The mighty Fish they, 'plaining, shall regret
> Having elected: time shall prove them wrong.
> He shall not wish with them to tarry yet,
> And be let down by those who speak his tongue.

Source: Yet again the Great Western Church Schism of 1378 when, under pressure from the local Roman mob who sacked the Vatican, the chosen Pope (the mentally ill Pope Urban VI) was reneged on by the formerly supportive cardinals in favor of Pope Clement VII, who duly became the first Avignon 'Antipope' of the Great Western Church Schism that was to split the Catholic Church down the middle for almost forty years. See V.46, VI.13, VII.23.

36. Original September 1557 text   Read as modern French:

Dieu le ciel tout le divin verbe à l'unde,   *l'eau*
Pourté par rouges sept razes à Bisance.   *Porté; cardinaux; moines*
Contre les oingz trois cens de Trebisonde,   *oingts*
Deux loix mettront, & horreur, puis credence.   *croyance*

> **Good heav'ns! Red-hats bear God's Word o'er the ocean!**
> **Seven monks at Istanbul they'll take ashore.**
> **Against th' Anointed Trabzon's fifteen score**
> **Shall pass two laws: first horror, then devotion.**

Source: The *Mirabilis Liber*'s confident prediction of Christendom's eventual defeat of Islam and invasion of the Middle East, with the final conversion of Muslims to Christianity. See I.55.

37. Original September 1557 text   Read as modern French:

Dix envoyés, chef de nef mettre à mort,
D'un adverty, en classe guerre ouverte:
Confusion chef, l'un se picque & mord,
Leryn, stecades nefz, cap dedans la nerte.   *Aux Îles de Lerins et d'Hyères; capitaine*

> **Ten sent the vessel's captain's life to strip**
> **With fleet at war, one such shall him alert.**
> **Chaos reigns, mutual conflict aboard ship**
> **Off Hyères, Lerins: but he is in La Nerthe.**

Source: Unidentified naval mutiny off France's Mediterranean coast. La Nerthe is a village west of Marseille.

38. Original September 1557 text   Read as modern French:

L'aisné Royal sur coursier voltigeant,
Picquer viendra, si rudement courir:
Gueule, lypee, pied dans l'estrein pleigant,   *lippée/lippue; dans l'étrier piégeant*
Traîné, tiré, horriblement mourir.

> **The eldest prince upon his prancing steed**
> **Shall spur it on, that it may run the faster:**
> **Swollen its mouth, from stirrup th' foot unfreed,**
> **He'll be dragged on to horrible disaster.**

Source: The accidental death of Henry II of Navarre in May 1555.[41]

39. Original September 1557 text Read as modern French:

Le conducteur de l'armee Francoise,
Cuidant perdre le principal phalange:
Par sus pavé de lavaigne & d'ardoise, *À cause du transport à travers les montagnes*
              [lat. supervehere]; l'avoine
Soy parfondra par Gennes gent estrange.

  The leader of the fighting force from France
  Doubts o'er the safety of his main formation
  Through fodder-train and shelter he'll advance.
  Through Genoa shall pour the alien nation.

Source: The *Mirabilis Liber*'s prophecy of a massive invasion of Europe via northern Italy, where this quatrain is evidently set. See I.9, I.75, II.24.

40. Original September 1557 text Read as modern French:

Dedans tonneaux hors oingz d'huille & gresse, *graisse*
Seront vingtun devant le port fermés:
Au second guet par mort feront prouesse,
Gaigner les portes & du guet assommés.

  In casks outside with grease and oil smeared tight
  Shall twenty-one before the port be sealed:
  At second watch unto the death they'll fight,
  They'll gain the gates, then by the watch be killed.

Source: Unidentified 'Trojan Horse' incident.

41. Original September 1557 text Read as modern French:

Les oz des piedz & des mains enserrés,
Par bruit maison long temps inhabitee: *rumeur*
Seront par songes concavant deterrés, *sons [?]*
Maison salubre & sans bruyt habitee.

  Of bones of hands and feet all shut away
  Noises shall keep the house untenanted:
  By hollow sounds they'll all be scared away.
  They'll find a nicer, noiseless home instead.

Source: Unidentified story of a haunted house, based on a letter by Pliny to his friend Sura.

Arles: the celebrated cloister of the cathedral of St-Trophime.

The ancient Tour de Bouc, now surrounded by a 17th century fort

*King François' celebrated spiral
staircase at the Château de Blois*

The former priory of St-Paul-de-Mausole just south of St-Rémy

The 'Antiques' at St-Rémy: the mausoleum of the Julii and city gate of ancient Glanum
Inset: the inscription on the mausoleum

The Mont Gaussier, overlooking the ruins of ancient Glanum

Distant view of the locally famous 'trous' (holes) in the rocky outcrop on the eastern flank of the Mont Gaussier

The 'Pyramide' still stands in the middle of the ancient Roman stone-quarry at Glanum

The massive Roman Pont du Gard aqueduct north of Nîmes

Nîmes: The former distribution point of the Pont du Gard aqueduct in the high part of the city

Nîmes: The ancient Roman amphitheatre known as the 'arènes', still used for bullfights today

The ruins of the ancient 'Temple of Diana' beside the Sacred Lake at Nîmes

Marseille: remains of the ancient Greek harbour

Marseille: the old harbour, guarded by the Tour St-Jean

The castle at the village of Vernègues, just east of Salon, ruined in 1909 by a violent earthquake that also destroyed much of Salon itself and rendered Nostradamus's house unsafe

Good King René's favorite castle beside the Rhône at Tarascon, on the western frontier of Provence

42. Original September 1557 text   Read as modern French:

Deux de poison saisiz, nouveau venuz,
Dans la cuisine du grand Prince verser:
Par le souillard tous deux au faict congneuz,   souillon; reconnus
Prins qui cuidoit de mort l'aisné vexer.   Pris; pensait

> **Two newcomers in Prince's kitchen act**
> **To pour out poison: they'll be ta'en at will.**
> **The scullion shall catch them in the act**
> **And hold the one who thought the Prince to kill.**

Source: Unidentified assassination-attempt.

Note: As explained in the Introduction, it is at this point that Century VII as originally published on 6 September 1557 concludes. It is worthy of note that it contains no omen-reports. This presumably reflects the fact that Nostradamus had by
this point largely lost interest, if not in Julius Obsequens, at least in the three other
major books of recent omens (Peucerus, Frytschius and Fincelius) that had evidently so excited him when they first appeared.

Century VIII

1. Original text of 1568 edition

PAU, NAY, LORON plus feu qu'à sang sera.
Laude nager, fuir grand aux surrez.
Les agassas entree refusera.
Pampon, Durance les tiendra enserrez.

Read as modern French:

Oloron
l'Aude; aux ruisseaux voisinants [lat. surrasos]
Aux agassas [Aux Pies?]
Le Pempotan [Le tout-puissant] [voir X.100]

> **More fire than blood at Oloron, Pau, Nay:**
> **Chief swims the Aude and flees to streams around.**
> **To those of Pius access ta'en away,**
> **Durance's chief shall hold them locked and bound.**

Source: Unknown. If the word for 'magpies' is, as I have assumed, a coded reference to the representatives of Pope Pius (*Pie* in French), the original incident has to have occurred either between 1458 and 1464 (the reign of Pius II, who in 1460 unsuccessfully summoned a council to try and unite Europe in a grand crusade against the invading Turks) or in 1503 (Pius III). Line 2 is another evident back-reference to the story of the fleeing Roman general Marius, one of Nostradamus's favourite historical characters. See II.17, VI.1, VI.36.

2. Original text of 1568 edition

Condon & Aux & autour de Mirande
Je voy du ciel feu qui les environne.
Sol Mars conjoint au Lyon puis marmande
Fouldre, grand gresle, mur tombe dans Garonne.

Read as modern French:

Condom; Auch

> **Condom and Auch and all around Mirande**
> **I see with fires girt from the sky that fall.**
> **Sun, Mars in Leo: lightning at Marmande**
> **With hail: then falls into Garonne the wall.**

Source: Julius Obsequens and the *Mirabilis Liber*; see the quatrain's twin verse at I.46. The astrology in line 3 occurs every two years or so. For the falling wall of the Garonne, compare Nostradamus's recollection of events at Toulouse in 1536 at IX.37.

3. Original text of 1568 edition   **Read as modern French:**

Au fort chasteau de Viglanne & Resviers   *San Vigilio; Riviera*[41]
Sera serré le puisnay de Nancy:
Dedans Turin seront ards les premiers,   *brûlés*
Lors que de dueil Lyon sera transy.

> **In forts Riviera, San Vigilio**
> **Shall Nancy's younger prince be locked and barred.**
> **In Turin to be burned the first shall go,**
> **When Lyon shall with grief be stricken hard.**

Source: Unidentified.

4. Original text of 1568 edition   **Read as modern French:**

Dedans Monech le coq sera receu,   *Monaco*
Le Cardinal de France apparoistra
Par Logarion Romain sera deceu   *l'Ogmion*
Foiblesse à l'aigle, & force au coq naistra.

> **In Monaco the Cock shall be received:**
> **The Cardinal from France shall duly show.**
> **By Ogmion shall the Roman be deceived:**
> **Weaker the Eagle, stronger the Cock shall grow.**

Source: Apparently another of Nostradamus's ill-advised 'window-forecasts' regarding contemporary politics, with 'Ogmion' – the French Hercules (i.e. Henri II) – seen as about to pull the wool over the eyes of the representatives of the Holy Roman Empire. For the familiar symbolism of Eagle and Cock, see III.52.

5. Original text of 1568 edition   **Read as modern French:**

Apparoistra temple luisant orné,
La lampe & cierge à Borne & Breteuil.   *Bornel*
Pour la lucerne le canton destorné,   *Par la lumière [lat. lucerna]; détourné*
Quand on verra le grand coq au cercueil.

> **At Bornel and Breteuil lamps, candles burn:**
> **He shall appear in church ornate and shining.**
> **To see that light shall every canton turn**
> **When in his coffin Cock is seen reclining.**

Source: The funeral cortege of King François I in 1547, which processed all over the country, stopping each night for a service in a different Catholic church – each brilliantly lit, unlike those of the Protestants – before finally arriving for the burial at Notre-Dame-des-Champs.[60] Clearly Nostradamus is enjoying playing with the 'Swiss-sounding' Latin word *lucerna*.

6. Original text of 1568 edition   **Read as modern French:**

Clarté fulgure à Lyon apparante
Luysant, print Malte subit sera estainte,
Sardon, Mauris traitera decepvante,   *Sardaigne; Maures*
Geneve à Londes à coq trahyson fainte.   *Gênes à l'onde*

> **A blazing light at Lyon seen shall be,**
> **Then, Malta taken, be snuffed out again.**
> **Sardinia Moors shall treat deceitfully.**
> **Genoa at sea. To Cock treason they'll feign.**

Source: The *Mirabilis Liber*'s familiar scenario of massive Arab invasion from the Mediterranean (see I.9, I.75), assimilated to Julius Obsequens's various 'fire-from-the-sky' omens (see I.46, II.96).

7. Original text of 1568 edition   **Read as modern French:**

Verceil, Milan donra intelligence,
Dedans Tycin sera faite la paye.   *plaie*
Courir par Siene eau, sang, feu par Florence.
Unique choir d'hault en bas faisant maye.

> **Milan, Vercelli each a news-supplier:**
> **Pavia is where the bloody blow shall fall.**
> **Florence fills Siena with blood, water, fire.**
> **At maying shall the One and Only fall.**

Source: The disastrous Battle of Pavia of 25 February 1525, at which almost the entire body of French chivalry was slain and King Francois I captured – subsequently, in May, being carted off to imprisonment in Madrid.

8. Original text of 1568 edition   **Read as modern French:**

Pres de linterne dans de tonnes fermez,   *Cisterna*
Chivaz fera pour l'aigle la menee,   *Chivas*
L'esleu cassé luy ses gens enfermez,   *chassé*
Dedans Turin rapt espouse emmenee.   *saisie*

> **Near Cisterna, all sealed in casks with hoops,**
> **Chivasso shall for th' Eagle plot a move:**
> **The elected one repulsed, cut off his troops**
> **Within Turin: his seized wife they'll remove.**

Source: The events of 1543, when a 'wooden horse' operation was attempted by Imperial troops at Turin during an ultimately unsuccessful campaign on the part of Charles V (the elected Holy Roman Emperor), and when the pirate Barbarossa landed on the Italian coast in search of water, duly carrying off and marrying Doña

Maria, daughter of the governor of Gaeta, who subsequently converted to Islam and followed him to Turkey.[60] Compare IV.58.

9. Original text of 1568 edition   Read as modern French:

Pendant que l'aigle & le coq à Savone
Seront unis Mer Levant & Ongrie,
L'armee à Naples, Palerne, Marque d'Ancone   Palerme
Rome, Venise par Barb' horrible crie.   Barbares

> **With Cock and Eagle locked around Savona**
> **The Eastern fleet to Hungary sails in.**
> **Troops at Palermo, Naples and Ancona,**
> **Venice and Rome ring with Barbaric din.**

Source: The *Mirabilis Liber's* prophecy of a massive Islamic invasion of Europe via both the Black Sea and the Mediterranean. See I.9, I.75, II.24.

10. Original text of 1568 edition   Read as modern French:

Puanteur grande sortira de Lausanne,
Qu'on ne saura l'origine du fait,
Lon mettra hors toute la gent loingtaine   L'on
Feu veu au ciel, peuple estranger deffait.

> **From Lausanne shall a mighty stench arise**
> **Whose origin no one alive shall know.**
> **Expelled the alien folk; fire in the skies.**
> **The foreigners they'll surely overthrow.**

Source: The *Mirabilis Liber's* forecast of the eventual Western liberation of Europe from its Muslim invaders, apparently coupled with a prediction by Nostradamus of the collapse of the Calvinism that he found so repulsive and, by way of a suitable omen, with one of Julius Obsequens's reports of fire in the sky. See I.46 and I.55, and compare II.16.

11. Original text of 1568 edition   Read as modern French:

Peuple infiny paroistra à Vicence
Sans force feu brusler la Basilique
Pres de Lunage deffait grand de Valence,   Lunigiane
Lors que Venise par more prendra pique.   par Maures

> **A countless folk appears before Vicenza,**
> **But not by force th' basilica's ablaze.**
> **Near Lunigiana falls the Lord Valenza,**
> **While Venice in the Moors attack shall face.**

Source: The accidental burning of the Palazzo della Raggione at Vicenza in 1496 (not fully rebuilt by Palladio until 1545) and the defeat of Cesare Borgia, Duke of Valentinois, at nearby Urbino in 1502,[60] both assimilated to the *Mirabilis Liber*'s prediction of a vast invasion of Italy by forces from North Africa. See I.9, I.75.

12. Original text of 1568 edition   Read as modern French:

Apparoistra aupres de Buffalorre
L'hault & procere entré dedans Milan   et grand *[lat. procerus]*
L'Abbé de Foix avec ceux de saint Morre   *Saint-Moritz*
Feront la forbe abillez en vilan.   *fourberie; habillés*

> **Near Buffalora he'll appear that day,**
> **Who high and mighty in Milan now sits,**
> **The Abbot of Foix, with those of St Moritz.**
> **As humble peasants dressed, the rogue they'll play.**

Source: The mission of Odet de Grailly de Foix-Lautrec to engage Swiss mercenaries on behalf of François I before the Battle of Marignano in 1515 – troops who then proceeded to loot the convoy carrying their own wages.[60]

13. Original text of 1568 edition   Read as modern French:

Le croisé frere par amour effrenee
Fera par Praytus Bellerophon mourir,   *Proetus*
Classe à mil ans la femme forcenee   *armée; à Milan*
Beu le breuvage, tous deux apres perir.

> **The monk-crusader made by love insane**
> **Bellerophon like Proetus shall make die.**
> **Troops at Milan; the woman made insane:**
> **The potion drunk; then both of them shall die.**

Source: Seemingly a garbled version of Machiavelli's account, in his *Istorie Fiorentine* of the 1520s, of an episode from sixth-century Lombard history. In exchange for marrying Longinus, the governor of Byzantine Italy, and thus making him King of the Milanais, the then queen Rosamunda first agreed to give her lover Amalchidus a cup of poisoned wine, but was then caught in the act and decided to die with him.[60] The mythological back-reference is to the story of King Proetus, who, on his spurned wife Anteia's insistence, deliberately sent her guest Bellerophon on a fatal mission – even though, unexpectedly, he survived it.

14. Original text of 1568 edition   Read as modern French:

Le grand credit d'or, d'argent l'abondance
Fera aveugler par libide l'honneur
Sera cogneu d'adultere l'offence,   *d'adultération*
Qui parviendra à son grand deshonneur.

Of gold great credit, and of silver mounds,
Shall blind with greed the eyes of honor bright:
The crime of coin debasing comes to light
Which to his great dishonour then redounds.

Source: The demise of Chancellor Antoine Duprat, Cardinal Archbishop of Sens and papal legate, suspected in 1530 of having debased and sold gold from the huge ransom collected for handing over to the Empire for the release of Francois I in 1526. See IV.88.

15. Original text of 1568 edition   Read as modern French:

Vers Aquilon grand efforts par hommasse
Presque l'Europe & l'univers vexer,
Les deux eclypses mettra en telle chasse,   *Les chefs [lat. duces] faillis*
Et aux Pannons vie & mort renforcer.

Great efforts by a northern woman mannish
Shall Europe vex and well-nigh all Creation.
She'll hound failed leaders till they're fit to vanish,
Through life, death strengthening Pannonia's nation.

Source: The dramatic activities of Isabella, daughter of Sigismund, King of Poland, who married John Zápolya, satrap of Pannonia, an ally of the Ottoman Suleiman the Magnificent, in 1539. On his death in 1540, she summoned Suleiman in aid against her own Chancellor, Cardinal George Martinuzzi, with the result that the Ottomans became firmly established in the region between 1541 and 1547. Nostradamus's contemporary Agrippa d'Aubigné would record the resulting chronic insecurity on the very borders of Christendom.[8]

16. Original text of 1568 edition   Read as modern French:

Au lieu que HIERON feit sa nef fabriquer,   *Jason [Hieson]; fit*
Si grand deluge sera & si subite,
Qu'on n'aura lieu ne terres s'atacquer   *auquels s'attacher*
L'onde monter Fesulan Olympique.   *l'Olympe fessan*

In th' place where Jason built his famous ship
So huge a flood there'll be, and such a fount,
That there'll be neither place nor land to grip,
And waves shall climb broad-based Olympus' mount.

Source: The *Mirabilis Liber*'s prophecies of huge floods presaging the end of the world, and particularly: 'The cities and provinces of the Islanders shall be swallowed up by floods . . . There shall no longer be on earth any eminence or unevenness, for the azure waters of the sea shall roll in level with the mountaintops' (Prophecy of the Tiburtine Sibyl). See I.69.

17. Original text of 1568 edition

Read as modern French:

Les bien aisez subit seront desmis   *mis à bas*
Par les trois freres le monde mis en trouble,
Cité marine saisiront ennemis,
Faim, feu, sang, peste, & de to⁹ maux le double.   *tous*

> **Put down the well-to-do shall quickly be:**
> **By brothers three the world is sorely troubled.**
> **The foes shall seize the city of the sea.**
> **Famine, fire, blood and plague – all ills redoubled.**

Source: Once again the pre-apocalyptic expectations floated by the *Mirabilis Liber*, and not least the promised invasion of Europe. See I.9, I.75, II.24. The 'city of the sea' is presumably Marseille. Compare I.18, I.71, I.72, X.88.

18. Original text of 1568 edition

Read as modern French:

De Flora issue de sa mort sera cause,
Un temps devant par jeusne & vieille bueyre   *boire*
Par les trois lys luy feront telle pause,
Par son fruit sauve comme chair crue mueyre.   *mûre*

> **From Florence come, his early death she'll cause**
> **With what to drink she once gave young and old.**
> **On France's part they'll give him mighty pause,**
> **Through her fruit safe as meat that's raw and old.**

Source: The apocryphal dispensing of poisons by a (here) heavily disguised Catherine de Médicis from behind the secret panels of her study at the castle of Blois.

19. Original text of 1568 edition

Read as modern French:

A soustenir la grand cappe troublee,   *le grand Pape*
Pour l'esclaircir les rouges marcheront,   *les cardinaux/les rouges de sang [?]*
De mort famille sera presque accablee.
Les rouges rouges le rouge assomeront:

> **The great Pope to support, in trouble sore,**
> **The red-hats march to put him right and well.**
> **His family, o'erwhelmed, are at death's door.**
> **The reddest reds his Redness dead shall fell.**

Source: An unidentified dispute – one of many possible – over the papal succession.

20. Original text of 1568 edition

Le faux messaige par election fainte
Courir par urben, rompue pache arreste,
Voix acheptees, de sang chapelle tainte,
Et à un autre l'empire contraicte.

Read as modern French:

à travers la cité [lat. per urbem]

> **Through fake elections, rumors false shall flood**
> **The city through: broken, the pact is over.**
> **Votes bought, the holy chapel stained with blood,**
> **The Empire to another they'll hand over.**

Source: Unidentified: either disputed papal elections, as per the previous verse (compare V.46, V.92, VI.13, VII.22, VII.23, VII.35), or elections for the post of Holy Roman Emperor.

21. Original text of 1568 edition

Au port de Agde trois fustes entreront
Portant l'infect non foy & pestilence
Passant le pont mil milles embleront,
Et le pont rompre à tierce resistance.

Read as modern French:

la mer [lat. pontus]; raviront
la tête de pont [?]

> **Into the port of Agde three craft shall row –**
> **Infidels bringing foul disease and dread.**
> **From overseas they'll strike a million dead,**
> **Their bridgehead breaking out at the third go.**

Source: The arrival of the Plague in Europe in 1347–8 aboard three Genoan vessels that landed first at Marseille, then at Agde, assimilated to the *Mirabilis Liber's* prediction of a massive Muslim invasion of Europe. See I.9, I.75, II.24. Nostradamus often describes the expected invaders of Europe themselves in terms of plague.

22. Original text of 1568 edition

Gorsan, Narbonne, par le sel advertir
Tucham, la grace Parpignan trahye,
La ville rouge n'y vouldra consentir.
Par haulte vol drap gris vie faillie.

Read as modern French:

Corsan
Tuchan la grasse; Perpignan

drapeau [?]

> **Coursan, Narbonne shall warn regarding salt**
> **Prosperous Tuchan, Perpignan betrayed.**
> **With it the city red shall 'stablish fault.**
> **High-flying, gray, the flag shows life downlaid.**

Source: The south-western salt-tax revolt of 1548–9, so brutally put down by Montmorency.

23. Original text of 1568 edition   Read as modern French:

Lettres trouvees de la royne les coffres,
Point de subscrit sans aucun nom d'hauteur   *d'auteur*
Par la police seront cachez les offres.   *Par le gouvernement*
Qu'on ne scaura qui sera l'amateur.

> Letters are found inside the queenly coffers:
> No signature, no name of author writ.
> The government shall hide the secret offers,
> Such that none knows which love's the source of it.

Source: An unidentified piece of contemporary court scandal.

24. Original text of 1568 edition   Read as modern French:

Le lieutenant à l'entree de l'huys,   *de la porte*
Assomera le grand de Parpignan,
En se cuidant saulver à Montpertuis.
Sera deceu bastard de Lusignan.

> The officer who by the gate shall be
> Shall kill the mighty lord of Perpignan.
> Thinking it safe to Montpertuis to flee,
> Shall be deceived the bastard of Lusignan.

Source: Unknown.

25. Original text of 1568 edition   Read as modern French:

Coeur de l'amant ouvert d'amour fertive   *furtive*
Dans le ruysseau fera ravyr la Dame,
Le demy mal contrefera lassive,   *lascive*
Le pere à deux privera corps de l'ame.

> The lover's heart a secret love shall rend:
> He'll rape the Lady in the stream or dike.
> Lustful, she shall but half a wrong pretend.
> The sire both bodies from their souls shall strike.

Source: Unidentified.

26. Original text of 1568 edition   Read as modern French:

De Caton es trouves en Barsellonne,   *planches*
Mys descouvers lieu terrouers & ruyne,   *territoires*
Le grand qui tient ne tient vouldra Pamplonne.   *Nettingen [?]*
Par l'abbage de Monferrat bruyne.   *l'abbaye; Montserrat*

Of Cato timbers found in Barcelona
Found where they left them, rotting in the dirt.
The lord of Nettingen shall crave Pamplona:
Monserrat's abbey thick with drizzle girt.

Source: The discovery of archaeological remains connected with C. Porcius Cato, grandson of the famous Censor, taken as an omen for political moves within the Hapsburg empire.

27. Original text of 1568 edition   Read as modern French:

La voye auxelle l'une sur l'autre fornix   *aus eaux [eaues]; arche*
Du muy deser hor mis brave & genest,   *Du Muy; hormis; drave [ivraie]*
L'escript [trouvé?] d'empereur le fenix   *du général [lat. imperator]*
Veu en celuy ce qu'à nul autre n'est.

By th' aqueduct with arch on arch withal,
And Le Muy's desert (barring broom and tare)
Th' inscription's found of phoenix general,
And seen in't whereof none else is aware.

Source: Another archaeological discovery, this time possibly connected with Nostradamus's favorite story of the fleeing Roman general Marius, and featuring an aqueduct near le Muy that fed the coastal town of Fréjus. Line 1 is an almost direct translation of Pliny's *aqua fornicibus structis perducta* ('the water being led over arches placed one on top of the other' – *Natural History*, 31.iii.24). Nostradamus seems to reckon that he alone has the key to deciphering the inscription involved: such Roman ceremonial texts were usually full of abbreviations. In this case the printer seems to have had considerable difficulty in deciphering Nostradamus's writing, too!

28. Original text of 1568 edition   Read as modern French:

Les simulachres d'or & d'argent enflez,   *les idoles*
Qu'apres le rapt au lac furent gettez   *le vol/le sac; jetés*
Au descouvert estaincts tous & troublez.   *étonnés [?]*
Au marbre escript presciptz intergetez.

The puffed-up images of silver, gold,
After the sack all thrown into the lake,
When found, shall them amazed and worried hold.
What's on the marble scribed, for laws they'll take.

Source: Sticking with the current theme, as Nostradamus is wont to do – in this case the archaeological one – the discovery (following the disastrous floods of 9 September 1557) of numerous pagan ritual objects from the now-ruined temple of Diana[p] that had originally been thrown into the Sacred Lake at Nîmes with the coming of Christianity.[62]

29. Original text of 1568 edition

Au quart pillier lon sacre à Saturne.
Par tremblant terre & deluge fendu
Soubz l'edifice Saturnin trouvee urne,
D'or Capion ravy & puis rendu.

Read as modern French:

longtemps sacré

de St-Sernin [?]
de Caepion

'Neath Saint-Sernin's fourth pillar underground
(By earthquake split when floods are at the door)
Pot Saturnine beneath the building's found
Of Caepio's plundered gold; then handed o'er.

Source: Still with the archaeological theme, the familiar story of the Sacred Gold of Toulouse, looted and then misappropriated by Quintus Servilius Caepio in 106 BC, with an intuitive 'window-forecast' based on local tradition[41] thrown in. See I.27.

30. Original text of 1568 edition

Dedans Tholoze non loing de Belvezer
Faisant un puy loing, palais d'espectacle
Tresor trouvé un chacun ira vexer,
Et en deux locz tout & pres del vasacle.

Read as modern French:

belvéder
long

lieux

Not far from Belvedere within Toulouse,
Digging a trench for a *palais de spectacles*,
A treasure's found that all shall sore bemuse
In places twain quite close to the Basacle.

Source: Yet another piece of conjectural archaeology, this time sited in the mill-area of Toulouse, but presumably related to the previous verse.

31. Original text of 1568 edition

Premier grand fruit le prince de Pesquiere
Mais puis viendra bien & cruel malin,
Dedans Venise perdra sa gloire fiere
Et mys à mal par plus joyue Celin.

Read as modern French:

Pescara
deviendra

jeune [joyne]; lunaire [Selin]

At first Pescara's prince good fruit shall bear
But then a cruel villain he'll become.
In Venice he shall lose his glory fair
And be put down by younger lunar one.

Source: Contemporary squabbles between France and the Holy Roman Empire. The Marquis of Pescara had been the commander of the Imperial troops who defeated François I at the disastrous Battle of Pavia. The verse appears to be predicting – somewhat rashly, perhaps – that France's Henri II, with his shield famously bearing a lunar device, will avenge his father's defeat and subsequent imprisonment.

32. Original text of 1568 edition   Read as modern French:

Garde toy roy Gaulois de ton nepveu
Qui fera tant que ton unique filz.
Sera meurtry à Venus faisant voeu,
Accompaigné de nuict que trois & six.

> **Beware, French king, beware your nephew of,**
> **Who as your only son himself affects.**
> **He shall be smitten paying court to love**
> **In nightly company but three and six.**

Source: The death in 1492 of Charles VIII and the accession of his cousin (not nephew) Louis XII, who at the 'wake' made the acquaintance of the lady whom he would secretly marry some nine (3 + 6) months later.[60]

33. Original text of 1568 edition   Read as modern French:

Le grand naistra de Veronne & Vincence,   *Vicense*
Qui portera un surnom bien indigne.
Qui à Venise vouldra faire vengeance
Luy mesme prins homme du guet & signe

> **Verona or Vicenza'll see his birth,**
> **That lord to whom vile nickname they'll assign.**
> **He shall on Venice wish to wreak his wrath,**
> **Yet shall be captured through the watchman's sign.**

Source: Unidentified.

34. Original text of 1568 edition   Read as modern French:

Apres victoire du Lyon au Lyon
Sus la montaigne de JURA Secatombe   *son hécatombe*
Delues & brodes septieme million   *ôtés [lat. diluti] par Allobroges/noirs [?]*
Lyon, Ulme à Mausol mort & tombe.   *fouetté [lat. ulmeus]; à St-Paul-de-Mausole*

> **Once Lion shall the other Lion surmount**
> **Comes mighty sacrifice on Jura's mount.**
> **Removed by seven score thousand Moors he'll be,**
> **The Lion scourged, and killed at St-Rémy.**

Source: This is seemingly a highly speculative elaboration of the *Mirabilis Liber*'s prediction of the papal flight from Rome (see II.41, V.16, VI.25, X.3) in the face of a huge Muslim invasion from North Africa and the Middle East (see I.9, I.75, II.24), directly linked to the dramatic celestial vision reported at I.35 as having been seen over Switzerland in 1547 (*q.v*).

35. Original text of 1568 edition

Dedans l'entree de Garonne & Bayse	*dans la Garonne de la Baïse*
Et la forest non loing de Damazan	
Du marsaves gelees, puis gresle & bize	*marécages*
Dordonnois gelle par erreur de mezan.	*mois [lat. mensis]*

Read as modern French:

    Where into the Garonne flows the Baïse,
    And in the forest near to Damazan,
    Ere hail and north wind, shall the marshes freeze,
    Dordognois freeze through getting the month wrong.

Source: Recent severe weather in the south-west of France, close to Nostradamus's former home at Port Sainte-Marie, just west of Agen. Compare IX.48.

36. Original text of 1568 edition

Sera commis conte oingdre aduché	*comté; joindre à Duché*
De Saulne & sainct Aulbin & Bell'oeuvre	*Lons-le Saulnier; Bellevesvre*
Paver de marbre de tours loing espluché	
Non Bleteram resister & chef d'oeuvre.	*Le nom de Bletterans [lat. Castrum Bliterium]*

Read as modern French:

    The Franche-Comté to join the Duchy's set
    Of Lons-le-Saulnier, Bellevesvre, St-Aubin
    By marble slabs from towers surrounding robbing.
    The name of Bletterans survives it yet!

Source: The fifteenth-century operation launched by Louis de Chalon-Arlay to link the Franche-Comté with the Duchy of Burgundy further to the west, using the remains of existing Roman roads and materials plundered from various ancient watchtowers in the region.[60] The printer was clearly flummoxed – as he often was in such cases – by the unfamiliar place-names in the Jura.

37. Original text of 1568 edition

La forteresse aupres de la Tamise	
Cherra par lors le Roy dedans serré,	*Tombera*
Aupres du pont sera veu en chemise	
Un devant mort, puis dans le fort barré.	

Read as modern French:

    Beside the river Thames, the mighty fort
    Shall fall just when the King is trapped inside.
    Him near the bridge in shirtsleeves they'll report.
    One dead in front, then he'll be barred inside.

Source: The capture, imprisonment in the Tower of London and brief re-instatement of the pious, if near-imbecilic Henri VI of England following the seizure of the throne in 1461 by Edward of York, subsequently King Edward IV. Henry was then overthrown yet again and secretly put to death in 1471.

38. Original text of 1568 edition   Read as modern French:

Le Roy de Bloys dans Avignon regner
Une autre foys le peuple emonopolle,   *en monopole*
Dedans' le Rosne par murs fera baigner
Jusques à cinq le dernier pres de Nolle.   *Noelle [pour: Noël?]/Oulle [?]*

> **In Avignon Blois's king shall set his throne,**
> **Once more a ruler o'er a single land.**
> **Over the walls into the flowing Rhône**
> **Some five he'll throw; the last with Yule at hand.**

Source: Unidentified, but evidently tied in with the *Mirabilis Liber*'s prediction of the eventual liberation of France from its future Islamic occupiers. See I.55.

39. Original text of 1568 edition   Read as modern French:

Qu'aura esté par prince Bizantin,
Sera tollu par prince de Tholoze.   *toléré; Toulouse*
La foy de Foix par le chief Tholentin,   *Toulousain [?]*
Luy faillira ne refusant l'espouse.

> **Who shall by th' Turkish prince accepted be**
> **Shall by Toulouse's prince not be denied.**
> **The trust of Foix being lacking, though, shall he,**
> **Toulouse's prince, yet not refuse the bride.**

Source: Unidentified event, probably quite recent.

40. Original text of 1568 edition   Read as modern French:

Le sang du Juste par Taurer la daurade,   *pour les églises de St-Saturnin-du-Tour et de*
    Ste-Marie-de-la-Dorade
Pour se venger contre les Saturnins   *contre les Juifs*
Au nouveau lac plongeront la maynade,   *la bande*
Puis marcheront contre les Albanins.   *les Albanois/les troupes du duc d'Alba*

> **Innocent blood against old Saturn's Jew**
> **Into the new-found lake they'll cast that crew,**
> **Then march against Duke Alba's men again.**

Source: Unknown incident involving the persecution of the Jews of Toulouse.

41. Original text of 1568 edition

Read as modern French:

Esleu sera Renad ne sonnant mot,   Renard
Faisant le saint [/] public vivant pain d'orge,
Tyrannizer apres tant à un cop,   tout à coup
Mettant à pied des plus grans sus la gorge.

> **The Fox shall be elected, keeping mum,**
> **Playing the saint, seen living on barley bread;**
> **Then suddenly a tyrant he'll become,**
> **Trampling upon each noble's throat instead.**

Source: Presumably Pope Julius III (1550–5) – a devout priest who nevertheless not only re-opened the repressive Council of Trent, but for a while supported the Emperor Charles V in his wars against France – here assimilated to the *Mirabilis Liber*'s forecast of the decline and corruption of the Church. See I.44, II.10, II.12.

42. Original text of 1568 edition

Read as modern French:

Par avarice, par force & violence
Viendra vexer les siens chiefz d'Orleans,
Pres saint Memire assault & resistance,   St-Mamert-du-Gard
Mort dans sa tante diront qu'il dort leans.   tente; là-dedans

> **Through force and violence, though avarice,**
> **Troubled his chiefs Orléanais he'll keep:**
> **Near Saint-Mémert he'll fight and shall resist.**
> **Dead in his tent, they'll say he is asleep.**

Source: The story of an unidentified local warlord.

43. Original text of 1568 edition

Read as modern French:

Par le decide de deux choses bastars   déchu
Nepveu du sang occupera le regne
Dedans lectoyre seront les coups de dars   Lectoure; dards
Nepveu par peur pleira l'enseigne.   pliera

> **Through the demise of two things ill-conceived**
> **The monarch's nephew shall the kingdom hold.**
> **Within Lectoure shall point-thrusts be received:**
> **By fear the nephew shall his banner fold.**

Source: The two miscarriages of Anne de Bretagne which permitted Louis of Orléans, suspected by some of poisoning her at Lectoure with a drug injected into an orange, to succeed his uncle Charles VIII as king.[60]

44. Original text of 1568 edition   **Read as modern French:**

Le procrée naturel dogmion,   *d'Ogmion*
De sept à neuf du chemin destorner
A roy de longue & amy aumi hom,   *Arroi de loin; ami au mi-homme*
Doit à Navarre fort de PAU prosterner.

> **The offspring natural of Ogmion**
> **(One of from seven to nine) shall far from th' route**
> **Divert the array; and half-man's friend, to boot,**
> **Must in Navarre Pau's fort lay humbly down.**

Source: Unidentified military events in the far south-west of France, apparently projected as involving one of the seven surviving children of Henri II.

45. Original text of 1568 edition   **Read as modern French:**

La main escharpe & la jambe bandee,
Longs puis nay de Calais portera   *longtemps*
Au mot du guet la mort sera tardee,
Puis dans le temple à Pasques saignera.

> **The younger brother shall leg bandagèd**
> **And long his hand in sling from Calais show.**
> **On watch's word the death shall be delayed,**
> **Then in the church at Easter blood shall flow.**

Source: The highly topical capture of Calais from the English by the Catholic Duke of Guise (of the junior branch of the Lorraine family) in January 1558.

46. Original text of 1568 edition   **Read as modern French:**

Pol mensolee mourra trois lieuës du rosne,   *A Saint-Paul-de-Mausole*
Fuis les deux [/] prochains tarasc destrois: *près des détroits de Tarascon*
Car Mars fera le plus horrible trosne,
De coq & d'aigle de France freres trois.

> **At St-Rémy, three leagues from flowing Rhône,**
> **He'll die, both having fled Tarascon's strait[P],**
> **For Mars shall sit upon his awful throne**
> **Through Eagle, Cock: on France three brothers wait.**

Source: Current military conflicts between France and the Holy Roman Empire, using the animal symbolism of the *Mirabilis Liber*'s Prophecy of St Brigid of Sweden.

47. Original text of 1568 edition

Lac Trasmenien portera tesmoignage,
Des conjurez sarez dedans Perouse,
Un despolle contrefera le sage,
Tuant Tedesq de sterne & minuse.

Read as modern French:

Le lac Trasimène
serrez; Péruge [?]
despote
Teuton; accablé; haché

Lake Trasimeno shall bear witness to
The plotters in Perugia locked away.
A despot does his best the sage to play,
Killing the Teuton, chopping him in two.

Source: Unknown event involving the drowning of Italian suspects and the murder of a German one, apparently by a ruler intent on aping the biblical judgment (and wisdom!) of Solomon.

48. Original text of 1568 edition

Saturne en Cancer, Jupiter avec Mars,
Dedans Fevrier Chaldondon salvaterre.
Sault Castallon assailly de trois pars,
Pres de Verbiesque conflit mortelle guerre.

Read as modern French:

Kalende[s] en; Salvatierra
Les passes de Castille
Briviesca

With Mars near Jupiter, in Cancer Saturn,
In early February, at Salvatierra
Castile's high passes stormed in triple pattern:
Near Briviesca war and mortal terror.

Source: Once again Froissart's account, in his *Chroniques*, of the massive military campaign of Edward the Black Prince to restore Don Pedro the Cruel of Castile to his throne in 1367. Froissart specifically mentions (Luce I:37) that 'the army set out in mid-February', and (I:237) that in order to pass through the narrow ravines and canyons of the Pyrenees 'the army had to split itself into three parts,' each passing through on a different day before re-assembling for a week's rest in the vale of Pamplona. He also reports specifically (I:238–241) that the Prince advanced to Salvatierra just before engaging the enemy. Nostradamus must have looked up the wrong part of his astrological tables, however, since the astrology is completely awry, with Mars not joining Jupiter in Sagittarius until September, and Saturn in Scorpio throughout. Compare III.54, III.80, IV.99, VI.88.

49. Original text of 1568 edition

Satur. au beuf jove en l'eau, Mars en fleiche,
Six de Fevrier mortalité donra,
Ceux de Tardaigne à Bruge si grand breche,
Qu'à Ponteroso chef Barbarin mourra.

Read as modern French:

Saturne

Cerdagne [Catalogne?]
Ponterosso [Gênes?]/La Mer Rouge [lat.
pontus?]

> Saturn in Bull, Jove in the Water-carrier,
> Mars in the Archer, February 6th death deals:
> At Bruges Shall Catalans breach such a barrier
> That near Genoa the Muslim chief death feels.

Source: Unidentified link-up between events in the Netherlands under Philip the Fair of Burgundy and the expected future Muslim invasion of Europe. The astrological configuration is for 1499.

50. Original text of 1568 edition

Read as modern French:

La pestilence l'entour de Capadille,   *aux alentours de Capellades*
Un autre faim pres de Sagont s'appreste: *Sagonte/Sagunto*
Le chevalier bastard de bon senille,   *sénile*
Au grand de Thunes fera trancher la teste.

> T'wards Capellades mighty Plague is headed,
> While famine on Sagunto falls again:
> The knightly bastard of the good old thane
> Shall shortly have Tunisia's lord beheaded.

Source: The Plague epidemic that struck Spain in 1557, assimilated to the famine that struck Sagunto at the time of the siege of the town by the Carthaginians in 219 BC – and the beheading in 1557 by the King of Spain of the son of the old Count of Alcaudete for surrendering to the pirate Salah Reis (albeit in this case apparently recalled with a fair amount of confusion).[60]

51. Original text of 1568 edition

Read as modern French:

Le Bizantin faisant oblation,
Apres avoir Cordube à soy reprinse:
Son chemin long repos pamplation,   *à tailler les vignes [lat. pampinatio]*
Mer passant proy par la Colongna prinse.   *les Collones d'Hercule*

> Peace-offerings the Turkish chief shall send
> Once for himself he'll Cordoba retake:
> After long journey he his vines shall tend.
> Off cape Gibraltar prey at sea they'll take.

Source: The original Moorish invasions of Spain of the eighth century onwards, resulting in a long period of control over the Straits of Gibraltar and of peaceful Spanish occupation, assimilated to the *Mirabilis Liber*'s projected Arab invasion of Europe. See I.9, I.75, II.24.

52. Original text of 1568 edition

Le roy de Bloys dans Avignon regner,
D'amboise & seme viendra le long de Lyndre
Ongle à Poitiers sainctes aesles ruiner
Devant Boni.

Read as modern French:

[Voir VIII.38]
essaim; l'Indre

Devant Bonny viendra la guerre éteindre [?]

> **In Avignon shall reign of Blois the king:**
> **From Amboise shall his host the Indre ascend.**
> **A claw from Poitiers'll maim his sacred wing:**
> **Before Bonny [the war he'll shortly end].**

Source: Unidentified, but possibly, like VIII.38, tied in with the *Mirabilis Liber's* prediction of the eventual liberation of France from its future Islamic occupiers. See I.55. Last line left incomplete.

53. Original text of 1568 edition

Dedans Bolongne vouldra laver ses fautes,
Il ne pourra au temple du soleil,
Il volera faisant choses si haultes
En hierarchie n'en fut oncq un pareil.

Read as modern French:

Bologne
au Vatican [?]

> **There at Bologna he'd his faults wash out,**
> **Being excluded from the Vatican:**
> **He'll high aspire and things so haughty shout.**
> **Ne'er saw the Church's rulers such a man.**

Source: A so-far unidentified pope or senior cardinal.

54. Original text of 1568 edition

Soubz la colleur du traicte mariage,
Fait magnanime par grand Chyren selin,
Quintin, Arras, recouvrez au voyage
D'espaignolz fait second banc macelin.

Read as modern French:

St-Quentin
du boucher

> **Beneath the cover of a marriage pact**
> **Magnanimous shall lunar Henri be.**
> **Thereby Arras, St-Quentin he'll exact,**
> **Spain having done more grievous butchery.**

Source: The September truce in the aftermath of the huge French defeat at St-Quentin of August 1557, which proved as disastrous in terms of the slaughter of the cream of French chivalry as the Battle of Pavia had been in 1525. The terms were finalized in the celebrated Treaty of Cateau-Cambrésis of 1559, which provided for the marriage of Philip II of Spain to Henri II's daughter Elisabeth de Valois, and of the brilliant Imperial Commander-in-Chief Emmanuel-Philibert de

Savoie to her aunt Maguerite de Valois. It was at the subsequent marriage celebrations in Paris that Henri, whose shield bore a lunar device, was mortally wounded in the head, with huge effects both for the future of France and for the reputation of Nostradamus as a prophet (given that, although he in fact failed to predict it, it has long been popularly assumed that he did).

55. Original text of 1568 edition   Read as modern French:

Entre deux fleuves se verra enserré,
Tonneaux & caques unis à passer outre,   *casques*
Huict pontz rompus chef à tant enferré   *étant [estant] [?]*
Enfans parfaictz sont jugutez en coultre.   *nobles; jugulés; à couteau*

> **Shut in between two rivers he shall be,**
> **Barrels and casks linked up to cross the flood.**
> **Eight bridges down, chief stabbed repeatedly,**
> **And noble children's throats cut, pouring blood.**

Source: Unidentified military crisis. In Nostradamus the phrase 'between two rivers' normally means one or more of (a) Babylon, (b) Lyon, or (c) Avignon.

56. Original text of 1568 edition   Read as modern French:

La bande foible le tertre occupera
Ceux du hault lieu feront horribles crys,
Le gros troppeau d'estre coin troublera,   *sur la droite [dextre]*
Tombe pres D.nebro descouvers les escris.   *près de l'Èbre; écrits/inscriptions*

> **The feeble band the hill shall occupy;**
> **Those from above shall let out fearful cries:**
> **The mighty host the right flank shall surprise.**
> **On tomb near Ebro writings they'll descry.**

Source: Unidentified battle, possibly connected with the Black Prince's Spanish campaign of 1367. See III.54, III.80, IV.99, VI.88, VIII.48.

57. Original text of 1568 edition   Read as modern French:

De souldat simple parviendra en empire,   *au commandement [lat. imperium]*
De robe courte parviendra à la longue
Vaillant aux armes en eglise ou plus pyre,   *au*
Vexer les prestres comme l'eau fait l'esponge.

> **From simple soldier he to power shall burst,**
> **From tunic short to lordly robe attaining;**
> **Valiant in arms: in church, though, at his worst,**
> **As does a sponge to water, clerics draining.**

Source: The rise to power of Gaspard de Coligny, who was promoted from simple soldier first to Colonel General of the infantry and then, in 1552, to 'Admiral of France' on the strength of his military exploits, subsequently becoming a Huguenot and in 1557 the leader of the French Protestant faction.

58. Original text of 1568 edition   Read as modern French:

Regne en querelle aux freres divisé,
Prendre les armes & le nom Britannique
Tiltre Anglican sera tard advisé,   *aperçu*
Surprins de nuict mener à l'air Gallique.   *surpris*

> **The realm at odds twixt brothers deep divided,**
> **They'll take up arms and fight for Britain's name:**
> **The name of 'Anglican' comes late provided.**
> **At night he's ta'en: they'll play the Gallic game.**

Source: The rivalry between the religiously relatively easy-going Edward Seymour, Earl of Somerset, official Protector to the young King Edward VI, and the much more sternly Protestant John Dudley, Earl of Warwick (later Duke of Northumberland), who was responsible for Somerset's arrest in 1549 and execution in 1552, and who introduced the Second Prayer Book that finally defined the beliefs of the Anglican Church. It was also during his regency that Boulogne was surrendered to the French for a derisory sum and the Dauphin François was allowed to marry Mary Queen of Scots, so allowing Henri II to claim that he ruled over France, Scotland, *and* England.

59. Original text of 1568 edition   Read as modern French:

Par deux fois hault, par deux fois mis à bas
L'orient aussi l'occident foyblira   *s'affaiblira*
Son adversaire apres plusieurs combats,
Par mer, chassé au besoing faillira.

> **Twice raised to giddy height, then twice brought low,**
> **The East shall weaken – and the West, indeed.**
> **After full many battles shall its foe**
> **Pursued by sea, collapse in time of need.**

Source: The *Mirabilis Liber*'s forecast of a mighty Western counter-invasion against the Muslim world after the latter's invasion and occupation of Europe. See I.55. The two separate occasions referred back to would seem to be (a) the Saracen invasions of Sicily and Italy and Moorish invasions of Spain and (b) the Ottoman invasions of Europe of Nostradamus's own day.

60. Original text of 1568 edition

Premier en Gaule, premier en Romanie,
Par mer & terre aux Angloys & Parys
Merveilleux faitz par celle grand mesnie
Violant terax perdra le NORLARIS.

Read as modern French:

du Saint Empire Romain
et ses partenaires
par cette grande compagnie/bande
violent; monstre [gr. teras]; Lorraine

The first in Gaul and in Rome's Empire too,
By land and sea 'gainst th' English and their crew,
That mighty host shall wondrous things attain.
A monster violent shall lose Lorraine.

Source: The brilliant counter-attack by François Duke of Guise, just back from campaigning in Italy, against the forces of Charles V, only a year after the disaster of St-Quentin of 1557 – including those that were threatening Paris itself – together with his recapture of Calais from the English. The 'violent monster' is conceivably code for Charles's Commander-in-Chief, Emmanuel Philibert, Duke of Savoy.

61. Original text of 1568 edition

Jamais par le decouvrement du jour
Ne parviendra au signe sceptrifere
Que tous ses sieges ne soyent en sejour,
Portant au coq don du TAG amifere.

Read as modern French:

sceptifère [portant le sceptre]

de la légion [gr. tagma] armifère

Never shall it be seen by light of day,
That man to scepter-bearer's rank ascending,
Till every see's archbishop is away
Each armèd host as gift to th' Cock presenting.

Source: The *Mirabilis Liber's* prophecies of the 'Angelic Pastor' who would eventually restore the Church to rights, aided by the forces of the future French *Grand Monarque*. Compare I.4, I.55, I.92, VI.21.

62. Original text of 1568 edition

Lors qu'on verra expiler le saint temple,
Plus grand du rosne leurs sacrez prophaner
Par eux naistra pestilence si ample,
Roy fuit injuste ne fera condamner.

Read as modern French:

saccager [lat. expilare]

l'injustice

When Holy Church despoilèd they shall see,
And Pope beside the Rhône profane its rite,
Through them so dire a pestilence shall be.
He'll not condemn th' unjust, that King in flight.

Source: The Great Western Church Schism of 1378 to 1417 (see I.32, V.46, V.92, VI.13, VII.22, VII.23, VII.35, IX.4), projected into the future by the *Mirabilis Liber* in terms of its prophecy of the sack of Rome by invading Muslim forces and the consequent flight of the Pope. See I.9, I.75, II.24.

63. Original text of 1568 edition   Read as modern French:

Quant l'adultere blessé sans coup aura
Meurdry la femme & le filz par despit,
Femme assoumee [/] l'enfant estranglera:
Huit captifz prins, s'estouffer sans respit.

> **When th' adulterer, wounded yet not attacked,**
> **His wife and son shall murder out of spite –**
> **The wife once killed, the child he'll choke, in fact –**
> **Eight captives ta'en, all smothered *sans* respite.**

Source: Unidentified.

64. Original text of 1568 edition   Read as modern French:

Dedans les Isles les enfans transportez,
Les deux de sept seront en desespoir,
Ceux du terrouer en seront supportez,   *du territoire/du pays*
Nom pelle prins [/] des ligues fuy l'espoir.   *Montpellier*

> **Transported to the isles the children are,**
> **Two of the seven cast down in great despair.**
> **The local ones shall be supported there.**
> **Montpellier ta'en: from th' Leagues all hope is far.**

Source: Unidentified Protestant actions in the south of France, unresisted by the powerful Catholic League.

65. Original text of 1568 edition   Read as modern French:

Le vieux frustré du principal espoir,
Il parviendra au chef de son empire: *à la tête*
Vingt mois tiendra le regne à grand pouvoir,
Tiran, cruel en delaissant un pire.   *Tyrant*

> **The old one in his greatest hope frustrated,**
> **Once he'll the summit of his power attain,**
> **Some twenty months in mighty power shall reign –**
> **A tyrant, once an even crueler rated.**

Source: The story of Pope Adrian VI, the only Dutch pope, who reigned from 9 January 1522 (when he was 63) until 14 September 1523, having formerly been not merely the future Holy Roman Emperor Charles V's tutor, but a Grand

Inquisitor in the Spanish Inquisition to boot. He made strenuous efforts to reform the Church, but was frustrated in this by the Italian Cardinals, the German Protestants and the predations of the Ottoman Turks.

66. Original text of 1568 edition   Read as modern French:

Quand l'escriture D.M. trouvee,
Et cave antique à lampe descouverte,
Loy, Roy, & Prince Ulpian esprouvee,
Pavillon Royne & Duc sous la couverte.

> **When the inscription 'D.M.' shall be found**
> **And ancient vault by light of torches seen,**
> **'Twill prove to be of Ulpian King renowned,**
> **The chief wrapped in his banner with his queen.**

Source: Another piece of contemporary archaeology, with which Nostradamus was always fascinated, possibly either at Arles or at Glanum, just south of his hometown. The inscription was the standard abbreviation for *Diis Manibus* ('in the hands of Pluto', god of the underworld – the equivalent of the modern *RIP*) on Roman tombstones, and line 3 suggests that the vault is supposed to be either that of the Emperor Trajan (Marcus Ulpius Traianus) or one dating from his reign.

67. Original text of 1568 edition   Read as modern French:

PAR. CAR. NERSAF, à ruine grand discorde,   Paris, Carcassonne, France
Ne l'un ne l'autre n'aura election,
Nersaf du peuple aura amour & concorde,   France
Ferrare, Collonne grande protection.   Cologne

> **From Paris to Carcassonne French ruin, discord:**
> **Nor one nor th' other shall approval gain.**
> **Yet what French folk shall want is love, concord.**
> **Cologne, Ferrara sheltered shall remain.**

Source: The contemporary French Wars of Religion, contrasted with the relative (but temporary) tranquility of the Imperial domains.

68. Original text of 1568 edition   Read as modern French:

Vieux Cardinal par le jeusne deceu,
Hors de sa charge se verra desarmé,
Arles ne monstres double soit aperceu,   doubles soient aperçus
Et Liquiduct [/] & le Prince embausmé.   l'aqueduc

> **By younger cardinal the old's deceived:**
> **Out of his ground he shall disarmed appear,**

Unless two miracles at Arles appear –
Both th' Aqueduct, and perfumed Prince perceived.

Source: The quarrel between Cardinal Jean du Bellay and Cardinal François de Tournon over the latter's appointment as French *chargé d'affaires* in Italy in 1554 – the very year when Nostradamus's young friend Adam de Craponne, by now a distinguished architect and hydraulic engineer, sought and obtained the permission of the parliament at Aix-en-Provence to dig an irrigation canal from the river Durance to water-starved Salon, designed to irrigate not merely the town itself, but the vast desert of the *Crau* to the west of it as far as Arles. The 'aqueduct' was a project in which Nostradamus and his wife were in due course to invest a vast sum, equivalent to some £41,000 in modern sterling, or a thirteenth share in the total investment. And it was on 13 May 1557 that, thanks to this miracle of modern engineering, the first trickle of water finally reached Salon for the first time. Whether there was some princely promise at the time officially to open the canal when it eventually arrived at Arles is unknown. In fact it didn't happen until 1585, well after the deaths of Craponne (d. 1576), Nostradamus (d. 1566), and his wife (d.1582).

69. Original text of 1568 edition   Read as modern French:

Aupres du jeune le vieux ange baisser,
Et le viendra surmonter à la fin:
Dis ans esgaux au plus vieux rabaisser,
De trois deux l'un l'huitiesme seraphin.   *d'eux; fera fin*

The older 'Angel' bows before the young,
For over him he'll gain the mastery.
Ere ten years he shall bring down th' older one:
The eighth shall put an end to one of three.

Source: Villehardouin's account in his *Conquest of Constantinople* (14) of the deposing and death of the old Emperor Isaac II Angelus of Constantinople (actually referred to by name) and the savage murder of one of his sons (Alexius IV) in 1204.[60] Compare I.35.

70. Original text of 1568 edition   Read as modern French:

Il entrera vilain, meschant, infame
Tyrannisant la Mesopotamie,
Tous amys fait d'adulterine d'ame.   *dame*
Tertre horrible noir de phisonomie.   *Monstre [gr. teras/teratos?]; physiognomie*

Wicked and vile, a man of ill repute
In Babylon his tyranny he'll base.
With the Great Whore all then shall plead their suit.
A monster horrible, and black his face.

Source: The *Mirabilis Liber*'s prophecy of the future Antichrist, here seen as swarthy, if not actually Moorish. See I.47, I.76, II.9.

71. Original text of 1568 edition | Read as modern French:

Croistra le nombre si grand des astronomes
Chassez, bannis & livres censurez,
L'an mil six cens & sept par sacre glomes   *assemblées [lat. glomus]*
Que nul aux sacres ne seront asseurez.

      Astronomers so multiply 'neath heaven
      That they'll be hounded, banned, censored their work
      By sacred councils in 1607:
      At sacred rites danger for them shall lurk.

Source: Another of Nostradamus's ill-advised 'window-forecasts'. No such persecution in fact took place, nor is there any truth in the 'urban myth' that there was a Council of Malines in 1607 that imposed such a ban. Compare IV.18.

72. Original text of 1568 edition | Read as modern French:

Champ Perusin o l'enorme deffaite   *de Péruge*
Et le conflit tout au pres de Ravenne,
Passage sacre lors qu'on fera la feste,   *de sacre/de bandit*
Vainqueur vaincu cheval manger la venne.   *l'avoine*

      O on Perugia's field what huge defeat!
      And hard by old Ravenna what affray!
      Bandits at large upon a holiday:
      The victor's horse the loser's oats shall eat.

Source: The *Mirabilis Liber*'s prediction of a huge Arab invasion of Europe via Italy. See I.9, I.75.

73. Original text of 1568 edition | Read as modern French:

Soldat Barbare le grand Roy frappera,   *Arabe*
Injustement non eslongné de mort,
L'avare mere du fait cause sera   *ambitieuse*
Conjurateur & regne en grand remort.

      An Arab soldier shall assail the King
      Almost to death, yet without reason due.
      Ambitious mother is behind the thing.
      That day both plotter and the realm shall rue.

Source: Unidentified.

74. Original text of 1568 edition

Read as modern French:

En tetre neufve bien avant Roy entré

terre

Pendant subges luy viendront faire acueil,

sujets

Sa perfidie aura tel recontré

rencontré

Qu'aux citadins lieu de feste & recueil.

et de recollection

Long ere the King shall into th' new land sail
While subjects come to bid him welcome all,
His perfidy such awesome heights shall scale
That they shall think it worth memorial.

Source: Presumably the actions of Philip II of Spain in the Netherlands from his accession in 1556 onwards.

75. Original text of 1568 edition

Read as modern French:

Le pere & filz seront meurdris ensemble

Le prefecteur dedans son pavillon

La mere à Tours du filz ventre aura enfle.

enflé

Caiche verdure de feuilles papillon.

de papier

Father and son shall murdered be as one
By the Count lurking in his ducal tent.
At Tours the mother, pregnant with her son,
Hides under leaves of green and paper rent.

Source: Unidentified.

76. Original text of 1568 edition

Read as modern French:

Plus Macelin que roy en Angleterre

boucher [< lat. macellum, 'marché de viande']

Lieu obscur nay par force aura l'empire:

Lasche sans foy, sans loy saignera terre,

Son temps s'approche si pres que je souspire.

More butcher, he, than ever English king,
Obscurely born, by force in power he'll sit.
Lawless and faithless, blood from the land he'll wring.
The wretch's time's so close I sigh at it.

Source: The story of King John of England, born at Oxford, who respected neither family, rank nor religion in his murderous efforts to seize and maintain power. Nostradamus seems to associate him with the expected Antichrist, whose advent he regards as imminent.

77. Original text of 1568 edition   Read as modern French:

L'antechrist trois bien tost annichilez,
Vingt & sept ans sang durera sa guerre,   *en sang*
Les heretiques mortz, captifs, exilez,
Sang corps humain eau rogie gresler terre.

> **The Antichrist – three very soon laid low –**
> **His war of blood shall last seven years and twenty.**
> **Heretics dead, captives to exile go:**
> **Blood, corpses: water red on earth a-plenty.**

Source: The contemporary Wars of Religion, presided over by John Calvin, leader of the Protestant cause from late 1536 until his death in May 1564, and widely regarded by Catholics as the Antichrist in person, who had persecuted Pierre Ameaux, exiled Ami Perrin and Jérôme Bolsec and burned at the stake Jacques Gruet and, in 1553, Michael Servetus.[60]

78. Original text of 1568 edition   Read as modern French:

Un Bragamas avec la langue torte   *bragueur [?]*
Viendra des dieux [rompre] le sanctuaire,
Aux heretiques il ouvrira la porte
En suscitant l'eglise militaire.

> **A real glib-talker with a serpent-tongue**
> **Of sacred sanctuary shall ope the door,**
> **Fling wide the gates, the heretics let in,**
> **And so stir up the Church to bloody war.**

Source: The alleged role of Chancellor Michel de l'Hospital in stirring up the Wars of Religion by allegedly being altogether too soft with the Protestants in the first place.

79. Original text of 1568 edition   Read as modern French:

Qui par fer pere perdra nay de Nonnaire,   *né*
De Gorgon sur la sera sang perfetant   *sûr; là; concevant de nouveau*
En terre estrange fera si tout de taire,
Qui bruslera luy mesme & son entant.   *enfant*

> **Through father's sword who'll lose the nunnery-born,**
> **Of Gorgon sure, a new kin is conceived.**
> **In foreign land to silence he'll be sworn**
> **Who'll burn himself and his own child so grieved.**

Source: Unidentifiable – indeed, barely fathomable.

80. Original text of 1568 edition

Des innocens le sang de vefve & vierge.
Tant de maulx faitz par moyen se grand Roge
Saintz simulachres trempez en ardant cierge
De frayeur crainte ne verra nul que boge.

Read as modern French:

veuve
du grand Rouge [de sang?]
brûlant
bouge

> **With innocents bleed maids and widowed dames –**
> **So many woes commits the Great Red lord.**
> **The holy icons dipped in candle-flames:**
> **For fear and dread not one shall move abroad.**

Source: The *Mirabilis Liber*'s grim prophecy of a vast and brutal Muslim invasion of Europe (see I.9, I.75, II.24), headed by the Antichrist in person (see I.47, I.76, II.9), which will destroy and desecrate the Roman Catholic Church (see I.15).

81. Original text of 1568 edition

Le neuf empire en desolation,
Sera changé du pole aquilonaire.
De la Sicile viendra l'esmotion
Troubler l'emprise à Philip tributaire.

Read as modern French:

l'entreprise

> **Desolate shall the empire new become,**
> **O'erthrown by power that further northward lies.**
> **From Sicily shall great upheaval come**
> **To trouble mighty Philip's enterprise.**

Source: Another of Nostradamus's somewhat ill-advised instant 'window-forecasts', based on his conviction that Philip II and his uncle, the Holy Roman Emperor Ferdinand (both of whom had come to power in 1556) would soon be at odds – possibly assimilated to the *Mirabilis Liber*'s prediction of a great Muslim invasion of Europe via the Mediterranean. See I.9, I.75. The suggested altercation never in fact happened.

82. Original text of 1568 edition

Ronge long, sec faisant du bon valet,
A la parfin n'aura que son congie
Poignant poyson & lettres au collet
Sera saisi eschappé en dangie.

Read as modern French:

Rongé
congé

danger

> **Emaciate, tall, at his lord's call and beck,**
> **He'll in the end gain nothing but the sack.**
> **Sharp bane and letters hung about his neck,**
> **Once he's the danger fled, they'll haul him back.**

Source: Unidentified.

83. Original text of 1568 edition   **Read as modern French:**

Le plus grand voile hors du port de Zara,
Pres de Bisance fera son entreprinse,
D'ennemy perte & l'amy ne sera
Le tiers à deux fera grand pille & prinse.

> **The biggest fleet that Zara e'er did see**
> **Near to Byzantium its task shall ply.**
> **Loss to the foe, nor friendly shall he be,**
> **That third that both shall plunder, rape and try.**

Source: Villehardouin's account of the infamous Fourth Crusade in his *Conquest of Constantinople*, whose whole fifth chapter he devotes to the Crusaders' capture of the port of Zara in the former Yugoslavia in 1202 on behalf of the Venetians, prior to sacking Constantinople itself in 1204. As he himself puts it, 'No finer fleet of ships ever sailed from any port.' The projected context, inevitably, is the great Western counter-invasion of the Middle East predicted by the *Mirabilis Liber*. See I.55.

84. Original text of 1568 edition   **Read as modern French:**

Paterne orra de la Sicile crie,   *entendra*
Tous les aprests du goulphre de Trieste,   *préparatifs*
Qui s'entendra jusqu'a à la trinacrie.   *Qui s'étendra jusqu'a Sicile/Rhodes*
De tant de voiles fuy, fuy l'horrible peste.

> **Unto Paterno Sicily's cries ascend:**
> **Trieste's gulf's with signs of war replete**
> **Which soon to Sicily itself extend.**
> **Flee, flee the plague of ships, the ghastly fleet!**

Source: The *Mirabilis Liber*'s familiar prophecy of a vast Muslim sea-invasion of southern Europe. See I.9, I.75.

85. Original text of 1568 edition   **Read as modern French:**

Entre Bayonne & à saint Jean de Lux
Sera posé de Mars le promottoire   *L'avance/la tête de pont [promontoire]*
Aux Hanix d'Aquillon Nanar hostera lux   *Aux alliés [lat. annixus]; Nana [nymphe];*
                                                    ôtera la lumière
Puis suffocqué au lict sans adjutoire.   *aide*

> **Between Bayonne and port St-Jean-de-Luz**
> **Shall war have made its martial inroads dread.**
> **To allies north the whore shall light refuse.**
> **Then he'll be smothered, helpless, on a bed.**

Source: A slightly garbled version of Froissart's account in his *Chronicles* (Luce I:245) of the murder of Don Pedro the Cruel (now cut off from his English ally Edward the Black Prince, who had become ill and retired to Aquitaine) by his illegitimate brother and rival Henry the Bastard of Castile, after Pedro had called him 'the son of a whore', in the course of a mortal struggle on a couch at the castle of Montiel. See III.54, III.80, IV.99, VI.88, VIII.48.

86. Original text of 1568 edition   Read as modern French:

Par Arnani tholoser ville franque,   *Ernani, Tolosa et Villafranca*
Bande infinie par le mont Adrian,   *la Sierra de San Adrian*
Passe riviere, Hurin par pont la planque   *hutin*
Bayonne entrer tous Bihoro criant.   *Bigorre*

> **Through Villafranca, Tolosa, Ernani**
> **A mighty host San Adrian shall pass o'er.**
> **Crossing the river, rushing the bridge shall many**
> **Enter Bayonne, crying 'Bigorre! Bigorre!'**

Source: Unidentified Spanish attack on Bayonne.

87. Original text of 1568 edition   Read as modern French:

Mort conspiree viendra en plein effect,
Charge donnee & voiage de mort,
Esleu, crée, receu par siens deffait.
Sang d'innocence devant foy par remort.

> **The plotted death to be shall surely come,**
> **The charges laid and voyage to his death.**
> **Chosen, created, by his own undone.**
> **Innocent blood before remorseful faith.**

Source: The capture, trial and eventual death of the head of the Templars, elected in 1295, who was forced in 1307 to sail from Cyprus to France to justify himself before the Pope.[60] Compare I.81, II.51.

88. Original text of 1568 edition   Read as modern French:

Dans la Sardeigne un noble Roy viendra.
Que ne tiendra que trois ans le royaume,
Plusieurs coulleurs avec soy conjoindra,
Luy mesmes apres soin someil marrit scome.   *après son sommeil matrimonial [?]*

> **Into Sardinia shall come a noble King**
> **Who shall the realm no more than three years keep:**
> **To him he'll various friends and allies bring.**
> **After his efforts comes his wedding-sleep.**

Source: The invasion of Sardinia by the King of Aragon between 1323 and 1326.

89. Original text of 1568 edition   **Read as modern French:**

Pour ne tumber entre mains de son oncle,
Qui ses enfans par regner trucidez,
Orant au peuple mettant pied sur Peloncle   *Plaidant; Pélion [?]*
Mort & traisné entre chevaulx bardez.

> **Lest he into his uncle's hands should fall**
> **Who'd killed his children to acquire the throne,**
> **Praying the people, aping the Giants' fall,**
> **He'll die, twixt armored horses cruelly drawn.**

Source: Unidentified.

90. Original text of 1568 edition   **Read as modern French:**

Quand des croisez un trouvé de sens trouble   *troublé*
En lieu du sacre verra un boeuf cornu
Par vierge porc son lieu lors sera comble,   *Pour; surmonté*
Par roy plus ordre ne sera soustenu.

> **When a Crusader with a mind unwhole**
> **In holy place a hornéd ox shall see,**
> **Then shall a pig take o'er the Virgin's role,**
> **And king no longer order oversee.**

Source: The *Mirabilis Liber*'s curious Prophecy of the Blessed Vincent, attributed by some sources to St Vincent Ferrer, by others to Vincent of Aquila, but actually a fairly late prophecy dating from about 1503, here evidently assimilated to the same book's familiar scenario of apocalyptic invasion and counter-invasion: 'When you shall hear the first Ox bellow within the Church of the Lord, then the Church shall start to go lame; but when three other signs shall be presented to you, and when you shall see the Eagle joined to the Snake, and when the second Ox bellows in the Church, it is the time of tribulations. For the Snake and the Ox shall summon up a king with a great name from the west who shall devastate the kingdom of the Assyrians, and after disposing of his conquered booty, he shall return barely safe and sound to his estates: then shall appear an adulterer who shall arrange for Snakes to be hidden in the shadows. Woe to the inhabitants of Sicily; for they shall see the dangers, without being able to ward them off. Finally, with Divine permission, the second Ox shall bellow; then there shall be more or less a schism in the Church: two Popes at the same time, of whom the one, schismatic, shall triumph by banishing the true Pope to Venice after usurping his pulpit by violence. Then three powerful armies shall enter Italy: one coming from the west; another from the east; a third from the north. They shall arise one against the other, and Italy, drowned in waves of blood, shall never have seen such a slaughter. The Eagle shall seize the adulterous king, and with fear and force shall subdue all. There shall be a new reform in the city, and the sects shall cease to be.'

91. Original text of 1568 edition

Frymy les champs des Rodanes entrees
Ou les croysez seront presque unys,
Les deux brassieres en pisces rencontrees
Et un grand nombre par deluge punis.

Read as modern French:

Entre [emmy]; de ceux du Rhône

Les deux planètes brûlantes [Mars et Soleil]

Great crowds shall tread the fields of flowing Rhône,
Where folk can most Crusaders gathered see.
Both Mars and Sun in Pisces shall be one
And a great many scourged by floods shall be.

Source: On the face of it, the Seventh Crusade of 1248, for which King Louis IX first built the still-impressive fortified port of Aigues-Mortes on the Rhône delta, then constructed a huge fleet of 1500 vessels, and finally assembled a vast army of Crusaders to man them numbering some 35,000, plus their horses, supplies, and equipment, which for each Crusader had to include a long box to serve as seat, trunk and, in the final event, coffin. After the Crusade failed when King Louis was taken prisoner, he tried again in 1270, only to die of the Plague at Tunis. The astrology in fact fits February and March on the second occasion. Possibly Nostradamus, as ever slightly vague about the half-remembered details, should in this case have written *peste* instead of *deluge*. His source appears not to have been the *Life of Saint Louis* by Joinville, however, since the latter did not join the 1270 Crusade, and made his own way to join the earlier one at Cyprus via Arles and Marseille, then in the kingdom of Provence. Hence, presumably, the last line's reference to '*most Crusaders*'.

92. Original text of 1568 edition

Loin hors du regne mis en hazard voiage
Grand ost duyra pour soy l'occupera,
Le roy tiendra les siens captif ostrage
A son retour tout pays pillera.

Read as modern French:

armée; il conduira; foi [?]
captifs en otage

Far from the realm on voyage hazardous
He'll lead his host, them to the Faith commit.
The king shall hold his captives hostage thus.
The land he'll sack on his return to it.

Source: Possibly the same Crusade as in the previous verse.

93. Original text of 1568 edition

Sept moys sans plus obtiendra prelature
Par son deces grand scisme fera naistre:
Sept moys tiendra un autre la preture
Pres de Venise paix union renaistre.

Read as modern French:

prélature [?]

> Seven months without the prelature regaining
> Through his decease he'll make a schism grow.
> Seven months from thence another bishop's reigning:
> Near Venice peace and union new they'll sow.

Source: Unidentified incidents involving Church politics.

94. Original text of 1568 edition   Read as modern French:

Devant le lac ou plus cher fut getté	*jeté*
De sept mois, & son host desconfit	*son armée*
Seront Hyspans par Albannois gastez	*Espagnols*
Par delay perte en donnant le conflict.	

> Before the lake in which his dearest thrown
> Of seven months was, discomfited his host.
> Spaniards by Alba's men are overthrown,
> Through hesitation many of them lost.

Source: Unknown.

95. Original text of 1568 edition   Read as modern French:

Le seducteur sera mis en la fosse,	
Et estaché jusques à quelque temps,	
Le clerc uny le chef avec sa crosse	
Pycante droite attraira les contens.	*Piquant à droite*

> Within the pit the great seducer's cast
> And for a time staked out as an outlaw.
> The clerk with crozier-wielding lord stands fast,
> Who, laying about him, shall supporters draw.

Source: Unidentified incident, possibly drawn from the contemporary Wars of Religion.

96. Original text of 1568 edition   Read as modern French:

La synagogue sterile sans nul fruit	
Sera receu entre les infideles	
De Babylon la fille du porsuit	
Misere & triste luy trenchera les aisles.	

> The sterile, fruitless synagogue of yore
> Shall 'midst the infidels be welcomèd
> Till Babel's daughter, chasing all before,
> Shall, sad and wretched, clip its wings instead.

Source: The contemporary emigration of persecuted Jews from Spain and Italy to the more tolerant Ottoman – even though Muslim – dispensation of Suleiman the Magnificent in Turkey. One of them, named Don Joseph Nassi, who emigrated to Constantinople in 1553, even became a powerful figure there.[41] However, Nostradamus expects them to be persecuted at the time of the *Mirabilis Liber's* predicted Arab invasion. See I.9, I.75, II.24.

97. Original text of 1568 edition   Read as modern French:

Aux fins du VAR changer le pompotans,   *le tout-puissant*
Pres du rivage les trois beaux enfans naistre.
Ruyne au peuple par aage competans
Regne au pays changer plus voir croistre.

> **On Var's long border shall the great lord change:**
> **Near to the bank three fair babes see the day,**
> **Then ruin the people once they are of age.**
> **They'll change the realm, increase the country's sway.**

Source: Unidentified.

98. Original text of 1568 edition   Read as modern French:

Des gens d'eglise sang sera espandu,   *épanché [espanché] [voir rime!]*
Comme de l'eau en si grande abondance:
Et d'un long temps ne sera restanché
Ve Ve au clerc ruyne & doleance.   *Hélas! Hélas!; chagrin*

> **The blood of churchmen shall be freely shed:**
> **As though t'were water such a flood shall flow.**
> **Longtime unstaunched that flood shall flow full red.**
> **Woe to the priests! Ruin, pain they'll undergo.**

Source: The *Mirabilis Liber's* grisly predictions of ruin for the Church in the wake of its expected Muslim invasion of Europe. See I.15.

99. Original text of 1568 edition   Read as modern French:

Par la puissance des trois rois temporelz,
En autre lieu sera mis le saint siege:
Où la substance de l'esprit corporel,
Sera remys & receu pour vray siege.

> **By power of the three kings temporal**
> **The Holy Seat shall elsewhere be removed,**
> **Where presence physical of spirit shall**
> **Be reaffirmed and ratified as proved.**

Source: The Council of Trent of 1545, designed to promote a counter-reformation in Europe and specifically to reaffirm the Catholic doctrine of the literal transubstantiation of Christ's body and blood in the Eucharist in the face of Protestant assertions to the contrary. Nostradamus was correct in assuming that that would indeed be its conclusion, finally reached in 1563.

100. Original text of 1568 edition   Read as modern French:

Pour l'abondance de larme respandue   *[ou: l'arme]*
Du hault en bas par le bas au plus hault
Trop grande foy par ieu vie perdue,   *pour Dieu*
De soif mourir par habondant deffault.

Through arms so many, tears so freely shed
From high to low and low to high above
Faith overdone shall lose lives for God's love,
Through all their faults from such a thirst soon dead.

Source: The developing Wars of Religion (with a deliciously apt pun in the first line).

Century IX

1. Original text of 1568 edition

Dans la maison du traducteur de Bourc
Seront les lettres trouvees sus la table,
Bourgne, roux, blanc, chanu tiendra de cours,
Qui changera au nouveau connestable.

Read as modern French:

Bourg

Borgne; chenu; au courant

> **Within the house of Bourg's translator, there**
> **The writings on the table they'll discover.**
> **One-eyed, red-haired, white-head he'll keep aware**
> **Till all shall change when constables change over.**

Source: The original writings of the classical translator Étienne de la Boétie of Bordeaux, and especially his seditious *La servitude volontaire* or *Contr'un*, written at the age of 18 in 1548 and circulated in manuscript, but not published until 1570, which covertly criticized the Constable of France, Anne de Montmorency, for his brutal suppression of the Salt-Tax Revolt of the same year in the south-west of France, and which has been celebrated as a seminal democratic text ever since.

2. Original text of 1568 edition

Du hault du mont Aventin voix ouye,
Vuydez vuydez de tous les deux costez,
Du sang des rouges sera l'ire assomye,
D'Arimin Prato, Columna debotez.

Read as modern French:

Assoupie/apaisée [assovye]
Rimini [?]; colonnes

> **A voice is heard from the Mount Aventine:**
> **'Away! Away! On either side, away!**
> **Once cardinals shall bleed shall wrath decline:**
> **From Prato, Rimini columns driv'n away.'**

Source: A self-invented 'augury', based on the semi-legendary King Numa's founding of the original state oracle on the Aventine Hill in Rome in around 710 BC (Livy, *History of Rome*, I.21), and used to reinforce the *Mirabilis Liber*'s prophecies of a brutal Islamic invasion of Europe via Italy, and via Rome in particular, resulting in the ruin and downfall of the Roman Church with its red-hatted and red-robed cardinals. See I.9, I.75.

301

3. Original text of 1568 edition   **Read as modern French:**

La magna vaqua à Ravenne grand trouble,   *La grande vache [it. – jeu de mots sur*
                                             Magnavacca]

Conduitz par quinze enserrez à Fornase   *à Farnèse [le Pape Paul III et ses successeurs]*
A Romme naistre deux monstres à teste double   *naîtront*
Sang, feu, deluge, les plus grands à l'espase.   *à la poutre [esparre]*

> The mighty cow, Ravenna's nightmare too,
> Shall fifteen tie and bring before the Pope:
> Rome sees two double-headed monsters new.
> Blood, fire and flood, the leaders hanged by rope.

Source: A somewhat muddled version of various omens reported by Conrad Lycosthenes in his huge and recently published *Prodigiorum ac ostentorum chronicon* of 1557:[44] first of all the famous Ravenna monster of 1511 (see II.32 above), and secondly the calf with a bearded human face born at Kleisdorf in 1556 – while a second monster mentioned in the same paragraph was indeed taken to be brought before the Pope. In Batman's translation:[5] *The 24 of July a Cow brought forth a deformed Monster* [Nostradamus, with his notably vague approach to reading Latin (compare his *Preface* in Appendix A below), has evidently taken Lycosthenes' *monstrum vacca enixa est* to mean 'a monster cow was born'] *in the vilage of Clesdorf 3 miles distant from Pabenberg, which Fincelius also described, he had foure feete like a Calfe, his head like a man, a black beard, two mens eares, indifferent well heared, likewise a mans brest with dugges, the monster was brought forth at the farme of a noble women, a widowe. So Volaterranus writeth that a childe was borne of a woman, begotten by a Dogge, having a mans shape in the upper part, but the lower parte the ful forme of a dogge, and to purge the sinne he was brought to the Pope, of which matter Cardanus maketh mention, Booke. 14. Chap. 64 of the variety of thinges.* Obviously, then, this latter case especially was

causing a considerable stir – not to say scandal – at the time, and so it is no surprise that Nostradamus should have referred to it. Line 3 could be based on any two of the many twin-headed births reported in the same volume. The two-headed child and

conjoined twins (in this case, though, with only *one* head between them!) reported from Italy in 1514 seem the most likely, given that they were taken to portend
the wars that indeed devastated Italy in that year as per the last line of the verse,
which possibly refers once again to the *Mirabilis Liber*'s menacing predictions of an
Arab invasion of Europe via Italy. See I.9, I.75. Evidently Nostradamus's interest in
omens had revived somewhat by the time he reached this point in his manuscript,
presumably under the influence of Lycosthenes' newly published book.

4. Original text of 1568 edition   **Read as modern French:**

L'an ensuyvant descouvertz par deluge,
Deux chefs esleuz le premier ne tiendra
De fuyr umbre à l'un d'eux le refuge,
Saccagee case qui premier maintiendra.   *maison*

> **The following year, revealed by mighty deluge,**
> **Two heads elect, but the first shall not hold:**
> **Fleeing eclipse, one of them shall seek refuge,**
> **The house be sacked which shall the first uphold.**

Source: The Great Western Church Schism of 1378, when two popes – Urban VI
and Clement VII – were elected at the same time. At the conclave of 6 April 1378,
after a huge thunderstorm that left the Vatican awash and caused the vote to be
postponed by one day, the former was elected under pressure from the mob, who
invaded and sacked the Vatican. On 20 September, the non Italian cardinals who
had sought refuge at Anagni then declared the election null and void because it
had been carried out under duress, and elected the latter instead – who promptly
fled Rome first for Naples, then for Avignon, where the resulting huge papal palace
remains to this day.

5. Original text of 1568 edition   **Read as modern French:**

Tiers doit du pied au premier semblera.   *doigt*
A un nouveau monarque de bas hault   *de petite taille [lat. altum]*
Qui Pyse & Lucques Tyran occupera
Du precedant corriger le deffault.

> **As is the third toe to the first shall he**
> **Seem but a tiny king, a monarch who**
> **Pisa and Lucca shall attack, and see**
> **Corrected what the former failed to do.**

Source: Probably the Duke of Tuscany, a member of the Medici clan.[41] Compare
IX.80.

6. Original text of 1568 edition   Read as modern French:

Par la Guyenne infinité d'Anglois
Occuperont par nom d'Anglaquitaine
De Languedoc Ispalme Bourdeloys.   *Lapalme*[44]
Qu'ilz nommeront apres Barboxitaine.

> **Unnumbered English occupiers bestow**
> **Upon Guyenne the name 'Anglaquitania':**
> **From Languedoc to Lapalme near Bordeaux**
> **Thereafter called the Arab Occitania.**

Source: The *Mirabilis Liber*'s prophecies of a future Arab invasion of southern Europe, which Nostradamus sees as akin to the long English occupation of the west of France from which it had only recently freed itself in his own day. See I.9, I.75, II.24.

7. Original text of 1568 edition   Read as modern French:

Qui ouvrira le monument trouvé,
Et ne viendra le serrer promptement.
Mal lui viendra & ne pourra prouvé,   *prouver*
Si mieux doit estre roy Breton ou Normand.

> **Him who the new-found monument flings wide**
> **And shall not shut it up right instantly,**
> **Evil befalls, nor can he best decide**
> **A Breton or a Norman king to be.**

Source: Once again – on the basis of the last line, at least – possibly Froissart's account of the exploits in Western France of Edward the Black Prince. Compare VIII.56.

8. Original text of 1568 edition   Read as modern French:

Puisnay Roy fait son pere mettre à mort,
Apres conflit de mort tres inhoneste: *malhonnête*
Escrit trouvé soubson donra remort,   *soupçon*
Quand loup chassé pose sus la couchette.   *sera posé*

> **The younger, once made King, shall kill his sire**
> **After a deadly conflict full of shame.**
> **A letter found shall some remorse inspire**
> **When hunted wolf upon the couch is lain.**

Source: Unidentified, but probably a quite recent event, unless it is a distorted memory of the fraught relationship between King John of England and his father Henry II.

9. Original text of 1568 edition

Read as modern French:

Quand lampe ardente de feu inextinguible
Sera trouvé au temple des Vestales,
Enfant trouvé feu, eau passant par trible: *crible*
Perir eau Nymes, Tholose cheoir les halles.

> **When they shall find the lamp that's ever living,**
> **Still burning 'midst the Vestal temple's walls**
> **(The flame found by a child who's water sieving),**
> **Floods destroy Nîmes; down fall Toulouse's halls.**

Source: The vast floods that struck France and much of Western Europe in September 1557, which not only devastated Toulouse, but (as various documents of the time reveal[62]) uncovered all sorts of ancient remains and artifacts (including, allegedly, an 'ever-burning lamp') in and around the ruins of the ancient Temple of Diana[P] on the edge of the Sacred Lake at Nîmes, following a seven-hour cloudburst.[41, 60]

10. Original text of 1568 edition

Read as modern French:

Moyne moynesse d'enfant mort exposé,   *De moine et nonne l'enfant*
Mourir par ourse & ravy par verrier.   *verrat*
Par Fois & Pamyes le camp sera posé   *Pamiers*
Contre Tholose Carcas dresser forrier.   *Toulouse; Carcassonne*

> **The child of monk and nun exposed to die**
> **Is killed by she-bear, taken by a boar.**
> **Near Foix and Pamiers shall the army lie;**
> **Against Toulouse Carcassonne's scouts shall war.**

Source: Unknown incident involving a religious scandal, taken as a presage of military activities.

11. Original text of 1568 edition

Read as modern French:

Le juste à tort à mort lon viendra mettre   *l'on*
Publiquement, & due millieu estaint: *du*
Si grande peste en ce lieu viendra naistre,
Que les jugeans fouyr seront constraint.   *fuir*

> **The innocent unjustly shall be killed,**
> **And from the place removed, quite publicly:**
> **With such great plague the place shall soon be filled**
> **That all the judges shall be forced to flee.**

Source: Unidentified incident, serving as an omen for a local Plague outbreak that evidently had the same effect on the local judges as it routinely did on local doctors.

12. Original text of 1568 edition   **Read as modern French:**

Le tant d'argent de Diane & Mercure
Les simulachres au lac seront trouvez,   *Les images*
Le figulier cherchant argille neufve   *Le potier [lat. figulus]*
Luy & les siens d'or seront abbrevez.   *abreuvés*

> **So many silver icons shall be found**
> **Of Hermes and Diana in the lake**
> **By potter seeking new clay underground**
> **As him and his their thirst for gold to slake.**

Source: Once again the discovery (following the disastrous floods of 9 September 1557) of numerous pagan ritual objects from the now-ruined temple of Diana[P] that had originally been thrown into the Sacred Lake at Nîmes with the coming of Christianity.[62]

13. Original text of 1568 edition   **Read as modern French:**

Les exilez autour de la Soulongne
Conduis de nuit pour marcher à Lauxois,
Deux de Modene truculent de Bologne,
Mys descouvers par feu de Burançoys.   *Buzançais/Bisançois*

> **The exiles living round about Sologne**
> **Shall be on foot led to Auxois by night.**
> **Two from Modena by the fierce Bologna**
> **Shall by 'Greek fire' be found and brought to light.**

Source: Unknown incident.

14. Original text of 1568 edition   **Read as modern French:**

Mys en planure chaulderons d'infecteurs,
Vin, miel & huyle, & bastis sur forneaulx
Seront plongez sans mal dit mal facteurs   *malfaiteurs*
Sept. fum extaint au canon des borneaux.   *fumée; bourreaux*

> **Placed on the flat the dyers' cauldrons, topped**
> **With wine, oil, honey up, and set o'er fire,**
> **Therein the blameless so-called crooks are dropped:**
> **While seven 'midst murderers' cannon-smoke expire.**

Source: Unidentified atrocity.

15. Original text of 1568 edition

Read as modern French:

Pres de Parpan les rouges detenus,   *Perpignan*
Ceux du milieu parfondrez menez loing:
Trois mis en pieces & cinq mal soustenus,
Pour le Seigneur & Prelat de Bourgoing.   *Bourgogne*

Near Perpignan they'll cardinals detain,
Those cast forth from the center led away:
Three cut to shreds and five half-starved remain
Upon Bourgogne's Lord Bishop's mighty say.

Source: More unidentified atrocities, presumably in connection with France's current religious disputes, this time affecting renegade clerics within the Catholic Church itself.

16. Original text of 1568 edition

Read as modern French:

De castel Franco sortira l'assemblee,   *Castelfranco [Castelfranco Véneto, en Italie]*
L'ambassadeur non plaisant fera scisme: *schisme*
Ceux de Ribiere seront en la meslee,   *Ceux de la côte [lat. vulg. riparia]*
Et au grand goulphre desnier ont l'entree.   *dénieront*

From Castelfranco th' assembled force shall go;
Th' unpleasant envoy, though, shall break away.
Those from the coast into the fray shall go,
And to the mighty Gulf shall bar the way.

Source: An unidentified historical military attack from the direction of Castelfranco Véneto towards the Gulf of Venice, possibly assimilated to the *Mirabilis Liber*'s expected eventual expulsion of future Muslim occupiers from Europe, and specifically from Italy: 'The great Gallic lion shall go to meet the eagle, and shall strike it on the head; a terrible struggle shall ensue. And the country of Ravenna, which shall then be queen of Italy, shall receive the crown' (Prophecy of St Severus); 'A swordsman shall be crowned king of the triple crown . . . And he shall place beneath him the Saracen criminals, and before him the good and bad of all Italy shall tremble and forsake their evil ways' (Prophecy of Merlin).

17. Original text of 1568 edition

Read as modern French:

Le tiers premier pys que ne feit Neron,   *fit*
Vuidez vaillant que sang humain respandre: *Vu des vaillants*
R'edifier fera le forneron,   *Réédifier; fourneau*
Siecle d'or, mort, nouveau roy grand esclandre.

The third estate shall worse than Nero act:
As all the brave shall see, much blood they'll shed.

The furnace they shall once again construct:
A shameful king, the Age of Gold once dead.

Source: Unknown, but possibly a gloomy premonition of the downfall of the monarchy amid an age of rabid religious conflict and public burnings.

18. Original text of 1568 edition	**Read as modern French:**
Le lys Dauffois portera dans Nansy	*Dauphinois; Nancy*
Jusques en Flandres electeur de l'empire,	
Neufve obturee au grand Montmorency,	*Réclusion/emprisonnement [lat. obturatio]*
Hors lieux provez delivre a clere peyne.	*livré au bûcher flambant [lat. pyra]*

Dauphiné's Lily shall to Nancy send
Th' Elector of the Empire, Flanders-bound.
For Montmorency new imprisonment:
Far from known paths he'll soon his pyre have found.

Source: Current events: Constable Anne de Montmorency had been captured by the Spaniards at the disastrous Battle of St-Quentin in 1557, and would not be released from prison, far away in Spain, until after the Treaty of Cateau-Cambrésis had been signed on the then border with Flanders in 1559. In 1557–8 Nostradamus fears a more sinister fate for him, though.

19. Original text of 1568 edition	**Read as modern French:**
Dans le millieu de la forest Mayenne,	
Sol au lyon la fouldre tombera,	
Le grand bastard yssu du gran du Maine,	*fils*
Ce jour fougeres pointe en sang entrera.	

Deep in the leafy forest of Mayenne,
With sun in Leo, lightning bright descends.
The mighty bastard of the lord of Maine
That day a bloody point at Fougères rends.

Source: Unknown.

20. Original text of 1568 edition	**Read as modern French:**
De nuict viendra par la forest de Reines,	*Rennes [Rennes-en-Grenouille, près de Lassay]*
Deux pars vaultorte Herne la pierre blanche,	*Duc [lat. dux] [?]; par Vautorte; Ernée; la Pierre Blanche [Maine]*
Le moine noir en gris dedans Varennes	
Esleu cap. cause tempeste feu, sang tranche.	*tranche sanglante*

> Through Woods of Rennes by night shall make his way
> The Duke via Pierre Blanche, Ernée and Vautorte:
> Within Varennes the black monk turned to gray
> Made captain, brings a firestorm, blood and sword.

Source: Still in Maine, the contemporary Wars of Religion, and in particular the defrocking of a Benedictine monk named Antoine du Plessis in 1557, who then became a notoriously brutal soldier (thereafter known, inevitably, as *le moine*) on the Catholic side, subsequently appointed captain of a company of royal arquebusiers. Curiously, though, both this particular 'election' (at one of the various 'Varennes', presumably) and his subsequent bloody exploits around Tours under the Duke of Montpensier seem to have taken place in 1562, *after* the writing of the quatrain.[60] But then it is not impossible that the seer's secretary Chavigny tampered with the last two lines before they appeared in the 1568 edition so as to 'prove his Master right'.[38] Most of the place-names mentioned are listed on pages 137–40 of Charles Estienne's *Guide des Chemins de France* of 1552.

21. Original text of 1568 edition

Au temple hault de Bloys sacre Solonne,
Nuict pont de Loyre, prelat, roy pernicant
Curseur victoire aux maretz de la lone
Dou prelature de blancs à bormeant.

Read as modern French:

à [Saint] Solenne [maintenant St-Louis]

Courier [lat.] aux marais de l'Olonne
d'où; Protestants [?]; abhorrables [abhorreants]

> Near lofty church at Blois of Saint-Solenne
> At night, on Loire bridge, king shall bishop kill.
> From Sables d'Olonne comes news of victory then,
> Whence dreaded Protestants the see shall fill.

Source: Unidentified event from the contemporary Wars of Religion, leading to a temporary Protestant take-over of Blois.

22. Original text of 1568 edition

Roy & sa court au lieu de langue halbe,
Dedans le temple vis à vis du palais
Dans le jardin Duc de Mantor & d'Albe,
Albe & Mantor poignard langue & palais.

Read as modern French:

habile [hable]/de l'antique halle [?]

Mantoue
par Mantoue; à la langue et au palais

> The King and Court in the debating-place
> Inside the church just opposite the palace:
> In th' garden, Dukes of Mantua, Alba pace:
> Mantua stabs Alba in the tongue and palates.

Source: Unknown dispute between nobles in Italy.

23. Original text of 1568 edition

Puisnay jouant au fresch dessouz la tonne,
Le hault du toict du milieu sur la teste,
Le pere roy au temple saint Solonne,
Sacrifiant sacrera fum de feste.

Read as modern French:

au frais

Saint-Solenne

fumée

>The younger playing outside, the barrel then
>From th' roof shall fall square on his head, alas!
>For his sire the King at th' church of Saint-Sologne
>Shall sanctify the incense at the Mass.

Source: The accidental death of the Comte d'Enghien, when a coffer fell on him from the roof while playing outside in the snow with the Dauphin François and his young playmates in February 1546, and François I's consequent expiatory Easter pilgrimage to the abbey of Ferrières in Sologne, just south of Blois.[60]

24. Original text of 1568 edition

Sur le palais au rochier des fenestres
Seront ravis les deux petits royaux,
Passer aurelle Luthece Denis cloistres,
Nonain, mallods avaller verts noyaulx.

Read as modern French:

Orléans [lat. Aurelianum]; Paris
marrons [?]

>From out the windows of the rock-built palace
>The two small princes to be snatched are seen,
>Then via Orleans to St-Denis at Paris
>With nun, both munching chestnuts with husk green.

Source: Unknown.

25. Original text of 1568 edition

Passant les pontz venir pres des rosiers,
Tard arrivé plustost qu'il cuydera,
Viendront les noves espaignolz à Besiers,
Qui icelle chasse emprinse cassera.

Read as modern French:

pensera
nouveaux; Béziers
cette; entreprise

>Near the rose-bushes he'll the bridges force:
>Much sooner than he thought he shall arrive.
>To Béziers comes the latest Spanish force,
>Whose enterprise is broken by his drive.

Source: Unidentified skirmish between Spanish and French forces in the southwest.

26. Original text of 1568 edition

Nice sortie sur nom des letres aspres,
La grande cappe fera present non sien,
Proche de vultry aux murs de vertes capres
Apres plombin le vent à bon essien.

Read as modern French:

surnom
Le Pape; nonscient
Voltri
Piobino; escient

When he of harsh-writ name from Nice shall 'vance
The Pope unwittingly a present grants
Near Voltri with its walls of capers green.
After Piombino shall the wind blow keen.

Source: Possibly the Imperial expedition of 1527 to sack Rome, co-commanded by Georg von Frundsberg, the hero of the Battle of Pavia, on the barbaric appearance of whose name written in German Gothic script Nostradamus also seems to comment at X.65. On the other hand, there seem to be certain similarities of theme with the next verse . . .

27. Original text of 1568 edition

De bois la garde vent cloz rond pont sera,
Hault le receu frappera le Daulphin,
Le vieux teccon bois unis passera,
Passant plus oultre du duc le droit confin.

Read as modern French:

le fort

ravaleur [lat. tector]; dans les vaisseaux réunis
au-delà [lat. PLUS ULTRA, devise de Charles V]

In wooden fort with tunnel 'gainst the gale,
High Guest shall Dauphin ritually rebuke:
Then the old fudger, fleets combined, shall sail
Out of the jurisdiction of the Duke.

Source: The celebrated voyage of Pope Clement VII against high winds to Marseille in the autumn of 1533 to celebrate the wedding of the Dauphin Henri (later Henri II) to the then Catarina de' Medici, departing again via Nice, which was part of the Duchy of Savoy at the time. A special wooden palace was constructed for him on the square next to the royal palace, and connected to it by a covered bridge.[60] Compare II.14.

28. Original text of 1568 edition

Voille Symacle port Massiliolique,
Dans Venise port marcher aux Pannons:
Partir du goulfre & sinus Illirique,
Vast à Socile, Ligurs coups de canons.

Read as modern French:

alliée [gr. symmachos]; de Marseille [lat.]
[Dedans]; pour
et gouffre [lat.]
Dévastation; Sicile; parmi les Liguriens

The allied fleet ships shall put in at Marseille,
At Venice, too, to march on Hungary:
They'll leave the Gulf and the Dalmatian bay.
Havoc in Sicily: gunfire in Italy.

Source: The *Mirabilis Liber*'s gruesome forecast of a massive sea-borne invasion of Europe via Italy and the Mediterranean coast. See I.9, I.75, II.24

29. Original text of 1568 edition

Read as modern French:

Lors qu celuy qu'à nul ne donne lieu,
Abandonner vouldra lieu prins non prins: *pris, mais non pas pris*
Feu nef par saignes, bitument à Charlieu,   *marais; Charleroi [?]*
Seront Quintin Balez reprins.   *et Calais repris*

> **When he who to no other place shall yield**
> **Shall wish to cede a captured place not taken,**
> **Fireships in swamps, and pitch on Charleroi's field,**
> **And St-Quentin and Calais'll be retaken.**

Source: The recapture of Calais from the Empire in January 1558 by the brilliant François duc de Guise, and the truce of September 1557, which anticipated the crucial Treaty of Cateau-Cambrésis of 1559, whereby St-Quentin, just captured by the Spanish with huge French losses, was restored to France.

30. Original text of 1568 edition

Read as modern French:

Au port de POULA et de saint Nicolas,   *de Pula/de la Pouille*
Perir Normande au goulfre Phanaticque,   *Normands; au gouffre de Kvarner [Flanatique]*
Cap. de Bisance rues crier helas,   *rués [?]*
Secors de Gaddes & du grand Philipique.   *secours; Cadiz; et du seigneur Philippien*

> **At blessed Nicholas and Pula's port**
> **In Kvarner's Gulf shall Norman troops succumb.**
> **In old Byzantium's streets they'll mourn, once caught,**
> **Till from Cadiz with aid Spain's lord shall come.**

Source: The invasion mounted on behalf of the Normans of Apulia against the Byzantine Empire by Robert Guiscard in 1081–2, and the subsequent appeal for aid sent by the Byzantine Emperor Alexius I Comnenus to Venice, following which Guiscard and his forces were driven out and forced to return to Italy. The facts seem to have got somewhat distorted either by Nostradamus himself or by his historical sources, however. The future context seems once again to be the *Mirabilis Liber*'s prophecy of a future invasion of Europe. See I.9, I.75, II.24.

31. Original text of 1568 edition

Read as modern French:

Le tremblement de terre à Mortara,
Cassich saint George à demy perfondrez,   *Caltagirone [Sicile]; abattu [lat. profondere]*
Paix assoupie, la guerre esveillera,
Dans temple à Pasques absysmes enfondrez.

The earth shall quake around Mortara's town,
Saint George Caltagirone half knocked down.
Peace once asleep, war shall awake again:
At Easter schisms rend the Church in twain.

Source: The earthquakes of 1542 both in the north of Italy and in Sicily, where the campanile of the church of St George at Caltagirone, near Catania, consequently collapsed – taken as omens for future military earthquakes and the future collapse of the Church itself respectively, as per the *Mirabilis Liber*'s predictions listed at I.15 above.

32. Original text of 1568 edition

	Read as modern French:
De fin porphire profond collon trouvee	*colonne*
Dessoubz la laze escriptz capitolin:	*Sous le pied [gr. laz]*
Os poil retors Romain force prouvee,	*Aux poils retordus/Aux barbes retroussées*
Classe agiter au port de Methelin.	*flotte; Mytilène*

Of porphyry a shaft found buried deep:
Beneath its foot, Imperial documents.
Against the curved-beards Rome its strength shall heap:
At Mitilini's port the fleet ferments.

Source: The discovery of the obelisk of Augustus Caesar in 1502, during the closing years of the reign of Pope Alexander VI, who pursued vigorous hostilities against the Ottomans until he actually had to call on the help of the Sultan Beyezid II against his own European enemies.

33. Original text of 1568 edition

	Read as modern French:
Hercule Roy de Romme & d'Annemarc,	*Danemark*
De Gaule trois Guion surnommé,	*Chef/Leader*
Trembler l'Itale & l'unde de sainct Marc	*L'Italie*
Premier sur tous monarque renommé.	

From Rome to Denmark Hercules shall be
Surnamed the leader of tripartite Gaul.
Of Venice quakes th' lagoon, and Italy.
Renowned he'll be as High King over all.

Source: The *Mirabilis Liber*'s prediction of a future *Grand Monarque* (elsewhere referred to as *Ogmion*, the Gallic Hercules) who would free Europe from its occupiers and go on to rule over the whole continent. See I.4, I.55, I.92.

34. Original text of 1568 edition　　　Read as modern French:

Le part soluz mary sera mittré,　　　　*Le partage rompu, l'évêque sera marri*
Retour conflict passera sur le thuille:　*En riposte; sur le pays des toits en tuiles*
Par cinq cens un trahyr sera tiltré,
Narbon & Saulce par coutaux avons d'huille.　*Salces; compte aux denrés alimentaires [lat.*
　　　　　　　　　　　　　　　　　　　　　annona]

> **The canceled share the Mitered One dismaying,**
> **The counter-conflict sweeps the tiled roofs by.**
> **One shall be blamed five hundred for betraying**
> **At Salces, Narbonne in terms of oil supply.**

Source: D'Auton's account, in his *Chroniques de Louis XII*, of the revenge-campaign launched against Spain by Louis XII in 1503 in support of the furious Cardinal Georges d'Amboise – then French foreign minister – when the Spaniards reneged on their secret agreement to share out Italy with France. In the course of it, the then town of Salces, on the Spanish frontier near Narbonne, was besieged, but the campaign threatened to fall apart when provisions of oil and candles intended for the French were allowed to fall into Spanish hands – a piece of organizational incompetence, if not betrayal, for which Marshal Gié was investigated and Marshal de Rieux, the commander of a company of five hundred men, was dismissed.[60]

35. Original text of 1568 edition　　　Read as modern French:

Et Ferdinand blonde sera descorte,　　　*d'escorte*
Quitter la fleur suyvre le Macedon.　　　*Florence; [le royaume de Philippe]*
Au grand besoing defaillira sa routte,
Et marchera contre le Myrmidon.　　　　*son Serviteur Fidèle*

> **So Ferdinand – with fair-haired escort, he –**
> **Shall quit fair Florence, follow Philip's might.**
> **In hour of need his course t' have failed he'll see,**
> **And march against his former acolyte.**

Source: Another of Nostradamus's risky 'window-forecasts', predicting that the new Holy Roman Emperor Ferdinand I would first ally with his nephew Philip II of Spain (here referred to obliquely in terms of his ancient namesake, Philip II of Macedon, father of Alexander the Great), then turn against him. Needless to say, the latter didn't happen.

36. Original text of 1568 edition　　　Read as modern French:

Un grand Roy prins entre les mains d'un Joyne,　*Jeune*
Non loing de Pasque confusion coup cultre:　　*de couteau [lat. culter]*
Perpet. captifs temps que fouldre en la husne,　*hune*
Lors que trois freres se blesseront & murtre.

A mighty King is held by Young King fast:
Near Easter great confusion, cutting knives.
Captives for life when lightning strikes the mast
And brothers three wound, take each others' lives.

Source: Unidentified.

37. Original text of 1568 edition   Read as modern French:

Pont & molins en Decembre versez,   *moulins*
En si haut lieu montera la Garonne:
Murs, edifices, Tholose renversez,   *à Toulouse*
Qu'on ne sçaura son lieu autant matronne.   *de même la Marne [lat. Matrona]*

In cold December bridges, mills cast down –
To such a point the high Garonne shall swell.
Buildings and walls throughout Toulouse's town
Destroyed beyond recall: the Marne as well.

Source: The *Annales de Toulouse* for 1536, recording severe floods in December of that year, seemingly as per the huge floods forecast by the *Mirabilis Liber*. See I.69.

38. Original text of 1568 edition   Read as modern French:

L'entree de Blaye par Rochelle & l'Anglois,
Passera outre le grand Aemathien,
Non loing d'Agen attendra le Gaulois,
Secours Narbonne deceu par entretien.

English inroads via La Rochelle and Blaye
Past latter-day King Philip shall sail on.
The Gaul awaits, to Agen very nigh:
Deceived by talks, he'll go to help Narbonne.

Source: Unidentified contemporary military activities in the south-west of France.

39. Original text of 1568 edition   Read as modern French:

En Arbissel à Veront & Carcari,   *Albisola Marina; Vérone [?]; Carcare*
De nuict conduitz pour Savonne atrapper,
Le vifz Gascon Turbi, & la Scerry   *Les vifs; la Turbie [?]; L'Escarène [?]*
Derrier mur vieux & neuf palais gripper.

At Arbisola, Verona, Carcara then,
Once led by night to trap Savonans all,
Lithe Gascons at Turbie and l'Escarène
Shall palace new seize there behind old wall.

Source: Another unidentified contemporary military campaign, this time in the Duchy of Savoy and the republic of Genoa.

40. Original text of 1568 edition   Read as modern French:

Pres de Quintin dans la forest bourlis,
Dans l'abbaye seront Flamens ranches,   *tranchés*
Les deux puisnais de coups my estourdis
Suitte oppressee & garde tous aches.   *hachés*

> **Near St-Quentin, in Bourlon wood quite deep,**
> **In th' Abbey Flemings are cut down like sheep.**
> **Two younger brothers stunned by blows to heads,**
> **Their train hard-pressed, their guard all hacked to shreds.**

Source: A further unidentified military encounter (though with distinct First World War echoes!), this time involving the continuing wars between France and the Empire on the French north-eastern frontier, probably during 1557–8.

41. Original text of 1568 edition   Read as modern French:

Le grand Chyren soy saisir d'Avignon,   *Le grand Henri se saisira*
De Romme letres en miel plein d'amertume
Letre ambassade partir de Chanignon,   *Canino [Farnese?]*
Carpentras pris par duc noir rouge plume.

> **The mighty Henri Avignon shall seize.**
> **From Rome come letters sweet and sour together –**
> **An embassy sent to him from Farnese.**
> **Carpentras seized by black duke with red feather.**

Source: The temporary seizure of Avignon from the Papacy by Henri II's father, François I, in 1536, followed by the inevitable protests by the Pope, who was then Paul III – i.e. Alessandro Farnese, possibly the former employer at St-Rémy of Nostradamus's father Jaume – for whom Canino, some six miles from the town of Farnese, just north-west of Rome, is here used as a code-name.

42. Original text of 1568 edition   Read as modern French:

De Barsellonne, de Gennes & Venise,
De la Secille peste Monet unis,   *contre Monaco [d'habitude 'Monech']*
Contre Barbare classe prendront la vise,
Barbar, poulse bien loing jusqu'à Thunis.   *repoussé*

> **The plague from Barcelona, Genoa, Venice**
> **And Sicily on Monaco shall prey:**
> **Against the Muslim fleet they'll sail with menace**
> **And chase them back to Tunis far away.**

Source: The centuries of Muslim raids on the Mediterranean coast of Europe, followed by the triumphant expedition against the Ottoman pirate Barbarossa in Tunis led by the Emperor Charles V in June 1535 – all assimilated to the *Mirabilis Liber*'s prophecy of a huge Muslim invasion of Europe from the Mediterranean (see I.9, I.75) followed by an equally huge Christian counter-invasion of the Muslim heartlands (see I.55).

43. Original text of 1568 edition

	Read as modern French:
Proche à descendre l'armee Crucigere	*chrétienne*
Sera guettee par les Ismaëlites	*par les Arabes*
De tous cottez batus par nef Raviere,	*ravisseuse*
Prompt assaillis de dix galeres eslites.	*élues/choisies*

> **Ready to land, Crusader troops approach,**
> **Watched by the Arabs with suspicious eyes.**
> **On every side marauding ships encroach:**
> **By ten choice galleys taken by surprise.**

Source: As in the previous verse, Charles V's expedition to Tunis of June 1535, assimilated to the *Mirabilis Liber*'s prophecy of an eventual Christian invasion of the Arab lands (see I.55). The 'suspicious eyes', though, are my own invention, inserted to make both the line and the rhyme!

44. Original text of 1568 edition

	Read as modern French:
Migres, migre de Genesve trestous	*Migrez*
Saturne d'or en fer se changera,	
Le contre RAYPOZ exterminera tous,	*Zopyra [Charles V] [anagr.]*
Avant l'a ruent le ciel signes fera,	*Avant l'arrivée [l'advent]*

> **Flee! Flee Geneva, each and every one!**
> **Saturn's pure gold shall into iron change –**
> **The opposite! Charles shall wipe out each one.**
> **Before he comes shall signs the sky derange.**

Source: Another of Nostradamus's ill-conceived 'window-forecasts', wrongly anticipating an eventual attack by the Emperor Charles V on the Protestant enclave at Geneva, and incorporating the seer's fervent belief that nothing happens on earth that is not foreshadowed in the heavens, not least by the planet Saturn with its promise either of general bliss or of equally general disaster. On the more detailed level, too, there were all those worrying celestial omens that had just been described in their dozens by Conrad Lycosthenes in his huge *Prodigiorum ac ostentorum chronicon* of 1557,[44] some of them apparently portending specific actions by the Emperor. 'At Erfurt twin parheliacal suns were seen,' he had reported for the year 1520; 'A burning beam of fearful magnitude was observed in the sky . . .' Dr Stephen Batman's English translation of 1581 records the sequel: *The Souldiours of* *the Emperoure Charles the fifth tooke not onelye the Castell of Milan, but the Citie also, driving awaye the French.* The celestial phenomena were duly illustrated in Lycosthenes' book (seemingly more from report than from observation). *Zopyra* or *Zopyro* is meanwhile known to have been a pseudonym chosen by Charles V for one of his heraldic devices, after the name of an ancient Persian hero.[41]

45. Original text of 1568 edition	Read as modern French:
Ne sera soul jamais de demander,	
Grand Mendosus obtiendra son empire	*Le grand Fautif/Vendôme [Vendosme, anagr.?]*
Loing de la cour fera contremander,	
Pymond, Picard, Paris, Tyron le pire.	*Tyran*

> **His lust and greed shall ne'er be satisfied:**
> **The False One's sway shall spread unceasingly.**
> **Worst of all tyrants, far from the Court he'll ride,**
> **Subverting Piedmont, Paris, Picardy.**

Source: If not merely an incident from contemporary politics, the *Mirabilis Liber*'s prediction of a vast Muslim invasion of Europe (see I.9, I.75, II.24), headed by the Antichrist in person (see I.47, I.76, II.9). Compare IX.50 below.

46. Original text of 1568 edition	Read as modern French:
Vuydez, fuyez de Tholose les rouges	*Toulouse*
Du sacrifice faire expiation,	
Le chef du mal dessouz l'umbre des courges	*de l'imbécilité [prov. coucoureou?]*
Mort estrangler carne omination.	*étranglé; par divination des entrailles [lat.]*

> **Away! Flee now the Red Ones of Toulouse**
> **And make your sacrificial expiation!**

The evil lord, 'neath shadow of the gourds,
Lies strangled as foretells the divination.

Source: Possibly Nostradamus's own former brush with the Inquisition of Toulouse in the 1530s, together with some unknown dire prediction that he himself reckoned to have made at the time.

47. Original text of 1568 edition

Read as modern French:

Les soulz signes d'indigne delivrance,
Et de la multe auront contre advis,
Change monarque mis en perille pence,
Serrez en caige se verront vis à vis.

soussignés
multitude
Changé; pense

The signers of a pact that's a disgrace
Shall find the people minded otherwise:
The change of king's a risk, they'll them advise.
Locked up in cage, they shall each other face.

Source: The aftermath of an unidentified recent truce.

48. Original text of 1568 edition

Read as modern French:

La grand cité d'occean maritime,
Environee de maretz en cristal:
Dans le solstice hiemal & la prime,
Sera temptee de vent espouvantal.

marais; glace
hivernal; au printemps
affligée

The mighty city of the ocean sea
Shall girt about with icy marshes be:
At winter solstice and the spring withal
It shall be tried by gales phenomenal.

Source: Presumably recent bad winter weather at Bordeaux, though there are no known specific records of this for 1557–8 (presumably the most likely date).

49. Original text of 1568 edition

Read as modern French:

Gand & Bruceles marcheront contre Envers
Senat de Londres mettront à mort leur roy
Le sel & vin luy seront à l'envers,
Pour eux avoir le regne en desarroy.

Anvers

Brussels and Ghent shall march against Antwerp
And London's parliament its king shall slay.
Wine shall for him the role of wit usurp,
Thus placing all the realm in disarray.

Source: Froissart's account in his *Chroniques* of the official deposition of the frivolous King Edward II of England in 1326 at the behest of a specially summoned parliament of nobles, followed by his secret murder, the former at least having been originally connived at from Flanders by his runaway Queen Isabella. Compare X.40.

50. Original text of 1568 edition   **Read as modern French:**

Mandosus tost viendra à son hault regne	*Le Fautif/Vendôme [anagr.?]*
Mettant arriere un peu de Norlaris:	*de Lorraine [anagr.?]*
Le rouge blaisme, le masle à l'interregne,	*blâme*
Le jeune crainte & frayeur Barbaris.	*du Barbare*

> **The False One, at the zenith of his reign,**
> **Shall of Lorraine o'ertake a goodly part,**
> **The cardinal the male shall meanwhile blame**
> **So young, for fear of th' Arabs sick at heart.**

Source: Once again the *Mirabilis Liber's* forecast of an Arab invasion of Europe extending northwards as far as the Low Countries (see I.9, I.75, II.24), and led by the Antichrist in person (I.47, I.76, II.9). Compare IX.45 above.

51. Original text of 1568 edition   **Read as modern French:**

Contre les rouges sectes se banderont,	
Feu, eau, fer, corde par paix se minera,	*seront affaiblis*
Au point mourir ceux qui machineront,	
Fors un que monde sur tout ruynera.	

> **Against the cardinals the sects unite:**
> **Peace shall confound fire, sword, rope, waves to drown.**
> **At point of death those who shall plot to fight,**
> **Save one who most of all the world brings down.**

Source: The contemporary Wars of Religion, and the temporary success of the Catholic French Establishment in suppressing the Protestants who demonstrated in the rue St-Jacques in Paris in May 1557, except in the case of the movement's chief leader John Calvin, safely ensconced in Geneva, who was continuing to send both missionaries and literature to spread his 'seditious' message all across Catholic France.

52. Original text of 1568 edition   **Read as modern French:**

La paix s'approche d'un costé, & la guerre	
Oncques ne feut la poursuitte si grande,	*Jamais*
Plaindre homme, femme, sang innocent par terre	
Et ce sera de France à toute bande.	

Peace shall approach from one side, war the other.
Ne'er did such persecution e'er befall.
Innocent blood spilt: moan, each sister, brother!
For such in France shall be the case for all.

Source: Once again the French Wars of Religion, made ten times more potent by the sudden disbanding of tens of thousands of royal troops following the disastrous Battle of St-Quentin and the subsequent truce between France and the Empire that was to lead to the Treaty of Cateau-Cambrésis in 1559 – but no doubt, too, with a worried glance at the *Mirabilis Liber*'s prophecy of a huge and brutal Arab invasion. See I.9, I.75, II.24.

53. Original text of 1568 edition

Read as modern French:

Le Neron jeune dans les trois cheminees
Fera de paiges vifz pour ardoir getter   pour brûler; jeter
Heureux qui loing sera de telz menees,
Trois de son sang le feront mort guetter.

The youthful Nero in fireplaces three
Shall have young pages thrown to burn alive.
Blessed is he who far from such shall be:
Through kinsmen three he shall fear for his life.

Source: The legendary cruelties of the Emperor Nero – though it was in fact Nero who terrorized and killed three of his closest relations – Claudius, Britannicus, and his mother Agrippina - and not the other way around. Possibly the story represents a borrowing from the story of Nebuchadnezzar and the Fiery Furnace (Daniel chapter 3).

54. Original text of 1568 edition

Read as modern French:

Arrivera au port de Corsibonne,   Porto Corsini
Pres de Ravenne qui pillera la dame,
En mer profonde legat de la Vlisbonne   Lisbonne
Souz roc cachez raviront septante ames.

At Porto Corsini there shall arrive,
Ravenna by, one who the dame shall harry.
Far out at sea shall Lisbon's envoy tarry.
Hidden 'neath rock, they'll seventy snatch alive.

Source: Unidentified raid on the Papal States.

55. Original text of 1568 edition   Read as modern French:

L'horrible guerre qu'en l'occident s'apreste
L'an ensuivant viendra la pestilence,
Si fort horrible que jeune, vieulx, ne beste,   *ni [forme normale chez Nostradamus]*
Sang, feu, Mercure, Mars, Jupiter en France.   *s'enfuira [s'enfuir]; en Aries [? – signe dit de*
                                                       la France]

> After dread war that westward is prepared
> They'll pestilence the year thereafter see,
> So dread nor young, nor old, nor beast is spared.
> In Aries Mars, Jupiter, Mercury.

Source: The *Mirabilis Liber*'s familiar prediction of a vast Muslim invasion of Europe (see I.9, I.75, II.24) bringing – as such military campaigns virtually always did at the time – widespread disease in its wake (see I.9, IV.48). As it happens, the conditions (though not the astrology) would very nearly fit the circumstances of the massive influenza outbreak during the last year of the First World War – an epidemic that killed far more people worldwide than the war itself.

56. Original text of 1568 edition   Read as modern French:

Camp pres de Noudam passera Goussan ville   *L'armée; Goussonville*
Et a Maiotes laissera son enseigne,   *aux Scythes [gr. maiotai]*
Convertira en instant plus de mille,
Cherchant les deux remettre en chaine & legne.   *les ducs/chefs [lat.duces]; et bois*

> Past Goussonville shall Houdan's army pass,
> Leaving its standard to the Scythian host.
> A thousand plus at once convert, alas!
> Seeking their chiefs to chain to pillar and post.

Source: The *Mirabilis Liber*'s forecast of a massive Muslim invasion of Europe, and of France in particular, though with some additional unidentified historical input.

57. Original text of 1568 edition   Read as modern French:

Au lieu de DRUX un Roy reposera   *Dreux/Druse*
Et cherchera loy changeant d'Anatheme,
Pendant le ciel si tres fort tonnera,
Portee neufve Roy tuera soy mesme.

> At th' place of 'Dreux' a King shall rest awhile
> And seek to change the curse upon his head.
> When – mighty thunder roars in heaven the while –
> It's re-imposed, he'll kill himself instead.

Source: Unknown, unless a rather mangled version of the death of the Roman general and Praetor *Drusus*, father of the Emperor Claudius, who was (according to some classical writers, at least) poisoned on the orders of the Emperor Augustus in 9 BC at his camp known for ever thereafter as *Scelerata* – i.e. 'The Accursed Camp' (Suetonius, *The Twelve Caesars*, Claudius, 1).

58. Original text of 1568 edition

Read as modern French:

Au costé gauche a l'endroit de Vitry
Seront guettez les trois rouges de France,
Tous assoumez rouge, noir non murdry,   *meurtri*
Par les Bretons remis en asseurance.

> On the left bank at Vitry, duly armed,
> They'll wait for the French cardinals, all three:
> All shall be killed, the dark one left unharmed
> And by the Bretons led to safety, he.

Source: Apparently a further incident in the French Wars of Religion.

59. Original text of 1568 edition

Read as modern French:

A la Ferté prendra la Vidame   *la Ferté-Vidame; Chartres [?]*
Nicol tenu rouge qu'avoit produit la vie.
La grand Loyse naistra que fera clame.   *qui hurlera*
Donnant Bourgongne à Bretons par envie.

> Of la Ferté the Vidame's soon required
> By red-garbed Nicholas who life had sired –
> Big baby Louise, new-born, who loud shall scream –
> To Bretons ceding Burgundy on a whim.

Source: Probably the contemporary activities of Nicholas de Lorraine, whose daughter Louise, born in 1553, would eventually marry King Henri III. The verse suggests intimate knowledge of the family on Nostradamus's part.

60. Original text of 1568 edition

Read as modern French:

Conflict Barbar en la Cornere noire.   *cornette*
Sang espandu trembler la d'Almatie,   *Dalmatie*
Grand Ismaël mettra son promontoire   *Le grand Arabe s'avancera*
Ranes trembler secours Lusitanie.   *Poissons de mer [amiraux?]*

> Muslims at war, all clad in headdress black:
> Blood shall be shed, the great Dalmatia quake.
> The mighty Arabs press home their attack:
> Lisbon shall help, but all the admirals shake.

Source: The *Mirabilis Liber*'s prediction of a huge Muslim invasion of southern Europe from the Mediterranean. See I.9, I.75.

61. Original text of 1568 edition

La pille faite à la coste marine,
In cita nova & parentz amenez
Plusieurs de Malte par le fait de Messine,
Estroit serrez seront mal guerdonnez.

Read as modern French:

et villes pareilles
Beaucoup de gens

> **Pillaged shall be the shores along the sea.**
> **To Cita Nova and the like are sent**
> **Many Maltese by Messinan decree:**
> **Locked up they'll be – a poor acknowledgment.**

Source: Possibly the *Mirabilis Liber*'s prediction of an Arab invasion of Europe via the Mediterranean islands. See I.9, I.75.

62. Original text of 1568 edition

Au grand de Cheramon agora
Seront croisez par ranc tous attachez,
Le pertinax Oppi, & Mandragora,
Raugon d'Octobre le tiers seront laschez.

Read as modern French:

d'Usak [Asie Mineure]

opium
Par rançon

> **For Usak's lord Crusaders hand and foot**
> **Shall be staked out in rows or by degree.**
> **For opium long-lasting, mandrake-root,**
> **October's ransom shall a third set free.**

Source: An unidentified episode from the various accounts of the Crusades.

63. Original text of 1568 edition

Plainctes & pleurs crys & grands urlemens
Pres de Narbon à Bayonne & en Foix
O quel horrible calamitz changemens,
Avant que Mars revolue quelques foys.

Read as modern French:

hurlements

> **Wailing and tears and screams and cries galore**
> **Near to Narbonne, in Foix and at Bayonne:**
> **What dread calamities and change before**
> **Mars round his path shall many times have gone!**

Source: Presumably the current Wars of Religion, with the word 'change' referring, as it generally does in Nostradamus, to upheavals threatening the established religious and social order, usually on the part of the Protestants. However, a simultaneous reference to the *Mirabilis Liber*'s prediction of a huge Muslim invasion of Europe cannot be ruled out.

64. Original text of 1568 edition   Read as modern French:

L'Aemathion passer montz Pyrennees,   *Le 'nouveau Philippe II de Macédoine'*
En Mars Narbon ne fera resistance,
Par mer & terre fera si grand menee.
Cap. n'ayant terre seure pour demeurance.   *Capitaine*

> The latter Philip vaults the Pyrenees
> In March: resistance none Narbonne presents.
> Such schemes he'll hatch by land and on the seas,
> The chief has nowhere safe to pitch his tents.

Source: Current hostilities between France and Spain.

65. Original text of 1568 edition   Read as modern French:

Dedans le coing de luna viendra rendre,   *Au coin de lune*
Ou sera prins & mys en terre estrange,   *pris*
Les fruitz immeurs seront à grand esclandre
Grand vitupere à l'un grande louange.

> Within the patch of moonlight he'll submit,
> Where he'll be taken, sent to land abroad.
> The unripe fruit as scandal great shall sit:
> Great blame on one, great praise on th' other poured.

Source: Unknown, possibly connected with a case of attempted poisoning.

66. Original text of 1568 edition   Read as modern French:

Paix, union sera & changement,
Estatz, offices bas hault, & hault bien bas,
Dresser voiage le fruict premier torment,
Guerre cesser, civil proces debatz.

> Peace, unity there'll be, and many a change,
> High offices brought low and low raised high,
> The first fruit of the torment trips to arrange.
> War over, quarrels, civil suits they'll try.

Source: Another of Nostradamus's occasional 'window-forecasts', this time envisioning an eventual end to the contemporary Wars of Religion, then projecting it forward in connection with the situation in the wake of the expected future Arab invasion of Europe and the subsequent liberation.

67. Original text of 1568 edition   Read as modern French:

Du hault des montz à l'entour de Lizer   *l'Isère*
Port à la roche Valen, cent assemblez   *de Valence*
De chasteau neuf pierre late en donzere,   *Châteauneuf, Pierrelatte; et Donzère*
Contre le crest Romans foy assemblez.   *croissant [lat. crescentem]; Romains [?]; s' [soy?]*

Upon the mountains all about th' Isère
Mass five score at Valence's mighty rock
From Châteauneuf, Pierrelatte and Donzère:
Against the Muslim power shall Romans flock.

Source: Apparently the *Mirabilis Liber*'s prophecy of a Muslim invasion of Europe (see I.9, I.75, II.24), involving a wordplay in the last line on the two names of the local towns of Crest and Romans.

68. Original text of 1568 edition   Read as modern French:

Du mont Aymar sera noble obscurcie,   *Montélimar*
Le mal viendra au joinct de sonne & rosne   *Saône et Rhône*
Dans bois caichez soldatz jour de Lucie,
Qui ne fut onc un si horrible throsne.   *jamais*

Obscured Montélimar's most noble light:
Where Saône runs into Rhône shall evil strike.
On Lucy's day, troops hid in woods from sight
Horror commit. None ever saw the like.

Source: Unidentified incident on 13 December, probably taken from the contemporary Wars of Religion.

69. Original text of 1568 edition   Read as modern French:

Sur le mont de Bailly & la Bresle   *Bully et l'Arbresle*
Seront caichez de Grenoble les fiers,
Oultre Lyon, Vien. eulx si grande gresle,   *Au-delà de Lyon et Vienne; à eux*
Languoult en terre n'en restera un tiers.   *Des locustes [langoustes]*

On Bully's mount and up there at l'Arbresle
Grenoble's proud ones shall be hidden away.
Beyond Lyon, at Vienne, they'll see great hail:
Of locusts in the land no third shall stay.

Source: Unidentified events possibly associated with recent omens reported by Conrad Lycosthenes in his *Prodigiorum ac ostentorum chronicon* of 1557,[44] which mentions huge hailstones on at least six occasions (mainly in Switzerland, Germany, and northern Italy) and swarms of locusts on a further seven (largely in the same areas).

70. Original text of 1568 edition

Harnois trenchant dans les flambeaux cachez
Dedans Lyon le jour du Sacrement
Ceux de Vienne seront trestout hachez
Par les cantons Latins Mascon ne ment.

Read as modern French:

construction de murailles [maçonnement]

> **Sharp swords concealed within the torches see**
> **In Lyon on the day of Sacred grace.**
> **All those of Vienne shall cut apart soon be:**
> **In Latin cantons walls go up apace.**

Source: Another episode from the contemporary Wars of Religion, which, as Conrad Lycosthenes' *Prodigiorum ac ostentorum chronicon* of 1557[44] reports, affected his homeland of Switzerland just as seriously as France, where some 1,600,000 deaths would eventually result.

71. Original text of 1568 edition

Aux lieux sacrez animaux veu à trixe,
Avec celuy qui n'osera le jour:
A Carcassonne pour disgrace propice,
Sera posé pour plus ample sejour.

Read as modern French:

> **In sacred places hairy beasts they'll see**
> **With him who dares not show his face by day:**
> **At Carcassonne to shame him suitably**
> **He shall be placed to spend an ampler stay.**

Source: Unknown incident, possibly assimilated to the *Mirabilis Liber*'s Prophecy of St Vincent: 'When you shall hear the first Ox bellow within the Church of the Lord, then the Church shall start to go lame; but when three other signs shall be presented to you, and when you shall see the Eagle joined to the Snake, and when the second Ox bellows in the Church, it is the time of tribulations. For the Snake and the Ox shall summon up a king with a great name from the west who shall devastate the kingdom of the Assyrians, and after disposing of his conquered loot, he shall return barely safe and sound to his estates: then shall appear an adulterer who shall arrange for Snakes to be hidden in the shadows. Woe to the inhabitants of Sicily; for they shall see the dangers, without being able to ward them off. Finally, with Divine permission, the second Ox shall bellow; then there shall be more or less a schism in the Church: two Popes at the same time, of which the one, schismatic, shall triumph by banishing the true Pope to Venice after usurping his pulpit by violence.'

72. Original text of 1568 edition

Encor seront les saincts temples pollus,
Et expillez par Senat Tholassain,
Saturne deux trois cicles revollus,
Dans Avril, May, gens de nouveau levain.

Read as modern French:

pillés

> **Once more to holy churches comes pollution,**
> **Their ransack by Toulouse's senate passed.**
> **Two or three turns of Saturn's revolution**
> **In April, May'll bring folk of different cast.**

Source: The contemporary struggles between the Protestants of Toulouse, as represented by its Consuls, and the established Catholic religion. The last two lines, however, hint at something much more threatening – the eventual take-over by Muslims from North Africa long forecast by the *Mirabilis Liber* (see I.9, I.75), which Nostradamus evidently expects to happen only sixty or so years in the future. See next verse.

73. Original text of 1568 edition

Dans Fois entrez Roy ceiulee Turbao,
Et regnera moins revolu Saturne
Roy Turban blanc Bizance cœur ban
Sol Mars, Mercure pres la hurne.

Read as modern French:

Fez [?]; au turban cérulé [couleur du ciel]

à Bizance se courbant [?]
dans l'urne [Aquarius]

> **Blue-turbaned chief takes Foix and enters it.**
> **E'er Saturn's back he'll no more rule the land:**
> **White-turbaned shall in Istanbul submit.**
> **Sun, Mars and Mercury in Aquarius stand.**

Source: Following on from the previous verse, once again the *Mirabilis Liber*'s prediction of a mighty Muslim invasion and occupation of Europe, which Nostradamus evidently expects to last less than thirty years from the date of composition. In his 1566 *Almanach* Nostradamus makes it clear that the 'blue-turbans' and 'white turbans' are contemporary warring Muslim sects – namely the Shi'ites of Persia and the Sunni of Turkey. The astrology for what is evidently expected to be the eventual collapse of the Ottoman empire is for 1586.[8] Needless to say, it didn't happen. See II.2.

74. Original text of 1568 edition

Dans la cité de Fertsod homicide,
Fait & fait multe beuf arant ne macter,
Retour encores aux honneurs d'Artemide,
Et à Vulcan corps morts sepulturer.

Read as modern French:

de sol fertile [Toulouse, d'après Augier Ferrier]
labourant [lat. arare]; immoler [lat. mactare]

> **In city murderous of rich return**

Lest plowing ox repeatedly be offered,
To Artemis's honors they'll return
And bury corpses unto Vulcan proffered.

Source: Nostradamus's dire paganistic expectations for Protestant Toulouse, a former center of animal sacrifice – a tradition that still persists in the popular cult of the bull – for opposing which its local saint, St Sernin, was originally martyred. See IX.72 above.

75. Original text of 1568 edition   Read as modern French:

De l'Ambraxie & du pays de Thrace,
Peuple par mer mal & secours Gaulois,   *malle*
Perpetuelle en Provence la trace,
Avec vestiges de leur coustume & loix.

Far overseas in Arta and in Thrace
Shall France by sea take sacks and sacks of aid
To folk who in Provence have left their trace
And many laws and customs yet to fade.

Source: The *Mirabilis Liber*'s long-promised liberation – albeit a bloody one – of the European territories occupied by Muslim invaders in Nostradamus's own day, as also allegedly in the future. See I.55.

76. Original text of 1568 edition   Read as modern French:

Avec le noir Rapax & sanguinaire
Yssue du peaultre de l'inhumain Neron,
Emmy deux fleuves main gauche militaire,   *Entre*
Sera murtry par Joyne chaulveron.   *jeune chauve [ou Jean Calvin/ Chauvin]*

With the rapacious, bloody Black,
Born from the bed of Nero, scarce a man,
Between two rivers, on the host's left flank
He shall be murdered – killed by Jean Calvin.

Source: If this reading of the last phrase is correct, the burning alive in 1553 of the 'heretic' Michael Servetus at Geneva, after being tried and condemned by the Protestant leader John Calvin, who was popularly regarded by Catholics as the Antichrist in person. Geneva does indeed lie at the confluence of two rivers – the Arve and the Rhône – but it may be that this typical Nostradamian reference is really to Mesopotamia, the 'land between the rivers', and is thus the seer's way of equating Protestant Geneva with the 'brothel' of ancient Babylon, from which the future Antichrist is expected to emerge.

77. Original text of 1568 edition   Read as modern French:

Le regne prins le Roy conviera,   *pris*
La dame prinse [//] à mort jurez à sort,   *prise*
La vie à Royne fils on desniera,
Et la pellix au fort de la consort.   *maîtresse*

> The throne once ta'en, the King shall ask all by,
> His dame held fast, condemned to death by lot.
> Life to a son of th' Queen they shall deny,
> And lodge the mistress in the consort's fort.

Source: Apparently the marital antics of King Henri VIII of England, and in particular his marriages to Catherine of Aragon and Anne Boleyn, which failed to produce a male heir.[60]

78. Original text of 1568 edition   Read as modern French:

La dame Greque de beauté laydique,   *de Lais [la dame la plus belle de Corinthe antique]*
Heureuse faicte de procs innumerable,   *d'amoureux [lat. procus]*
Hors translatee au regne Hispanique,   *déplacée*
Captive prinse mourir mort miserable.   *prise*

> The lady Greek and fair beyond compare
> Shall happy be with suitors without end:
> Sent far away to breathe Hispanic air
> She'll captured be and have a wretched end.

Source: The story of Helen of Epirus, the daughter of Michael VIII Angelus, Emperor of Constantinople, who, besieged by numerous suitors, eventually married the son of the Emperor Frederick II von Hohenstaufen, only to be widowed, captured on her way back to Greece and imprisoned at Naples (then under Spanish control), where she died in 1272.[60]

79. Original text of 1568 edition   Read as modern French:

Le chef de classe par fraude stratageme,
Fera timides sortir de leurs galleres,
Sortis murtris chef renieur de cresme,   *du chrisme*
Puis par l'embusche luy rendront les saleres.   *salaires*

> The admiral by fraud and stratagem
> Shall coax the timid from their galleys forth:
> The Christ-denying chief shall batter them,
> Then they shall trap him, paying him his worth.

Source: Unknown.

80. Original text of 1568 edition   **Read as modern French:**

Le Duc voudra les siens exterminer,
Envoyera les plus forts lieux estranges,
Par tyrannie Pize & Luc ruiner,   Lucca
Puis les Barbares sans vin feront vendanges.

> **The Duke, resolved to wipe out all his kin,**
> **Shall make the strongest far abroad to fare,**
> **As tyrant doing Pisa, Lucca in.**
> **Grape-picking Muslims shall no wine prepare.**

Source: Unidentified incident from Italian politics, together with the opportunistic Arab pirate raids of the day, no doubt assimilated to the *Mirabilis Liber*'s prediction of a future Muslim invasion and occupation. See I.9, I.75.

81. Original text of 1568 edition   **Read as modern French:**

Le Roy rusé entendra ses embusches
De trois quartiers ennemis assaillir,
Un nombre estrange larmes de coqueluches   *d'armes [?]*
Viendra Lemprin du traducteur faillir.   *l'entreprise; de son agent*

> **The crafty King by ambushes intends**
> **His enemy on three sides to assail:**
> **A number strange of monkish arms forfends**
> **That what his agent does should ere prevail.**

Source: Unidentified, but apparently once again based on the contemporary Wars of Religion.

82. Original text of 1568 edition   **Read as modern French:**

Par le deluge & pestilence forte
La cité grande de long temps assiegee,
La sentinelle & garde de main morte,
Subite prinse, mais de nul oultragee.

> **With floods and ghastly pestilence about,**
> **The mighty city shall be long beset.**
> **The mortmain's watch and guards are taken out:**
> **Sudden its fall, but never looted yet.**

Source: The ceding of Boulogne to France by England against a payment of 800,000 golden crowns, or some two million pounds, in June 1546.[60]

83. Original text of 1568 edition   Read as modern French:

Sol vingt de taurus si fort terre trembler,
Le grand theatre rempli ruinera,
L'air, ciel & terre obscurcir & troubler,
Lors l'infidelle Dieu & sainctz voguera.   *invoquera*

> **When sun in Taurus twenty they'll remark,**
> **The crowded theatre shall an earthquake raze.**
> **Air, sky and sea it shall disturb, turn dark.**
> **Godless, they'll call on God and saints for days!**

Source: An almost gleeful re-evocation of the *Mirabilis Liber's* end-of-the-world prophecies. See I.46. I.87, II,13.

84. Original text of 1568 edition   Read as modern French:

Roy exposé parfaira l'hecatombe,
Apres avoir trouvé son origine,
Torrent ouvrir de marbre & plomb la tombe
D'un grand Romain d'enseigne Medusine.

> **The King shall hold great games of ritual slaughter**
> **Once he their source and origin unmasks.**
> **The lead-and-marble tomb's revealed by water**
> **Of a great Roman, with Medusan masks.**

Source: Persistent legends of the French royal family's classical ancestry, linked to recent classical archaeological discoveries resulting from huge local floods. Compare V.7, V.66, VIII.66, IX.9, IX.12, X.66.

85. Original text of 1568 edition   Read as modern French:

Passer Guienne, Languedoc & le Rosne,
D'Agen tenens de Marmande & la Roole   *la Réole*
D'ouvrir [par foy] par roy Phocen tiendra son   *paroi [expression répétée en deux formes]*
*   trosne*
Conflit aupres saint Pol de Manseole.   *St-Paul-de-Mausole*

> **They'll pass Guyenne, the Languedoc, the Rhône,**
> **Thanks to Agen, Marmande and la Réole.**
> **Through walls thrown down Marseille's lord takes his throne:**
> **Conflict there'll be near St-Paul-de-Mausole.**

Source: Either the Wars of Religion or the earlier campaigns in southern France of Charles V.

86. Original text of 1568 edition

Du bourg Lareyne parviendront droit à Chartres
Et feront pres du pont Authoni panse,
Sept pour la paix cautelleux comme martres
Feront entree d'armee à Paris clause.

Read as modern French:

Bourg-la-Reine
Antony; pause [voir rime]

close

> From Bourg-la-Reine to Chartres they'll duly come,
> Near Pont St-Antony to seek repose:
> Seven, for peace as polecats sly become,
> Shall bring the army into Paris closed.

Source: Contemporary military movements. The lists of place-names in this and the next verse seem to be lifted directly from page 92 of Charles Estienne's *Guide des Chemins de France* of 1552.

87. Original text of 1568 edition

Par la forest du Touphon essartee,
Par hermitage sera posé le temple,
Le duc d'Estampes par sa ruse inventee,
Du Mont Lehori prelat donra exemple.

Read as modern French:

Torfou; écartée [escartée]

Montlhéry; au prelat

> By wood of Torfou, from the way remote,
> The church they'll set, as hermitage designed:
> The duc D'Étampes shall through the ruse he wrought
> Bishop Montlhéry of his job remind.

Source: An unidentified lesson given by a lay noble to a lazy cleric who was possibly too interested in politics and good living. It seems to involve the erection of a dummy church. For the place-names, see previous verse.

88. Original text of 1568 edition

Calais, Arras secours à Theroanne,
Paix & semblant simulera lescoutte,
Soulde d'Alabrox descendre par Roanne
Destornay peuple qui deffera la routte.

Read as modern French:

l'écoute
Soldats [souldartz]
Détournés par

> Calais, Arras shall aid to Thérouanne send:
> Peace and the like the spy shall make pretend.
> Savoyard troops shall through Roanne descend,
> Diverted far by folk who'll roads unmend.

Source: More military activities, some of them set in the same area as the preceding verse, and apparently related to the Imperial siege of Thérouanne in 1553.

89. Original text of 1568 edition   Read as modern French:

Sept ans sera Philip. fortune prospere,
Rabaissera des Arabes l'effaict,   *l'effort [voir rime!]*
Puis son mydi perplex rebors affaire
Jeusne ognyon abysmera son fort.   *Hercule [Ogmion]*

> **Seven years shall Philip's fortunes prosper much:**
> **The Arabs' efforts he shall batter down.**
> **Then in the south shall things turn upside down:**
> **A youthful Hercules his power shall crush.**

Source: The 'fortunate years' of Philip II from 1554 (the year of his marriage to Queen Mary of England), taking in his more successful escapades as King of Spain against the North African pirates at Oran and Tripoli. However, this would suggest that the evident defeat in the last line, apparently at the hands of Henri II of France, is forecast for 1561. As it happened, Philip *would be* defeated, not by the French, but by the Ottoman fleet under Pyali Pasha at the battle of Djerba, and in 1560 rather than 1561, at that – by which time Henri would in any case be dead. Could this 'window-forecast', then, possibly be counted as at least a *half*-success on Nostradamus's part?

90. Original text of 1568 edition   Read as modern French:

Un capitaine de la grand Germanie
Se viendra rendre par simulé secours
Un Roy des roys ayde de Pannonie,
Que sa revolte fera de sang grand cours.

> **A captain of the greater Germany**
> **Shall make his way in guise of help pretended**
> **To help a King of kings of Hungary**
> **Whose great revolt much blood shall have expended.**

Source: Presumably the successful military campaigns of the Emperor Charles V, King of Germany, against the invading Ottomans in Hungary in the early 1530s.

91. Original text of 1568 edition   Read as modern French:

L'horrible peste Perynte & Nicopolle,   *Eski Eregli; Preveza*
Le Chersonnez tiendra & Marceloyne,   *Le Péloponnèse; Macédoine*
La Thessalie vastera l'Amphipolle,
Mal incogneu & le refus d'Anthoine.   *le refus de [contact social par Saint] Antoine*

> **Dread Plague Perinthus and Nicopolis**
> **Shall sweep, all Macedonia and western Greece,**
> **Thessaly ravage, and Amfipolis –**
> **A woe unknown. All social life shall cease.**

Source: Possibly the inevitable medical aftermath of the massive Muslim invasion threatened by the *Mirabilis Liber*. See I.9, IV.48.

---

92. Original text of 1568 edition

Le Roy vouldra dans cité neufve entrer
Par ennemys expunger lon viendra
Captif libere faulx dire & perpetrer,
Roy dehors estre, loin d'ennemys tiendra.

Read as modern French:

Naples/Villeneuve/Villanova/Cita Nova
l'on

> Into that 'City New' the King would go,
> And so to drive the foe out they're agreed
> To do and say false things to a captive freed.
> The King shall stay outside, fight off the foe.

Source: More unidentified military activities, possibly around Naples.

---

93. Original text of 1568 edition

Les ennemis du fort bien eslongnez,
Par chariots conduict le bastion,
Par sur les murs de Bourges esgrongnez,
Quand Hercules battra l'Haemathion.

Read as modern French:

Le nouveau 'Philippe II de Macédoine'

> Far from the fort the foes are driven back,
> A wall of stones, on wagons borne, they'll seat
> Atop Bourges' walls that shall already crack
> When Hercules shall 'Macedon' defeat.

Source: A further episode – whether historical or merely anticipated – in the wars between France and Spain, headed respectively by Henri II and Philip II (namesake of the father of Alexander the Great of Macedon).

---

94. Original text of 1568 edition

Faibles galleres seront unies ensemble,
Ennemis faux le plus fort en rampart:
Faible assaillies Vratislave tremble,
Lubecq & Mysne tiendront barbare part.

Read as modern French:

Bratislave
Meissen

> The weakest groups alliances shall make,
> Of treacherous foes the strongest soon allied.
> Attacked and weakened, Bratislavans quake:
> Lübeck and Meissen take the Muslims' side.

Source: The contemporary wars between the Holy Roman Empire and the Ottomans in central and eastern Europe, assimilated to the *Mirabilis Liber*'s forecast of a massive future Muslim invasion of the continent. See I.9, I.75, II.24.

95. Original text of 1568 edition

Le nouveau faict conduyra l'exercite,
Proche apamé jusques au pres du rivage,
Tendant secour de Milannoile eslite,
Duc yeux privé à Milan fer de cage.

Read as modern French:

l'armée
Presqu'isolée [gr. apamao]
Milanaise [Milannoise]; choisi

> **The new-appointed then shall lead the host,**
> **Almost cut off, towards the nearest shore,**
> **Helped by Milan's elite along the coast.**
> **Blinded the chief; Milan shall cage him sure.**

Source: Unidentified military activities in northern Italy.

96. Original text of 1568 edition

Dans cité entrer exercit desniee,
Duc entrera par persuasion,
Aux foibles portes clam armee amenee,
Mettront feu, mort [//] de sang effusion.

Read as modern French:

l'armée

fermées

> **To th' army access to the town denied,**
> **The Duke shall enter by cajolery.**
> **Brought up the weakened gates, still closed, outside,**
> **They'll sow fire, death – and bloodshed great there'll be.**

Source: A further unidentified military episode of the day.

97. Original text of 1568 edition

De mer copies en trois parts divisees,
A la seconde de vivres failleront,
Desesperez cherchant champs Helisees,
Premiers en breche entrez victoire auront.

Read as modern French:

les forces

Elysées

> **The force from th' sea in three parts they shall split,**
> **The second lack wherewith themselves to feed**
> **Seeking th' Elysian Fields, and desperate.**
> **The first the breach to enter shall succeed.**

Source: The Empire's invasion and widespread devastation of Provence in 1524 under Charles de Bourbon. The 'Elysian Fields' reference suggests an attack on Arles in particular, with its *Alyscamps*. See IV.20.

98. Original text of 1568 edition

Read as modern French:

Les affligez par faute d'un seul taint,
Contremenant à partie opposite,
Aux Lygonnois mandera que contraint
Seront de rendre le grand chef de Molite.

teints [accord habituel par proximité]

Lyonnais
de Malte [Melite]

> **By fault of one th' afflicted hurt shall be,**
> **Turning them over to the other side:**
> **He'll tell the folk of Lyon that they'll be**
> **Forced to surrender Malta's chief denied.**

Source: Unidentified incident from contemporary politics.

99. Original text of 1568 edition

Read as modern French:

Vent Aquilon fera partir le siege,
Par murs geter cendres, chauls, & pousiere,
Par pluye apres qui leur fera bien piege,
Dernier secours encontre leur frontiere.

du nord
chaux
pire [prov. piegi]

> **The north wind them the siege shall force to quit:**
> **They'll throw lime, dust and ashes o'er the walls.**
> **Through rain thereafter (e'en worse comes of it)**
> **Their last help lies towards where the frontier falls.**

Source: Unidentified unsuccessful siege.

100. Original text of 1568 edition

Read as modern French:

Navalle pugne nuit sera superee,
Le feu aux naves à l'Occident ruine:
Rubriche neufve la grand nef coloree,
Ire a vaincu, & victoire en bruine.

bataille; vaincu[e]
aux bateaux
D'argile rouge

> **Night shall o'ertake the battle on the sea:**
> **Fire shall destruction bring to th' Western fleets.**
> **Red new-bedecked shall then the flagship be.**
> **Wrath to the fall'n: mist the victory greets.**

Source: Possibly the Battle of Actium of 31 BC – which, as reported by Suetonius, went on so late that Octavian, the victor (later the Emperor Augustus), had to spend the night aboard his flagship – adapted to the *Mirabilis Liber*'s prophecy of a Muslim invasion of Europe via the Mediterranean. See I.9, I.75.

Century X

1. Original text of 1568 edition   **Read as modern French:**

A L'ennemy l'ennemy foy promise
Ne se tiendra, les captifs retenus:
Prins preme mort & le reste en chemise,   *Pris; près de*
Damné le reste pour estre soustenus.

> From foe to foe the promise that ensued
> Shall not be met, the captives be retained:
> One captive near to death, the rest half nude,
> Yet others damned for being by serfs maintained.

Source: Unidentified. The last line suggests some kind of peasant revolt.

2. Original text of 1568 edition   **Read as modern French:**

Voille gallere voil de nef cachera,
La grande classe viendra sortir la moindre   *flotte*
Dix naves proches le torneront poulser,   *repousser*
Grande vaincue unies à soy joindre.   *avec elles-mêmes*

> The galley's sails shall veil the ship from sight:
> The greater fleet as lesser shall emerge.
> Ten nearby ships shall put them straight to flight,
> The allied fleets with beaten great one merge.

Source: Unidentified naval battle.

3. Original text of 1568 edition   **Read as modern French:**

En apres cinq troupeau ne mettra hors un   *Ci-après/Après cinq ans [?]; hors [fin du vers]*
Fuytif pour Penelon l'ashera,   *Un fugitif; pour peines l'on; lâchera*
Faulx murmurer secours venir par lors,
Le chef le siege lors habandonnera.

> After five years his flock he'll not lead out:
> A fugitive for all his pains he'll free.

> **Of help false rumors shall spread thereabout:**
> **Then shall the mighty chief forsake the see.**

Source: Either an unidentified prolonged siege, presumably from recent history, or more likely (in the light of the words *troupeau* and *siege* together), the Pope's eventual flight from Rome as predicted by the *Mirabilis Liber*.

4. Original text of 1568 edition

Read as modern French:

Sus la minuict conducteur de l'armee
Se saulvera, subit esvanouy,
Sept ans apres la fame non blasmee,
A son retour ne dira oncqu ouy.   *n'en avoir jamais entendu [ouï] parler*

> **Upon the midnight shall the leader act**
> **To quit the host, vanishing suddenly:**
> **Seven years thereafter, fame still quite intact**
> **Once back, of it all knowledge he'll deny.**

Source: Unidentified military incident.

5. Original text of 1568 edition

Read as modern French:

Albi & Castres feront nouvelle ligue,
Neuf Arriens Lisbon & Portugues,
Carcas, Tholosse consumeront leur brigue   *Carcassonne, Toulouse*
Quand chief neuf [ ] monstre de Lauragues.   *[vu?]*

> **Albi and Castres conclude a new-born league**
> **With a new Arrianus Portuguese.**
> **Toulouse and Carcassonne scotch their intrigue**
> **When th' new chief monster sees from th' Pyrenees.**

Source: Further unidentified troubles in the contemporary south-west of France. The original Arrianus was the second-century soldier-statesman who first wrote the history of Alexander the Great's campaigns.

6. Original text of 1568 edition

Read as modern French:

Sardon Nemans si hault desborderont,   *Gardon/Gard; Nîmes [lat. Nemausus]*
Qu'on cuidera Deucalion renaistre,
Dans le collosse la plus part fuyront,   *le Colisée [les Arènes]*
Vesta sepulchre feu estaint apparoistre.

> **At Nîmes shall Gardon's waters flood so high**
> **That they shall think Deucalion's returning.**
> **Into the Coliseum most shall fly,**
> **In vestal tomb flame once extinguished burning.**

Source: Once again the vast floods that struck France and much of Western Europe in September 1557 which (as various documents of the time reveal[62]) uncovered all sorts of ancient remains and artifacts (including, allegedly, an 'ever-burning lamp') in and around the ruins of the ancient Temple of Diana (or Vesta)[P] whose ruins still stand on the edge of the Sacred Lake at Nîmes, following a seven-hour cloudburst. The Roman amphitheater ('Coliseum'), nowadays known as the Arènes,[P] was traditionally used as a place of refuge by the citizens. See also V.66, IX.9, IX.12. The river Gard, or Gardon, does not in fact enter the city at all, though it is certainly prone to severe flooding (as, for example, in 2002).

7. Original text of 1568 edition

Le grand conflit qu'on appreste à Nancy.
L'aemathien dira tout je soubmetz,
L'Isle Britanne par vin, sel en solcy,
Hem. mi deux Phi. long temps ne tiendra Metz.

Read as modern French:

Le 'nouveau Philippe II de Macédoine'
pour vin, sel en souci
en mi-défi

> **When mighty war at Nancy is prepared,**
> **'New Philip' says, 'I am the conqueror, I.'**
> **For wine and salt shall Britain's isle be scared:**
> **Metz shall not long continue to defy.**

Source: The disastrous Imperial invasion of north-eastern France in August 1557, which nevertheless failed to overrun Metz as anticipated by the verse.

8. Original text of 1568 edition

Index & poulse parfondera le front
De Senegalia le Conte a son filz propre
La Myrnarmee par plusieurs de prinfront

Trois dans sept jours blesses mors [...].

Read as modern French:

l'armée des Myrmidons; tout de suite [de prin front]

[rime manque]

> **With thumb and finger shall the Count of th' day**
> **Of Senigallia wet his own son's brow:**
> **Many shall of his followers straight away**
> **To death wound three in seven days, I trow.**

Source: Events surrounding the current della Rovere rulers of Senigallia, in Italy.

9. Original text of 1568 edition

De Castillon figuieres jour de brune,

De feme infame naistra souverain prince
Surnom de chausses perhume luy posthume,
Onc Roy ne feut si pire en sa province.

Read as modern French:

Castillan voiturier [? – voir commentaire]; brume

parterre [lat. per humum]
Jamais

> Of Spanish carter, on a misty morn,
> A shameful slut shall bear a sovereign prince.
> 'Pantsdown' they'll call him, after he is gone:
> Ne'er worse king ever ruled there 'fore or since.

Source: Prévost associates the verse with the cruel and debauched Duke Alessandro de' Medici of Florence, who was said at the time to be worse even than Nero or Caligula, and who was murdered by his own cousin in 1537.[60] Quite how this ties in with *figuieres* is not explained, but rumor had it that he was the son of a carter's wife or a female African slave . . .

10. Original text of 1568 edition   Read as modern French:

Tasche de murdre enormes adulteres,
Grand ennemy de tout le genre humain
Que sera pires qu'ayeulx, oncles, ne peres
En fer, feu, eau, sanguin & inhumain.

> With murder stained and with corruption vast,
> He'll be the foe of all the human race.
> Far worse than any like him in the past,
> By sword, fire, flood, inhuman, bloody, base.

Source: The *Mirabilis Liber*'s prophecies of the Antichrist. See I.47, I.76, II.9.

11. Original text of 1568 edition   Read as modern French:

Dessoubz Jonchere du dangereux passage   Junquera
Fera passer le posthume sa bande,
Les monts Pyrens passer hors son bagaige
De Parpignam courira duc à tende.   attendre [?]

> On past Junquera, through its perilous gate,
> Son posthumous shall with his army press,
> Then o'er the Pyrenees, quite baggageless.
> From Perpignan Duke hastes him to await.

Source: An unidentified Spanish incursion into south-western France.

12. Original text of 1568 edition   Read as modern French:

Esleu en Pape, d'esleu sera mocqué,   élu
Subit soudain esmeu prompt & timide,
Par trop bon doulx à mourir provocqué,
Crainte estainte la nuit de sa mort guide.

> Elected Pope, as Pope-elect soon mocked,
> At once distressed, suddenly full of fear.

Too good, too gentle, unto death provoked –
Yet fearless, he, when death by night draws near.

Source: Unidentified papal election and death.

13. Original text of 1568 edition

Soulz la pasture d'animaux ruminant
Par eux conduicts au ventre herbipolique
Soldatz caichez les armes bruit menant,
Non loing temptez de cite Antipolique.

Read as modern French:

Sous

d'Antibes

Beneath the fodder for the chewing cattle,
And thereby brought up to the grass-girt town,
Soldiers all hidden bring the sound of battle
And almost bring that place near Antibes down.

Source: An ancient account of an attack by the ancient Segobrigenses of classical times on the inhabitants of Marseille at the annual feast of Flora, using troops hidden under leaves piled in wagons.[60]

14. Original text of 1568 edition

Urnel Vaucile sans conseil de soy mesmes
Hardit timide par crainte prins vaincu,
Accompaigné de plusieurs putains blesmes
A Barcelonne aux chartreux convaincu.

Read as modern French:

Humilié, vacillant [Humil. vacil.]

à emprisonnement

Made small, uncertain, not knowing what's th' best for,
First brave, then scared, by fear o'ercome, constricted,
Accompanied by many a painted whore,
To jail at Barcelona he's convicted.

Source: The story of Cesare Borgia following the poisoning of his father, Pope Alexander VI. At his wits' end to know whether he also had been poisoned, he seems to have gone to pieces, finishing up in a Spanish prison before escaping again, only to be assassinated at Viana in 1507.[60]

15. Original text of 1568 edition

Pere duc vieux d'ans & de soif chargé,
Au jour extreme filz desniant les guiere
Dedans le puis vif mort viendra plongé,
Senat au fil la mort longue & legiere.

Read as modern French:

l'aiguière
puits; plonger
le vieux [lat. senex]

To th' Duke his father, aged and thirsty sore,
On day of death his son denies a ewer:

Down in the pit to living death he'll lower
His sire by rope to long, slow death most sure.

Source: A somewhat garbled version of the famous story of the scandalous mal-treatment by the Duke of Guelders of his own father in the 1470s, as reported by Commynes in Book IV of his *Mémoires*: 'There was a young Duke of Guelders called Adolf. He had performed a truly horrible deed, for he had taken his father [Duke Arnold] prisoner . . . He then let him down into the bottom of a tower where there was no light other than from a tiny skylight, and there he kept him for five years . . . Finally the Pope and the Emperor exerted heavy pressure on him and the Duke of Burgundy was ordered on pain of severe penalty to extricate Duke Arnold from prison . . . [Duke Adolf] answered that he would rather have thrown his father in head-first into a pit and then to have thrown himself in after him than to have reached this accommodation, and that, with his father having been Duke for 44 years, it was high time that *he* was.'

16. Original text of 1568 edition   Read as modern French:

Heureux au regne de France, heureux de vie
Ignorant sang mort fureur & rapine,
Par non flateurs sera mys en envie,
Roy desrobé trop de foy en cuisine.

Happy in France's realm, happy to live
Knowing nought of blood, death, rape or mad desire!
Those who'll not flatter him he'll scarce forgive.
Rescued the king: in th' kitchen too much fire!

Source: The pontificate of the French Pope Benedict XII at Avignon – despite much criticism of him by Petrarch and others, but at least well away from the bloody intrigues of Rome – and the visit there of King Pedro IV of Aragon in 1340, during which the new papal palace had to be evacuated when fire broke out.[60]

17. Original text of 1568 edition   Read as modern French:

La royne Ergaste voiant sa fille blesme,   reine ; 'ayant des projets' [lat. ergastica]; boiter
Par un regret dans l'estomach encloz,
Crys lamentables seront lors d'Angolesme,
Et au germain mariage fort clos.

The scheming queen who sees her daughter lame
And in her bosom secret sorrow knows,
Shall hear loud cries from out of Angoulême
But on the German marriage sure foreclose.

Source: The marriage-plans that Anne de Bretagne, Queen of France, had for her daughter Claude (curiously, Latin for 'lame'). Having had her proposal to marry her off to the future Emperor Charles V thwarted by the French Estates General, she betrothed her instead to the future French King François I, while herself hoping to give birth to a son to preclude him from ever taking the throne, and thus to safeguard her own hereditary interests. Each time she became pregnant, consequently, there were loud lamentations from François's mother, Louise de Savoie. However, nothing came of it, and François duly ascended the throne on Louis XII's death in 1515.[60]

18. Original text of 1568 edition — Read as modern French:

Le ranc Lorrain fera place à Vendosme,
Le hault mys bas & le bas mys en hault,
Le filz d'Hamon sera esleu dans Rome   *de Jupiter*
Et les deux grands seront mys en deffault.

> **Lorraine's great clan shall give way to Vendôme,**
> **The low raised up on high, the high brought low.**
> **Jupiter's son shall chosen be in Rome,**
> **And the two lords shall both frustration know.**

Source: Nostradamus's dark conviction, in the light of the current religious troubles, that 'the times, they are a' changing', and that everything that he and his fellow Catholics held most dear was about to be turned upside-down – in particular by a revival of classical paganism and by the Protestants of the house of Navarre, whose prince, the young Henri duc de Vendôme (the future Henri IV), he would allegedly pick out specifically for future glory during the royal visit to Salon of 1564.

19. Original text of 1568 edition — Read as modern French:

Jour que sera par royne saluee,   *reine*
Le jour apres le salut, la priere,
Le compte fait raison & valbuee,   *valuée*
Par avant humble oncques ne feut si fiere.   *jamais*

> **One day she shall be greeted by the Queen,**
> **The next, thereafter, unto prayer devoted.**
> **After the matter duly weighed has been,**
> **Once humble, with rare pride she shall be bloated.**

Source: Unidentified incident involving a female member of the royal court.

20. Original text of 1568 edition   Read as modern French:

Tous les amys qu'auront tenu party,
Pour rude en lettres mys mort & saccagé,
Biens publiez par fixe grand neanty,   *Biens publics parfaits [parfaictz], grands, anéantis*
Onc Romain peuple ne feut tant outragé.   *jamais*

All of the friends who are partisanized
By him of crude-writ name are killed and sacked,
Great, perfect public works to pieces hacked:
Never were Roman folk so scandalized.

Source: Events surrounding the sacking of Rome in 1527 by Imperial troops under Georg von Frundsberg in 1527, to whose 'harsh-writ name' in German Gothic script Nostradamus also seems to refer at IX.26 and X.65

21. Original text of 1568 edition   Read as modern French:

Par le despit du Roy soustenant moindre,
Sera meurdry luy presentant les bagues,
Le pere au filz voulant noblesse poindre
Fait comme à Perse jadis feirent les Magues.   *firent*

Through the King's spite, he who the lesser fuels,
Shall then be put to death who gives him jewels.
Sire wishing son his nobleness to show
Shall act like Persian Magi long ago.

Source: Unidentified case of a father showering his son with precious gifts.

22. Original text of 1568 edition   Read as modern French:

Pour ne vouloir consentir au divorce,
Qui puis apres sera cogneu indigne,   *reconnu comme*
Le roy des Isles sera chassé par force
Mis à son lieu que de roy n'aura signe.

For being so loth to let the divorce be,
Which afterwards unworthy might be deemed
The Islands' king shall be constrained to flee,
Replaced by one who never kingly seemed.

Source: Unidentified, despite its surface similarities with the much later case of King Edward VIII and the divorcee Mrs Wallis Simpson which led to the former's dramatic abdication in 1936.

23. Original text of 1568 edition   Read as modern French:

Au peuple ingrat faictes les remonstrances,
Par lors l'armee se saisira d'Antibe,
Dans l'arc Monech feront les doleances,   *Dans la citadelle de Monaco*
Et à Frejus l'un l'autre prendra ribe.   *la rive*

The ungrateful people shall be argued with:
The troops shall seize Antibes subsequently.

In Monaco's citadel they'll complain forthwith
And Fréjus' shore by each side taken be.

Source: Contemporary hostilities between French and Imperial forces in the southeast.

24. Original text of 1568 edition   Read as modern French:

Le captif prince aux Italles vaincu
Passera Gennes par mer jusqu'à Marseille,
Par grand effort des forens survaincu   *des étrangers [lat. foranus]*
Sauf coup de feu barril liqueur d'abeille.

> The captive prince, in Italy o'ercome
> By sea via Genoa to Marseille shall come:
> Through mighty foreign force he'll lose his quarrel,
> But for explosion in a honey-barrel.

Source: Unidentified, if curious, incident in the same general area as the previous verse.

25. Original text of 1568 edition   Read as modern French:

Par Nebro ouvrir de Brisanne passage,   *l'Èbre; Bretagne [?]*
Bien eslongnez el tago fara muestra,   *du Tage; un phare se monterera [esp. faro*
                                              muestra]
Dans Pelligouxe sera commis l'outrage   *Périgueux*
De la grand dame assise sur l'orchestra.   *sur/devant la scène [de l'amphithéâtre antique]*

> From th' Ebro they'll take ship for Brittany,
> Far from where Tagus' light shines out to sea.
> In Périgueux shall take place the outrage
> Against the lady seated on the stage.

Source: Unidentified double incident.

26. Original text of 1568 edition   Read as modern French:

Le successeur vengera son beau frere,
Occuper regne souz umbre de vengeance,
Occis ostacle son sang mort vitupere,   *Tué l'otage [ostaige]*
Long temps Bretaigne tiendra avec la France.

> The heir'll avenge his lady's brother's name:
> In vengeance' name to power he shall advance.
> Him, hostage killed, his kin for th' death shall blame.
> Brittany long shall loyal stay to France.

Source: Unidentified, but possibly the accession of Louis XII in 1498, following his predecessor Charles VIII's acquisition of Brittany for France.

27. Original text of 1568 edition	**Read as modern French:**
Par le cinquieme & un grand Hercules	
Viendront le temple ouvrir de main bellique,	
Un Clement, Jule & Ascans recules,	*reculés*
Lespe, clef, aigle, n'eurent onc si grand picque.	*L'épée; jamais*

> **For him that's fifth, a mighty Hercules,**
> **The church by warlike act they'll open wide:**
> **Never such strife twixt eagle, sword and keys:**
> **Julius Ascanius (Clement) steps aside.**

Source: Once again the shock invasion and sacking of Rome by Charles duc de Bourbon and Georg von Frundsberg in 1527 on behalf of the Holy Roman Emperor Charles V. As a result, with the imperial eagle and the keys of St Peter holding a sword to other's throats, the current Pope, Clement VII (whose name was indeed Julius, after Julius Ascanius, the son of Virgil's Aeneas, alleged forerunner of the Roman Julii) did 'step aside': he was held under virtual house-arrest for several months in the Castel del' Angelo to which he had fled. Compare IX.26, X.20 and X.65, and specifically II.93.

28. Original text of 1568 edition	**Read as modern French:**
Second & tiers qui font prime musicque	
Sera par Roy en honneur sublimee,	*Seront [liaison 'par proximité' avec 'musicque']*
Par grasse & maigre presque demy eticque	
Raport de Venus faulx randra deprimee.	*rendra*

> **Second and third who music best shall make**
> **Shall by the King be raised to honor high:**
> **Through thick and thin – thin, almost, as a rake –**
> **False talk of love shall make him moan and sigh.**

Source: Story of an unidentified lovelorn king.

29. Original text of 1568 edition	**Read as modern French:**
De Pol MANSOL dans caverne caprine	*des chèvres [lat. caverna caprina]*
Caché & prins extrait hors par la barbe,	
Captif mené comme beste mastine	*comme un chien*
Par Begourdans amenee pres de Tarbe.	*Par ceux de Bigorre*

> **At Saint-Paul-de-Mausole, in th' goat-cave found**
> **He'll hide, be captured, by his beard hauled out:**

> They'll lead him captive like some lowly hound
> To Tarbes, shall those from far Bigorre, no doubt.

Source: In the view of Prévost,[60] the story of Eustache Marron, a sixteenth-century Waldensian leader who was captured by troops from Béarn on their way back from Piedmont. On this basis, he would have taken refuge in one of the galleries (since used to shelter goats) of the ancient Roman stone-quarry at Glanum, just south of St-Rémy,[P] before being led off to Avignon, where he was executed. Alternatively, this verse may represent a piece of purely local knowledge that has found no place in the history books.

30. Original text of 1568 edition   Read as modern French:

Nepveu & sang du sainct nouveau venu,
Par le surnom soustient arcs & couvert
Seront chassez mis a mort chassez nu,
En rouge & noir convertiront leur vert.

> Of new-come holy man the kith and kin
> Shall use his name to maintain homes of taste.
> Expelled they'll be, put to death, naked chased:
> To red and black they'll change their green young skin.

Source: The contemporary story of the notoriously nepotistic Pope Paul IV (reigned 1555–9), who was famous for showering his own nephews with ill-gotten riches filched from the Colonnas, a prominent Roman family who opposed his policies.

31. Original text of 1568 edition   Read as modern French:

Le saint empire viendra en Germanie,
Ismaelites trouveront lieux ouverts.
Anes vouldront aussi la Carmanie,
Les soustenens de terre tous couverts.

> Germany th' Holy Empire is assigned:
> The Arabs shall the lands all open find.
> Those asses also far Carmania crave,
> But their supporters go unto their grave.

Source: The *Mirabilis Liber*'s prophecy of a vast Arab invasion of Europe, following the election as Holy Roman Emperor in 1520 of Charles V, King of Germany, rather than France's François I.

32. Original text of 1568 edition   **Read as modern French:**

Le grand empire chacun an devoir estre   *en*
Un sur les autres le viendra obtenir,
Mais peu de temps sera son regne & estre,
Deux ans aux naves se pourra soustenir.

> The mighty empire each shall sure retain:
> One above all shall take it as he may.
> But not for long shall last his power and sway:
> Two years by ship he shall himself sustain.

Source: The *Mirabilis Liber*'s prophecy of various kings to come, culminating in the Antichrist himself, as spelt out by the Tiburtine Sibyl: 'Then shall come a king called B., under whose reign there shall be many wars. He shall reign for two years, and after him shall come a prince A., who shall remain a long time on the throne. He shall march against Rome and shall seize it. The Lord shall not deliver it into the hands of his enemies during his lifetime. He shall be good and great, and shall render justice to the poor. He shall be from the race of the Lombards. After him there shall be another prince, named B., from whom twelve other B.s shall spring. Himself a Lombard, he shall reign a hundred years. Then shall appear, after him, a Salic [i.e. Frankish] prince, named L., a frightful prince, under whom shall begin a series of sufferings whose like has never been since the beginning of the world: battles, tribulations, bloodshed, earthquakes, cities in captivity. The Lord in his wrath shall send a man whose yoke nobody shall be able to shake off, other than the Lord himself. The Romans shall be beaten, and the Roman city shall be destroyed. The earth shall be covered in ruins: never shall monarch have done such a thing. This city [i.e. Rome] shall be called Babylon; this kingdom shall be of iron, and Rome shall be prey to persecution and the sword. Men shall be greedy, despots, hard on paupers, oppressors, unjust, wicked. Resistance shall be impossible at the time, but the Persians, Macedonians, and Turks, hearing of this tyrant, shall form an alliance, shall come to Rome, and shall seize the Salic prince, whom they shall cause to undergo a cruel death, and the burning of Rome shall be avenged.'

33. Original text of 1568 edition   **Read as modern French:**

La faction cruelle à robbe longue,
Viendra cacher souz les pointus poignars
Saisir Florence le duc & lieu diphlongue   *diphtongue [Fiesole?]*
Sa descouverte par immeurs & flangnards.   *par immûrs et flatteurs*

> The cruel faction in their robes full long
> Shall hide beneath them daggers sharp as razors.
> The Duke takes Florence and the place 'diphthong',
> Which youthful flatterers, finding out, amazes.

Source: Unidentified.

34. Original text of 1568 edition　　**Read as modern French:**

Gauloys qu'empire par guerre occupera
Par son beau frere mineur sera trahy,
Par cheval rude voltigeant trayneta,　　*traînera*
Du fait le frere long temps sera hay.

　　The Frenchman who the Empire shall invade
　　Is by his younger brother-in-law betrayed.
　　His prancing horse, untrained, shall drag that lord,
　　For which the brother shall be long abhorred.

Source: Unidentified incident.

35. Original text of 1568 edition　　**Read as modern French:**

Pusnay royal flagrand d'ardant libide,　　*désir*
Pour se jouyr de cousine germaine,
Habit de femme au temple d'Arthemide:　　*au mausolée/au temple de Diane [?]*
Allant [,] murdry par incognue du Marne.　　*assassiné/blessé; Maine [voir rime]*

　　The younger prince, burning with flagrant lust
　　T' enjoy the favors of his cousin first,
　　As woman dressed, and to Diana's fane
　　Going, is hurt by unknown wench from Maine.

Source: Unidentified but nevertheless curious incident.

36. Original text of 1568 edition　　**Read as modern French:**

Apres le Roy du soucq guerres parlant,　　*sud [?]*
L'isle Harmotique le tiendra à mepris,　　*Hermétique [?]*
Quelques ans bons rongeant un & pillant
Par tyrranie à l'isle changeant pris.　　*d'avis [?]*

　　When th' King of Arab souks shall speak of war
　　Shall Hermes' island simply him despise.
　　A good few years of raids and plunder o'er,
　　Shall tyranny the island's view revise.

Source: The *Mirabilis Liber*'s prophecy of an invasion of Europe via the Mediterranean islands (see I.9, I.75, II.24), though the exact identity of the island in question is undetermined.

37. Original text of 1568 edition   Read as modern French:

Lassemblee grande pres du lac de Borget,   *L'assemblée*
Se ralieront pres de Montmelian,
Marchans plus oultre pensifz feront proget
Chambry, Moriane combat sainct Julian.   *À Chambéry, St-Jean-de-Maurienne*

> **The mighty force quite near to Bourget's lake**
> **Shall gather hard against Montmélian,**
> **Marching *plus ultra*, thinking war to make**
> **On Chambéry, Maurienne, St-Julien.**

Source: Unidentified military operations in Savoy, almost certainly (in view of the inclusion of the Emperor Charles V's Latin motto 'Further beyond' in line 3) on the part of the Holy Roman Empire.

38. Original text of 1568 edition   Read as modern French:

Amour alegre non loing pose le siege,   *D'Amoura en Algers; posé*
Au sainct barbar seront les garnisons,
Ursins Hadrie pour Gaulois feront plaige,
Pour peur rendus de l'armee aux Grisons.

> **Quite near Amoura they'll the siege engage:**
> **The garrison for the Arab Prophet is.**
> **Orsinis, Venice for the French shall pledge,**
> **For fear by troops surrendered to the Swiss.**

Source: Unidentified recent events involving war with Algerian Muslims.

39. Original text of 1568 edition   Read as modern French:

Premier fils vefve malheureux mariage,   *veuf*
Sans nuls enfans deux Isles en discord,
Avant dixhuict incompetant eage,
De l'autre pres plus bas sera l'accord.

> **The first son, widower after marriage glum,**
> **Shall, childless, see two Isles in discord dread.**
> **Ere he's eighteen, not yet of age become,**
> **The next e'en younger they'll engage to wed.**

Source: Reported prophecies by contemporary astrologers[8] concerning the prospects of the young François II, who was 14 years old at the time of writing (1557–8) and would follow his late father Henri II to the grave only two years later. The last line could then be taken to refer to the even younger brother who would succeed him as the ten-year-old Charles IX, and who would indeed be promised to Elizabeth of Austria the same year. If so, however, this raises some doubt as to whether the verse – mirrored, if the sources are to be believed, by a prediction in the seer's *Almanach* for 1560 that seems to have caused something of a furor at the time[8] – might not have been 'edited' by Nostradamus's faithful secretary Chavigny before the publication of the 1568 edition (which is the earliest edition in which it has come down to us) so as to make it seem even more 'successful' than it already was, given that we have actual evidence of such editing on his part in respect of the *Presages* published in the 1605 edition.[8, 38]

40. Original text of 1568 edition   **Read as modern French:**

Le jeune nay au regne Britannique,   *né*
Qu'aura le pere mourant recommandé,
Iceluy mort LONOLE donra topique,   *La mort de celui-ci à Londres*
Et à son fils le regne demandé.

> **The youthful prince in Britain's kingdom born**
> **Whose dying father shall to them commend –**
> **His death shall then much talk in London spawn:**
> **Back from his son the kingdom they'll demand.**

Source: Froissart's account, in his *Chroniques*, of the death of the mighty Edward I and the controversial reign of his unpopular and effeminate son Edward II: 'On his deathbed Edward publicly summoned his eldest son who was about to become King, and made him swear by all the Saints that as soon as he had died he would have his corpse boiled in a cauldron until the flesh fell off the bones, and have the flesh buried and the bones preserved, and that whenever the Scots rebelled he would summon his army and bear his father's bones with him . . . However, King Edward II failed to fulfill his oath, and instead had his father's corpse borne back to London, where it was buried. For this he would suffer great harm' [Luce I:26] . . . 'And when all the deeds done or authorized by the King [Edward II] and the full details of his private life had been read out, the leading members of the assembly took counsel together, and concluded from their own experience that most of it was true, and that such a man was unworthy to bear the crown or be called King. Instead, they agreed that his eldest son and true heir should be crowned in the place of his father . . . and that his father should be well guarded and kept prisoner . . . for the remainder of his life' [Luce I:14]. Compare IX.49.

41. Original text of 1568 edition   **Read as modern French:**

En la frontiere de Caussade & Charlus,   *Caylus*
Non guieres loing du fonds de la vallee,
De ville Franche musicque à son de luths,   *Villfranche-de-Rouergue*
Environnez combouls & grand myttee.   *cymbales; mitré [évêque]*

> **Caussade's and Caylus' borders, there around,**
> **From th' bottom of the valley distant bare,**

> From Villefranche music, and of lutes the sound,
> Cymbals about, and mighty bishop there.

Source: Probably personal memories of a religious ceremony in the region of Nostradamus's former stamping ground of Agen.

42. Original text of 1568 edition   Read as modern French:

Le regne humain d'Anglique geniture,
Fera son regne paix union tenir,
Captive guerre demy de sa closture,
Long temps la paix leur fera maintenir.

> The cultured realm of English ancestry
> Shall keep its realm in peace and unity.
> War half shut up and almost captive ta'en,
> She'll long make them that peace and quiet maintain.

Source: A rather daring projection into the future of the current reign of Queen Mary of England, allied by marriage with Philip II of Spain and devoted (much to Nostradamus's approval) to the restoration of Catholicism, the 'old religion'. Unfortunately, he was not to know that Mary would die within a year of his writing the verse, and that the Protestant Elizabeth would therefore succeed.

43. Original text of 1568 edition   Read as modern French:

Le trop bon temps trop de bonté royalle:
Fais & deffais prompt subit negligence,
Legier croira faux d'espouse loyalle,
Luy mis à mort par sa benevolence.

> Too good a time, too much largesse full royal
> Granted, ungranted, sudden negligence:
> False rumors he'll believe of wife full loyal,
> And then be killed for his benevolence.

Source: Astonishingly, not so far identified. Consequently, more likely a favored aristocrat than the actual King himself.

44. Original text of 1568 edition   Read as modern French:

Par lors qu'un Roy sera contre les siens,
Natif de Bloys subjuguera Ligures:
Mammel, Cordube & les Dalmatiens,   Mahomet [Mahmet?]
Des sept puis l'ombre à Roy estrennes & lemures.   pris

> Whenas a King against his own shall stir,
> A Blésois'll soon th' Ligurians shall have broken,

Muslims, Dalmatians, too, and Cordoba.
Seven captured – one th' King's image, ghostly token.

Source: Unidentified.

45. Original text of 1568 edition

Read as modern French:

Lombre du regne de Navarre non vray,   *L'ombre*
Fera la vie de sort illegitime: *fort [?]*
La veu promis incertain de Cambray,   *Le voeu*
Roy Orleans donra mur legitime.

**Of th' Kingdom of Navarre the untrue shade
Shall bring to life a destiny unlawful:
The promise made at Cambrai doubtful made,
Orléans' King defense erects quite lawful.**

Source: In the case of the last two lines, the collapse of the Treaty of Cambrai of 1529, broken by the French in 1556 with catastrophic results for themselves the following year. In the case of the first two lines, presumably some event in the career of Antoine, the current King of Navarre, rather than of his son Henri (the future Henri IV of France), who was only five at the time of writing.

46. Original text of 1568 edition

Read as modern French:

Vie sort mort de L'OR vilaine indigne,   *l'ordure [L'ORDE]*
Sera de Saxe non nouveau electeur: *de Saxonie*
De Brunsuic mandra d'amour [le] signe,
Faux le rendant au peuple seducteur.

**In life, death, fate, the turd – unworthy, base –
Of Saxony's th' Elector yet again:**
From Brunswick he demands of love some trace
To make him falsely popular to men.

Source: Probably the Elector Maurice who, although a Lutheran (to Nostradamus's anagrammatically disguised disgust), did not openly support Luther against the Emperor until 1552, and thus retained his position as a significant German power-broker longer than he might otherwise have done.

47. Original text of 1568 edition

Read as modern French:

De Bourze ville à la dame Guyrlande,   *Bourgos*
L'on mettra sus par la trahison faicte,
Le grand prelat de Leon par Formande,   *[l'île de] Formentera*
Faux pellerins & ravisseurs defaicte.

> At Burgos, at Our Lady of the Flowers,
> They'll come down heavy on the treason done:
> Leon's great bishop in the Baléares
> By thieves and pilgrims false shall be undone.

Source: Unidentified religiously related events in Spain.

48. Original text of 1568 edition   Read as modern French:

Du plus profond de l'Espaigne enseigne,
Sortant du bout & des fins de l'Europe,
Troubles passant aupres du pont de Laigne,   *du détroit maritime [lat. pontus, lagena]*
Sera deffaicte par bandes sa grand troppe.   *troupe*

> Marching from deepest Spain their banners see!
> From Europe's furthest borders they shall come.
> Troubles they'll have passing the narrow sea:
> Large troops of men their army shall o'ercome.

Source: The *Mirabilis Liber's* familiar prediction of a huge Islamic invasion of Europe via both the Hellespont and the Strait of Gibraltar. See I.9, I.75, II.24. The expression at the end of line 3 evidently refers via the Latin to 'the bottle-necked sea'.

49. Original text of 1568 edition   Read as modern French:

Jardin du monde au pres de cité neufve,   *d'Eden [héb. = plaisance]; Villeneuve*
Dans le chemin des montaignes cavees,
Sera saisi & plongé dans la Cuve,   *Il sera*
Beuvant par force eaux soulfre envenimees.   *Buvant; envenimées avec du soufre*

> Seized at 'World's Garden', quite near 'City New',
> Upon the road to th' mountains dug out hollow,
> Plunged in the cask, he shall be made to swallow
> Waters with sulfur poisoned through and through.

Source: Unknown, but evidently based on the Inquisition's known methods of assassinating suspected heretics at the time, as confirmed in Nostradamus's own correspondence for the early 1560s, and applied to an unidentified victim at the village of Plaisance just north of Villeneuve-sur-Lot, on the road to the Dordogne with its famous caves – and especially, perhaps, the village of Aubeterre-sur-Dronne, with its celebrated rock-hewn church and tombs.

50. Original text of 1568 edition   Read as modern French:

La Meuse au jour terre de Luxembourg,   *autour de*
Descouvrira Saturne & trois en lurne,   *en Aquarius [l'urne]*
Montaigne & pleine, ville, cité & bourg,
Lorrain deluge trahison par grand hurne.   *par un noble; cette année [lat. horno]*

> **Saturn plus three within Aquarius,**
> **The Meuse shall Luxembourg around assail,**
> **Flooding Lorraine, cities and strongholds various,**
> **Mountains and plains: this year the lord's betrayal!**

Source: The great Lorraine floods of February 1523, the year when the Lord Constable of France, Charles de Bourbon, defected to the Empire in a fit of pique over his wife's inheritance, prior to invading Provence on Charles V's behalf the following year.[60]

51. Original text of 1568 edition   Read as modern French:

Des lieux plus bas du pays de Lorraine,
Seront des basses Allemaignes unis,
Par ceux du siege Picards, Normans, du Maisne,
Et aux cantons ce seront reunis.

> **Some lower parts of th' country of Lorraine**
> **Shall be made one with Lower Germany,**
> **While Picards, Normans, Swiss and those of Maine,**
> **All sore besieged, united too shall be.**

Source: Unidentified line-up of contemporary opposing forces.

52. Original text of 1568 edition   Read as modern French:

Au lieu où LAYE & Scelde se marient,   *Leie et Schelde*
Seront les nopces de long temps maniees,
Au lieu d'Anvers où la crappe charient,
Jeune vieillesse consorte intaminee.

> **There where the Leie and Schelde both do marry**
> **The marriage rites shall long arrangèd be,**
> **Instead of Antwerp where the chaff they carry.**
> **Too old too young, wife undefiled shall be.**

Source: Unidentified (though no doubt either noble or royal) fruitless marriage at Ghent.

53. Original text of 1568 edition

Les trois pellices de loing s'entrebatron,
La plus grand moindre demeurera à l'escoute:
Le grand Selin n'en sera plus patron,
Le nommera feu pelte blanche routte.

Read as modern French:

maîtresses

lunaire
peau [pelle]; rompue [lat. rupta]

> **Mistresses three shall from afar dispute,**
> **From least to greatest stay on watch, alert.**
> **No longer Lunar One shall rule her suit:**
> **She'll call him 'former white-skin torn apart'.**

Source: Evidently the celebrated extramarital affairs of King Henri II.

54. Original text of 1568 edition

Nee en ce monde par concubine fertive,
A deux hault mise par les tristes nouvelles,
Entre ennemis sera prinse captive,
Et amené à Malings & Bruxelles.

Read as modern French:

Par duc [lat. a duce]
prise
amenée

> **Born in this world a secret concubine's,**
> **By Duke raised high on hearing news so grim,**
> **By foes she shall be captured, far from him,**
> **And led away to Brussels and Malines.**

Source: Unknown.

55. Original text of 1568 edition

Les malheureuses nopces celebreront,
En grande joye, mais la fin malheureuse:
Mary & mere nore desdaigneront,
Le Phybe mort, & nore plus piteuse.

Read as modern French:

la belle-fille

> **They'll celebrate the ill-starred wedding-morn**
> **With joy untold, but a sad end shall see.**
> **Husband and mother daughter-in-law shall scorn:**
> **Her Phoebus' dead, more piteous still she'll be.**

Source: On the face of it, a genuine prophetic insight. The details fit almost exactly the marriage of the 14–year-old François II and the plight of his almost equally young queen, Mary Queen of Scots, who on his premature death in 1560 was promptly sent back to Scotland. The marriage of April 1558 Nostradamus would have known about prior to first publication of the verse in around July (his dedication to King Henri II was dated 27 June), but the subsequent death of the bridegroom and the shameful subsequent treatment of Mary – seemingly actually named via wordplay in line 3 – suggests a piece of judicious 'editing' by Chavigny for the 1568 edition (the earliest one we have), ten years after the original verse was written and eight years after the event. Were that the case, however, one would have expected him to mention the verse triumphantly in his own *La premiere Face du Janus François* of 1594 – which he does not. Given that his main aim in the book was to prove how right his late Master had always been, this seems distinctly odd. It is worth noting, though, that Nostradamus himself uses neither the name *Phybe* (as such) nor the word *nore* anywhere else in the *Propheties*. Compare the equally suspicious X.39 above.

56. Original text of 1568 edition

Read as modern French:

Prelat royal son baissant trop tiré,
Grand fleux de sang sortira par sa bouche,
Le regne Anglicque par regne respiré,   *réaspiré; par reine [?]*
Long temps mort vif en Tunys comme souche.

> **The royal prelate too deep his bow performing,**
> **Shall a great gush of blood surge from his throat.**
> **The English realm revived by Queen reforming,**
> **Long time, log-like, 'twixt death and life he'll float.**

Source: An unidentified mishap to an unknown bishop, with a line thrown in about the reign of Queen Mary of England and her (to Nostradamus) welcome efforts to revive Roman Catholicism in England.

57. Original text of 1568 edition

Read as modern French:

Le sublevé ne cognoistra son sceptre,   *soulevé*
Les enfans jeunes des plus grands honnira:
Oncques ne fut en plus ord cruel estre,   *Jamais; plus sale*
Pour leurs espouses à mort noir bannira.

> **The parvenu his scepter shall disgrace:**
> **He'll shame the children of the noblest men.**
> **Never was man more cruel, filthy, base:**
> **Their wives unto the Black Death he'll condemn.**

Source: Conceivably the *Mirabilis Liber*'s prophecies of the coming Antichrist. See I.47, I.76, II.9.

58. Original text of 1568 edition

Read as modern French:

Au temps du deuil que le felin monarque,   *lunaire [selin]*
Guerroyera le jeune Aemathien: *le 'nouveau Philippe II de Macédoine'*
Gaule bransler perecliter la barque,   *l'église*
Tenter Phossens au Ponant entretien.   *Marseille; à l'ouest*

> The lunar chief at time of mourning dark
> Shall war declare upon young Philip Two,
> Who'll shake his rod, make totter Peter's barque,
> Harass Marseille, with the West deal anew.

Source: The current rivalry between King Henri II of France, whose device included a crescent moon, and Philip II of Spain, whose Spanish troops, following the French military disaster of St-Quentin in 1557, were currently menacing Rome itself. The resumption of military activities against the Empire in the north had indeed happened, thanks to the efforts of the brilliant François duc de Guise, fresh from campaigning on the Italian front, who had then returned quickly to Marseille to deal with matters there.[60]

59. Original text of 1568 edition

Read as modern French:

Dedans Lyon vingt cinq d'une alaine,   *haleine*
Cinq citoyens Germains, Bressans, Latins,
Par dessous noble conduiront longue traine,
Et descouvers par abbois de mastins.

> In Lyon two dozen of a single mind,
> Five Germans, Latins, Bresseans among them,
> Long files shall lead the noble's back behind.
> But barking of the dogs shall soon have sprung them.

Source: Unidentified – and unsuccessful – covert operation.

60. Original text of 1568 edition

Read as modern French:

Je pleure Nisse, Mannego, Pize, Gennes,   *Monaco*
Savone, Sienne, Capue, Modene, Malte:
Le dessus sang & glaive par estrennnes,
Feu, trembler terre, eau, malheureuse nolte.   *non pas voulue [lat. nolita]*

> Weep, Nice, Savona, Monaco, Siena,
> And Malta, Pisa, Genoa, Capua, Modena,
> Upon you sword and blood as gifts shall fall,
> Fire, earthquake, flood, not wanted there at all.

Source: Once again the *Mirabilis Liber*'s forecast of a massive Arab invasion of southern Europe via the Mediterranean (see I.9, I.75, II.24) accompanied by earthquakes (see I.20, I.46. I.87, II.43).

61. Original text of 1568 edition

Betta, Vienne, Emorre, Sacarbance,
Voudront livrer aux Barbares Pannone:
Par picque & feu, enorme violance,
Les conjurez descouvers par matrone.

Read as modern French:

Buda; Comarno; Sopron
la Hongrie

Komarno, Buda, Sopron and Vienna
Would Hungary to Arab Muslims yield:
Huge violence, clashes, fires as in Gehenna.
The plotters by an old crone are revealed.

Source: The *Mirabilis Liber's* prophecy of a vast Arab invasion of Europe, partly from the east. See I.9, I.75, II.24. Nostradamus seems suddenly to have realized that he has spent so long projecting relatively small, local events into the future by way of 'page-fillers' that he is in danger of finishing his book without returning to his major theme . . .

62. Original text of 1568 edition

Pres de Sorbin pour assaillir Ongrie,
L'heroult de Bude les viendra advertir:
Chef Bizantin, Sallon de Sclavonie,
A loy d'Arabes les viendra convertir.

Read as modern French:

Serbie/Sopron [?]
détourner [abvertir: lat. a(b)vertere]
Solin/Salona/saillissant [saillant]

Via Sopron he shall Hungary attack,
Of which shall Buda's envoy them alert:
The Turkish chief, Slavonia at his back,
To Islam shall the whole of them convert.

Source: Once again, the *Mirabilis Liber's* forecast of a Muslim invasion of Europe, clearly based on the contemporary Ottoman invasion of south-eastern Europe. See I.9, I.75, II.24.

63. Original text of 1568 edition

Cydron, Raguse, la cité au sainct Hieron,
Reverdira le medicant secours,
Mort fils de Roy par mort de deux heron,
L'Arabe Ongrie feront un mesme cours.

Read as modern French:

Khania; Dubrovnik; Stridon

héros

Khania, Dubrovnik, th' town of St Jerome
Shall healing help cause to grow green again.
The King's son dead through deaths of heroes twain,
To Arab Hungary it too shall come.

Source: Still on the eastern front, apparently the *Mirabilis Liber's* prediction of an eventual counter-invasion against the occupying Muslims. See I.55.

64. Original text of 1568 edition   **Read as modern French:**

Pleure Milan, pleure Luqes, Florance,
Que ton grand Duc sur le char montera,
Changer le siege pres de Venise s'advance,   *Pour renverser*
Lors que Colomne à Rome changera.   *les Collonas; tomberont*

> **Weep Lucca, weep Milan, weep Florence too,**
> **When he, your Duke, on war-chariot shall prance:**
> **To ruin the See near Venice he'll advance**
> **When Rome's Colonnas fall, as they must do.**

Source: Unidentified, but possibly connected with the *Mirabilis Liber*'s threatened Arab invasion of Europe. See I.9, I.75, II.24.

65. Original text of 1568 edition   **Read as modern French:**

O vaste Romme ta ruyne s'approche,
Non de tes murs de ton sang & sustance:
L'aspre par lettres fera si horrible coche,   *tranche*
Fer poinctu mis à tous jusques au manche.

> **O mighty Rome, your ruin is at hand –**
> **Not to your walls, but to your living part:**
> **He of the harsh-writ name such woes has planned,**
> **His sword shall pierce all to the hilt and heart.**

Source: The dramatic and truly epoch-making Imperial sacking of Rome of 1527 under the partial command of Georg von Frundsberg, the savage appearance of whose Gothic German signature the shocked Nostradamus also picks up on elsewhere (see II.93, X.20. X.27) – presumably assimilated to the *Mirabilis Liber*'s prediction of a future Arab invasion of Europe via Rome (see I.9, I.75).

66. Original text of 1568 edition   **Read as modern French:**

Le chef de Londres par regne l'Americh,   *[de] dame erist[ique] [gr. eristikos, disputé –*
                                                     voir rime]
L'isle d'Escosse tempiera par gellee: *templera*
Roy Reb auront un si faux antechrist,   *En Roy rebelle*
Que les mettra trestous dans la meslee.   *Qui*

> **Through lady's realm disputed, London's lord**
> **In icy winds shall rack the Scottish isle:**
> **A rebel king and Antichrist abhorred**
> **Shall draw them all into the fray awhile.**

Source: The brutal military campaigns against Scotland mounted by King Edward I of England (ever since known as the 'Hammer of the Scots'), which grew out of the power vacuum that resulted when King Alexander III of Scotland died and the kingdom fell to his granddaughter Margaret (ever since known as the 'Maid of Norway'), who herself died on her way back to Scotland from Norway to claim her crown in 1290. This was the same year when Edward notoriously expelled all the Jews from England – which might explain why Nostradamus knew about it, presumably from his family. The verse, in other words, has the standard Nostradamian format of 'omen plus corollary': just as Edward I mounted a brutal and ruinous invasion of Scotland as a consequence of the premature ending of Margaret's reign – so causing King Robert the Bruce eventually to embark on his famous counter-campaign as recorded in Froissart's *Chroniques* – so the rebellious Antichrist (rebellious, this time, against the Word of God) will conduct an equally brutal and ruinous invasion of Europe, as predicted by Nostradamus's prime source, the *Mirabilis Liber*. Compare I.9, I.75, II.24 for the invasion, and I.47, I.76, II.9 for the Antichrist. The reading *erist[ique]* for the last word of line 1 is suggested by the fact that *Americh* simply does not rhyme with *Antechrist* in line 3 as printed: one assumes that the printer was currently rather obsessed with the latest news from the New World, which for people of the day evoked all the excitement of today's news from outer space. The 'icy winds', one imagines, reflect the warm Provençal Nostradamus's idea of what the weather away up there in snowy Scotland's 'island' must be like . . .

67. Original text of 1568 edition   **Read as modern French:**

Le tremblement si fort au mois de May,
Saturne, Caper, Jupiter, Mercure au beuf: *en Capricorne*
Venus aussi [/] Cancer, Mars, en Nonnay,   *à Annonay*
Tombera gresse lors plus grosse qu'un euf.   *grêle [gresle]*

> **So great an earthquake in the month of May –**
> **Saturn in Goat; Jove, Mercury in Taurus**
> **And Venus, Mars in Crab – at Annonay:**
> **Hail bigger than an egg shall fall down o'er us.**

Source: Jean Perrat's description in his contemporary *Chronique d'un notaire d'Orange* of the violent earthquake of 4 May 1549 at Montélimar that left buildings split apart, assimilated to the same source's report for the same year of huge hail: 'On Saturday the 15th day of June of the present year, between five and six o'clock of the afternoon . . . there fell so much hail at Orange and places round about that the ground was covered with it, with wheat, grapes and all fruit severely damaged; and it was a big as hazel and other nuts.' One of the 'places round about' Orange

and Montélimar was and is Annonay just south-west of Roussillon, further up the Rhône valley. On the former date, moreover, the planets' positions had been precisely as the verse describes.[8] Nostradamus had presumably been reminded of the occasion when he came to page 567 of Conrad Lycosthenes' *Prodigiorum ac ostentorum chronicon* of 1557,[44] which described how, in 1538, 'Basel was repeatedly struck by earthquake . . . In Switzerland, and principally in the countryside around Zurich, enormous hail, whose stones were bigger than hens' eggs, devastated everything far and wide.' Moreover, it had gone on to illustrate both events with customary verve (see woodcuts).

68. Original text of 1568 edition   Read as modern French:

L'armee de mer devant cité tiendra.
Puis partira sans faire longue alee,
Citoyens grande proye en terre prendra,
Retourner classe reprendre grand emblee.

> **The sea-borne troops before the city stay,**
> **Then leave again, nor further much shall pass:**
> **By land shall many folk be ta'en away.**
> **The fleet returns: much looting then, alas!**

Source: The Muslim pirate raids from North Africa that continually blighted the Mediterranean coast just south of Salon during Nostradamus's lifetime, notably between 1526 and 1531, in 1534 and in 1536.

69. Original text of 1568 edition   Read as modern French:

Le fait luysant de neuf vieux eslevé   *Les faits luisants*
Seront si grand par midi aquilon,
De sa seur propre grandes alles levé.   *ailes*
Fuyant murdry au buysson d'ambellon.

> **The shining deeds done by the new-raised sire**
> **Shall gleam so bright from south to north withal**
> **That on his sister's wings he'll rise yet higher.**
> **Fleeing, in Ambel's bushes he shall fall.**

Source: Unidentified, despite the evident personal fame described.

70. Original text of 1568 edition   Read as modern French:

L'œil par object fera telle excroissance,
Tant & ardante que tumbera la neige,
Champ arrousé viendra en descroissance,
Que le primat succumbera à Rege.   *Quand; Reggia*

Through object struck, the eye such size shall gain,
So much, so burning, as the snow shall fall:
Fields rained upon, it shall go down again,
When th' Primate, too, at Reggia shall fall.

Source: Apparently the story of an eye-problem that Nostradamus himself suffered in 1554, when the Cardinal Hippolyte D'Este was replaced as Henri II's representative in Ferrara by Piero Strozzi, a cousin of Catherine de Médicis.[60] Inevitably, he treats the one as an omen of the other.

71. Original text of 1568 edition   Read as modern French:

La terre & l'air gelleront si grand eau,
Lors qu'on viendra pour jeudi venerer,
Ce qui sera jamais ne feut si beau,
Des quatre pars le viendront honnorer.

Both land and sea shall freeze: such rain there'll be
When they shall come Thursday to venerate.
Nought finer than what shall take place they'll see:
From the world's corners they'll it celebrate.

Source: Apparently the blasphemous celebration of the Sabbath on a Thursday ascribed by some Catholics to certain Protestant sects of the time. If so, the last two lines are presumably ironic.

72. Original text of 1568 edition   Read as modern French:

L'an mil neuf cens nonante neuf sept mois
Du ciel viendra un grand Roy deffraieur

        De la part du ciel; pourvoyeur/commis aux
           vivres/hôte

Resusciter le grand Roy d'Angolmois.   *Viendra résusciter/Résuscitera; Angoumois*
Avant apres Mars regner par bon heur.   *Avant, après Mars, de régner; de manière*
           fortunée

When 1999 is seven months o'er
Shall a great King and host – on heaven's part, he –
Restore the King from Angoumois once more,
Ere, after March, he'll reign propitiously.

Source: The miraculous restoration to health in his Madrid prison of the dying King François I, duc d'Angoulême, which apparently resulted from a personal visit from his host and jailor the Holy Roman Emperor Charles V in August 1525, projected (with some adaptation) into the future in accordance with the *Mirabilis Liber*'s description of the similar function of a future 'Angelic Pastor': 'According to all the prophets, this new Pope shall be full of holiness and very pleasing to God, and during his life and at his death shall perform miracles . . . Pure and full of grace, he shall annul everything [untoward that has taken place hitherto], and shall redeem with his amiable virtues the State of the Church and the dispersed temporal powers' (Prophecy of the Angelic Pastor). François was duly released to resume his reign the following March. Nostradamus has evidently calculated the celebrated date in the first line (July 1999) by simple comparative horoscopy, given that Jupiter, Mars, Venus, Mercury, and the moon were each in the same signs (Taurus, Scorpio, Virgo, Leo, and Cancer-to-Scorpio respectively) on both occasions.

73. Original text of 1568 edition   Read as modern French:

Le temps present avecques le passé
Sera jugé par grand Jovialiste,   *Prélat/Noble/Juriste[8]*
Le monde tard luy sera lassé,   *en sera fatigué*
Et desloial par le clergé juriste.

> **The present time as well as all the past**
> **The mighty man of God shall judge that day,**
> **And yet the world shall tire of him at last,**
> **And priestly lawyers shall the man betray.**

Source: The *Mirabilis Liber*'s prophecies of a future 'Angelic Pastor' who would reform the entire Church. See VI.21.

74. Original text of 1568 edition   Read as modern French:

Au revolu du grand nombre septiesme
Apparoistra au temps Jeux d'Hacatombe,   *des jeux Olympiques*
Non esloigné du grand eage milliesme,
Que les entres [//] sortiront de leur tombe.   *entrés*

> **When mighty Number Seven shall quit the stage,**
> **At time of Games Olympic, 'fore their eyes,**
> **Not long ere dies the great Millennial Age,**
> **Those who have entered graves shall from them rise.**

Source: The resurrection of the dead at the Last Judgment, as per the *Mirabilis Liber*'s Bible-based prophecies. See II.13. On the basis of contemporary calculations by Roussat[67] and others, the seventh millennium since the world's creation (the subject referred to in the above verse) was due to end in 1800 or 1887, though Roussat himself (and apparently Nostradamus, too) suggested a considerable extension to the system, effectively until the year 4722 . . .

75. Original text of 1568 edition   Read as modern French:

Tant attendu ne reviendra jamais
Dedans l'Europe, en Asie apparoistra
Un de la ligue yssu du grand Hermes,   *sorti*
Et sur tous roys des orientz croistra.

So long awaited, ne'er to come again
To Europe, Asia Minor him shall breed
From Hermes' robber-band of desperate men,
And all the eastern kings he'll far exceed.

Source: The *Mirabilis Liber*'s prophecies of the coming Antichrist. See I.47, I.76, II.9. For readers unfamiliar with classical mythology, I have expanded on the traditional qualities of Hermes, from whose robber-band the original line 3 merely describes him as coming.

76. Original text of 1568 edition   Read as modern French:

Le grand senat discernera la pompe,
A l'un qu'apres sera vaincu chassé,
Ses adherans seront à son de trompe,
Biens publiez ennemys deschassez.

The senate shall a triumph then award
To one whom they shall later beat and banish:
His followers shall with loud trumpet-chord,
Their assets published, foes be named – and vanish.

Source: Unidentified, but possibly the story of Julius Caesar, as recorded by Suetonius.

77. Original text of 1568 edition   Read as modern French:

Trente adherans de l'ordre des quyretres   *Quirites [citoyens romains]*
Bannys leurs biens donnez ses adversaires,
Tous leurs bienfais seront pour desmerites
Classe espargie delivrez aux corsaires.

Of th' title 'citizen' shall thirty be
Banished, their goods to adversaries rendered:
All their good deeds as vices they shall see.
The scattered fleet to pirates is surrendered.

Source: Unidentified, but possibly connected with the previous verse.

78. Original text of 1568 edition   Read as modern French:

Subite joye en subite tristesse
Sera à Romme aux graces embrassees
Dueil, cris, pleurs, larm. sang excellant liesse   *larmes*
Contraires bandes surprinses & troussees.

Full sudden joy to sudden sadness turning
Shall be at Rome of the Embracing Graces:

Grief, cries, tears, blood: then wondrous joy returning.
Enemy bands surprised and placed in traces.

Source: The sequence first of joyful liberation and then of pillage experienced by Rome at the hands of the French troops of the Duke of Guise and the Spaniards of the Duke of Alba respectively during the course of 1557,[60] assimilated to the *Mirabilis Liber*'s prophecy of the capture of Rome and its eventual liberation as a result of the expected Muslim invasion of Europe. See I.9, I.75, II.24, I.55.

79. Original text of 1568 edition   Read as modern French:

Les vieux chemins seront tous embelys,
Lon passera à Memphis somentrée,   *L'on; comparable [gr. symmetros]*
Le grand Mercure d'Hercules fleur de lys
Faisant trembler terre, mer & contree.

Old roads with new embellishments they'll fit:
As though to ancient Memphis they shall go,
As Gallic Hercules' mercurial writ
Earth, sea and all the land shall quaking know.

Source: The triumphant liberation of Arab-occupied Europe and re-establishment of classical civilization under a future *Grand Monarque* (see I.4, I.55, I.92), as promised by the *Mirabilis Liber* (see I.55).

80. Original text of 1568 edition   Read as modern French:

Au regne grand du grand regne regnant,
Par force d'armes les grands portes d'arain
Fera ouvrir le roy & duc joignant,
Port demoly nef à fons jour serain.   *au fond*

When o'er the realm the regent comes to reign,
By force of arms the gates of bronze are seen
To be flung wide by King and Duke again.
Port ruined, shipping sunk, yet day serene.

Source: The liberation of Rome from Muslim occupation by a future *Grand Monarque*, as per the previous verse. I have not attempted to reproduce Nostradamus's undignified and rather ridiculous wordplay in the first line, though.

81. Original text of 1568 edition   Read as modern French:

Mys tresor temple citadins Hesperiques
Dans iceluy retiré en secret lieu,   *celui-ci*
Le temple ouvrir les liens fameliques.   *familiaux*
Reprens ravys proye horrible au milieu.   *repris [reprins]; dans le saint des saints [mi-lieu]*

The Spaniards shall hide treasure in their fane
Securing it deep in a secret place:
Descendants then shall ope it up again,
And therein awful plunder it shall face.

Source: Unknown story of Spanish gold and silver, probably from the New World.

82. Original text of 1568 edition   Read as modern French:

Cris, pleurs, larmes viendront avec coteaux
Semblant fouyr donront dernier assault
Lentour parques planter profons plateaux,   *Aux alentours la mort [lat. Parca]*
Vifs repoulsez & meurdrys de prinsault.   *dès le début*

As the knives slash, of cries, moans, tears the sound:
Seeming to flee, they'll mount a last attack.
Death all around, they'll sink planks in the ground:
Those left alive are murdered or pushed back.

Source: Possibly the last stand of King Harold's house-carls at the Battle of Hastings, undermined by a feigned withdrawal on the part of the attacking Normans.

83. Original text of 1568 edition   Read as modern French:

De batailler ne sera donné signe,
Du parc seront contraint de sortir hors
De Gand lentour sera cogneu l'ensigne,   *alentour*
Qui fera mettre de tous les siens à mors.

Of giving battle no sign shall be made:
From the enclosure they'll be forced to flee.
All around Ghent the signal is displayed
That put to death, of all, its own should be.

Source: Unknown.

84. Original text of 1568 edition   Read as modern French:

La naturelle à si hault hault non bas   *La fille illégitime*
Le tard retour fera martis contens,   *marris*
Le Recloing ne sera sans debatz   *La réunion [rejoinct]*
En empliant & perdant tout son temps.

The lord's love-child shall lordly be, no less:
The late return shall make th' aggrieved content.
Th' reunion shall not be quarrel-less
And fill his time, which shall be quite misspent.

Source: Totally unidentifiable.

85. Original text of 1568 edition   **Read as modern French:**

Le vieil tribung au point de la trehemide   *du tremblement*
Sera pressee captif ne deslivrer,   *livrer*
Le veuil non veuil le mal parlant timide   *vieux*
Par legitime à ses amys livrer.

> **The ancient tribune, on the point of trembling,**
> **He'll be sore pressed as captive to hand o'er.**
> **He'll speak with pain, that old but old dissembling,**
> **Too scared by law him to his friends t' restore.**

Source: Cicero, *Oratio pro Milone*: the well-known and still-extant oration of the panicking and trembling Cicero in defense of the Tribune Milo, accused of assassinating his adversary and co-tribune Claudius in 52 BC, in the face of threats from a packed audience of Pompey's troops.[60]

86. Original text of 1568 edition   **Read as modern French:**

Comme un gryphon viendra le roy d'Europe
Accompaigné de ceux d'Aquilon,   *du nord*
De rouges & blancz conduira grand troppe   *troupe*
Et yront contre le roy de Babilon.   *iront*

> **The King of Europe, Gryphon-like indeed,**
> **Accompanied by forces from the North,**
> **Of reds and whites a mighty host shall lead**
> **'Gainst Babylon's great ruler boldly forth.**

Source: The Third Crusade of 1189–92, led by the French King Philippe Auguste, the Emperor Frederick Barbarossa and their illustrious ally from the North, King Richard I of England who, in addition to the standard Crusaders' uniform of red cross on white coverall, had his shield emblazoned with gryphons and finished up in virtual sole command. One of the titles of their chief adversary, the Arab Saladin, was indeed 'King of Babylon'. All this is of course assimilated to the *Mirabilis Liber's* by-now familiar theme of an eventual counter-invasion against the future Arab occupiers of Europe. See I.55.

87. Original text of 1568 edition   **Read as modern French:**

Grand roy viendra prendre port pres de Nisse   *Nice*
Le grand empire de la mort si enfera
Aux Antipolles posera son genisse,   *Antibes; son genêt/balai*
Par mer la Pille tout esvanoira.

> **Near Nice the mighty king shall shoreward ride**
> **To stab to death the empire as he may.**

At Antibes he his broom shall lay aside:
By sea all pillage then shall fade away.

Source: An ill-advised 'window-forecast' about the future success of French operations against both the Holy Roman Empire and the perennial Arab pirates in the south, possibly assimilated to the *Mirabilis Liber*'s prediction of an eventual Christian counter-invasion against the future Muslim occupiers of Europe. See I.55.

88. Original text of 1568 edition   Read as modern French:

Piedz & Cheval à la seconde veille
Feront entree vastient tout par la mer,   *dévastant*
Dedans le poil entrera de Marseille,
Pleurs, crys, & sang, onc nul temps si amer.   *jamais*

At second watch shall horse and foot alike
Force their way in and sack all from the sea:
Within the heart of Marseille they shall strike.
Tears, screams and blood: ne'er bitterer times there'll be.

Source: Previous frequent raids on France's Mediterranean coast by Arab pirates from North Africa, to say nothing of the earlier Saracen incursions, assimilated to the *Mirabilis Liber*'s prediction of a massive Muslim invasion of Europe. See I.9, I.75, II.24.

89. Original text of 1568 edition   Read as modern French:

De brique en marbre seront les murs reduits
Sept & cinquante annees pacifiques,
Joie aux humains renové Laqueduict,   *renouvelé ; l'aqueduc*
Santé, grandz fruict joye & temps melifique[s].

In marble they shall brick walls reconstruct:
Of peace seven years and fifty they shall see.
For humans, joy; renewed each aqueduct;
Health, honeyed times, joy, rich fecundity.

Source: The famous reported claim by the Emperor Augustus, at the end of his 57 years in power, that he had 'found Rome of brick and left it of marble', assimilated to the *Mirabilis Liber*'s forecast of a golden age following the final defeat of the future Muslim invaders of Europe, and possibly with a sideways glance at Nostradamus's own activities in encouraging and helping to finance the construction of the local Canal de Craponne. Compare I.55.

90. Original text of 1568 edition   Read as modern French:

Cent foys mourra le tyran inhumain.
Mys à son lieu scavant & debonnaire,
Tout le senat sera dessoubz sa main,
Faché sera par malin themeraire.

>   A hundred deaths the brutal tyrant dies:
>   Put in his place instead a gentle scholar.
>   The senate 'neath his hand like putty lies;
>   Troubled, though, by a scoundrel full of choler.

Source: The reign of the gentle Emperor Claudius – following the death of the brutal Caligula at the hands of a conspiracy – featuring the difficulties he had with his two unscrupulous advisers Pallas and Narcissus who, for a while, virtually took over power.

91. Original text of 1568 edition   Read as modern French:

Clergé Romain l'an mil six cens & neuf,
Au chef de l'an feras election
D'un gris & noir de la Compagne yssu,   Campanie[?]
Qui onc ne feut [ ] si maling.   jamais; [pontife?]

>   You, Roman clergy, in 1609
>   At the year's turning shall election make:
>   Campanian, he, who'll gray and black combine.
>   Never worse Pope; never more grave mistake!

Source: Another of Nostradamus's ill-advised 'window-forecasts', apparently based directly on a fifty-year projection into the future of the coronation of Pope Pius IV on 6 January 1559.[60] Needless to say, *no* Pope was in fact elected in 1609, which fell almost four years after the start of the long reign of Paul V. Moreover, although I have rhymed my translation, this verse is the only one in the whole collection that is totally *un*rhymed.

92. Original text of 1568 edition   Read as modern French:

Devant le pere l'enfant sera tué:
Le pere apres entre cordes de jonc,
Genevois peuple sera esvertué,
Gisant le chief au milieu comme un tronc.

>   Before its father they the child shall kill:
>   The father in rush ropes they then shall tie.
>   Geneva's folk to live shall lose the will
>   When in their midst, log-like, their chief shall lie.

Source: Another 'window-forecast', this time linked to an omen, predicting the eventual death of the pre-eminent Protestant leader John Calvin – which duly happened (as death usually does!) some six years later.

93. Original text of 1568 edition   Read as modern French:

La barque neufve recevra les voyages,
Là & aupres transfereront l'empire,
Beaucaire, Arles retiendront les hostages,
Pres deux colomnes trouvees de porphire.

> **The new barque shall know voyages untold:**
> **Here, there and everywhere they'll shift the See.**
> **At Arles, Beaucaire the hostages they'll hold,**
> **Near two shafts, newly found, of porphyry.**

Source: The Great Western Church Schism of 1378 to 1417 (see I.32, V.46, V.92, VI.13, VII.22, VII.23, VII.35), in the course of which the French branch of the papacy fled to Avignon, as projected into the future in the form of the *Mirabilis Liber*'s prediction of the eventual flight of the Pope from Rome. See I.32. An archaeological 'omen' in the form of two newly discovered classical columns is thrown in for good measure, partly as a 'timer' and partly as a symbol of the dual papacy that resulted.

94. Original text of 1568 edition   Read as modern French:

De Nismes, d'Arles, & Vienne contemner,
N'obey tout à l'edict Hespericque: *espagnol*
Aux labouriez pour le grand condamner,   *À être torturés*
Six eschappez en habit seraphicque.

> **Of Nîmes, Arles and Vienne they'll scorn all them**
> **Who'll not obey what Spain on them impressed:**
> **For the lord they'll to torture them condemn,**
> **But six shall 'scape, in robes Franciscan dressed.**

Source: Unknown.

95. Original text of 1568 edition   Read as modern French:

Dans les Espaignes viendra Roy trespuissant,
Par mer & terre subjugant or midy,   *l'ordure*
Ce mal fera rabaissant le croissant,
Baisser les aesles à ceux du vendredy.

> **Down into Spain the mighty King shall sweep,**
> **By land and sea the southern filth defeat.**

> Such ill he'll do the crescent, down it beat,
> And clip the wings of those who Friday keep.

Source: The *Mirabilis Liber*'s prophecy of a final, triumphant liberation of Europe from its future Muslim occupiers (see I.55) by a future *Grand Monarque* of all Europe. See I.4, I.55, I.92.

96. Original text of 1568 edition   Read as modern French:

Religion du nom des mers vaincra,
Contre la secte fils Adaluncatif,   *d'Abdalah calif*
Secte obstinee deploree craindra,
Des deux blessez par Aleph & Aleph.   *Aleph et Alif [voir rime!]*

> **The sect with sea-like name shall victory gain**
> **Against the heirs of Abdalah Caliph.**
> **The stubborn sect deplored shall fear the twain,**
> **Wounded alike by Aleph and Alif.**

Source: Another 'window-forecast' confidently predicting the eventual victory of the Jews (whose alphabet starts with the letter *aleph*) over the Muslims (whose Arabic first letter is *alif*, and whose last Arab Caliph was the seventh-century Abd Allah ibn al-Zubayr). The 'sect with the sea-like name' is of course the *Marranos*, from whom Nostradamus's family may well have been descended. The 'stubborn, deplored sect' appears to be the contemporary Protestants, unable to make much headway with either side.

97. Original text of 1568 edition   Read as modern French:

Triremes pleines tout aage captif,
Temps bon à mal, le doux pour amertume:
Proye à Barbares trop tost seront hastifs,
Cupid de veoir plaindre au vent la plume.   *Désirant*

> **Triremes with captives of all ages packed,**
> **The weather ripe for evil, fair for ill,**
> **Being Arab prey, shall rush too soon to act,**
> **Anxious to see which way the wind shall fill.**

Source: Unidentified.

98. Original text of 1568 edition   Read as modern French:

La splendeur claire à pucelle joyeuse,
Ne luyra plus [//] long temps sera sans sel:
Avec marchans, ruffiens loups odieuse,
Tous peste mele monstre universel.   *pêle-mêle; augures partout*

That brilliant light that so rejoiced the Maid
Shall shine no more: long shall no sense abide,
With hawkers, ruffians, wolves of hateful shade,
All topsy-turvy, omens on every side.

Source: Nostradamus's familiar conviction that things generally are falling apart, with all the ancient ideals of the age of Joan of Arc gone for ever.

99. Original text of 1568 edition   Read as modern French:

La fin le loup, le lyon, beuf, & l'asne,
Timide dama seront avec mastins,
Plus ne cherra à eux la douce manne,   *tombera*
Plus vigilance & custode aux mastins.   *et garde*

At length lies wolf with ox and lion with ass:
The timid deer lies down amid the hounds.
Yet no more gentle manna falls, alas!
See that more care the hungry dogs surrounds!

Source: Presumably Nostradamus's personal worry lest the eventual advent of the promised Golden Age be scuppered by current religious animosities.

100. Original text of 1568 edition   Read as modern French:

Le grand empire sera par Angleterre,   *pour*
Le pempotam [//] des ans plus de trois cens: *Le tout-puissant*
Grandes copies passer par mer & terre,   *armées [lat. copia]*
Les Lusitains n'en seront pas contens.

For England the all-powerful shall be
More than three hundred years' imperial sway.
Great armies shall set out by land and sea:
The Portuguese shall surely rue the day.

Source: A slightly confused reading of Richard Roussat's *Livre de l'estat et mutations des temps* of 1549–50, under the terms of which the world had just entered (in 1533) the 354-year 'Age of the Moon'. This was traditionally associated with the Roman Empire, while the eventual zodiacal 'Air Triplicity' (due after some 330 years of it) would see the coming of the Antichrist and the supremacy of the powers of the North. The proposed link with England arises from Roussat's statement that 'under this triplicity of Air, which causes the Northerners to triumph, hold sway, and be victorious, there flourished the Noble Knights of King Arthur of Britain, being of the number of the Round Table; and since this triplicity . . . also applies to the Prophets, Merlin was of their number, too . . .' On this basis, then, what Nostradamus is projecting into the future, along lines already laid down by Roussat, is nothing less than a new British Camelot, a prospect that would, of course, hardly appeal to Spain and Portugal, the major imperial powers of the day. Probably the seer never knew how close he came, in this respect at least!

Appendix A

Translation of Nostradamus's dedicatory Preface to the 1555 edition of *Les Propheties*, addressed to his son César

(with annotations based on Pierre Brind'Amour's seminal research in his *Nostradamus: les Premières Centuries ou Propheties*)[9]

The original text – basically, a restatement without acknowledgment of Marsilio Ficino's ideas in his *Disputatio contra iudicium astrologorum* on how divination might be achieved, supplemented by passages borrowed, equally without acknowledgment, from Petrus Crinitus and Savonarola (the latter as quoted in Nostradamus's major source, the *Mirabilis Liber* of 1523–44[5]) – was not divided into either paragraphs or sections, any more than were most printed texts of the time. Numbers between square brackets simply correspond to the sections into which I divided the original French text for ease of reference in my *Nostradamus Encyclopedia*.[37]

PREFACE
BY M. MICHEL
NOSTRADAMUS TO
His Prophecies.
Ad Caesarem Nostradamum filium
[To César Nostradamus his son],
Long life and felicity.

[1] YOUR LATE arrival, CESAR NOSTRADAME [*sic*] my son, has caused me to set out in writing the [results of the] long periods that I have spent in ceaseless night watches, in order to leave you a memorandum, after the physical extinction of [this] your progenitor, and for the general benefit of mankind, of that about which the Divine Being has granted me knowledge through [the calculation of] astronomical cycles. And since it has pleased Immortal God that you have not reached this earthly shore with instinctive knowledge [of the future],

not to mention your years – still less your months of March – which are not yet more than one in number, and so cannot permit your weak understanding to take in what I shall be obliged to specify [for the times] after my death: seeing that it is not possible to leave you in writing what shall be obliterated by the ravages of time – for the hereditary gift of prediction shall be shut up within my bosom; considering, too, that the outcome of human events is uncertain, and that all of it is ruled and governed by the power of God Inestimable, inspiring us not by drunken frenzy, nor yet by melancholic emotion, but by astronomical facts: *Soli numine divino afflati praesagiunt & spiritu prophetico particularia* [Latin: 'Only those inspired by the divine godhead can prophesy, and only those inspired by the spirit of prophecy can prophesy detailed events' – quote from Pseudo Ptolemy's *Centiloquium*, 1st aphorism, in Pontano's translation].

[2] Although I have long repeatedly predicted, well in advance, what has since come to pass [translated directly from the Latin of Savonarola's *Compendium revelationum*, as quoted at length in the important *Mirabilis Liber*[45]], and in particular regions, too – asserting the whole of it to have been done through God's power and inspiration – and having deliberately said nothing of, and refrained from putting in writing, other events both happy and unfortunate that were foreshadowed as increasingly imminent, and that have since come to pass in [various] regions of the world, for fear of attack [!] – indeed, concerning not only time present, but most of the future, too – because regimes, sects, and religions shall undergo such diametrical changes with respect to the present that if I were to disclose what shall come to pass, members of governments, sects, religions, and faiths would find it so out of accord with the fantasies they have heard that they would condemn what will [eventually] be recognized as having been [truly] seen and perceived about future ages; considering also the statement of the true Lord: *Nolite sanctum dare canibus nec mittatis margaritas ante porcos ne conculcent pedibus & conversi dirumpant vos* ['Do not give what is holy to the gods or cast pearls before swine, lest they trample them under their feet, turn upon you, and tear you in pieces' – Matthew 7:6, quoted amidst another passage borrowed from Savonarola in the *Mirabilis Liber*[45]]. This is what caused me to refrain from public utterance and prevented my putting pen to paper. Besides, I had determined to go as far as declaring in abstruse and puzzling utterances the future causes of the 'common advent' [i.e. the coming of the common people to power], even those truly cogent ones that I have foreseen. Yet lest whatever human changes may be to come should scandalize delicate ears, the whole thing is written in nebulous form, rather than as a clear prophecy of any kind. True, *Abscondisti haec à sapientibus, & prudentibus, id est potentibus & regibus, & enucsleasti ea exiguis & tenuibus* ['Thou hast hidden these things from the wise and prudent, i.e. the mighty and kings, and hast revealed

them to the small and weak' – a typically vague, expanded Nostradamian version of Matthew 11:25, apparently quoted from memory, and once again echoing Savonarola] – and to the Prophets.

[3] By the grace of immortal God and the good angels these have received the spirit of prophecy, by which they see distant things and succeed in foreseeing future events, for nothing can be achieved without Him. So great is Their* power and goodness to their subjects that all the while they abide in these two – while still subject to all other influences – that prophetic heat and power visits us in the similitude of the essence of the spirit of goodness, just as the rays of the sun reach us, casting their influence over elementary and non elementary bodies alike. [The whole of this section is translated directly – and so badly as to suggest that Nostradamus didn't fully understand it – from the Latin of Petrus Crinitus's *De Honesta Disciplina* of 1504, as reprinted by Gryphius of Lyon in 1543, even failing to adjust the 'their' at *, which in the original refers to the gods in the plural!]

[4] As for us humans, we can by our [own] instinctive knowledge and the application of [our own] ingenuity know nothing of the hidden secrets of God the creator, *Quia non est nostrum noscere tempora, nec momenta* etc. [Latin version of Acts 1:7: 'For it is not for us to know the times or moments . . .', as found in Joachim of Fiore⁴⁵] However, it is possible that even today there may appear and exist people to whom God the creator has deigned to reveal, through imaginative impressions, some secrets of the future as harmonized with judicial astrology, just as in the past a certain power and faculty of will came through them, appearing like a flame of fire, and inspiring them in such a way as to allow others to appreciate their divine and human inspirations [much of this is once again based on Crinitus]. For [those] divine works that are totally absolute are performed by God; the one that is medial, or contingent, by the angels; and the third one by those who are evil [Nostradamus's text here is a hopeless word-for-word translation from Crinitus (based in turn on Ficino) in which neuter plurals are mistaken for feminine singulars in a way that suggests once again that Nostradamus hadn't much idea of what Crinitus really meant].

[5] But my son, I am speaking to you here a little too obscurely [!]: but as for the occult predictions that one manages to receive through the subtle spirit of fire which sometimes, as the disturbed intellect contemplates attentively the highest of the stars, surprises one with the written pronouncements [that emerge] – pronouncements made with neither fear nor expectation, nor with immodest loquacity – what shall I say? The whole of it has proceeded from the divine power of Almighty and Eternal God, from whom all bounty proceeds.

[6] Although, my son, I have used the word 'prophet', I would not attribute to myself a title of such lofty sublimity in these presents: for *qui propheta dicitur, hodie, olim vocabatur videns* [Latin Vulgate: 'He who is nowadays described as a prophet was formerly called a seer' – I Samuel 9:9]. For, properly speaking, my son, a prophet is one who sees far off things with the natural perception that every creature has [paraphrased from Savonarola]. Even in the case where the prophet seems, by dint of the pure light of prophecy, to perceive clearly not merely things human, but things divine – this [simply] cannot be, seeing that the effects of future prediction extend [into the future so] far [more Savonarola]. For the secrets of God are unfathomable, and the manifesting power that is contingent upon long exercised instinctive gnosis, taking its immediate rise from free will, brings about the revelation of things that cannot of themselves reveal themselves to the mind, whether by human auguries or by any other occult knowledge or power beneath the concavity of the sky – [things, that is, concerning] each present moment out of the whole of eternity which embraces within itself the whole of time [end of passage vaguely borrowed from Savonarola]. But thanks to some indivisible timelessness [perceived] via epileptic trance, things are known [to us] through the movement of the heavens.

[7] I do not say, my son – lest you misunderstand me, given that knowledge of such matters cannot [yet] imprint itself upon your weak mind – that future, very distant things cannot be known by any reasonable creature: on the contrary, the intellectually minded person is well able to perceive things both present and far off [provided] that [these] are not too utterly occult or obscure. But the perfect appreciation of things cannot be acquired without that divine inspiration, given that that all prophetic inspiration takes its prime moving principle [first] from God the creator, then from chance and instinct. It is in this way that – various things being produced or not produced in various ways – the prophecy is partially arrived at, or has been arrived at [another paraphrase from Savonarola]. For intellectually based understanding is incapable of seeing occultly in what direction things to come will tend – other than through the voice [that is heard] with the aid of the hem, and through the tiny flame [two familiar direct references to Iamblichus's *De Mysteriis Aegyptiorum* – as republished in Crinitus's *De honesta disciplina* of 1504, reprinted by Gryphius of Lyon in 1543, an edition that was in César's library, and thus no doubt in his father's – as per quatrains I.2 and I.1 respectively].

[8] And also, my son, I beg you never to devote your mind to such fancies and vanities, which desiccate the body, drive the soul to perdition, and disturb the feeble intelligence – even that vanity of more then execrable magic that was long ago condemned by the sacred scriptures and divine precepts – from which

the main exception is the judgment of judicial astrology, by means of which (and thanks to the divine inspiration and revelation [emerging from] continual night watches and calculations) we have drawn up our prophecies in writing [here Nostradamus once again echoes Savonarola, but contradicts him at the end in the matter of astrology, instead echoing Cornelius Agrippa's view that 'no perfect divination can take place without astrology'].

[9] And even where that occult philosophy was not forbidden, I never wished to promulgate their wild views, even though many volumes that have been hidden for long ages have presented themselves to me. Instead, for fear of what might happen, after I read them I offered them to Vulcan [i.e. the fire] such that, while he was devouring them, the flames that licked the air gave out an extraordinary brightness, brighter than natural flame [the salts formerly used for tanning parchment often contained quantities of saltpetre!], illuminating the house like the light of a flashing jet of fire as if [the building] had suddenly caught alight. It is for this reason, in order that you should not be deceived by studying the supreme transmutation both lunar and solar, whether of the incorruptible metals under the earth or hidden underwater [i.e. recoverable from rivers, generally by panning], I reduced them to ashes.

[10] But as for the conclusions that can be attained by means of astrological exegesis, that is what I should like to reveal to you [here]. It is by this means that one has knowledge of things to come, while rejecting out of hand all imaginary fantasies – and can through divine inspiration pin down precise places supernaturally in accordance with the celestial patterns. [Indeed, not only] places, [but] to some extent times, by hidden virtue of the divine power and intelligence, in the presence of which all three [dimensions of] time[s] are included in eternity, holding circuit with past, present, and future causes. *Quia omnia sunt nuda & aperta etc.* [Latin: 'For all things are naked and open' – half remembered version of Matthew 10:26, as quoted by Savonarola in the *Mirabilis Liber*[45]].

[11] In this way, my son, you can easily understand, despite your tender brain, how things to come can be foretold [both] by the nocturnal and celestial lights [i.e. the stars] – which are [perfectly] natural – and by the spirit of prophecy. Not that I wish to attribute to myself either the name or the function of a prophet, but [rather rely on] inspired revelation, like any man whose senses are no less distant from heaven than his feet are from the ground.

[12] *Possum non errare falli decipi* [Latin: 'I am able *not* to err, fail, or be deceived': elsewhere, in his letter to the canons of Orange of February 1562, Nostradamus quotes the phrase without its *non* and adds the admission

Humanus sum ('I am human'): certainly the word seems superfluous in context here, as the following sentence suggests]: I am a bigger sinner than anybody in this world, and subject to all human afflictions. But being overtaken several times a week by [the spirit of] prophecy that lends a sweet odor to my nocturnal studies, I have by dint of long calculation composed [these] books of prophecies, each containing 100 prophetic astronomical quatrains, which I have intentionally put together a little obscurely. They contain perpetual predictions for [the period] from now until the year 3797 [oddly, this figure is the sum of the contemporary Richard Roussat's date for the end of the current cycle – 2242 – and the date of this current Preface – 1555]. Which will possibly cause some people to raise their eyebrows on seeing such a long prognosis; [yet these] things shall take place and shall be known everywhere beneath the sphere of the moon – by which I mean throughout all the earth, my son. For if you live [to] the natural human age you shall see in the area of your own native clime and heaven [these] future events take place.

[13] God eternal, though, is the only one who knows the eternity of His light which proceeds from Himself. And I tell [you] frankly that into those to whom His immense greatness, which is immeasurable and incomprehensible, has deigned to reveal [things] through long and melancholic [i.e. introspective] revelation – by way of that hidden thing which is divinely manifested – is poured one of the two main things that condition the understanding of the inspired prophet, illumining with supernatural light the person who is predicting via the doctrine of the stars, as well as prophesying through inspired revelation: namely a certain participation in the eternity of God, through [which] the prophet comes to judge what his divine [guiding] spirit has revealed through the agency of God the creator, as well as through an instinctive impulse: in other words, what he predicts is true and of celestial origin. Such light and tiny flame is totally efficacious and sublime, no less than the natural brilliance or natural light [that] makes philosophers [i.e. scientists and academics] so assured that, on the basis of the principles of the First Cause, they have succeeded in penetrating to the profoundest depths of the loftiest doctrines.

[14] But in order, my son, that I may not stray [into waters] too deep for the future capacity of your mind, and also because I find that literacy shall undergo such a huge and unparalleled collapse [Brind'Amour relates this prediction to verse I.62], I find that so many deluges and such deep floods [Roussat] shall befall the world before the universal conflagration [Roussat] that there shall be scarcely any land that is not covered by water: and for a long time things shall be such that, were it not for written accounts of peoples and countries, all would be lost. Moreover, both before and after these floods, the rains in many

countries shall be so slight, and so much fire and so many meteorites shall fall from the sky, that nothing shall remain that is not consumed [Roussat]. And all this is to occur, in brief, before the final conflagration. [Most of this fire and flood scenario reflects the Babylonian Berosus, as reported by Seneca.] For now that the planet Mars is completing its cycle [under the terms of contemporary cosmology, this had actually happened in 1533, and the age of the Moon (governed by Gabriel) had already taken over – see I.48], and is at the end of its most recent period, so it shall take it up again [this piece especially scandalized Laurent Videl[70] and other contemporary astrologers] – but with some [of the planets] grouped in Aquarius for several years, and others grouped in Cancer for longer and more continuous periods. And – given that we are now governed by the moon – before it has completed its full circuit, thanks to the omnipotence of God eternal, the [age of the] sun shall come [again], and then [that of] Saturn [to the horror of the professional astrologers of his day, Nostradamus here extends the accepted three-age, 7000 year system long espoused by Trithemius, Gaurico, Turrel, Roussat, and others into a fourth cycle of ages, with the new Age of the Sun (governed by the Archangel Michael) theoretically starting in 1887, and the subsequent Age of Saturn (governed by the angel Orifiel) starting in 2242]. For according to the signs in the sky the reign of Saturn shall return, and the world is nearing an age of denouement [Roussat]; and before 177 years and 3 months from what I am writing about here [*or:* from when I am writing this], through pestilence, long drawn out famine, wars, and additionally floods, the world shall – between now and the time that I have just laid down in advance, as well as several times before and afterwards – be so diminished, and there shall be so few people, that nobody shall be found willing to take to the fields, which shall be free [of cultivation] for as long as they have been subject [to the plow]. And all this by interpreting what can be seen in the stars. Furthermore, we are now in the midst of the seventh count of a thousand [years] which brings everything to a close [Roussat] [compare X.74], and approaching the eighth that corresponds to the eighth [celestial] sphere, which is at the altitude where God eternal shall accomplish the cycle during which the [former] patterns in the sky shall return to exert themselves [again], as well as being the upper driving force that makes our earth stable and firm, [so that] *non inclinabitur in saeculum saeculi* ['It shall not vary from age to age'] [badly mangled misquotation of Roussat,[76] pp. 139–40: 'Know, therefore, dear readers, that the Kingdom of God is at hand, that is to say in the seventh millennium where we are now – when the eighth Sphere, which is the lofty Firmament and the beauty of God, is about to complete a(nother) revolution, and the celestial bodies (having arrived back) at the point where they first began their motion, shall return and cease to move']. Yet all this shall be when His will is accomplished, and not otherwise. [Note how Nostradamus's distinctly unpopular idea that there would be a fourth cycle of ages which would thus take humanity into an eighth millennium from the alleged Creation seems to be derived from the fact that even though there were supposed to be only seven celestial spheres, these were governed by an eighth known as the *Primum Mobile* – the *grand moteur des siecles* or 'great mover of the cycles/ages' mentioned at II.46.]

[15] Nevertheless, whether by vague hunches that exceed all natural reason or by inspired dreams, it also happens from time to time that God the creator, through the ministry of his messengers of fire, proposes in the form of the flame that he sends, even to our eyes, the causes of future predictions signifying the future events that are to appear to the one who prophesies. For the prophecy arrived at via the exterior light must inevitably be arrived at with – and by the grace of – the interior light, even though in truth that part which seems to see through the eye of the understanding does so only by inhibiting the imaginative faculty. The reason is only too obvious – namely that all of it is predicted through divine inspiration and by means of the angelic spirit that is breathed into the one prophesying [Nostradamus elsewhere claimed to be inspired by the Archangel Michael, whom he regarded (naturally enough) as his own Guardian Angel], pouring prophecies into him, illumining him, stirring his imagination with various nocturnal visions such that, in the [more certain] light of day he prophesies through the application of astronomy in conjunction with the most holy revelation of the future – which consists, moreover, in nothing less than the exercise of free will [from Savonarola].

[16] It should be understood at this point, my son, that I find through my [calculations of astrological] cycles, in accordance with revealed inspiration, that the sword of death is now about to descend on us through plague, war more horrible that has been for three generations, and famine which shall befall the world and often return, for the stars agree with the[se calculations of] cycles. Moreover, [God] has said *Visitabo in virga ferrea iniquitates eorum, & in verberibus percutiam eos* ['I will visit their sins with an iron rod and strike them with lashes' – half remembered version of Psalm 89:32, filtered through Savonarola in the *Mirabilis Liber*[45]], for the [ultimate] mercy of the Lord shall not have time to be spread abroad, my son, before most of my prophecies shall be fulfilled and reach the time of their fulfillment.

[17] Then, over a repeated period, [there shall be] ominous storms (*Centeram ergo*, the Lord shall say, *& confringam, & non miserebor* [Latin: 'I will trample and break them, and will have no mercy' – vague reference to Isaiah 63:3, filtered through Savonarola in the *Mirabilis Liber*[45]]) and many other things to come that shall occur through floods and continual rains, as I have set out more fully in writing in my other prophecies which are written out at length, *in soluta ora-*

tione [Latin: 'in plain prose' (Cicero) – presumably his annual *Almanachs*, which had been entirely in prose up until 1554], specifying the places, times, and the pre-ordained period – as future human beings shall see [for themselves], recognizing that the future things [predicted] have [indeed] unerringly come to pass, just as we have noted in the other [prophecies] in clearer language. Their meanings shall admittedly be understood only vaguely, *sid quando submovenda erit ignorantia* ['but when the time comes for the removal of ignorance'] the matter shall become clearer.

[18] To bring this to a close then, my son, take this gift from your father M. Nostradamus, who hopes to explain to you [one day] every one of the prophecies set out in these quatrains. Praying God immortal that he will grant you long life, in good and prosperous happiness. From Salon, this 1st of March 1555.

Appendix B

Translation of Nostradamus's dedicatory foreword of 1558 to the final installment of *Les Propheties*, addressed to 'Henri King of France the Second'

Relatively few of the strange prophecies elaborated in this intriguing and highly disordered document are Nostradamus's exclusive copyright. As with the *Propheties* themselves, many of their originals are to be found in a variety of existing prophetic sources that we know were available to him at the time. However, the underlying framework probably owes most to the twelfth-century Abbot Joachim of Fiore, whose celebrated attempt to predict the future of the world had been based on the idea that the chronology of the Old Testament stood as a kind of cyclic paradigm for each succeeding age (of which he distinguished three in all). This idea had had a huge influence on religious and even secular life ever since the thirteenth century, being at least partially responsible for the contemporary identification of the Emperor Friedrich II von Hohenstaufen either as Messiah or as Antichrist, as well as for the rise of the Franciscans and Dominicans. In particular, Joachim had claimed that the Old Testament's leading players and developments would each be reflected in later and often direr counterparts. The roles of Jacob, Joshua, King David, Elias, Hezekiah, the Babylonian captivity, and Malachi, for example, were destined to be reflected in Zacharias, St John and his Gospel, Constantine, Justinian, Charlemagne, the current age, and the expected Antichrist, a seductively attractive figure who would in some sense present an exact negative image of Christ himself.

Joachim's initiative having rather come to grief in the late thirteenth century following the failure of his (admittedly reluctant) prediction of the start of his final 'Third Age' for the year 1260, Nostradamus here takes up the challenge once again. After the customary ritual groveling to King Henri II (sections A1 to A4), he sets out what he takes to be the religious chronology to date (A5) – specifically pinpointing Adam, Noah, Abraham, Moses, King David, and Christ, and throwing in Muhammad for good measure so as to achieve, like Joachim, a sevenfold paradigm – then starts to apply it to the immediate future (sections B1 to B15), while muddying the water somewhat by claiming to have thrown astronomical calculation (i.e. Roussat's supposed planetary ages) into the mix as well. In the event, Noah's flood fails to put in any reappearance, but there are due echoes of Abraham, Moses, David, Christ (or rather the Antichrist), and the rise of Islam – albeit heavily masked by the usual layers of allegorical and scholastic verbiage and vague historical borrowings.

At section B16, however, rather as per his practice in his annual *Almanachs*, he decides to have a second bite at the cherry, starting all over again with a new biblical chronology. This time he pinpoints the dates of Adam, Noah, the Flood, Abraham, Isaac, Jacob, the entry into Egypt, the Exodus, the building of the Temple, and the birth of Christ – a tenfold paradigm instead of a sevenfold one, whose figures, though correct, do not in fact match the earlier ones. Of these, though, he adduces only Noah's flood (B21), the Exodus (B17), and the (re)building of the Temple (B26) for his future scenario, and then (following an astrological rigmarole pinpointing the year 1606 as especially significant) turns his attention to those events expected to accompany and follow the advent of the Antichrist and lead up to the final Golden Age. In this he freely plunders the existing prophecies, especially Richard Roussat's *Livre de l'estat et mutations des temps* of 1549–50[67] and a Lyon edition of the *Mirabilis Liber qui prophetias revelationesque, necnon res mirandas, preteritas, presentes et futuras, aperte demonstrat . . .*[10, 45] published (to judge by its trademark motto *Spes mea Deus*, or 'God is my hope') by Jehan Besson in 1523. This – perhaps the most celebrated of all contemporary collections of ancient prophecies – is thought by some to have been compiled by none other than Nostradamus's father Jaume. Certainly it seems to have been known to the seer's secretary, Jean de Chavigny, who apparently quoted from it, just as it clearly was to Roussat.[11] As already outlined in my Introduction, it includes the prophecies of:

A. (in Latin)

- ✧ Bishop Bemechobus (Pseudo-Methodius – Syrian, seventh century)
- ✧ The Tiburtine Sibyl (Syrian, ninth century)
- ✧ 'St Augustine of Hippo' (actually the tenth-century Adso of Montier-en-Der)
- ✧ 'St Severus' (in fact a fifteenth-century composition)
- ✧ Johann Lichtenberger (a composite collection from various named sources, first printed in 1488)
- ✧ A set of papal prophecies (fourteenth century)
- ✧ Telesphorus of Cosenza (fourteenth century)
- ✧ Another composite source combining (among others) St Brigid of Sweden, St Hildegard of Bingen, the Cretan Sibyl, the Hermit Reynard and the celebrated Abbot Joachim of Fiore
- ✧ Joannes de Vatiguerro (sixteenth century)

✧ Joachim of Fiore himself (twelfth century)

✧ 'St Vincent' (actually a sixteenth-century compilation from St Thomas Aquinas and other sources)

✧ 'St Catuldus' (actually a sixteenth-century prophecy)

✧ Jerome of Ferrara (Savonarola – late fifteenth century)

✧ Fra Bonaventura (sixteenth century)

✧ Johannes de Rupescissa (Jean de la Roquetaillade – fifteenth century)

✧ St Brigid of Sweden (fourteenth century)

B. (in French)

✧ An anonymous composite source including a collection of late thirteenth-century prophecies elsewhere attributed to 'Merlin'

The fact that Nostradamus re-presents his borrowings from the above and other books in his own words, rather than actually quoting them verbatim, suggests that they were texts that he had had plenty of time to digest at leisure before embroidering their predictions *ad lib*, more or less after the manner of his *Almanachs*. He was, after all, much more given to quoting sources from memory than to religiously copying them out word by word.

The original text of Nostradamus's letter was not divided into either paragraphs or sections, any more than were most printed texts of the time. Letters and numbers between square brackets simply correspond to the sections into which I divided the original French text for ease of reference in my *Nostradamus Encyclopedia*,[37] as already referred to above. Prophecies similarly indicated between square brackets are those that seem to parallel those of Nostradamus – albeit often rather vaguely and generally – and that consequently may well have served as a basis for them.

[Preamble]

[A1] *TO THE MOST INVINCIBLE, MOST PUISSANT and most Christian Henry King of France the Second, Michel Nostradamus his most humble and obedient servant and subject [bids] victory and felicity.*

[A2] BY VIRTUE OF that sovereign esteem that I have had, O most Christian and victorious King, ever since my long since obscure face did present itself before the deity of your immeasurable Majesty – since when I have been perpetually dazzled, never ceasing to honor and worthily to venerate that day when first I presented myself before it, as before a Majesty at once so unique and so cultured; Now, seeking for some occasion whereby I might manifest the goodness and sincerity of my heart, so that in this way I might amply extend my gratitude towards your most serene Majesty; Now, seeing that to declare it in terms of deeds was beyond my power – and this combined with my singular desire to be suddenly illuminated and transported from my over long darkness and obscurity before the face of the sovereign eye and Prime Monarch of the World – in such wise I was long in doubt as to whom I should dedicate these three Centuries of my remaining Prophecies that complete the thousand, and after cogitating thereon for a long time have taken the daringly audacious step of addressing your Majesty, without being daunted thereby – just as the most eminent author Plutarch recounts in his *Life of Lycurgus* that, in view of the offerings and gifts that were presented as sacrifices to the temples of the immortal gods of that time, people did not dare to present themselves at the temples, lest they be too frequently daunted by [the sheer cost of] the said fees and vestments. This notwithstanding, seeing that your Royal splendor is accompanied by an incomparable humanity, I have addressed myself not as to the kings of Persia, whom it was in no wise permitted to visit, still less to approach: But it is to a Prince most prudent and wise that I have dedicated my nocturnal and prophetic computations, [which I have] put together by natural instinct, accompanied by poetic frenzy, rather than by poetic rule, [and which are] for the most part composed and harmonized with Astronomical calculations relating by the year, month, and week to the regions, countries, and most of the Towns and Cities of all Europe, taking in those of North Africa and part of Asia Minor, as modified in respect of those regions that come closest to all these latitudes; and which I have composed in an instinctive manner.

[A3] The stuffy nosed will retort that the scansion is as easy as understanding the meaning is difficult. And since, O most cultured King, most of the prophetic quatrains are so difficult that people would not know how to approach them, still less interpret many of them, nevertheless – in the hope of setting out in writing the years, towns, cities, and regions where most of them will occur, notably those of the years 1585 and 1606, starting from the present day, which is the 14th March 1557, and extending far beyond to the advent (which will be thoroughly calculated thereafter) of the beginning of the seventh millennium [Roussat] (in so far as my astronomical calculation and other knowledge has been able to extend thereto) when the adversaries of Jesus Christ and his Church shall begin to multiply more vigorously [Tiburtine Sibyl] – the whole has been composed and calculated in days and hours, carefully chosen and set out, and as accurately as I have been able. And the whole of it *Minerva libera, et non invita* [Latin ref. to Horace – 'insofar as my natural ability allows, and not otherwise'], by calculating almost as many of the events of future times as of ages past, including the present [Roussat] – and of whatever can be ascertained about future events in all regions as time rolls by – precisely as this has been recorded, and without adding anything superfluous [note this evident admission of direct historical borrowing],

[A4] ... even though it is said *Quod de futuris non est determinata omnino ver-itas* [Latin: 'For concerning future events the truth is not fully determined', as quoted by Savonarola]. It is true, Sire, that not [?] thinking to prophesy, and to prophesy, by the natural instinct which has been bequeathed to me by my ancestors, and adjusting and harmonizing this natural instinct in conjunction with my lengthy calculations, and emptying my soul, spirit, and heart of all care, worry, and unease through mental calm and tranquility [end of sentence: not for the first time Nostradamus seems to have lost track of his own syntax]. All of it harmonized and foretold partly *trepode aeneo* [Latin reference to Iamblichus's *De Mysteriis* . . . , as reprinted by Crinitus in 1504 and republished in Lyon by Gryphius in 1543 – 'by the bronze tripod']. Although they be many who attribute to me what is as much mine as nothing of the kind, only God Eternal, who is the holy, just, and merciful examiner of human hearts, is the true judge of it – whereupon I pray that he will defend me from the slanders of the wicked, who for equally slanderous reasons would also inquire how it was that your most ancient forebears the Kings of France cured people of the scrofula, while those of other nations cured them of snake bites, and yet others had a certain instinct for the divining art, [to say nothing of] other examples that would be [too] long to recount here. Notwithstanding those in whom the malignity of the evil spirit shall *not* [my italics] be apprehended, over the course of time after my earthly extinction my writings shall be more so than during my lifetime.

[A5] Nevertheless, if I should fall short in my calculation of the ages [note the Joachimite parallel] or if it should not be according to the will of some, may it please your more than imperial Majesty to pardon me, for I protest before God and his Saints that I do not claim to put anything whatever in writing in the present epistle that is against the true Catholic faith, but have collated the Astronomical calculations to the best of my knowledge: for the space of time since our first ancestors is such (deferring as I do to correction by the soundest judgment) that the first man, Adam, lived about 1242 years before Noah, not calculating the time by the Gentile method, as Varro wrote, but solely according to the sacred Scriptures, and according as my poor mind has been able to cope with my Astronomical calculations. Around 1080 years after Noah, from him and the world flood, came Abraham, who was a consummate astrologer according to some, and was the first inventor of Chaldean writing; around 515 or 516 years after him came Moses, and between the time of David and Moses was about 570 years. After that, between the time of David and the time of our Savior and Redeemer Jesus Christ, born of the only Virgin, was (according to some chronographers) 1350 years – though it could be objected that this calculation is not accurate because it differs from that of Eusebius. And from the time of man's redemption until the detestable blandishments of the Saracens there were 621 years or thereabouts, and therefrom one can easily add together how long has passed [overall], if my reckoning be but good and valid for all nations. And thus it is that the whole of it has been calculated according to the celestial revolutions, by association with impressions absorbed at certain desolate hours from affections [that I have] inherited from my ancient ancestors.

[A6] But the violence of the times requires, O most serene King, that such secret events be expressed only in enigmatic terms, [even though] having but one sole sense and single meaning, free of ambiguous or equivocal reckoning – nay, rather under a cloudy obscurity, in the form of an instinctive inpouring akin to the utterances of the one thousand and two prophets that have been since the world began. As the reckoning and Punic Chronicle of Joel has it, *Effundam spiritum meum super omnem carnem, et prophetabunt filii vestri, et filiae vestrae* [I will pour out my spirit upon all flesh, and your sons shall prophesy, and your daughters' – Joel 2:28]. But such prophecy proceeded from the mouth of the Holy Spirit, which was the sovereign eternal power, in conjunction with the celestial, and some of this number predicted great and marvelous happenings; [though,] for me, I in no way attribute to myself such a title here. God forbid! I confess truly that the whole of it comes from God, and render him thanks, honor, and immortal praise, without having adulterated it with any of that divination that comes *a fato* [from any direct prophetic gift], but *a Deo, a natura* [from God, from the natural order of things], and most of it confirmed by the movements of the celestial round, rather like seeing in a burning mirror [a concave mirror for concentrating the sun's rays], as though with clouded sight, the great and ominous events and the calamitous happenings that [now] loom at the hands of members of the major religious groups.

[Main text]

[B1] Firstly in respect of God's churches, secondly in respect of those who depend upon the land, such collapse shall draw near [Tiburtine Sibyl], together with a myriad of other calamitous events, as through the course of time shall become apparent; for God shall look upon the long sterility of the Great Lady [reference to Abraham's wife Sarai?], who thereafter shall conceive two princely children [St Brigid]; but she being at risk – the female one (who shall be most helpful to her) being in danger of dying in her eighteenth [year] through the temerity of the age [anonymous French prophecy?] – [shall be] unable to survive her thirty sixth year, [and] shall leave behind three male children and one female – who [in turn] shall have two of them, one of these being the one who never had [more than one] of them by the same father. Such differences shall there be between the three brothers [St Brigid], who shall thereafter be united and brought into harmony, that three, [if not all] four parts of Europe shall tremble. The Christian monarchy shall be sustained and extended by the youngest, sects shall rise up and then be dashed again [St Hippolytus], Arabs shall be driven back [Pseudo-Methodius; Torquato], kingdoms united, new Laws promulgated [Hermit Reynard]. Of the other children the first shall seize the furious crowned Lions, holding their paws above the brave coat of arms. The second shall advance so far, accompanied by the Italians, that the second ascent of the Mount of Jove [ostensible reference either to the Mons Capitolinus, Rome, seat of government and sacred to Jupiter Capitolinus, or the Montjuich in Barcelona – but, at a prior level, referring to Moses' ascents of Mount Sinai] shall be made trembling and prophetically inspired. Coming back down to pass over the Pyrenees [which rather suggests the Barcelonan connection] he shall not be translated to the ancient monarchy [just as Moses did not survive to rule over the Promised Land]. The third human bloodbath shall take place [Roussat], and war shall for a long time not occur in Lent. And the daughter shall be given for the preservation of the Christian Church. Her lord and master falling to the pagan sect of the new infidels, she shall have two children, the one legitimately and the other illegitimately, as confirmed by the Catholic Church, and the other who to her great confusion and tardy repentance shall wish to ruin her. There shall be three regions corresponding to the sharp differences between the [various] leagues – namely Italy, Germany, and Spain – which shall be the military wings of divers sects, starting from the 50th and 52nd degrees of latitude. All of the distant religions shall pay homage to the regions of Europe and of the North [Roussat; Tiburtine Sibyl] around the 48th degree of latitude [i.e. France] – for they that shall be the first to tremble out of futile timidity, then the most westerly, southerly, and easterly shall tremble. Such shall be their power that what shall be created through [their] cooperation and union [shall be] invulnerable to warlike conquest. They shall be of equal nature, but greatly different in faith.

[B2] After this, the sterile Lady [who is] more powerful than the second shall be received by two peoples – the first made stubborn by him who [formerly] had power over all, and the second and third which shall extend its powers in the region of the perimeter of Eastern Europe towards the already subdued and beaten Hungary [Torquato], and shall spread her sway to the 'Adriatic Sicily' [Rhodes] with the aid of mercenaries from a completely beaten Germany [this, plus most of the previous section, is perhaps the most original of the prophecies in the Epistle]. And the barbarian sect [i.e. the Muslims] shall be greatly afflicted and chased away by the Italians [St Cesarius; Torquato].

[B3] Then the great Empire of the Antichrist shall arise in the Atila [this word seems to make little sense here, unless it is a misprint or anagram for *Altai*, home-area of Genghis Khan; the original 1558 edition may have had 'the Arda' i.e. the province of Ardalan in north-Western Persia], and [a new] Xerxes shall descend [on the world] with a great and countless host [Tiburtine Sibyl]. As a result, the religion centered on the 48th degree of latitude [once again, there is reason to suspect interference with this figure (presumably by the nationalistic Chavigny), given that no known religion is or was centered on Paris (!): the original 1558 edition may have said '24th', the latitude of Medina – thus referring to Islam] shall migrate abroad [Pseudo-Methodius], driving [everybody] before it with the abomination of the Antichrist, and making war on the Prince who is the great Vicar of Jesus Christ on earth and on his Church and Kingdom [Joachim of Fiore; Tiburtine Sibyl; Pseudo-Methodius; St Cesarius] *per tempus et in occasione temporis* [Latin – 'for a time, and at the end of time'].

[B4] Before this shall come a solar eclipse darker and more gloomy than there has ever been either from the world's creation until the death and passion of Jesus Christ, or since then until our own time.

[B5] And it shall be in the month of October that some great upheaval shall occur, such that people shall think that the weight of the earth has lost its natural movement and has been cast down into perpetual darkness. During the previous spring and thereafter, there shall be extreme changes and transformations of kingdoms [Roussat; Hermit Reynard], accompanied by great earthquakes [Tiburtine Sibyl; St Cesarius, together with an anonymous prediction reported by Chavigny[11]], together with the swarming of the New Babylon [Tiburtine Sibyl], [that] miserable daughter, plus the abomination of the first holocaust. And it shall remain so for no more than 73 years and seven months [the precise period of the Russian October Revolution and subsequent Communist regime!]. Then afterwards shall spring from the branch that has for so long time remained barren, proceeding from the 50th degree [latitude of Cracow, Poland], one who shall renew the entire Christian Church [anonymous French prophecy; Savonarola; Joachim of Fiore; Joachim's and Telesphorus's 'Angelic Pastor']. And great peace, union and concord shall be established [St Severus] between one of the children with distracted faces and [those] separated by different kingdoms [sense unclear]. And such a peace shall be made that the promoter and sustainer of the warlike faction shall be consigned to the deepest pit by the various religious [movements]. And the Kingdom of the Rabid shall be united in counterfeiting the good [Hermit Reynard]. And the countries, towns, cities, kingdoms, and provinces that will have forsaken their original ways in the hope of freeing themselves, only to imprison themselves [all the] more deeply, shall be secretly enraged at the loss of their freedom and perfect religion, and shall start to attack the left, in order to turn to the right, as well as restoring their long abandoned sanctity [Hermit Reynard], together with their original scriptures.

[B6] And after the Great Dog shall emerge the Great Hound [the expression normally referred to Cerberus, but here presumably the biblical Gog and Magog], who shall inflict destruction on everything, even that which has previously been perpetrated [Tiburtine Sibyl]. The churches shall be rebuilt as in former times, the priesthood shall be restored to its original status [Hermit Reynard; Lichtenberger], and [then] shall start to prostitute and indulge itself, and to commit countless crimes [St Cesarius].

[B7] And being close to a further desolation [Roussat], at the time when she [?] shall be at her highest and most sublime dignity, military potentates and forces shall arise and her two swords shall be removed, and only her banners shall remain. And [those potentates and forces] shall be forced from the crooked path that attracts them into a straight path by the people, who shall resist submitting to them with the aid of the other end of the distaff [or possibly of the drawing-bench] from the hand that does the winding – the one that touches the ground – preferring [merely] to prod with it until, . . .

[B8] . . . from a branch of the long sterile Lady, shall be born one who shall deliver all the people from their meek and willing slavery, placing himself under the protection of Mars and robbing Jupiter of all his honors and dignities [St Brigid] for the sake of the free city set up and sited in a second mini Mesopotamia [Avignon, as per Petrarch?]. The leader and governor shall be flung into the midst and strung up on high, [still] ignorant of the conspiracy mounted against him with the help of a second Thrasybulus [Athenian general who not only staged a successful coup against the ruling oligarchy in 404 BC to re establish democracy, but nine years later brought about a similar democratic revolution in Byzantium, too (now, of course, Istanbul)], who will have been plotting all this for some time. Then [all] the shameful impurities and abominations shall be done away with and consigned to the shadows that have resulted in a veiling of the light – [a veiling which itself will cease] towards the end of the overthrow of his regime.

[B9] And the keys of the Church [i.e. those of St Peter, and thus the Papacy] shall fall short of the love of God, and many of them shall abandon the true Faith [Joachim], and of the three sects [from north to south: Protestantism, Catholicism, and Islam], the middle one shall be allowed by its members to fall somewhat into decay [St Brigid]. The first [the Protestants] [shall spread] throughout Europe, while most of North Africa shall be wiped out by the third [i.e. the Muslims] [Pseudo-Methodius] on account of the 'poor in spirit' whom maniacs shall rouse up against [all forms of] extravagance and immorality and [whose faith they shall] corrupt. Again and again the common folk shall rise, hounding out government supporters. With regimes everywhere weakened by the Middle Easterners, it shall seem as though God the Creator had unleashed Satan from his infernal prison to give birth to the great Dog and Doham [presumably Gog and Magog, the symbolic names given by the Revelation of John to Satan's forces at his last battle with the 'people of God' – a literary deformation that seems to confirm that Nostradamus was working from memory, rather than directly from the printed Bible text] [Pseudo-Methodius; Tiburtine Sibyl; Roussat]. These shall create such an abominable schism within the Churches [St Severus; St Brigid; Cretan Sibyl; Hermit Reynard; St Cyril; Joachim – a repetition of the Great Western Schism of the fourteenth century?] that neither reds nor whites [i.e. the judiciary], who shall fail either to see or to act, shall be able to judge the situation properly any more, and their power shall be taken away from them [compare quatrain I.3].

[B10] At that time more persecutions shall be visited on the Church than ever before [St Cyril; Tiburtine Sibyl; St Cesarius]. And even while these are in progress, such a great pestilence shall arise [Roussat; Tiburtine Sibyl] as to wipe out over two thirds of the population [Hermit Reynard]. Such shall be its extent that it will no longer [even] be possible to establish the ownership of fields or houses, and grass shall grow knee high and more in the city streets. The clergy shall be totally wiped out [St Cyril; Hermit Reynard], while the military shall seize all the revenues of the City of the Sun [either Rhodes, sacred to Helios, or, by astrological and zoological analogy, Lyon], of Malta and of the Iles d'Hyères, and the great chain of the port which takes its name from the sea bull shall be broken [Latin *phoca* = 'seal': *Phocaea* = Marseille].

[B11] And a new sea-borne invasion shall be mounted, in an attempt to free the Sierra Morena from the first retaking of it by the Muslims. And this shall in no wise be unsuccessful, and the place which was formerly the dwelling of Abraham shall be attacked by those who shall venerate the rulers of Christendom [Pseudo-Methodius]. And this city of Hashem [Medina] shall be surrounded and attacked from all quarters in very great strength by armed troops. Their naval forces shall be weakened by the Westerners.

[B12] And great desolation shall be inflicted on this kingdom [Roussat]. The biggest cities shall be depopulated, and those who take over shall embody the vengeance of an angry God [Roussat; Pseudo-Methodius]. For a long time the Holy Sepulcher, so long venerated, shall remain open to the sky, exposed to those all seeing eyes of heaven, the sun and moon. The sacred site shall be turned into a stable for farm animals large and small [Hermit Reynard], as well as put to other profane uses [Tiburtine Sibyl?; St Cesarius].

[B13] O what calamitous afflictions shall befall women with child in those days [Joachim of Fiore; Tiburtine Sibyl]! Most of [the forces of] the supreme Middle Eastern leader, driven out by the Northerners and Westerners, shall be defeated and put to death [Tiburtine Sibyl; Pseudo-Methodius], and the rest shall be put to flight, and his children (by a number of women) imprisoned. Then shall be fulfilled the prophecy of the Royal Prophet [i.e. King David]: *Ut audiret gemitus compeditorum, Ut solveret filios interemptorum* ['that he may hear the groaning of the prisoners and set free the children of the dead' – Psalm 102:20, here misquoted in Latin, as was Nostradamus's wont. The quotation should actually conclude: 'and set free those who are condemned to death']. What mighty oppression shall be visited in those days on Princes and on those who govern the nations, even the maritime and Middle Eastern ones whose languages will by then have become mixed with those of the world at large – and in particular Arabic, by way of Africa, with the Latin tongues!

[B14] All the Middle Eastern leaders shall be pursued, cut down, and extermi-nated [Anonymous French prophecy] – not so much as a result of any action on the part of the Northern leaders' forces, nor of any resemblance to events now current, but of the secret alliance of the trio who shall be secretly seeking their death, and of their own plotting and ambushing of each other. The new Triumvirate shall last for seven years, during which the renown of their religion shall spread throughout the world, and the sacrifice of the Holy and Immaculate Host shall be maintained. And at this time the bipartite Northern leadership shall be victorious over the Middle Easterners [Anonymous French prophecy; Tiburtine Sibyl; Torquato], and they shall make such a great noise and tumult of war that the whole of the Levant shall tremble for fear of these Northern brothers [St Brigid; Tiburtine Sibyl] who are nevertheless not broth-ers.

[B15] And since, Sire, in this address I am presenting these predictions almost confusedly – both in respect of when each may occur and in respect of the amount of time which shall elapse until the events themselves – in a way that conforms little, if at all, with the above; [and since,] whether by means astro-nomical or by other means (namely the Holy Scriptures, which can in no wise fail), if I wished to set a definite term [i.e. date] to each quatrain, this could be done; yet this would not be pleasing to all, still less [that I should] interpret them, [at least] until, Sire, your Majesty should have fully authorized me to do so, lest any occasion be given to the slanderers to savage me.

[B16] However, counting the years from the creation of the world until the birth of Noah, there passed 1506 years [misprint for 1056]; and from the birth of Noah to the completion of the construction of the Ark in the run up to the world flood there passed 600 years (whether the data were solar or lunar or mixtures of the two – though I maintain that the Holy Scriptures hold them to be solar). And at the end of these six [hundred] years, Noah entered the Ark in order to be saved from the flood: and this flood was world wide, and lasted a year and two months. And from the end of the flood to the birth of Abraham there passed a total of 295 years. And from the birth of Abraham until the birth of Isaac there passed 100 years. And from Isaac to Jacob, sixty years, [and] from the time when he entered Egypt until he left it again there elapsed 130 years. And from the time when the latter entered Egypt until the exodus therefrom there elapsed 430 years. And from the exodus from Egypt to the building of the Temple, which Solomon constructed in the fourth year of his reign, there passed four hundred and eighty (or fourscore) years. And from the building of the Temple to Jesus Christ, according to the calculation of the sacred scribes, there passed 490 years. And so it is that, according to the calculations that I have carried out in conjunction with the sacred scriptures, this amounts [in all] to some 4173 years and four months more or less [possible misprint for '4713', the starting date for Joseph Justus Scaliger's subsequent 'Julian Period', though the actual total here is 4092; this would make the theoretical terminal date of the then conventional 7000 years of earth history AD 2828, as opposed to AD 2242, as per both Roussat and the earlier chronology!]. Now as regards [the time] from Jesus Christ to now, given the diversity of sects, I shall say nothing. And [I have] reckoned and calculated the present prophecies entirely accord-ing to the order of the chain that contains its own revolution [i.e. periodic recurrence], entirely according to Astronomical teaching and to my [own] nat-ural instinct. After some time, and taking in the time when Saturn shall go ret-rograde beginning on the 7th of the month of April until 25th August; Jupiter from 14th June to 7th October; Mars from 17th April until 22nd June; Venus from 9th April to 22nd May; Mercury from 3rd February to 24th of the same – and afterwards from 1st June until the 24th of the same, and from 25th September until 16th October – Saturn [being] in Capricorn; Jupiter in Aquarius; Mars in Scorpio; Venus in Pisces; Mercury in Capricorn, Aquarius, and Pisces [all] within one month; the Moon in Aquarius; the head of the Dragon in Libra; its tail in the opposite sign following a conjunction of Jupiter with Mercury, with a quartile aspect between Mars and Mercury; and the head of the Dragon alongside a conjunction of the sun with Jupiter the year [which all of the above indicates to be 1606, as per section A3 above] shall be peace-ful without any eclipse whatever, and it shall be the start, among other things, of a dispensation that shall endure.

[B17] And as from that year there shall be inflicted on the Christian Church a greater persecution [Tiburtine Sibyl; St Cesarius] than was ever carried out in North Africa [back-reference to the biblical Exodus], and this shall last until the year 1792 [Roussat[67] mentions both 1789 and 1791], which shall be considered as the beginning of a new age. After this the Roman people shall begin to stand up [for themselves] again and to banish certain dark shadows while recovering something of their original light, [though] not without great divisions and continual upheavals.

[B18] Thereafter shall Venice with great force and power raise its wings to such a lofty height as barely to fall short of the power of ancient Rome.

[B19] And at that time great ships from Byzantium, joined with the Italians thanks to the support of powers to the north [Russia and/or Ukraine?], shall in some way prevent both [or: the leaders of the] Cretans from holding to their promises. Vessels built by the former military shall sail in company through Neptune's waves. In the Adriatic there shall be vast discord, what was united shall be split asunder, and present and former cities (including the all powerful European Babylon) shall be reduced to a single house on the forty-fifth, forty-first, forty-second and thirty-seventh degrees of latitude [presumably – despite the apparently confused order – Turin, Naples, Rome (here identified as 'Babylon', as in John's Revelation and the Tiburtine Sibyl) and Syracuse in Sicily]. And at that time and in those countries the power of hell shall confront the Church of Jesus Christ with all the might of those who oppose its teachings [Tiburtine Sibyl], who shall be the second Antichrist [John of Rupescissa; Hermit Reynard; St Brigid], and who shall persecute the said Church and its true Vicar [Tiburtine Sibyl; Pseudo-Methodius; St Cesarius] via the authority of the temporal rulers who in their ignorance shall be seduced by tongues that shall cut more deeply than any maniac's sword.

[B20] The said reign of the Antichrist [Hermit Reynard; St Brigid] shall last only ['St Vincent'] until the death of him who was born near [our] age [i.e. Christ?] and of the other in the city of Plancus [Lyon, founded by Lucius Munatius Plancus in 43 BC], accompanied by the elected [ruler] of Modena Fulcy [unidentified place name], near a Ferrara that is supported by Adriatic Italians [Venetians?], as well as by a not far distant Sicily. Then the Gallic Ogmion [the Gallic version of the classical Hercules, noted for his eloquence] shall pass the Mountain of Jove [either the Montjuich in Barcelona, or the Capitoline Hill in Rome], accompanied by such a vast host that the Empire shall be presented from afar with a greater dispensation [Pseudo-Methodius; St Cesarius], and then for some time the blood of innocents shall be shed profusely [Tiburtine Sibyl] by villains of middle rank.

[B21] Then in the course of great floods [Roussat; Anonymous French prophecy] the memory of what is preserved in the documents shall suffer countless losses, as shall even the knowledge of writing itself, especially in the northern hemisphere [back-reference to Noah's flood]. And by the will of God Satan shall be bound once more [Pseudo-Methodius].

[B22] And world peace shall be established among humans [Tiburtine Sibyl; St Severus], and the Church of Jesus Christ shall be delivered from all its tribulations [Pseudo-Methodius; St Hippolytus], despite all the efforts of debauched hedonists to adulterate the honey with the gall of their pestilent seduction [St Hippolytus]. This shall be near the seventh millennium [by the best contemporary calculations of Trithemius and Roussat, either 1800 or 1887, but more like 2828 if Nostradamus's figures advanced above are used], when the sanctuary of Jesus Christ shall no longer be trampled underfoot by infidels from the north [Roussat; Anonymous French prophecy], and when the world shall be approaching some great conflagration [Tiburtine Sibyl] (though my prophetic calculations reveal that time itself will go on for a good while longer).

[B23] In the Letter that I dedicated years ago to my son César Nostradamus I declared a number of points fairly openly, without casting them in prophetic form. But here, Sire, are contained many great and awesome events, as those who come after shall see. And during [the period covered by] these astrological calculations, carried out in conjunction with the Sacred Scriptures, the persecution of the clergy [St Cyril; Hermit Reynard; St Cesarius] shall find its origin in the power of the Northern rulers [Roussat; Tiburtine Sibyl], united with the Middle Eastern ones. This persecution shall last eleven years or a little less, whereupon the power of the main northern ruler shall collapse. At the end of these years his southern ally shall move to persecute the clergy [St Cyril; Hermit Reynard] even more severely for three years, thanks to the seductive apostasy of one who holds absolute power in the Church Militant [St Cyril]. The holy people of God who do still observe its laws shall, like the religious orders themselves, be greatly persecuted and afflicted, to such an extent that the blood of true churchmen and churchwomen shall flow far and wide [St Cyril; Pseudo-Methodius; St Cesarius]. One of the most horrible of the political rulers, indeed, shall be praised by his followers for having spilt more of the blood of innocent church people than anybody could possibly have wine in his wine cellar. This ruler shall commit the most incredible crimes against the Church [Tiburtine Sibyl; St Cesarius]. Human blood shall flow through the city streets and churches like water after heavy rain. Nearby rivers shall run red with blood, just as shall the sea after a naval battle that shall cause one ruler to report to another that *Bellis rubuit navalibus aequor* [Latin: 'The sea blushed red with blood of naval war']. Then, in that same year and in those following, there shall ensue the most terrible pestilence [Roussat; Tiburtine Sibyl], made even more awful by the famine that shall precede it [Roussat; Anonymous prediction reported by Chavigny]. And there shall be tribulations, even throughout the Latin nations, greater than any that have occurred since the first foundation of the Christian Church [Pseudo-Methodius], such as to leave their traces even in various countries of the Iberian Peninsula.

[B24] Then the third Northern ruler, hearing the pleas of the people of his principal domain, shall raise a huge army. Re-crossing the straits once traversed by his most recent predecessors and those before them, he shall restore most things to rights [Tiburtine Sibyl; St Cesarius].

[B25] The great Vicar of the Cope, too, shall be restored to his original state [Roussat; Hermit Reynard].

[B26] ... that shall have been laid waste [St Brigid] and then completely abandoned, and he shall return to his Holy of Holies (now destroyed by paganism) [Roussat; Pseudo-Methodius; Anonymous French prophecy; Hermit Reynard; Tiburtine Sibyl; St Cesarius] from which Old and New Testaments alike shall have been thrown out and burnt [back-reference to the rebuilding of the Temple following the Babylonian captivity].

[B27] And thereafter the Antichrist [Pseudo-Methodius; Roussat] shall be the Prince of Hell. And so yet again – though for the last time – all the Kingdoms of Christendom shall tremble, as shall the heathen too, for the space of twenty five years. There shall be even more terrible wars and battles, and towns, cities, castles, and all other buildings shall be burnt, sacked, and destroyed [Anonymous French prophecy; Anonymous prediction reported by Chavigny]. There shall be a great shedding of virgin blood; married women and widows shall be raped; suckling babes shall be dashed and broken against town walls. So many evils shall be committed through the agency of Satan, Prince of Hell that almost the entire world shall find itself undone and destroyed [Joachim of Fiore].

[B28] And before these events a number of unusual birds shall cry in mid air 'Huy! Huy!' [in Old French, 'Today! Today!', but in Hebrew, 'Woe! Woe!' as per the premonitory eagle of John's Revelation], and after some time they shall [be found to have] disappear[ed] again [Anonymous French prophecy?].

[B29] And after this period has lasted for a good long time, what shall be virtually a new reign of Saturn or Golden Age shall be established [Roussat]. Paying heed to the afflictions of His people, God shall order Satan to be bound and thrown into the deep pit of the bottomless abyss [Pseudo-Methodius]. Then a universal peace shall commence between God and man [Tiburtine

Sibyl], while Satan shall stay bound for around the space of a thousand years, before being unleashed again to turn all his might against the power of the Church [Joachim of Fiore].

[Valediction]

[C1] In order that all these figures might be more precisely collated by means of the sacred scriptures with visible celestial phenomena – i.e. in conjunction with Saturn, Jupiter, Mars, and so on – as might be seen in greater detail by applying various quartiles, I could have gone more deeply into my calculations and adapted the one to the other. But seeing, O Most Serene King, that some critics will have difficulty [with it], and that this will be the reason for my withdrawal of my pen for the sake of my nightly rest: *Multa etiam ô Rex omium potentissime praeclara et sane in brevi ventura, sed omnia in hac tua epistola innectere non possumus nec volumus: sed ad intelliganda quaedam facta horrida fata, pauca libanda sunt, qamvis tanta sit in omnes tua amplitudo et humanitas homines, deosque pietas, ut solus amplissimo et Christianissimo Regis nomine, et ad quem summa totius religionis auctoritas deferatur dignus esse videare* ['Many remarkable things, O most puissant King of all, are doubtless shortly to happen, but we neither can nor will include them in this your letter; yet in order that you should understand such horrible events as are predicted, it is necessary to divulge some of them, even though your generosity and humanity toward all men are so great, as is your Divine piety, that you alone are seen to be worthy of the full Christian title of King, to whom the highest authority in all religions should be accorded'].

[C2] But I beseech you, O most merciful King, by this your unique and wise humanity rather to hearken to the desire of my heart – and the sovereign care that I have had to obey your most serene Majesty ever since my eyes were so near to your sunlike splendor – [but] only to the extent that the magnitude of my labor achieves and deserves it. From Salon this 27th June, one thousand five hundred and fifty eight.

Faciebat Michael Nostradamus
Salonae Petreae
Provinciae

[standard Latin formula: 'Written by Michael Nostradamus of Salon of the Stones (Salon de Craux) in Provence']

Reference-Bibliography

(European/American publishers are indicated by slash-marks)

1. Allemand, J., *Nostradamus et les hiéroglyphes* (Maison de Nostradamus, Salon, 1996/).
2. Alciatus, A., *Toutes les Emblemes de M. André Alciat* [tr] (Lyon, Rouille, 1549).
3. Amadou, R., *L'Astrologie de Nostradamus* (ARRC, Poissy, 1992/).
4 Anon, *Palinodies de Pierre de Ronsard* (1563).
5. Batman, Dr S., *The Doome, warning all men to the Judgemente* (1581), including partial English translations of Lycosthenes and Obsequens (below).
6. Benazra, R., *Répertoire Chronologique Nostradamique (1545–1989)*, 1990.
7. Breysse, J., *Adam de Craponne et son canal* (Office de Tourisme, Lamanon, 1993).
8. Brind'Amour, P., *Nostradamus astrophile* (/klincksieck; University of Ottawa, 1993).
9. Brind'Amour, P., *Nostradamus: Les premières centuries ou propheties* (Droz, 1996/).
10. Britnell, J. and Stubbs, D., 'The *Mirabilis Liber*, its Compilation and Influence' in the *Journal of the Warburg and Courtauld Institutes*, Volume 49, 1986.
11. Chavigny, J. A. de, *Commentaires du Sieur de Chavigny Beaunois, sur les Centuries et Prognostications de feu M. Michel de Nostradamus . . .* (Paris, 1596) and *Les Pleiades de Sieur de Chavigny, Beaunois...* (Lyon, Pierre Rigaud, 1607).
12. Chavigny, J. A. de, *La Premiere Face du Janus François . . .* (Lyon, les héritiers de Pierre Roussin, 1594).
13. Chavigny, J. A. de, *Recueil des Presages Prosaiques de M. Michel de Nostradame* (unpublished MS, 1589).
14. Cheetham, E., *The Final Prophecies of Nostradamus* (Futura/Perigree, 1989).
15. Cheetham, E., *The Prophecies of Nostradamus* (Corgi; Perigree, 1973/Berkley, 1981).
16. Chevignard, B. *Présages de Nostradamus* (Ed. du Seuil, 1999/).

17. Chomarat, M., Dupèbe, J. and Polizzi, G., *Nostradamus ou le savoir transmis* (Chomarat, 1997/).

18. Chomarat, M. and Laroche, Dr J.-P., *Bibliographie Nostradamus* (Koerner, 1989/).

19. Dagueniere, J. de la, *Le Monstre d'Abus* (Paris, Barbe Regnault, 1558).

20. Dufresne, M., *Dictionnaire Nostradamus* (JCL, 1989).

21. Dupèbe, J. *Nostradamus. Lettres Inédites* (Droz, 1983/).

22. Erickstad, H. G. B., *The Prophecies of Nostradamus in Historical Order* (Janus, 1996/Vantage, 1982).

23. Fincelius, Jobus (Fincel, Job), *De miraculis sui temporis* (1556).

24. Frytschius, Marcus (Fritsch, Markus), *De meteoris* (1555).

25. 'Hercules le François', *La Premiere Invective du Seigneur Hercules le François, contre Monstradamus . . .* (Paris, Simon Calvarin, 1558).

26. Hippocrates, *De aere et aqua et regionibus* in *Articella nuperrime impressa...* (de la Place, Lyon, 1515 ; also 1526, 1529, 1538, 1542, 1546).

27. Hogue, J., *Nostradamus and the Millennium* (Bloomsbury, 1987/).

28. Hogue, J., *Nostradamus: The Complete Prophecies* (Element/Element, 1997).

29. Hogue, J., *Nostradamus: The New Revelations* (Element/Element 1994).

30. Iamblichus, *De Mysteriis Aegyptiorum, Chaldaeorum, Assyriorum* (Lyon, De Tournes, 1549).

31. Ionescu, V., *Les dernières victoires de Nostradamus* (Filipacchi, 1993/).

32. Kidogo, Bardo (Popkess, Barry), *The Keys to the Predictions of Nostradamus* (Foulsham, 1994/).

33. King, Francis X., *Nostradamus: Prophecies Fulfilled and Predictions for the Millennium and Beyond* (BCA, 1993/).

34. Laver, J., *Nostradamus or the Future Foretold* (Mann, 1942–81/).

35. Lemesurier, P., *The Essential Nostradamus* (Piatkus, 1999/).

36. Lemesurier, P., *Nostradamus Beyond 2000/Nostradamus and Beyond* (Godsfield/Sterling, 1999).

37. Lemesurier, P., *The Nostradamus Encyclopedia* (Godsfield/St Martin's, 1997).

38. Lemesurier. P., *Nostradamus in the 21st Century* (Piatkus, 2000).

39. Lemesurier, P., *Nostradamus: The Final Reckoning* (Piatkus, 1995/Berkley, 1997).

40. Lemesurier, P., *Nostradamus – The Next 50 Years* (Piatkus, 1993/Berkley, 1994).

41. Leoni, E., *Nostradamus and His Prophecies* (/Wings, 1961–82/).

42. Leroy, Dr E., *Nostradamus: ses origines, sa vie, son œuvre* (Lafitte, 1993/).

43. LeVert, L. E., *The Prophecies and Enigmas of Nostradamus* (/Firebell, 1979).

44. Lycosthenes, C., *Prodigiorum ac ostentorum chronicon* (Basel, 1557).

45. *Mirabilis Liber qui prophetias revelationesque, necnon res mirandas, preteritas, presentes et futuras, aperte demonstrat . . .* (Paris, 1522-3: Lyon, 1523, but claiming 'Rome, 1524').

46. 'Moult, T.-J.', *Propheties Perpetuelles*, '1269' (assumed 1740 reprint of ditto by Friar Joseph Illyricus, 1530).

47. Nostradamus, C., *L'Histoire et chronique de Provence...* (Lyon, Simon Rigaud, 1614).

48. Nostradamus, M., *Almanach pour l'an M.D.LXVI* (Volant & Brotot, 1565).

49. Nostradamus, M., *Ein Erschecklich und Wunderbarlich Zeychen . . .* (Nuremberg, Heller, 1554).

50. Nostradamus, M., *Orus Apollo*, Ed. Rollet, P., as *Interprétation des hiéroglyphes de Horapollo* (Marcel Petit, 1993/).

51. Nostradamus, M., *Paraphrase de C. Galen sus l'exhortation de Menodote* (Du Rosne, 1557).

52. Nostradamus, M., *Les Propheties* (Bonhomme, 1555: Albi copy).

53. Nostradamus, M., *Les Propheties* (Du Rosne, September 1557).

54. Nostradamus, M., *Les Prophéties, Lyon, 1557* (Chomarat, 1993/).

55. Nostradamus, M., *Les Prophéties, Lyon, 1568* (Chomarat, 2000).

56. Nostradamus, M., *Lettre à Catherine de Médicis* (Chomarat, 1996/).

57. Nostradamus, M., *'Traité des fardemens et des confitures'*, published as *Excellent & moult utile opuscule . . .* (Lyon, Antoine Volant, 1556), *Le Vray et Parfaict Embellissement de la Face* (Antwerp, Plantin, 1557).

58. Obsequens, Julius, *De Prodigiis* (fourth century: republished Jean de Tournes, 1553).

59. Peucerus, Gaspar (Peucer, Kaspar), *Teratoscopia* (Book XV) in *Commentarius de praecipuis divinationum generibus* (1553).

60. Prévost, R., *Nostradamus: le mythe et la réalité* (Laffont, 1999/).

61. Rabelais, F., *Pantagrueline Prognostication pour l'an 1533* (1533).

62. *Revue des langues romanes*, 1914.

63. Rollet, P. (ed), *Interprétation des hiéroglyphes de Horapollo* (Marcel Petit, 1993/).

64. Ronsard, P. de, *Discours des miseres de ce temps* (1562).

65. Ronsard, P. de, *Elegie sur les Troubles d'Amboise* (Toulouse, Jaques Colomies, 1560).

66. Ronsard, P. de, *Prognostiques sur les miseres de nostre temps* (1584).

67. Roussat, R., *Livre de l'estat et mutations des temps*, 1549–50.

68. Trithemius, J., *De Septem Secundeis . . .* (1508).

69. Vesalius, *De humani corporis fabrica*, 1543.

70. Videl, L., *Declaration des abus, ignorances et seditions de Michel Nostradamus* (Avignon, Roux & Tremblay, 1558).

71. Ward, C. A., *Oracles of Nostradamus* (Society of Metaphysicians [facsimile of 1891 ed.], 1990, 1995 /Modern Library [Scribner], 1940).

72. Watts, P. M., *Prophecy and Discovery: On the Spiritual Origins of Christopher Columbus's 'Enterprise of the Indies'* in *American Historical Review*, February 1985, pp.73–102.

Index